... Sister ... ...es of the Romanov ... ...aterinburg: The Last Days of the Romanovs; ... ...aught in the Revolution: Petrograd, 1917. Helen was also historical consultant to the ITV drama series Victoria, and her books about the Victorians include Magnificent Obsession: Victoria, Albert and the Death that Changed the Monarchy. She lives in West Dorset.

Praise for The Race to Save the Romanovs

'What I always love about Helen Rappaport's books is that they appeal to the heart as well as the head. She's a writer of great compassion.'

Lucy Worsley

'Fascinating.'

Evening Standard

'Highly entertaining ... Rappaport introduces us to a colourful array of con men, charlatans and fantasists involved in ideas to free the Romanovs ... [Rappaport] is a vivid storyteller ... fascinating, she has found hitherto unknown material in royal archives belonging to many of the ruling houses in Europe.'

Sunday Times

'Gripping ... [Rappaport] has uncovered many missing pieces in t[...] ...ar's fate to a[...]

...he Times

'Superb ... There remain fresh angles and, crucially, unused evidence pertaining to the Romanovs ... [Rappaport] speaks to our continued fascination with them ... *The Race to Save the Romanovs* is a groundbreaking book that presents a convincingly alternative account from the scenario in which their chances of survival flourished or perished on George V's decision.'

Daily Telegraph

'Helen Rappaport's frank and brilliant study of the various efforts to save the Romanovs begins, intelligently, with the race to save them from themselves ... Though the last days of the Romanovs are among the most thoroughly ploughed fields of historical research, Rappaport nonetheless manages to unearth new material.'

Spectator

'A fascinating study that reads much like a detective story.'

Choice Magazine

ALSO BY HELEN RAPPAPORT

Caught in the Revolution

The Victoria Letters

Four Sisters

Magnificent Obsession

Beautiful for Ever

Conspirator

Ekaterinburg

No Place for Ladies

Queen Victoria

An Encyclopedia of Women Social Reformers

Joseph Stalin

Dark Hearts of Chicago (with William Horwood)

Capturing the Light (with Roger Watson)

The Race to Save the Romanovs

The Truth Behind the Secret Plans to Rescue Russia's Imperial Family

HELEN RAPPAPORT

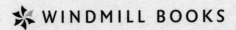 WINDMILL BOOKS

1 3 5 7 9 10 8 6 4 2

Windmill Books
20 Vauxhall Bridge Road
London SW1V 2SA

Windmill Books is part of the Penguin Random House group
of companies whose addresses can be found
at global.penguinrandomhouse.com

Copyright © Helen Rappaport 2018

First published by Hutchinson in 2018
First published in paperback by Windmill Books in 2019

www.penguin.co.uk

A CIP catalogue record for this book is available from the British Library.

ISBN 9781786090171

Typeset in 10.49/12.3 pt Bembo
by Integra Software Services Pvt. Ltd, Pondhicherry

Printed and bound in Great Britain by Clays Ltd, Elcograf S.p.A.

In memory of my parents,
Kenneth and Mary Ware

There is no worse punishment for a monarch than to lose the love of his people. It is hard for anyone other than he who has lived through it to understand.

King Alfonso of Spain, in exile, 1933

They have dragged all our world down crashing with them ... Everyone says what a fearful punishment but I say it is not a punishment, it is a pure logical result of their own acts. Just as if they had taken a match and put fire to their own garments.

Grand Duchess Kirill to her sister Marie,
Queen of Romania, Petrograd, 10 March 1917

Ever since then [1918], I have been haunted by the idea that had I been able to argue with the Ural Soviet for a longer period I might have been able to save the Russian Royal Family.

Sir Thomas Preston, former British consul
in Ekaterinburg, letter to *The Spectator*,
11 March 1972

Contents

List of Illustrations

20 Archangel: USS *Des Moines* on White Sea, 19 May 1919, Frank E. Lauer papers, the Frank E. Lauer family and the Bentley Historical Library, University of Michigan

21 Nikolay Markov ('Markov II'): Paul Fearn/Alamy Stock Photo

22 Cornet Sergey Markov ('Little Markov'): Author's Collection

23 Inner courtyard of the Governor's House, Tobolsk: Courtesy of Charles Gibbes

24 Courtyard at the Governor's House, Tobolsk: Courtesy of Charles Gibbes

25 Sisters' room, Tobolsk: Courtesy of Charles Gibbes

26 Alexandra's sitting room, Tobolsk: Courtesy of Charles Gibbes

27 Room plan for the Governor's House: Courtesy of Charles Gibbes

28 Pierre Gilliard, Petr Petrov and Sydney Gibbes: Author's Collection

29 Prince Vasily Dolgorukov: Courtesy of Charles Gibbes

30 Nicholas and his four children: TopFoto

31 Jonas Lied: Library of Congress, Prints & Photographs Division, LC-DIG-ggbain-19063

32 Count Benckendorff: Ullstein Bild Dtl.

33 Kaiser Wilhelm II: Public Domain/National Library of Norway

34 Vasily Yakovlev, aka Konstantin Myachin: Public Domain

35 Major Stephen Alley: Courtesy of Felix Jay

36 King Alfonso XIII: Hulton Archive

37 Carriages outside the Governor's House: Courtesy of Charles Gibbes

38 Postcard of Ekaterinburg: Azoor Photo/Alamy Stock Photo

39 Ipatiev House, Ekaterinburg: Heritage Images

40 Alexey and Olga: Courtesy of Charles Gibbes/Kirill Protopopov

41 Twenty-three steps: Public Domain

42 *Daily Mirror*, 13 September 1918: John Frost Newspapers/Alamy Stock Photo

TSARSKOE SELO
TO EKATERINBURG:
The Romanovs' Places
of Captivity, 1917–18

ARCTIC
OCEAN

Franz Josef Land

ARCTIC

OCEAN

Yamal Peninsula

Kara Sea

Spitsbergen

Barents
Sea

Novaya
Zemlya

Matochkin Strait

Obdorsk

Arctic Circle

U

Norwegian Sea

Murmansk

Kola
Peninsula

Tromsø

KINGDOM OF FINLAND

White

Archangel

Sea

Tornio

Vologda

Sølsnes

N O R W A Y

S W E D E N

Petrograd
(St Petersburg)

Bergen

Christiana
(Oslo)

Helsingfors
(Helsinki)

Gulf of Finland

Tsarskoe
Selo

Moscow

Stockholm

Baltic Sea

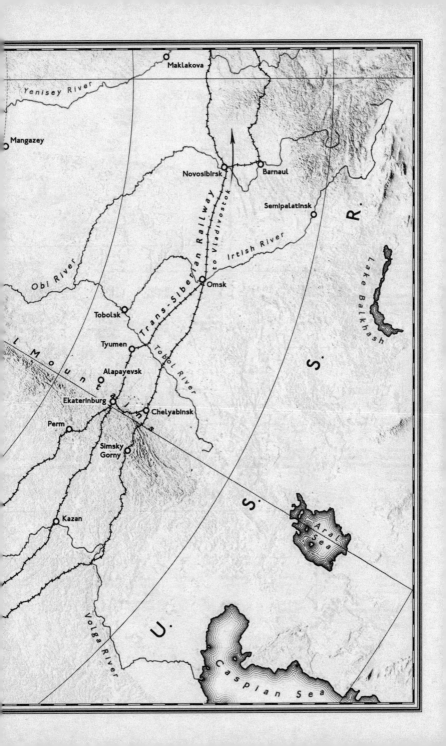

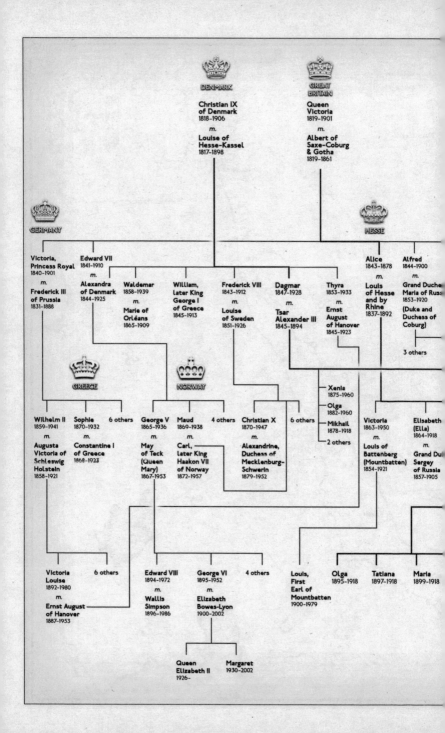

THE ROMANOVS
and their
European Royal Relatives

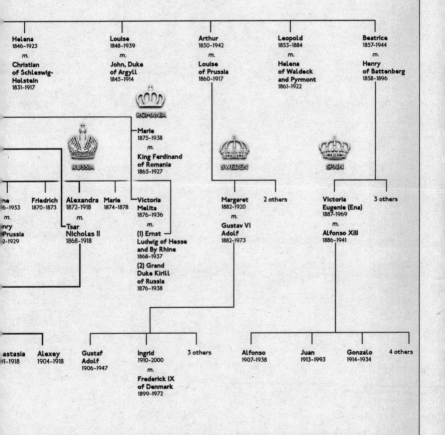

Helena
1846–1923

m.

**Christian
of Schleswig-
Holstein**
1831–1917

Louise
1848–1939

m.

**John, Duke
of Argyll**
1845–1914

Arthur
1850–1942

m.

**Louise
of Prussia**
1860–1917

Leopold
1853–1884

m.

**Helena
of Waldeck
and Pyrmont**
1861–1922

Beatrice
1857–1944

m.

**Henry
of Battenberg**
1858–1896

ROMANIA

Marie
1875–1938

m.

**King Ferdinand
of Romania**
1865–1927

RUSSIA

SWEDEN

SPAIN

...ne
...6–1953

m.

**...nry
...Prussia**
...2–1929

Friedrich
1870–1873

Alexandra
1872–1918

m.

**Tsar
Nicholas II**
1868–1918

Marie
1874–1878

**Victoria
Melita**
1876–1936

m.

**(1) Ernst
Ludwig of Hesse
and By Rhine**
1868–1937

**(2) Grand
Duke Kirill
of Russia**
1876–1938

Margaret
1882–1920

**Gustav VI
Adolf**
1882–1973

2 others

**Victoria
Eugenie (Ena)**
1887–1969

m.

Alfonso XIII
1886–1941

3 others

...astasia
...1–1918

Alexey
1904–1918

**Gustaf
Adolf**
1906–1947

Ingrid
1910–2000

m.

**Frederick IX
of Denmark**
1899–1972

3 others

Alfonso
1907–1938

Juan
1913–1993

Gonzalo
1914–1934

4 others

Glossary of Names

Alexandra/Alix/Alicky: Princess Alexandra of Hesse and by Rhine; Alexandra Feodorovna, Tsaritsa of Russia; wife of *Nicholas*

Alexeev, General Mikhail: Imperial Russian Army Chief of Staff from 1915 until the abdication of *Nicholas*, March 1917

Alexey Nikolaevich Romanov: the Tsarevich, son of *Nicholas* and *Alexandra; Wilhelm*'s godson

Alfonso XIII: King of Spain; husband of *Ena*

Alice: Princess Alice of Great Britain, later Grand Duchess of Hesse and by Rhine, mother of *Alexandra, Irene, Ella, Victoria Milford Haven* and *Ernie*; sister of *Bertie*

Alley, Major Stephen: British Secret Intelligence Service (SIS) agent based in Murmansk

Anastasia Nikolaevna Romanova: fourth daughter of *Nicholas* and *Alexandra*

Andersen, Hans Niels: Danish businessman and friend of the British and Danish royal families

Armitstead, Henry: agent of the Hudson's Bay Company based at Archangel

Avdeev, Alexander: *Yakovlev*'s deputy and later commandant of the Ipatiev House in Ekaterinburg

Balfour, Arthur: British Foreign Secretary, 1916–19

Beloborodov, Alexander: Chair of the Ural Regional Soviet from January 1918

Benckendorff, Count Pavel: Grand Marshal and Master of Ceremonies at the Russian Imperial Court

Bertie: Prince of Wales, later King Edward VII; father of *George V*; husband of Alexandra the *Queen Mother*

Bertie, Sir Francis: British ambassador in Paris, 1905–18

Bethmann-Hollweg, Theobald von: German Chancellor, 1909–July 1917

Botkin, Dr Evgeniy: physician to the Russian Imperial Family, who accompanied them to Tobolsk and Ekaterinburg

Botkin, Petr: Imperial Russian ambassador to Lisbon; brother of *Evgeniy Botkin*

Brändström, General Edvard: Swedish envoy to St Petersburg/ Petrograd, 1906–20

Brockdorff-Rantzau, Count Ulrich von: German envoy to Copenhagen, 1912–18

Buchanan, Sir George: British ambassador to St Petersburg/Petrograd, 1910–17, father of *Meriel Buchanan*

Buchanan, Meriel: British author, daughter of *Sir George Buchanan*

Buxhoeveden, Baroness Sophie: *Alexandra*'s honorary lady-in-waiting

Cecil, Lord Robert: Parliamentary Under-Secretary of State for Foreign Affairs, 1915–19

Chicherin, Georgiy: People's Commissar for Foreign Affairs, 1918–30, in the first Soviet government

Christian X: King of Denmark, 1912–47, nephew of the *Queen Mother, Dagmar* and *Valdemar* and first cousin to *Nicholas*

Coburg, Duchess of: Grand Duchess Maria Alexandrovna, daughter of Tsar Alexander II; wife of Prince Alfred of Great Britain, Duke of Coburg; aunt by marriage of *Alexandra, Ella, Irene, Victoria Milford Haven* and *Ernie*, and aunt by blood of *Nicholas*

Contreras, Fernando Gómez: Spanish business attaché in Petrograd, 1918

Cumming, Sir Mansfield: Head of MI1(c), the foreign division of the British SIS

Dagmar/Dowager Empress: Princess Dagmar of Denmark, Dowager Empress of Russia known as Maria Feodorovna, sister of the *Queen Mother*, mother of *Nicholas* and aunt of *Christian X*

Davidson, Sir Arthur: Equerry to *Bertie* and later to *George V*, 1910–22

Dehn, Lili: one of the ladies in *Alexandra*'s close entourage, but with no official court position

Dolgorukov, Prince Vasily: Major-general with *Nicholas* at Army HQ and followed him to Tobolsk; stepson of *Count Benckendorff*

Egan, Maurice: American ambassador to Denmark, 1907–December 1917

Ella: Princess Elizabeth of Hesse and by Rhine, later Grand Duchess Elizabeth of Russia, sister of *Alexandra, Irene, Victoria Milford Haven* and *Ernie*

Ena: Victoria Eugenie of Battenberg, Queen of Spain and wife of *Alfonso*; first cousin of *Alexandra* and niece of *Bertie*

Ernie: Grand Duke Ernst Ludwig III of Hesse and by Rhine, brother of *Alexandra, Ella, Irene* and *Victoria Milford Haven*

George V: King of Great Britain and Northern Ireland; first cousin of *Wilhelm, Nicholas* and *Alexandra*

George, Grand Duchess: wife of Grand Duke George Mikhailovich, daughter of King George I of Greece

Gilliard, Pierre: Swiss tutor, who taught French to the Grand Duchesses and the Tsarevich Alexey

Goloshchekin, Filipp: military commissar of the Ural Regional Soviet

Gustav V: King of Sweden, distantly related to the Romanovs through marriage

Haakon VII: King of Norway, married to his first cousin *Maud* who, like him, was a first cousin to *Nicholas*

Hanbury-Williams, Major-General Sir John: Chief of the British Military Mission in Russia, 1914–17; based at Stavka, adviser to *Nicholas*

Hardinge, Lord: 1st Baron of Penshurst, Permanent Under-Secretary of State for Foreign Affairs, 1916–20

Hardinge, Sir Arthur: British ambassador to Madrid, 1913–19

Hauschild, Herbert: First Secretary and acting German consul in Moscow, 1918

Howard, Sir Esmé: 1st Baron Howard of Penrith, Envoy Extraordinary and Minister Plenipotentiary to the King of Sweden, 1913–18

Irene: Princess Henry of Prussia, sister of *Alexandra, Ella, Victoria Milford Haven* and *Ernie*; sister-in-law of *Wilhelm*

Joffe, Adolph: first Soviet ambassador to Berlin, 1918

Kerensky, Alexander: Justice Minister of the Provisional Government, March 1917; War Minister, May 1917; Prime Minister, July–October 1917

Khitrovo, Rita (Margarita): a friend of *Olga* and fellow nurse at her hospital at Tsarskoe Selo

Kienlin, Albert von: German legation secretary to Stockholm

Kirill, Grand Duchess: Princess Victoria Melita, daughter of *Duchess of Coburg*, sister of *Marie of Romania*, first cousin of *Alexandra* and *Nicholas*

Kobylinsky, Colonel Evgeniy: Commandant of the Alexander Palace Garrison at Tsarskoe Selo; Commander of the Guard at the Governor's House, Tobolsk

Kokovtsov, Vladimir: former Prime Minister of Russia, 1911–14

Krivoshein, Alexander: Russian monarchist, former Imperial Minister of Agriculture, 1908–15

Kudashev, Prince Ivan: Russian ambassador to Madrid, replaced in July 1917 by *Neklyudov*

Kühlmann, Richard von: German Foreign Minister, August 1917–July 1918

Lied, Jonas: Norwegian businessman, shipping magnate and adventurer; pioneer of the Kara Sea passage to northern Russia

Lloyd George, David: British Prime Minister of the wartime coalition government of Conservatives and Liberals, 1916–22

Locker-Lampson, Oliver: Lieutenant Commander in the Royal Navy Volunteer Reserve, in command of the British Armoured Car Squadron in Russia, 1916–17

Lockhart, Robert Bruce: diplomat and spy; British Consul General in Moscow, 1917; first British envoy to the Soviets, 1918

Lvov, Prince: Prime Minister of the Provisional Government, March–July 1917

MacDonald, Ramsay: British Labour MP, leader of the opposition and first Labour Prime Minister in 1924

Maria Nikolaevna Romanova: third daughter of *Nicholas* and *Alexandra*

Marie of Romania: Crown Princess and later Queen; daughter of *Duchess of Coburg*, sister of *Grand Duchess Kirill*; first cousin to *Nicholas* and *Alexandra*

Markov, Nikolay: Russian collegiate counsellor and former Duma member. Leading monarchist, known as Markov II

Markov, Cornet Sergey: Russian monarchist, known as Little Markov

Mary, Queen: Princess May of Teck, wife of *King George V*

Maud, Princess: daughter of *Bertie* and Alexandra the *Queen Mother*; Queen of Norway and wife of *King Haakon VII*

Merry Del Val, Alfonso: Spanish ambassador to London, 1913–18

Mikhail Alexandrovich, Grand Duke: *Nicholas*'s brother and *Dagmar*'s son

Mikhail Mikhailovich, Grand Duke: 'Miche-Miche', son of Grand Duke Mikhail Nikolaevich; a grandson of Nicholas I and brother of *Sandro*

Milyukov, Pavel: Foreign Minister of the Provisional Government, March–May 1917, succeeded by *Tereshchenko*

Mirbach, Count Wilhelm von: German ambassador to Moscow, April–July 1918

Mosolov, Count Alexander: Head of the Russian Imperial Court Chancellery

Neidgart, Dmitri: Russian monarchist and representative of the Right Centre in negotiations with the Germans

Neklyudov, Anatoly: Imperial Russian ambassador to Stockholm, 1913–17; ambassador to Madrid, June–September 1917

Nicholas/Nicky/Niki: Tsar Nicholas II of Russia, husband of *Alexandra* and son of *Dagmar*

Nikolay Nikolaevich, Grand Duke: *Nicholas*'s first cousin once removed, but referred to as an uncle; former Commander in Chief of the Imperial Russian Army

Olga Nikolaevna Romanova: eldest daughter of *Nicholas* and *Alexandra*

Paléologue, Maurice: French ambassador to St Petersburg/Petrograd, 1914–17

Pankratov, Vasily: Commandant of the Governor's House at Tobolsk

Poole, Major General Frederick C.: British Commander in Chief of the Allied Intervention Forces in Northern Russia, May–October 1918

Preston, Thomas: British consul in Ekaterinburg, 1913–18

Queen Mother: Alexandra, Princess of Denmark, wife of *Bertie*, mother of *King George V*; aunt of *Nicholas* and *Alexandra*

Ratibor, Prince Maximilian von: German ambassador to Madrid

Rodzianko, Mikhail: Chair of the Imperial State Duma, 1911–17

Sandro: Grand Duke Alexander Mikhailovich, married to *Nicholas*'s sister *Xenia*

Scavenius, Harald: Danish ambassador to St Petersburg/Petrograd, 1912–18

Solovev, Lieutenant Boris: Russian monarchist and would-be Romanov rescuer; husband of Rasputin's daughter, Maria

Stamfordham, Lord: Arthur Bigge, 1st Baron Stamfordham, *George V*'s private secretary, 1910–31

Sverdlov, Yakov: Chair of the Central Executive Committee and Lenin's right-hand man; in close contact with the Bolsheviks of the Ural Regional Soviet, he played a key role in the fate of the Romanovs

Tatiana Nikolaevna Romanova: second daughter of *Nicholas* and *Alexandra*

Tereshchenko, Mikhail: Russian Foreign Minister, May–October 1917, successor to *Milyukov*

Trepov, Alexander: Russian monarchist and former Prime Minister, 1916–17

Valdemar: Prince of Denmark, brother of *Dagmar* and the *Queen Mother*; uncle of *Nicholas*

Vasiliev, Father Alexey: priest at the Church of the Annunciation, Tobolsk; associate of *Solovev*

Victoria Melita: see *Kirill Grand Duchess*

Victoria Milford Haven: Princess Victoria of Hesse and by Rhine; wife of Prince Louis of Battenberg, later Marchioness of Milford Haven. Sister of *Alexandra, Ella, Irene* and *Ernie*; niece of *Bertie*

Vladimir, Grand Duchess: aka Maria Pavlovna the Elder; aunt by marriage to *Nicholas*

Vorovsky, Vatslav: Soviet ambassador to Stockholm, 1917–18

Vyrubova, Anna: close friend and lady-in-waiting of *Alexandra*

Waters, Wallscourt Hely-Hutchinson, Brigadier General: Chief of the British Military Mission to the Imperial Russian Army in World War I; friend of *Wilhelm*

Wilhelm: Kaiser of Germany, first cousin of *Alexandra* and *George V*, godfather of *Alexey*

Woodhouse, Arthur: British consul in Petrograd, who looked after diplomatic interests there after the ambassador, *Sir George Buchanan,* returned to the UK in January 1918

Xenia: Grand Duchess Xenia Alexandrovna, daughter of *Dagmar* and sister of *Nicholas*; wife of *Sandro*

Yakovlev, Vasily: aka Konstantin Myachin, Soviet commissar entrusted with the transfer of the Romanovs from Tobolsk to Ekaterinburg

Yurovsky, Yakov: Urals Bolshevik and member of the Cheka (secret police); appointed commandant of the Ipatiev House on 4 July 1918 in order to organize and oversee the eventual murder of the Romanov family

Yusupov, Prince Felix: murderer of Rasputin; nephew by marriage of *Nicholas* and *Alexandra*; one of the conspirators wishing to remove *Alexandra* from power

By Way of a Beginning

After publishing two books on Russia's last Imperial Family, in 2008 and 2014, a book on Lenin in 2009 and one on the Russian Revolution in 2016, I really thought I had come to the end of my written love affair with the Romanovs and Russia. It seemed to me that I had exhausted all I had to say on the subject. From now on, as a writer, I was going to stay closer to home, and go back to my other love, the Victorians.

But something kept niggling away at me. The Romanovs would not let me go.

Romanovs. Russia. Revolution. Those three seductive words have drawn so many of us into the tragic story of Russia's last Imperial Family over the century since their deaths. They suggest a grandeur that in many ways runs entirely counter to the real family – albeit a royal one – at the heart of it. What is it about Tsar Nicholas II, his wife Alexandra and their five children, Olga, Tatiana, Maria, Anastasia and Alexey, that endlessly fascinates? Despite representing the apotheosis of 300 years of Romanov dynastic rule in Russia – as the possessors of fabulous wealth, vast lands and numerous grand palaces – it is not the epic scale of the Imperial Family's story that attracts, but rather the intensely moving and human one of a quiet, loving and deeply unostentatious family who liked nothing better than being in each other's company, but whose lives ended in hideous murder.

While it is their parents' story that will set the scene in the opening chapters of this book, and we shall see how they were in many respects the masters of their own violent destiny, it is the children who inspire a continuing sense of regret and of longing for a different outcome.

As rulers of the most powerful empire in the world, Nicholas and Alexandra had been desperate for a son and heir. The birth of four daughters – Olga, Tatiana, Maria and Anastasia – in quick succession between 1895 and 1901 had brought considerable public anguish, but also much private joy. The arrival, finally, in 1904 of a son and heir to the Romanov throne, Alexey, turned the family's life upside down. Its whole focus shifted onto the sickly Tsarevich and the unending battle to keep at bay the crippling attacks of haemophilia, passed on to him unknowingly by his mother, which could at any time have killed 'The Hope of Russia'.

With so much attention directed onto Alexey, less and less note was taken of his four sisters, who increasingly slipped into the background, an anonymous collective of pretty girls who seemed charming, uncontroversial – and dull. But despite living perpetually in the shadow of filial duty to their brother and loyalty to their controlling, invalid mother, the Romanov sisters by no means lost their striking individuality. Olga, kind and sensitive, who loved poetry but who tended to introspection and mood swings, felt the weight of responsibility, as the eldest, to set an example. Tatiana, in contrast, never betrayed her feelings, was brisk and capable and extremely good at getting things done. She had the same cautious personality and reserve as her mother, to whom she was devoted. Maria was sweet, gentle and loving, a natural care-giver who loved children. But as the middle child she was vulnerable to being bullied by the others, particularly the fourth sister, Anastasia. Much has been written about the youngest Romanov sister – perhaps at the expense of the others – but she was an extraordinary individualist, a wild spirit, flamboyant and extrovert, good at entertaining people and keeping up morale. And finally there was Alexey, a bright, inquisitive child who suffered from being spoilt by an overprotective mother – which encouraged bouts of bad behaviour – but who demonstrated great intelligence and intuition as he grew older, and a compassion for those, like him, who experienced ill health.

The intimate, highly protected domestic world created by their mama and papa, which these five children inhabited so contentedly till the outbreak of war in 1914, was very different from the public one occupied by Nicholas and Alexandra themselves. By 1917, the autocratic Tsar and Tsaritsa – once so beloved as the 'little father' and 'little mother' of the nation – were widely reviled in a rapidly changing revolutionary Russia. The country was worn down by the abuses of the old repressive tsarist regime and a growing voice of dissent demanded their overthrow and the establishment of a democratic constitutional government.

During the war years of 1914–18 the Romanov children had begun to see and experience at first hand the ugly truth of the widespread antipathy directed towards their parents. They had had to grow up fast – the eldest two sisters, Olga and Tatiana, training as nurses to work in the hospital set up by their mother at Tsarskoe Selo, and all of them, including Alexey, supporting Red Cross charities, hospital-visiting and other war work. But then war descended into revolution and chaos; in March 1917 the metaphorical cage that had protected the Romanov children till now became a very real and frightening one. The old tsarist government – the State Duma – fell, and Nicholas was prevailed upon to abdicate. Now prisoners of the new Russian Provisional Government, the Romanov family were held under house arrest, first at the Alexander Palace from March to July 1917, then transferred to Tobolsk from August to April 1918, and finally sent to the House of Special Purpose in Ekaterinburg.

It was here, in this centre of the Urals mining industry in Western Siberia, during the last ninety-eight days of their lives, that the Romanovs finally began to sense an ominous change in the atmosphere. Until then they had endured the monotony of their captivity with a combination of intense boredom and calm resignation. But, for the Bolshevik Revolution, the endgame was in sight; and that meant one thing: a brutal and vindictive act of retribution would be carried out against the entire Imperial Family. Nicholas and Alexandra must have sensed that sooner or later the revolution might take its revenge on them. But the children too?

The violent deaths of these seven royal victims, along with their doctor and three loyal servants, although horrific to us now, were soon forgotten at the time. They were rapidly swallowed up in a much more hideous catalogue of savage fighting and murder that saw eleven million Russians die during the years of upheaval and civil war of 1917–22.

Yet despite this, for some people the Romanov family will always represent, historically, the symbolic first victims of the new, Soviet regime and a system that would go on to kill even more millions in the decades of Stalinist repression that followed. There is also another element that keeps this story in the public consciousness: a persisting sense – often not fully understood – that regicide, the killing of a king or tsar, is the killing of God's anointed; that regicide is an act that crosses a line, after which any evil is possible.

But, ultimately, it is the murder of innocent children that horrifies us the most.

I had felt a strong sense of attachment to the Romanov family right from the very start – when walking the streets of Ekaterinburg in the summer of 2007, after flying there to research my book Ekaterinburg: The Last Days of the Romanovs. In the humid July heat and late into the eerie White Nights that lit up the city, I walked its streets from north to south, east to west, reimagining the Romanovs' last days at the Ipatiev House on Voznesensky Prospekt. I travelled out to the Koptyaki Forest nine miles away and stood with the pilgrims mourning the Romanovs in rapt silence at the place where the family's bodies, and those of their loyal retainers, had been thrown in chaotic haste that first night. I found my way to the modest wooden cross with plastic flowers in a woodland glade not far away, where they all – bar Maria and Alexey – had been tossed into a shallow grave forty-eight hours later. I pondered why exactly this story had gained such a hold over my imagination. I could understand the powerful, all-pervading sense of grief about the Romanov murders that was still nursed by devout Orthodox Russians; and, like everyone else, I had been sucked into its elements of high drama and tragedy. But my fundamental attraction to it was as a historian and a writer. I wanted answers to questions that had long been troubling me, and which I felt no one till now had really tried to answer. I wanted to try and get at the truth of what really happened in 1917–18.

The canonisation of the murdered Romanov family in the 1980s, followed by the resurgence of the Russian Orthodox Church after the collapse of communism in 1991, has fostered a level of veneration that has today turned Ekaterinburg into a major pilgrimage centre. As a result, a great deal of evidence has come to light in the last twenty-five years in post-Soviet Russia about the circumstances of the family's time in captivity, from their house arrest at the Alexander Palace to the final *haunting, foreboding days in Ekaterinburg. Russian historians have, since the 1990s, published valuable evidence that had long been languishing in the Soviet archives, and have written extensively on the circumstances of the murders and the identity of their perpetrators. The continuing controversy over the DNA testing of the remains – first carried out in the 1990s and repeated more recently at the behest of the Russian Orthodox Church – has meant that the story regularly resurfaces in the press. Every time it does, the inevitable tedious conspiracy theories and claims of miraculous survival follow in its wake; even now, they still refuse to go away.*

July 2018 marks the 100th anniversary of the Romanov murders. Now is undoubtedly the opportune and most fitting time to at last put the metaphorical lid on the coffin and bring closure to this story. For me as a historian, there remain several burning, unanswered questions that nobody has yet tackled – except piecemeal, here and there, and often based on conjecture rather than original, evidence-based research. And they are these:

Why was nobody able to save the Romanovs?

Why did the Imperial Family's many royal cousins in Europe collectively fail them? Why did all the Allied governments with which Russia had so doggedly been fighting a war for three and a half years let them down? Why did the Russian Provisional Government prove impotent in effecting a prompt and safe evacuation out of Russia, after Nicholas abdicated? Why did Germany not take advantage of its upper hand at the Brest-Litovsk peace talks with the Bolsheviks in 1918 and insist that the Romanovs be released? And why was everyone so easily taken in by the duplicitous game played by Lenin's Soviet government about the true circumstances of the Imperial Family's brutal murder?

Having spoken about the Romanovs on the literary-festival circuit for many years, I always get two predictable questions from audiences at the end of every talk. One is: 'Did Anastasia get away?'; and the other: 'Why did King George V betray his Romanov cousins and not grant them asylum in England?'

Ah, so it was all King George's fault? The British king had failed to come galloping to the rescue of his Romanov cousins. If only it were that simple. The story that I unravel here is much more complicated: it is a tale of intriguing personal family relationships; internal and inter-national political rivalries and prejudices; the vagaries of geography and the weather, and the logistical difficulties created by them; and – at its most basic level – a story of plain bad timing.

To make sense of it all, I wanted to begin by getting to grips with the attitudes and relationships of the royal cousins who found themselves at war – or clinging perilously to a neutral stance – in August 1914. This meant that I needed to go back to the close, incestuous world of European royalty of the 1890s.

Chapter 1

Happy Families

In April 1894 the last of a succession of royal dynastic marriages engineered by Queen Victoria as 'Grandmama of Europe' took place in Coburg, the capital of the German Duchy of Saxe-Coburg and by Rhine. The bride and groom were two of her grandchildren: Ernst, the reigning Grand Duke of Hesse and by Rhine, and Princess Victoria Melita, a daughter of Victoria's son Prince Alfred. It was a union that epitomised the close intermarriage of first and second cousins that had been a regular feature of Queen Victoria's family since the 1850s. By the time she died in 1901, her royal descendants in Europe had been drawn into a network of complex and often antagonistic dynastic ties and loyalties that would continue to be made right up to the eve of war in 1914.

This latest family marriage at Coburg, between first cousins Ernst (better known as Ernie) and Victoria Melita, was, however, almost upstaged by the behind-the-scenes drama surrounding the ten-year-long on–off romance between Nicholas Alexandrovich, heir to the Russian throne, and Ernie's sister, Princess Alix (as she was then known). Everyone thought Alix a great beauty and a desirable match, as a granddaughter of Queen Victoria. Nicholas had carried the torch for her for several years, but she had stubbornly resisted his entreaties to marry her. The seemingly insurmountable stumbling block was that, despite being deeply in love with Nicholas, the pious Alix steadfastly refused to give up her Lutheran faith and convert to Russian Orthodoxy. But at the Coburg wedding, and somewhat unexpectedly, the match was given the impetus it required by the intervention of one of the couple's least-likely relatives – the difficult and often antagonistic Wilhelm, Kaiser of Germany. Here, as German emperor on a par with his grandmother Victoria, who was Empress of India, Wilhelm revelled in presiding over this 'august reunion of the oldest dynasties in Europe'.[1] He had worked hard to persuade Alix to agree to convert, in order to cement further royal dynastic expansion in Europe, and on 21 April she had finally relented. Nicholas recorded in his diary that this was the 'most wonderful, unforgettable day of my life – the day of my betrothal to my dear beloved Alix'.[2] For ever after, Wilhelm would congratulate himself that he had acted as the *deus ex machina* behind the engagement of his Russian and German cousins. They owed their good fortune to him, and this unshakeable belief in his own magisterial powers would remain an integral part of the 'mythomania' of Wilhelm's eccentric world.[3]

Queen Victoria, however, had very serious apprehensions about what the future might hold for her beloved granddaughter Alix if she married into Russian royalty. 'My blood runs cold when I think of her so young most likely placed on that very unsafe throne,' she wrote to Alix's sister Victoria, for 'her dear life and above all her husband's' would be 'constantly threatened'.[4] As in many things, history would prove Queen Victoria right.

In earlier years, Wilhelm had himself held aspirations to marry one of the four beautiful Hesse sisters: Alix, Ella, Victoria and Irene. He had visited them frequently from his home in Berlin when they were growing up in Hesse and had always looked on Alix's older sister Ella as his 'special pet'.[5] By the time he was nineteen, Wilhelm hoped to make her his wife. She was a first cousin, a match that, despite the genetic risks of consanguinity, Queen Victoria might nevertheless have encouraged. But Wilhelm's mother, Crown Princess Victoria, had other thoughts. She favoured a Princess of Schleswig-Holstein-Sonderburg-Augustenburg, who was less closely related.

Wilhelm never liked being thwarted, especially by his mother, and persisted in visiting the Hesse sisters at Darmstadt. But just as Ella began to relent, the notoriously unpredictable Kaiser-in-waiting switched his affections to his mother's preferred candidate, Augusta Victoria of Schleswig-Holstein, with what his own father described as 'outrageous rapidity'.[6] Yet Wilhelm never forgot his early love for Ella and developed an obsessive hatred for the man she went on to marry in 1884 – Grand Duke Sergey Alexandrovich. Ella might have married a Russian, but in Wilhelm's eyes she was, and would remain, a German.

Privately it was clear that Crown Princess Victoria had feared that haemophilia – the 'Hesse disease' – might be passed by Ella into the German royal family. For Ella's mother, Princess Alice, the Grand Duchess of Hesse and the Crown Princess's sister, had been a carrier of the potentially fatal gene, passed on to her unknowingly by their mother, Queen Victoria. The closeness of the blood ties that bound the European royal families was thus, by the end of the century, increasingly being called into question. Still, at the wedding at Coburg in 1894 everyone tried to shut out these fears. It was such a happy time: 'No one seemed to remember all those horrid things which were said about cousins marrying,' Alix had reassured a friend about her engagement to Nicholas, 'look, half our cousins have married each other'. And besides, 'who else is there to marry?'[7]

The marriage in November 1894 of Nicholas and Alix (who now took the Russian names of Alexandra Feodorovna) forged new Russian–German–British family alliances. These would ensure that the Russian Imperial Family made regular family visits, with their five children – Olga, Tatiana, Maria, Anastasia and Alexey – to their relatives in Europe over the coming fifteen years. The favourite venue was Alexandra's home state of Hesse and by Rhine – usually the Neues Palais in the city of Darmstadt, where she had been born a princess of the ruling house in 1872. So regular were Romanov family visits that in the late 1890s Nicholas paid for a Russian Orthodox chapel to be specially built for Alexandra's use there, for she had become as devout in her Russian Orthodoxy as she had been in her Lutheranism. But the place in Hesse that the Romanov family loved most was Ernie's summer retreat, the hunting lodge known as Schloss Wolfsgarten, to which his and Alexandra's father, Grand Duke Louis, frequently retreated after the untimely death of their mother, Princess Alice, in 1878. Situated not far from the capital, the house was brick-built and modest, but it was set in beautiful, dense beech woods, with a sweet-smelling rose garden, ornamental fountain and orchards. Here the Romanovs enjoyed reunions with Alexandra's sisters Irene, married to Prince Henry of Prussia, and Victoria, married to Prince Louis of Battenberg and now resident in England. Ella joined them from Russia when she was able. These relaxed family holidays often went on for several weeks, with many happy hours of riding, games of tennis and picnics, much music and singing. They were in marked contrast to the tense atmosphere that prevailed when Wilhelm was present at family gatherings.

Like most of their European royal cousins, the Hesse and Romanov families always found Wilhelm abrasive and systematically cold-shouldered him; many held him in utter contempt. He had – as Count Mosolov, head of the Russian Imperial Court Chancellery, noted – 'a special gift of upsetting everybody who came near him'. Nicholas could not bear Wilhelm's overbearing manner and held him always at arm's length, as his father Alexander III had done before him. Alexandra too had always had 'an innate aversion' to her cousin and often contrived a 'bad head' when a lunch or dinner with Wilhelm loomed. She was scathing in her view of her cousin: 'He's an actor, an outstanding comic turn, a false person,' she told a member of her entourage.[8]

Wilhelm's English cousin, George – who had become Prince of Wales after the old queen's death in 1901 – and his wife, the half-German Mary, got on with the Kaiser rather better. Although privately Mary thought Wilhelm's erratic behaviour at times 'made royalty ridiculous', she and her husband showed a greater natural tolerance of his eccentricities. This was partly out of loyalty to the strong ties with Prussia that had been promoted by George's grandfather, Prince Albert, during his lifetime, when his and Queen Victoria's eldest daughter Vicky had married

Wilhelm's father, the future Prussian emperor.[9] For a time an inherent sense of a 'deep dynastic commitment' to all things German, based on a century or more of Hanoverians on the throne of Britain prior to Victoria, had existed between the two royal houses.[10] This was confirmed by a relative, Princess Marie of Battenberg (a daughter of Prince Alexander of Hesse and by Rhine), who remarked that she had 'never felt more German' than with Queen Victoria. During the Queen's lifetime, 'it was taken as a matter of course that German was widely and fluently spoken in the family'.[11] But after Victoria's death it was a struggle for Wilhelm to gain the approval of his uncle Bertie, now King Edward VII; Wilhelm's hectoring and bellicose manner did nothing to promote the alliance with Britain that his mother and father had long cherished. His aggressive colonial expansionism further antagonised the British and, by the end of the century, a chill political and diplomatic air between the two countries prevailed. During the reign of King Edward VII 'there was always a feeling of thunder in the air' whenever he was obliged to meet with his nephew the Kaiser.[12]

In contrast, the Danish royals, according to Queen Victoria, had always been the 'one remarkable' exception to the disharmony among so many of her other European relatives.[13] They enjoyed warm relations with their British and Russian relatives, thanks to the marriage into those royal houses of the Danish sisters Alexandra and Dagmar, in 1863 and 1866 respectively. As young parents, Nicholas and Alexandra made a few informal summer trips to 'amama' and 'apapa' (as they referred to the Danish king Christian IX and his wife Queen Louise) at Fredensborg. It was here that the cousins – Dagmar's son, Nicholas the Tsarevich, and Alexandra's son, George, Prince of Wales – had first developed a firm friendship. Indeed, it was as far back as 1883, on a family holiday at Fredensborg that George's sister Maud had first taken note of the fifteen-year-old 'darling *little* Nicky'. Like everyone else, she had noted how enamoured he was of Alix of Hesse and teased Nicholas about the fact that the object of his admiration was taller than him. Nonetheless, when Nicky and Maud were seen together at Prince George's wedding to Princess Mary of Teck in London in 1893, his father (then still Prince of Wales) had asked his mother-in-law Queen Louise whether there might perhaps be hope of a match between Nicky and Maud. The queen had thought this a bad idea; Maud was 'very sweet but far too headstrong'.[14]

Dynastic alliances were thus as much in the mind of the future King Edward VII as they were in that of the Kaiser, although Wilhelm's matchmaking ambitions had been part of a grandiose plan for the creation of a powerful new *Zollverein* – a continental alliance of Germany, Russia and France. Steering Alix of Hesse in the direction of Nicholas of Russia had been one way of shoring this up. Perhaps, in the wilder reaches of his vivid imagination, Wilhelm nursed visions of being another Frederick the Great, the Prussian monarch who had been instrumental in brokering the marriage of his German relative Sophie van Anhalt-Zerbst-Dornburg, and with it her rise on the Russian throne as Catherine the Great. The new Tsaritsa Alexandra would, however, never demonstrate any of Catherine's breadth of vision and energy as Empress. If anything, she inherited the prosaic, domestic Victorian values of her mother Alice – of example, duty, morality and a sense of service. But in one thing at least Alexandra would later demonstrate an instinct that she shared with her cousin Wilhelm: an entrenched belief in absolutist autocratic power.

Wilhelm's mother, the Dowager Empress Victoria, had certainly hoped that her niece Alexandra's succession to the Russian throne in November 1894, on the sudden death of Alexander III, might foster improved relations between Russia and Germany. In the years up to 1908 Nicholas and Wilhelm made frequent visits to each other for army manoeuvres, reviews of the fleet or simply to enjoy the shooting at their respective hunting lodges in Prussia and the Russian imperial game reserves in Poland. They had even gone yachting together – the Romanovs on the imperial yacht, the *Shtandart*, the Kaiser on the *Hohenzollern* – at Kiel and around the Finnish skerries. But far too often the prickly, meddlesome Kaiser had succeeded in upsetting those around him.[15] Despite this, in his letters to Nicky, Willy repeatedly assured him of his love and devotion; after all they shared the same fundamental belief in their divine right as sovereigns. 'We, Christian Kings and Emperors have one holy duty imposed on us by Heaven,' he told Nicky. 'That is to uphold the principle "*von Gottes gnaden*" [by the grace of God].'[16]

The Tsarevich Alexey's christening in 1904 would be the culmination of a period of rapprochement with Wilhelm, when he was asked to be godfather, in what may well have been an act more of diplomatic flattery than of familial affection. Wilhelm had been impatiently anticipating the birth of a 'nice little boy' since Nicholas and Alexandra's marriage in 1894, but had had to wait almost ten years – interspersed with the arrival of four baby girls – before the longed-for Tsarevich was born.[17] He was delighted to be honoured in this way, and hoped that little Alexey would 'grow to be a brave soldier and a wise and powerful statesman' and a 'ray of sunshine to you both during your life'.[18]

A year later, at the time of Russia's war with Japan, and in light of the 1902 alliance between Britain and Japan, Wilhelm worked hard on Nicholas's political loyalties. His long-term ambition had always been to keep his Russian cousin preoccupied with war in the East and Central Asia, leaving the way clear for his own ambitious German dominion-building in Europe.[19] He had spent years lecturing Nicholas by letter on his political and military options. Now, in July 1905, he took advantage of the Tsar's low morale at a time when he was worn down by a disastrous war, badgering him into a secret meeting at Björkö in Finland. Here Wilhelm talked the impressionable Nicholas into signing 'a little agreement' of their own, a defensive treaty under which Russia and Germany would come to each other's aid in the event of attack, an act clearly designed to undermine Russia's 1894 alliance with France. Thankfully Nicholas's advisers refused to endorse his signature and the treaty was aborted.

Thereafter, and in the long, slow burn towards the outbreak of war in 1914, it became increasingly evident that Nicholas and Alexandra's relationship with their German relative was 'tinged with a measure of latent and almost instinctive animosity' – a fact that would have a crucial bearing on events later in this story.[20] As for Nicholas, it was one thing for the two rulers to refer to each other by their pet domestic names, Willy and Nicky, but quite another for him 'to bow the Slavic head to German benevolent assimilation'. As the US ambassador to Denmark, Maurice Egan, observed, 'The Czar might call the Emperor by any endearing epithet, but that did not imply political friendship.' Neither Nicholas nor Alexandra was impressed by Wilhelm's brand of bombastic militarism, or by his manic sense of Hohenzollern grandeur.[21] Egan's conclusion was that 'Germany and Russia will fly at each other's throats as soon as the financiers approve of it.'[22]

In contrast, and much to Wilhelm's disgust, there had been a marked and growing closeness in recent years between the Russian and British royal families. People had always remarked on Nicholas's good manners and impeccable English, the result of having grown up with an English tutor, Charles Heath, who had educated him in the traditional public-school values of fair play and gentlemanly behaviour.[23] Ever since Nicholas first visited Queen Victoria at Windsor in 1894 he had referred to her with great affection as 'granny', writing to his cousin George when the Queen died in 1901, 'I am quite sure that with your help ... the friendly relations between our two countries shall become still closer than in the past ... May the new century bring England and Russia together for their mutual interests and for the general peace of the world.' From now on, the Prince of Wales (and future king George V) made repeated assurances in letters that he was 'Ever, dearest Nicky, your loving and truly devoted cousin and friend'.[24] They had much in common, notably an unostentatious domestic life and a love of the quiet of the countryside.

In tandem with warmer relations with Russia, a British entente with France was initiated in 1903 after King Edward made a triumphant state visit there. The *entente cordiale* had followed in 1904, and in 1907 a new Triple Entente of Britain, France and Russia. It was seen as a long-overdue and necessary defensive counterweight to the Triple Alliance that Wilhelm's grandfather had forged with Italy and Austria–Hungary in 1882. In Queen Victoria's time Russia had been a traditional enemy, and a country of whose expansionist ambitions in Central Asia she had had a pathological mistrust. By 1908, however, with cousin Willy embarking on an intensive shipbuilding programme and rapid expansion of his German battle fleet, there was clearly a pressing need for political rapprochement between Britain and Russia to counter this. Nevertheless, many in the British government and press perceived Nicholas as a despot and openly criticised the tsarist regime and its draconian prison and exile system.

It was the pragmatic Edward VII who saw the logic of this new alliance and what he came to call 'the Trade Union of Kings'. Nicholas, forever a straw in the wind susceptible to the influence of his more politically accomplished and domineering royal cousins, drifted increasingly into the British sphere of influence. For the time being, Edward's form of personal royal diplomacy remained effective. In June 1908 he finally made an official visit to Russia – albeit at sea, for security reasons – meeting Nicholas at the Estonian port of Reval (now Tallinn) in the Baltic, at this time still part of the Russian Empire. Superficially intended as a family affair, the visit added a 'personal touch of royal friendliness ... to clear away any lingering mistrust' and further cement Anglo–Russian relations. It also gave Edward the opportunity to offer Nicholas the weight of his own considerable political experience.[25]

Despite rumblings from Labour MP Ramsay MacDonald that the King should not be 'hobnobbing with a bloodstained creature' Edward made the grand gesture at Reval of creating Nicholas an admiral of the British fleet, and Nicholas returned the compliment by making Edward an admiral of the Imperial Navy.[26] By the end of the two-day PR exercise, designed, so *The Times* noted, 'to establish the world's peace', the atmosphere between the 'sovereigns of the two greatest empires under the sun' was one of 'cordial trust', a fact that infuriated the Kaiser when the news reached him.[27] Privately Edward had grave reservations about

Nicholas's competence as a monarch, thinking him 'deplorably unsophisticated, immature, and reactionary', but Edward was a skilful and tactful diplomatist who made his point by example and not by lecturing (unlike his nephew, the Kaiser), and the following year he invited the Romanovs to Britain.

August 1909 witnessed the last lovely imperial summer that the Romanovs would enjoy with their English relatives before war changed things irrevocably. Nicholas, Alexandra and all five children had sailed to the Isle of Wight to spend time with 'dear uncle Bertie' and his family. But such was the security nightmare of entertaining the Tsar of Russia that the four-day visit had to be conducted almost entirely at sea. Meetings, meals and receptions between the two families were held away from public view, on the two royal yachts, the *Shtandart* and the *Victoria and Albert*, anchored in the Solent outside Cowes harbour. The Romanovs were accorded a perfunctory tour of Osborne House, and afternoon tea with the Prince of Wales and his family at nearby Barton Manor, but at least the Romanov children had enjoyed a day ashore. They had taken great pleasure in visiting the royal family's private beach near Osborne House, where they dug sandcastles and collected seashells like any other children. On a shopping trip to west Cowes, with a bevy of detectives keeping a discreet distance, it was, however, the two eldest Romanov sisters, Olga and Tatiana, who had attracted the most attention and admiration. They seemed so natural, so modest and charming, and had shown such delight at their simple purchases of postcards and gifts for their parents and entourage.*

King Edward had been eager to organise this visit as an important gesture of support for the Anglo-Russian entente, at a time of increasing political tension. It was, he argued, 'politically of the highest importance'.[28] But in 1909 growing hostility from Ramsay MacDonald's Labour Party was reflected in a widening public

---

* For a description of the 1909 Cowes visit, see chapter 8, 'Royal Cousins', of my book *Four Sisters*.

hostility towards Russia's 'Nicholas the Bloody', which reached its zenith when the imperial yacht arrived at Cowes. This change had been coming ever since the brutal repressions of peaceful protesters in St Petersburg (from 1914 Petrograd) in January 1905 by Cossacks and other troops from the Imperial Guard, which was loyal to the government. Edward was accused of fraternising with a 'common murderer' and the Labour Party issued a formal protest. Nevertheless the atmosphere was in marked contrast to the stiff and uncomfortable visits made to the Kaiser by Nicholas at Swinemünde in 1907, and by Edward to Berlin six months before the Cowes visit, neither of which had done anything to mitigate deteriorating relations with Germany. Cowes, 1909, despite the anti-tsarist protests and worrying signs that Edward VII was now seriously ailing, reinforced the burgeoning new Anglo-Russian alliance. The Tsar's attendance at a naval review at Cherbourg en route to the Isle of Wight also further endorsed the Russian union with France in a power bloc against a now highly militant Germany.

Despite the wish to promote closer family relationships in the run-up to what seemed an inevitable European war, after 1909 Nicholas and Alexandra were increasingly forced to stay at home. The threat of revolutionary violence against them in Russia, as well as Alexandra's rapidly declining health, frequently made trips across the country, and beyond, untenable. With this heightened danger pressing inwards, the Imperial Family retreated within the protected walls of their palace at Tsarskoe Selo, fifteen miles south of St Petersburg. Journeys by rail were particularly open to attack, and the Romanovs now only travelled to visit relatives by sea. Even on a low-key visit to the Swedish king and queen in Stockholm in 1909 there had been rumours of an attempted attack on Nicholas, and for their protection the family had remained on board their yacht, with the Swedes coming to them. Such highly constrained visits allowed very little significant time in which the imperial children might enjoy the company of their young cousins, aside from precious trips to Wolfsgarten in Hesse.[29]

*

On 6 May 1910, Edward VII, the monarch at the heart of the old European royal order, died, his overweight body finally giving up on him after years of heavy smoking, drinking and eating. Edward might have begun his reign with the reputation of a self-indulgent playboy, but he ended it as a model constitutional monarch and one who had been universally loved and admired at home and abroad. Sadly, his good example had not rubbed off on his most stubbornly autocratic nephews – Wilhelm and Nicholas.

A great, solemn and dignified state funeral was arranged, but first the King's coffin lay in state in Westminster Hall for three days, in order to allow almost 250,000 members of the public – in a queue that was seven miles long on its final day – to file past and pay their respects. A cavalcade of royals in full rig – gold braid, feathers and cockades ablaze in the hot sunshine – processed on horseback behind the gun carriage carrying the King's coffin through the streets of London, to say farewell to this monarch, 'the most kingly of them all'.[30]

King Edward's funeral, larger even than that for his mother in 1901, undoubtedly marked the apotheosis of European monarchy. Among the dignitaries gathered from all over the world to pay their respects were nine reigning monarchs: eight kings and one emperor, aged from twenty-one to sixty-six years old. They sat together at Windsor Castle for a now-famous portrait: the new British king, George V; Kaiser Wilhelm of Germany; Frederick VIII of Denmark; George I of Greece; Haakon VII of Norway; Alfonso XIII of Spain; Manuel II of Portugal; Ferdinand I of Bulgaria; and Albert I, King of the Belgians – all related to the dead monarch either by blood or marriage. As too were most of the forty-five princes and seven queens in their entourages.[31]

Yet one monarch was conspicuous by his absence. Where was Nicholas? It was no surprise to anyone that he was unable to attend, being represented instead by his younger brother, Grand Duke Mikhail Alexandrovich, and his mother the Dowager, who was the dead king's sister-in-law. No official explanation was offered, but it is likely that the security nightmare of the Tsar of Russia marching in the funeral procession, where any political assassin could take a shot at him, was one that neither Nicholas's advisers nor British Special Branch had wished to take on. Cousin Wilhelm, however, was not slow to take advantage of Nicholas's absence and clasped George's hand in a moment's commiseration as they stood together by the King's coffin in Westminster Hall. The genuine sympathy that Wilhelm displayed that day prompted an invitation to return to England to attend the unveiling of a new statue of Queen Victoria – the grandmother he had revered as 'the creator of the greatness of modern Britain' – the following February.[32]

Even as people talked of an inevitable war between Britain and Germany, the Kaiser remained hopeful that he and his English cousin could still be best friends. But behind his back, George was already aligning himself firmly with his Russian cousin, exchanging letters of solidarity with Nicholas in which he reassured him that he hoped 'we shall always continue our old friendship to one another' and insisting that 'I have always been very fond of you'.[33] 'If only England, Russia and France stick together,' wrote George not long after his father's funeral, 'then peace in Europe is assured.' His correspondence with Nicholas over the following years became regular, frank and friendly. He was sure the Tsar shared his sentiments, for they were both by now convinced of the need to strengthen the entente in the face of increased German aggression. 'I know you don't mind me writing quite frankly what I think, as we have always been such good friends, I like to tell you everything,' George assured Nicholas a year later.[34]

As things turned out, 1910 also marked the last time Nicholas and Alexandra were able to make the journey to their German relatives in Hesse. A prolonged stay at Friedberg Castle provided a rare opportunity for all five Hesse siblings – Alexandra, Ella, Irene, Victoria and their brother Ernie – to be reunited. Friedberg, located between Darmstadt and Frankfurt, was perhaps the most unroyal venue of all the royal homes Nicholas and Alexandra visited. Here the Romanovs enjoyed a reduced entourage, no parades or ceremonies, relaxed etiquette and, for Nicholas, an escape into civilian clothes. He was able to go out, incognito, with his brother-in-law Ernie, and could sit and drink a glass of beer in a café and browse in the local shops.[35] But Alexandra was by now in serious physical decline, suffering from chronic sciatica, heart trouble, headaches and facial neuralgia, made worse by the constant mental strain of having a haemophiliac son. She had already undergone treatment at a spa in Bad Nauheim prior to their visit, and kept mainly to her rooms, spending much of her time in a wheelchair. Her five children, who had long since learned to be self-sufficient during their mother's frequent bouts of illness, enjoyed being left to their own devices and made the most of the time with their cousins.

Back in Russia, the nation enjoyed one final golden opportunity to see their sovereigns – their little mother and father – at close hand during the Romanov Tercentenary celebrations of 1913. In St Petersburg and Moscow the whole family joined in great religious parades, where ordinary Russians turned out in their thousands to catch a glimpse of them, followed in May by a river-boat tour along the Volga to Kostroma, Yaroslavl, Suzdal and other ancient cities of old Muscovy. The ceremonials held in Moscow also enabled many of the Russian public to see the elusive young Tsarevich at last, though people expressed concern at seeing him having to be carried by a Cossack. Alexey was still recovering from a severe episode of bleeding that had nearly killed him the previous year and had left him with permanent damage to his leg. The truth about his haemophilia and the constant threat to his life was still being kept from the Russian public.

Shortly afterwards, Nicholas left for Germany, for the last great European royal wedding to be held before the outbreak of war – in Berlin. By this time, one of the monarchs in King Edward's funeral procession has already lost his throne: King Manuel of Portugal had been deposed in a military coup just five months later.

Always keen to outdo his English cousins, Wilhelm had invited even more relatives than those who had gathered in London in 1910. Nicholas, however, travelled alone to the festivities under heavy guard in an armoured train, arriving at Berlin's Anhalter station where the security was so extensive it looked like 'a constabulary camp, police and detectives were everywhere'.[36] At the Berlin Schloss he joined George V and his wife Mary at the marriage of the Kaiser's only daughter, Viktoria Luise, to Duke Ernst Augustus of Brunswick, a grandson of the last King of Hanover, and Nicholas's first cousin. The assembled military dress uniforms were magnificent, the parades and other imperial German ceremonial impressive, the jewels lavish and the food spectacular. Yet the atmosphere, although superficially cordial, was strained by intensifying Anglo-German-Russian rivalries and by continuing concern over Germany's naval build-up.

During the visit Wilhelm seemed more paranoid and jealous than ever and had done his utmost to ensure that his two cousins did not have any private time together. Nevertheless George managed to have 'a long and satisfactory talk with dear Nicky' over tea at the Kaiserhof Hotel.[37] He found Nicholas still the same amiable cousin of his childhood memories, and observers noted the affectionate, if not jovial, atmosphere between them. To seal their continuing closeness they had their photograph taken, wearing the uniforms of their honorary German regiments – Nicholas's Westphalian Hussars and George's Rhenish Cuirassiers – that they had worn for the wedding. They looked even more uncannily alike than ever. It was an iconic photograph, and one that would go down in history as the last ever taken together of Nicky and Georgy, the 'Heavenly Twins'.

Sixteen months later the world was at war. Nicholas had agonised over his decision to mobilise in defence of the Serbs, as fellow Slavs, when Austria–Hungary had declared war on them. Although he did so in the face of dark warnings from Wilhelm about the consequences, the Tsar was confident of British and French support. With the English and Russian monarchs forging an even closer relationship as allies, George confided in Margot Asquith, wife of his Prime Minister, that his cousin the Tsar was 'the best, straightest, most clear and decided man I know'. Their cousin Wilhelm – his dreams of a vast continental alliance of

Germany, Russia and France in tatters – was now the enemy.[38] Orthodox Russia was now a wartime ally of socialist, freethinking France, an unlikely union that Nicholas found uncomfortable, despite his admiration for President Poincaré. But far better to be allies than the alternative. His mother the Dowager, like many in the Romanov family, expressed her enormous sense of relief: 'You cannot imagine, after having been obliged to hide my true feelings for forty years, what it feels like to be able to tell you at last how much I hate the Germans!' she told a member of the State Duma.[39] The wounds of the Schleswig-Holstein crisis and the ensuing Danish war with Prussia in 1864 still ran very deep. Nicholas vowed that he was 'determined to stick to my French Ally to the bitter end', he told Prince Nicholas of Greece. 'We cannot afford to lose this war, as the triumph of Prussian militarism would mean the end of all liberty and civilization.'[40]

There would be no more visits, however brief, to relatives in war-torn Europe, as royal families were forced to align with either the Allies (the Triple Entente of Britain, France and Russia) or the Central Powers (the Triple Alliance of Germany, Austria–Hungary and Italy). The finger of suspicion, however irrational, was now being pointed at anyone on the Allied side with familial links to Germany. Close royal relatives in Coburg and in Hesse would soon be cut off from their families in Russia and Britain. The Duchess of Coburg (Russian wife of Queen Victoria's son Prince Alfred), who was very pro-German, was forced to send messages to her English and Russian relatives via neutral embassies in Scandinavia and the offices of the Crown Princess of Sweden, who ran a kind of royal postal service for her warring relatives.

The three major Scandinavian powers – Norway, Sweden and Denmark – had been reluctant to take part in the conflict, all of them having their own historical loyalties. King Gustav V of Sweden was inherently sympathetic to the German side, Sweden having fought a succession of wars with Russia since the late fifteenth century. Gustav's wife Victoria was a daughter of the Grand Duke of the German duchy of Baden, and Sweden had long feared incursions from Russia, which still controlled neighbouring Finland. In 1915 Gustav wrote in secret to Nicholas telling him how, in an attempt to broker a separate deal between Russia and Germany, he would offer to mediate, but Nicholas would not countenance one. 'Never has Russia been so united and so determined as now,' he told Gustav; they would carry on with the war 'until it reaches a permanent end'.[41] But remaining neutral throughout a protracted war would leave Sweden increasingly isolated by harsh rationing and famine, to such an extent that King Gustav became fearful for his own throne.

Like Sweden, Denmark and Norway opted for neutrality, despite family ties with the major antagonists. George V and Nicholas II were closely related to the kings of Denmark and Norway: King Christian X was a nephew to Dagmar, the Dowager Empress and the Queen Mother; and King Haakon was also their nephew. Geographically, however, Denmark had always been considered 'part of Germany', wrote ambassador Maurice Egan; its capital Copenhagen was:

> so near what was that center of world politics – the German court – its royal family ... so closely allied with all the reigning and non-reigning royal families of Europe, and its diplomatic life so tense and comprehensive – that it ha[d] been well named the whispering gallery of Europe.[42]

Having such a close relationship with the Allies, through his two widowed aunts Alexandra and Dagmar, King Christian of Denmark offered to mediate in the war via messages that he sent through a wealthy Danish businessman and shipowner, Hans Niels Andersen, a personal friend of both the Danish and British royal families. In 1915 Christian had suggested hosting a peace conference in Copenhagen; as a neutral country, Denmark would be well placed economically to capitalise on the rebuilding of Germany and Russia after the war. Only that year the Danes had established a Russian trading company and had appointed their own commercial attaché, Harald Schou-Kjeldsen, to the Danish embassy in Petrograd. The export opportunities to Russia were huge, and the Danish-born Dowager was a key patron of Danish enterprise at the time.[43] Policy was what drove wartime loyalties, not blood ties; policy based on the needs for territory, markets and raw materials.

Andersen, like Kjeldsen, supported Danish trading interest during the war and travelled regularly between London, St Petersburg and Berlin. He seemed the perfect go-between; and already in 1915, with Berlin's encouragement, he had travelled to Petrograd to try and persuade the Tsar to negotiate a separate peace with Germany. This had greatly annoyed the British government, which wanted nothing less than a general peace between all parties, and only after Germany had been brought to its knees. But it was perhaps King Haakon of Norway, the furthest removed from Russia geographically and the most pragmatic and democratic monarch of the three, who seemed best placed to offer Nicholas serious advice at a time when Russia was not just worn down by a disastrous campaign on the Eastern Front, but also by the threat of civil disturbance at home. Haakon was in fact a Danish prince, Carl, who had been invited to take the newly vacant throne of Norway when the act of Union linking it with Sweden had been dissolved in 1905. His wife Maud was the young English princess who had teased Nicholas about his affection for Alexandra back in the 1880s.

Before agreeing to take the throne, Haakon had insisted on a national referendum being held, so that his accession was endorsed by the nation as a whole. It was, in his opinion, only by the will of the Norwegian people that he and his fellow monarchs ruled, and in a frank conversation with Nicholas some time before the war, Haakon had advised him on the best way to avoid revolution in Russia:

> Give the Poles autonomy. Let the little Russians [Ukrainians], Georgians and Armenians enjoy home rule and nationality undisturbed. Restore peace to the Caucasus by recognizing their rights and cease trying to Russianize Finland.

'That alone,' the King had told his Russian cousin, and 'there would be no desire for revolution.'[44]

This rare interview with Haakon, published by an American reporter, Mary Boyle O'Reilly, was lost for a century. Forgotten in a long-defunct newspaper – the *Fort Wayne Sentinel* – it is now, like so much valuable context on the period, retrievable, thanks to the digitisation of old newspapers. It encapsulates the sanest, most pragmatic advice ever offered to Nicholas II by a fellow monarch, who understood only too clearly what they all needed to do to survive: compromise, reform, democratise, enfranchise. If only Nicholas had listened …

But Nicholas never acted upon Haakon's or any other sensible advice offered to him by his relatives in the years leading up to the Revolution of 1917. Instead, he stubbornly turned his face away from what was logical and expedient, into the headwind of the vagaries of superstition and fate.

By the beginning of 1917, the royals of Europe were in a race to try and save Nicholas and Alexandra from their own folly. Having so far failed, how disposed would any of them be towards coming to their aid, when the inevitable, predicted crisis came?

Chapter 2

'Some Catastrophe Lurking in the Dark'

*I*t all began with a suitcase.

Into every historian's life some lucky breaks must fall, and one such presented itself just as I embarked on the research for the story of the failed Romanov asylum. A dedicated Romanov buff and friend, who knew I was on the lookout for new material, contacted me. She had recently been acting as co-executor of the literary estate of a fellow enthusiast who had spent a lifetime exhaustively transcribing royal correspondence (written in English) held in the Romanian Royal Archives. The collection was extensive, was in some disarray, had had to be moved at speed and nothing was catalogued ... 'Do you want to take a look at the files?' she asked, before they all got sent off to a royal archive in Spain that had agreed to take them.[1]

In such situations no sane historian ever says no. It is a measure of my friend's devotion to history, scholarship and camaraderie that she pulled out all the files and folders she thought would be of interest to me, put them in a very large suitcase and trundled it across London, then all the way on the train down to my house in the West Country.

A quick flip through a random file and I was taken aback by the damning comments about the Tsaritsa Alexandra: 'My innermost conviction is that she is suffering from a mild, but morally serious kind of insanity,' wrote Alexandra's aunt, the Duchess of Coburg, to her daughter, Crown Princess Marie of Romania, in February 1913; a year later she was even more scathing: 'Alix to my mind is absolutely mad, everything she does is dictated to her by this false prophet [Rasputin].'[2] The level *of vitriol levelled at the ailing Tsaritsa by her royal relatives seemed excessive. Did they all really hate Alexandra so much, I asked myself? Was this why so many of them had had such ambivalent feelings when Nicholas and Alexandra's whole world came crashing down in 1917?*

I was soon to discover that the hatred for Alexandra was far more widespread, and would colour attitudes to the Romanov asylum in the most profound and disturbing ways.

In 1896, when Nicholas and Alexandra visited Queen Victoria for the last time, at Balmoral, family perceptions of the sunny young Alexandra had dramatically changed. Now, as Empress of Russia, full of a sense of undisguised superiority over her lesser European relatives, she seemed so much grander and obsessed with her own precedence. Unlike other royal relatives, including her mother-in-law Dagmar who believed that the aristocracy had to work for their position, Alexandra considered it vulgar to make overt efforts to win the support or affection of her people. At the Imperial Russian Court, feelings were much the same. The Russian aristocracy had taken an almost instant dislike to Alexandra from the day she married Nicholas in November 1894. She had none of the grace, social skills or sartorial panache of her 'brilliant mother-in-law, Dagmar of Denmark, [who] was still beautiful and picturesque', as ambassador Maurice Egan observed. More importantly, the Dowager was truly 'imperial' in manner and understood the importance of court pomp and tradition, while her daughter-in-law refused to kowtow to any of it.[3] Alexandra had a pathological aversion to the very rituals of court life that Dagmar enjoyed. They intruded on her family life with Nicholas and were too protracted. The imperial entourage, to her mind, was unnecessarily large. From the outset, official public life in Russia tormented her and she contrived to find every possible way of avoiding it.[4]

In Alexandra's frequent absences from the St Petersburg social scene, the domineering presence – after the gregarious and stylish Dowager – had been Nicholas's aunt, Maria Pavlovna the Elder, better known as Grand Duchess Vladimir. It was her social pronouncements that set the trend for whoever was in or out. From the very first, the new serious and sober-minded Tsaritsa was most decidedly out; her reticent appearances at the Russian court were sneered at. She was no equal of the sophisticated and ostentatious *beau monde* who met at functions at the Vladimir Palace in St Petersburg. Alexandra's perceived social inadequacies, which none of her Romanov relatives ever tried to understand or make concessions for, gave increasing power to her most vocal critics within the family. Having also played a key role in persuading Alexandra to marry Nicholas, Grand Duchess Vladimir had expected a position as close adviser to her, when she became Tsaritsa. But this was not to be; and the Grand Duchess never forgave Alexandra when it became apparent that her advice and company were not welcomed. For ever after she 'gave full vent to her spleen in acid comment on everything that her niece did or did not do,' recalled Count Mosolov. 'The Court – *her* Court – followed the example set to it. It was from the immediate entourage of Marie Pavlovna that the most wounding stories about the Tsaritsa emanated.'[5]

Over the years, these wounding stories gathered strength and venom, particularly once Alexandra had embraced the spiritual guidance of the guru and healer Rasputin in 1907. There had always been a sense, among some of the female members of the family, that the highly strung and mistrustful Alexandra was emotionally damaged and difficult, and her behaviour seemed to prove that this was the case. These fires of family animosity were stoked by Alexandra's own cousin and former sister-in-law, Victoria Melita, now remarried as Grand Duchess Kirill; and the pot was vigorously stirred – when she visited St Petersburg – by Grand Duchess Kirill's mother, Marie, Duchess of Coburg. Their gossipy letters to each other testify to the levels of backbiting against Alexandra in St Petersburg society.

A growing and voluble resentment against the Tsaritsa gathered pace during the war years. In September 1915, after the Russian army suffered a series of crippling reverses on the Eastern Front,

Nicholas II decided to sack his Commander in Chief, his uncle Grand Duke Nikolay Nikolaevich, and take over command of the Russian army himself. He did so in the sincere belief that this would reassure his allies of his absolute determination to fight to the bitter end, and to counter persistent rumours that Russia was seeking an early exit from the war. Although his presence at the front did something to revive the flagging morale of the army, Nicholas's absence from Petrograd opened the floodgates to what by then had become a stream of rumour, gossip and accusation targeted at his wife. Alexandra stepped into the political vacuum and rapidly began overreaching herself by directly influencing the sacking and appointment of key ministers, replacing with sycophants those who were sympathetic to reform. Even worse, in the eyes of the Romanov family elders, they became convinced that she was soliciting the advice of Rasputin at every turn.

Alexandra repeatedly protested her great love for Russia, and there was no doubting her unquestionable devotion to the Russian Orthodox Church. Yet nothing could dispel the widely held conviction, not just in Russia but also abroad, that the Hesse-born Tsaritsa was a covert German sympathiser. People were convinced that she was machinating against the Allied war effort and passing military information on to the German High Command. In France they openly referred to her as 'La bochesse'; in Russia she was 'the German woman'.[6]* Many believed that Alexandra, Rasputin and her camarilla of reactionary ministers were traitors, and were secretly conniving for a separate peace with Germany.[7] Rumours were even circulating that the Empress had a 'special

---

* Other royal brides had also been vulnerable to nationalistic rabble-rousing during war or times of crisis. During the French Revolution the mob referred to Marie Antoinette as the 'Austrian woman'; and in World War I, Queen Sophie of Greece, who was Alexandra's cousin and the Kaiser's sister, was also referred to as 'the German woman'. Rumours even circulated that she kept a secret transmitter at the Tatoi Palace, on which she sent messages to the Germans.

radio-telegraph machine' hidden at the Alexander Palace, on which she transmitted intelligence on the Russian war effort to Berlin.[8] Such blatant character assassination prompted the French ambassador, Maurice Paléologue, to come to Alexandra's defence. The Empress was 'German neither in mind nor spirit and has never been so,' he insisted. She was English through her mother and her grandmother, Queen Victoria, and in 'the uncompromising and militant austerity of her conscience'. British statesman Lord Hardinge concurred: had Nicholas been an Englishman, he 'would have been the most perfect type of English gentleman' and there was no doubt that Alexandra 'though shy and reserved, was devoted to England and thoroughly English in all her tastes'.[9]

Believing that she, the Empress, had no need to explain herself, and trusting only Nicholas, Alexandra did nothing to counter the rumours. But her continuing absence from public life only fanned the flames. At the Alexander Palace at Tsarskoe Selo she had increasingly shut herself away from all but her closest entourage. Even her ladies-in-waiting hardly saw her and were bored and frustrated with so little to do. To a woman as *comme il faut* as the Duchess of Coburg, Alexandra's reclusiveness was outrageous; she had a duty to her public. Yet during her visit for the Tercentenary in 1913, the Duchess had found the atmosphere at Tsarskoe Selo 'exactly like living in a house with an invisible ghost in it'.[10] 'She never goes out now and lays most of the day on the sofa,' the Duchess complained. Alexandra had made no attempt to talk to her and had lain there with 'a suffering smile on her face'. For Alexandra's relatives, their patience was being stretched to the limit. She was always playing 'the victimized martyr'.[11]

But it was the welfare of Alexandra's daughters in particular that concerned the Duchess. They seemed so neglected and hardly went out, spending their days forever at their mother's beck and call. The sad reality of their lives was that, far from being out and about enjoying the company of people of their own age and social status, they had by now become carers and protectors of their ailing mother and haemophiliac brother. Alexandra had always disapproved of her daughters mixing in decadent St Petersburg society, as she saw it; a trip to the opera or ballet with their father before the onset of war had been a major event in their lives. And so their social circle was a tightly controlled one of a few close female members of Alexandra's entourage, and the hand-picked officers of the Imperial Yacht or the elite Cossack Escort that guarded them. Pleasure, for all the children, was gained from small things – in particular, walking, cycling and boating with their father and enjoying the fresh air. Otherwise, the four sisters spent interminable hours sitting at home with their mother, sewing and knitting. 'Does Mama ever read?' the Duchess of Coburg had asked them, shocked at the girls' narrow existence. '"Oh never," they answered, "as she always has headaches."'[12] The Duchess was convinced that Alexandra had succumbed to some kind of internal disease for which she refused to be operated on and that she was mentally disturbed. 'Uncle Serge [Ella's husband], more than ten years ago, told me that he was persuaded of it then already, *une douce folie* as he called it. How right he was!'[13]

With his wife in retreat, and preoccupied always with the fragile health of his son, Nicholas seemed to have closed his mind to the ongoing dangers of political and social unrest. Even the foreign diplomatic community was warning him of the looming danger of revolution, if he did not capitulate to some kind of democratic reform. At court, Prince Volkonsky told the Duchess of Coburg that whenever he or 'any well intentioned people who would like to open Niki's eyes and save Russia' tried to raise their concerns with him, Nicholas would avert his gaze, look out of the window and 'so completely drops the conversation that there is no possibility to go on!' Avoidance seemed to be his only, and perpetual, response. Every attempt to engage him in serious conversation was thwarted by the Empress: 'He tells her everything, shows her every letter, discusses everything with her and she puts a stop to all good resolutions and we all feel the utter hopelessness of getting at Niki without his spouse spoiling everything.' The only hope now, Prince Volkonsky suggested, was 'if all the influential members of the family united in one big demonstration and came to tell the truth. That, he felt, 'would impress him'.[14]

By December 1916 such was the mounting family hostility that even Alexandra's sister Ella came especially from Moscow to plead with the Empress to remove Rasputin from his position of influence and to cease interfering in matters of state. But no amount of reason ever worked with the Tsaritsa; she had, as her cousin Marie Louise of Schleswig-Holstein recalled, 'a strange impregnable obstinacy which nothing would overcome'.[15] For her own part, Alexandra was paranoid that the Romanov family were all plotting against her and stirring up ill feeling with their relatives abroad. By now, respect for the Russian throne among its own aristocracy was at an all-time low, not helped by a series of scandals involving adultery, divorce and morganatic marriages among Nicholas's uncles and cousins, all of which had dented Romanov prestige and family unity. Even his younger brother, Grand Duke Mikhail Alexandrovich, had broken the Romanov House law. He had travelled abroad without permission, dodging the tsarist police who were tailing him, to marry a commoner, Natalia Wulfert.

In the meantime, Nicholas and Alexandra's response to all appeals for political concessions had been to repeatedly meddle in the workings of the State Duma, while clinging ever more ferociously to their own stubbornly held values and moral principles.[16] Alexandra's response to her cousin Grand Duchess Kirill's plea was typical:

'Who is against us? Petrograd, a bunch of aristocrats playing bridge and understanding nothing. I have been sitting on the throne for twenty-two years, I know Russia, I have travelled around the whole place, and I know that the people love our family.'[17]

Diplomats in Petrograd recorded the sharp descent into crisis that winter of 1916–17, not just in the war, but within the Romanov family. Russia, having already endured catastrophic losses on the Eastern Front, was suffering the mass desertion of demoralised conscripts. Supply lines to the big cities were in disarray; the railways were in chaos, due to a chronic shortage of rolling stock; and much-needed food and fuel were not reaching the beleaguered populations of the major cities. People were tired of the war, tired of shortages, tired of a government that did not listen to their grievances about harsh working conditions, low wages and long hours. They despaired that they would ever see the introduction of a constitutional government. The rumble of dissent grew ever louder, with a succession of crippling strikes and workers' protest marches bringing the life of the city to a standstill. The old, moribund tsarist regime was about to collapse, but still Alexandra refused to recognise the dangers, dismissing the disturbances as the work of disorganised hooligans; at the front, Nicholas's right-hand man General Alexeev was, like Alexandra, underplaying their significance to the Tsar, who, in ignorance of the true gravity of the situation, thought it would all blow over.

In Petrograd, however, that was far from the case: with revolution at their door, members of the Romanov family were plotting a palace coup against an intransigent Tsar and Tsaritsa. Maurice Paléologue heard that Grand Duchess Vladimir's three sons were 'talking of nothing less than saving tsarism by a change of sovereign'. Another relative, Grand Duke Gavriil Konstantinovich, spoke of leading four Guards regiments in a march on Tsarskoe Selo by night and forcibly removing Alexandra.[18] She, according to her brother-in-law Sandro (Grand Duke Alexander, married to Nicholas's sister Xenia) – who had gone to plead with her at Tsarskoe Selo – was 'in a state of complete and incurable delusion'.[19] Alexandra had to be stopped: either sent away to a convent or locked up in a psychiatric hospital. A more outlandish plan involved luring her onto a destroyer, under some pretext, and transporting her off to England.[20] Even the highly restrained British ambassador, Sir George Buchanan, in later years admitted that he had come to the conclusion that the Tsar should disassociate himself from his wife and save himself.[21] 'Their hatred of the Empress has reached a terrible pitch,' admitted one Russian officer in conversation with the Tsaritsa's cousin Marie, Queen of Romania, 'they consider her a misfortune for the country and there is no one today who would not gladly get rid of her by any means'.[22] Even the Dowager could no longer contain her imperial discretion: her daughter-in-law 'must be banished ... I don't know how but it must be done. Otherwise she might go completely mad.' Shockingly, such was her contempt for Alexandra that Dagmar did not much care about her subsequent fate: 'Let her enter a convent or just disappear.'[23]

As for the Tsar, the consensus was increasingly that if Nicholas refused to concede to a responsible, constitutional government free of interference from himself and his wife, he should be deposed and his twelve-year-old son Alexey should take the throne under a regency of either Grand Duke Nikolay Nikolaevich or Grand Duke Mikhail Alexandrovich. But the situation had by now spiralled beyond all reasonable attempts at persuasion. Alexandra's knee-jerk response to all and any suggestions of reform was as arrogant as it was dogmatic: 'Nicky is an autocrat. How could he share his divine rights with a parliament?'[24] The Romanov family railed and plotted, but all their plans to oust Nicholas and Alexandra from power shared the fatal flaw of 'wishy-washiness', in the view of Duma president, Mikhail Rodzianko. A coup against Nicholas and Alexandra would be successful only 'with real force behind it' – in other words, the involvement of the military.[25]

At the end of December 1916 the murder of Rasputin, and with it the removal of Alexandra's perceived malevolent adviser, seemed to have defused a desperate situation. Prince Felix Yusupov and Grand Duke Dmitri Pavlovich had plotted his assassination, in the hopes that it would save Russia from imminent disaster. 'A desperate situation had required desperate measures,' Yusupov wrote later. 'One can't argue with anyone who is insane.' 'Everything was at boiling point,' recalled Grand Duke Pavel Alexandrovich,' ... there was a heaviness in the air.' The people did not need to agitate for revolution; the imperial house was doing the job for them.[26]

In Europe, none of Nicholas and Alexandra's royal cousins had made any attempt to disguise their enormous sense of relief when Rasputin was killed. In Britain, Alexandra the Queen Mother wrote that Rasputin's death was 'only regretted by poor dear Alicky who might have ruined the whole future of Russia through his influence … she thinks herself like the Empress Catherine.'[27] Grand Duchess Kirill agreed: Alexandra's conviction that 'on her depended the salvation and reconstruction of Russia … had created a tangled situation, out of which there was no exit'.[28]

'*What* a blessing that R[asputin] is now out of the way,' wrote Queen Maud of Norway to Dagmar on 27 January 1917.[29]* But for many in the Imperial Family the removal of Rasputin was not enough: 'we must entirely rid ourselves of Alexandra Fyodorovna and Protopopov [the Russian Minister of the Interior],' Grand Duke Nikolay Mikhailovich wrote to Dagmar, who, exasperated that her son and his wife would not listen to her advice, had removed herself to Kiev. 'I put before you the same dilemma,' he went on:

> Having removed the hypnotiser we must try and disable the hypnotised … This is a matter of *saving the throne* – not the dynasty, which still stands firm, but the current sovereign. It will otherwise be too late … all Russia knows that the late Rasputin and A. F. are one and the same. One has been killed, now the other must disappear.[30]

A deadly atmosphere of hostility and recrimination continued to prevail at court. Nicholas and Alexandra had seemed 'solely occupied with vengeance on all whom they think implicated' in the murder, wrote Grand Duchess Kirill. 'It's so awful here now that we are living like in a mad house.'[31] Nicholas's response to Rasputin's demise had certainly been harsh: the two perpetrators, Dmitri Pavlovich and Felix Yusupov, were sent to the Persian front and into internal exile respectively. The Romanov family wrote a collective letter of protest to Nicholas; his refusal to soften

---

* Note that all dates throughout are given according to the Gregorian calendar in use in Western Europe (New Style: NS), and to avoid confusion with the Julian calendar, which was in use in Russia until 13 February 1918 (Old Style: OS).

the punishment further galvanised some of them to talk seriously of the Tsar and Tsaritsa's removal. At a dinner held at Prince Gavriil Konstantinovich's home, the talk, as Maurice Paléologue recalled, was all about conspiracy. Other secret meetings to discuss the subject were held at Grand Duchess Vladimir's palace. The family feared that once Nicholas returned to the front, the 'Empress may make herself Regent'.[32]

By early 1917, the constant pressures from his family and his domineering wife, in addition to terrible worries over the Russian campaign, had aged Nicholas terribly. He seemed completely beaten down and was capitulating ever more to fatalism. 'His hair and beard were streaked with white, his eyes were sunken,' recalled the Russian ambassador to Stockholm, Anatoly Neklyudov. But that was not what had struck him most:

> I noticed a kind of weariness, a kind of constant preoccupation which seemed to prevent him concentrating his whole attention on the conversation in hand; the vivacity of his manner and of his mind seemed to have vanished … it seems to me that in the manner and appearance of the emperor Nicholas II, there was more than preoccupation, more than worry. Perhaps he already saw the abyss opening at his feet and perhaps he knew that to stop was impossible, that he must pursue his way towards the inevitable and fatal crash.[33]

Everyone pitied Nicholas for his weakness; but they hated Alexandra even more for her morbid hysteria. 'Her will is active, aggressive and restless,' Grand Duchess Vladimir observed to Paléologue. Nicholas's will, on the other hand, was 'merely negative. When he ceases to believe in himself and thinks God has abandoned him, he does not try to assert himself, but merely wraps himself up in a dull and resigned obstinacy.' Alexandra was becoming too powerful: 'Before long she'll be the sole ruler of Russia.'[34] The Dowager was in despair at her son's apathy. 'I feel that we are approaching some disaster with relentless steps and that His Majesty listens only to flatterers,' she confided to Prime Minister

Vladimir Kokovtsov. Her son could not see 'that there is something forming under his feet. Something he does not see yet, and
I feel it, instinctively, but can't make out what exactly we are in
for.'[35] A gathering tide of change was clearly heading Nicholas's
way, and within the State Duma, as Paléologue noted, even the
most 'ardent devotees of tsarism and reaction were now openly
discussing the possibility of the emperor's assassination'.[36]

The fate of Russia was, by now, the 'one subject of discussion
in diplomatic circles,' recalled Maurice Egan. 'It was the general
opinion that the Empress was the great obstacle to the Emperor's
giving a liberal constitution to his people.'[37] It was at this point
that Nicholas's brother-in-law Sandro composed a long letter
to the Tsar in which he begged Nicholas to make political
concessions and bring his autocratic wife under control. 'You
cannot govern a country without listening to the voice of the
people,' he wrote. 'With a few words and a stroke of the pen,
you could calm everything and give the country what it yearns
for, that is a government of confidence and freedom to the
forces of society.'[38] Sandro was distraught; Nicholas's advisers,
most of whom had been put in place by Alexandra in his
absence, were leading him and Russia 'towards certain ruin'. In
an uncompromisingly frank discussion with Mikhail Rodzianko,
Grand Duchess Vladimir was now urging that Alexandra 'must
be annihilated'.[39]

At a secret meeting in the capital, key members of the Duma,
the Council of the Empire and the Special Council discussed the
possibility of a *coup d'état*.[40] A group in the Duma, centring around
Prince Lvov, talked of sending Alexandra to Crimea and forcing
Nicholas to cede authority to his uncle, Grand Duke Nikolay
Nikolaevich, but the Grand Duke rejected the idea.[41] Instead 'it
was decided to force the boy [Alexey] to sign a document prepared
in advance,' recalled Duma deputy Boris Engelgardt, 'and to form
a ruling council around him', made up of various Duma ministers.[42] This was paramount in order to save the war effort from
being further undermined. A coup was planned for early March;
Mikhail Tereshchenko would travel to the front to recruit

sympathetic officers. But as with so many of the various conspiracies against Nicholas and Alexandra at this time, it barely progressed 'beyond salon talk'; and, like all of them, it came too late.[43]

In the National Archives at Kew there is an enormous, unindexed 573-page file marked 'Russia and Siberia', which comprises Foreign Secretary Arthur Balfour's papers for the war period. It is normally accessed for the extensive documents it contains on the Allied intervention of 1918, but also – and typical of the entirely eccentric organisation of Foreign Office documents of this period – the file contains key documents relating to the Romanov asylum and one of its key players, Sir George Buchanan, some of which have till now been largely overlooked and which will be drawn on in the course of this book. One such telegram from Buchanan in January 1917 sets the tone of his concerns about an imminent collapse of the regime in Russia; the official response to it is a significant indicator of how the British government, and the King, would respond throughout this affair.

Throughout the winter of 1916–17, at the British Embassy on Suvorov Square in Petrograd, Sir George Buchanan had been anxiously watching the escalating situation and begging permission from his government to make serious representations to the Tsar about the danger he was in. 'Revolution was in the air' and 'the only moot point was whether it would come from above or from below,' he recalled.[44] Despite Buchanan's repeated and urgent warnings that the Tsar must be made to confront the danger, the British government had been loath to meddle, advising him that it had 'grave doubts whether diplomatic advice, however friendly, on such a matter would be well received, or whether, if well received, it would lead to any practical result. After all, the facts of the case are notorious, and cannot be unknown to the Emperor.'[45]

But Sir George was adamant: the situation was 'becoming so serious,' he telegraphed on 7 January 1917, 'that it is in my opinion a duty which we owe to the Emperor himself, to Russia, and to ourselves as Russia's ally, to speak plainly'. Russia was on the brink:

With the exception of a small clique of interested persons, the whole country is united in opposition to the Emperor's present policy, which is also condemned by [the] majority of his Ministers ... Minister of Foreign Affairs to whom I spoke in private on the subject this morning, begged me to ask for an audience, and said that even if I spoke only in my own name, my support would be most useful at the present moment to those who had already expressed to the Emperor somewhat similar views. The French Ambassador ... [said] that *a word from our King would be invaluable* [my italics].[46]

Such was Sir George's strength of feeling on the matter that he stuck his neck out even further: if officialdom would not allow him, as ambassador, to appeal to the Tsar on behalf of King George and his government, might he be given permission to make an entirely personal approach to the Tsar? He was, he said, 'quite prepared to assume the whole responsibility for what I may say, and I believe I can put the case in such a way as would not offend the Emperor. The worst that can happen is that I may personally incur His Majesty's temporary displeasure.' Buchanan could not emphasise sufficiently the urgent state of affairs:

All that I ask is that I may be charged with some message from the King, that would show that His Majesty both as the Emperor's kinsman, and as Russia's Ally, is seriously pre-occupied by the turn which events are taking. I would humbly submit this suggestion for HM's gracious consideration. Unless the Emperor unexpectedly changes his present attitude, most leading Ministers will resign and it is in my opinion, the psychological moment for us to speak. If we defer doing so, it may be too late, and the consequences may be incalculable.[47]

In a telegram sent to Buchanan on 8 January, and in the light of the ambassador's strong views, Foreign Secretary Balfour withdrew his objection to him seeking an audience with Nicholas. But Balfour was adamant on one thing: he did not wish to 'press the King to send a private telegram to the Emperor'. 'The whole subject,' he stressed, was 'causing the King very great anxiety'. He relied on Buchanan's 'tact and discretion in handling the matter in a way that would not give offence to Nicholas', which might otherwise do 'more harm than good'.[48]

On 12 January, Buchanan finally had his meeting with the Tsar, but it proved stiff and formal, and Nicholas was more defensive and evasive than ever.[49] He adamantly refused to take seriously the talk of revolution. Sir George was horrified, and warned the British government that both the Russian sovereigns seemed 'possessed of madness and to be wantonly courting disaster'.[50]

It is clear from this exchange of telegrams on 7 and 8 January that the British king privately shared Buchanan's sense of urgency about the security of the Russian throne, but that his government was already setting up barriers to prevent him becoming embroiled in the whole contentious problem. Nevertheless, having been copied in on this latest message from his ambassador, and having read 'alarming accounts' of the Romanov family's involvement in the murder of Rasputin – with or without his government's advice – King George responded in the only natural way anyone would: as a close blood relative. He had, quite rightly, come to the conclusion that only a personal approach from a family member might, at this critical moment, make his cousin see sense.[51] Through his equerry Arthur Davidson, he therefore enlisted his Danish friend Hans Niels Andersen to undertake a special assignment, asking him 'most earnestly' if he could persuade King Christian to send him and Prince Valdemar (Christian and Nicholas's uncle) on a special mission to Petrograd to try to avert what King George saw as 'the menacing family catastrophe'.[52]

In response to the King's request, Andersen had a private meeting in London with Balfour on 21 January. 'In the event of a Revolution, or great social upheaval,' he told Balfour, he did not believe, 'as most other people do, that the Russian nation is sufficiently united to carry on the war with Germany to a victorious conclusion', adding a further warning that:

> Germany is watching all that is going on in Russia with the greatest eagerness and delight and ... at a suitable moment she will offer Constantinople to Russia as a bribe for a separate peace and 'standing aside' for the rest of the war.[53]

Andersen was very clear: if there was a revolution, 'the German task would be comparatively easy'. Russia would be pulled out of the war on the Eastern Front. Such a prospect would present the Allies with a crisis: 'the whole result of the War is at present literally trembling in the balance owing to what is going on in Russia.' Through his equerry Davidson, the King underlined the utmost urgency of the Andersen/Valdemar mission, not so much to save Nicholas from himself as to keep Russia in the war.

The only problem was Alexandra: Andersen was apprehensive that if she were privy to any conversations that he and Valdemar had with Nicholas, their message would be undermined by her negativity and she would persuade her husband otherwise. But perhaps she also needed to 'hear at first hand of the dangers that threaten the continuance of this Reactionary Regime'. Unless her influence over Nicholas could be 'deflected into another channel,' Andersen advised, 'disaster with all its train of inevitable consequences is almost certain'.[54] It was 'useless', he told Davidson, to try to preach to Nicholas about constitutional reform and how to run his own government, but he might listen to his uncle, Valdemar, if he spoke to him 'on family grounds'.[55]

As Nicholas's reign headed towards crisis, family loyalties were the British king's only hope of salvaging the situation. Unfortunately the reliance on dynastic connections in maintaining peace and stability had already been shown to be ineffectual, with the outbreak of hostilities in 1914; royal families were now fighting each other in a world war, as well as within Russia itself. The situation was critical, as far as King George was concerned. In London, Andersen and Valdemar, having been given the go-ahead by King Christian, prepared to leave for their mission, with Andersen carrying a letter dated 22 January, written on the King's behalf by Davidson and addressed to British Ambassador Sir George Buchanan. It bore instructions in red ink on the envelope: 'To be destroyed immediately once read.' The letter reiterated the King's concern that the Tsar and Tsaritsa should be made aware 'that the abyss lies before them'.[56]

Unfortunately the letter was never handed over: just as the two men were preparing to leave at the beginning of February, the Germans launched a full-scale submarine blockade of Great Britain. It was too dangerous to travel. Two days later, Sir George Buchanan was telegraphing the King and Cabinet that 'Alarming reports have reached me from more than one quarter of preparations being made either for a Palace revolution or for assassination in High quarters but I have no confirmation of them.'[57] On 10 February, Andersen telegraphed that the 'Danish minister at Petrograd has reported that there is a plot to remove Czar and either place Grand Duke Alexander [Sandro] on throne or to create republic'.[58]

On 27 February, three weeks after the initial shock of the German submarine war had subsided, King George once again telegraphed Hans Niels Andersen about the urgency of his and Valdemar's mission to Tsar Nicholas.[59] But it was too late. Revolution had already broken out on the streets of Petrograd.

The story of King George's initiative in early 1917, and this aborted act of intercession, has till now been confined to material in the Royal Archives and a brief discussion in Danish sources. It clearly demonstrates that the King was far from indifferent to the plight of his Russian relatives and the impact that their fall from power would have on the war. Perhaps it is time to give him a little more credit, where due.

In a statement made in May 1917 by the Duma president and moderate Mikhail Rodzianko – one of the most able men in Nicholas's government – we are confronted with the full horror of Nicholas and Alexandra's obduracy in the face of imminent disaster. Rodzianko was no monarchist, but he battled away for six years against the Tsar's resistance, trying to convince him of the pressing need for political concessions, having had a long-held premonition of what was to come. But even he had reached the regretful conclusion that 'he could not envision the salvation of Russia without a coup'.[60] Better the creation of a new government in place of the monarchy than the dangers of out-and-out revolution at a time when Russia was at war:

> I am convinced that, had a responsible ministry been granted on the 25th [February; 10 March NS] and Aleksandra Fedorovna sent to Livadia, the movement would have been stopped and revolution could have been avoided. The popular masses – and everyone agrees with this – were not inclined to excesses. This was the life-saver. Everything could have succeeded if vigorous, legal, and responsible measures had been quickly introduced.[61]

The 'catastrophe lurking in the dark' that Nicholas and Alexandra's royal relatives had for so long anticipated had finally broken.[62]

On 12 March 1917, news was telephoned to Tsarskoe Selo from Petrograd that key regiments – the Preobrazhenskys, Pavlovlskys and Volynskys – on whom the regime had always been able to rely – were mutinying. Sooner or later the mob of protesters in Petrograd would head out to Tsarskoe Selo. The Tsaritsa, however, had other, far more pressing concerns: Alexey, Tatiana and Olga were all seriously ill with measles and were running high temperatures of over 100 degrees Fahrenheit.[63] When she heard the news of the violent insurrectionist turn of events in Petrograd, she told her lady-in-waiting Baroness Buxhoeveden that 'it was all up'. She had to think of the safety of her children, and sent immediately for the Grand Marshal of the Court, Count Benckendorff, and Colonel Groten, commander of the palace garrison. Her first thought was to head out of the city by train with the sick children to meet Nicholas at Army HQ in Mogilev. But that was sixteen hours away by rail. Count Benckendorff telephoned this suggestion through to the Tsar's aide-de-camp (ADC), Vladimir Voeikov, who passed it on to Nicholas.[64] He was horrified at the idea: 'Under no circumstances whatsoever' should his wife do this, he responded. 'The sick children must not be brought by train … not for anything.'

At 10 p.m. that same evening Rodzianko telephoned Count Benckendorff, strongly advising Alexandra to take the children somewhere – anywhere – away from Tsarskoe Selo. Tomorrow might be too late. Alexandra baulked at the idea of being seen to run away, but decided she should at least have contingency plans in place and on the morning of the 13th told Baroness Buxhoeveden to 'quietly pack my bag to be able to start with them [the children] at any moment, should this prove necessary'.[65] Shortly afterwards, however, she received devastating news: at 3 p.m. on 15 March, 185 miles away in Pskov, her husband Nicholas had abdicated.

On Monday, 12 March, Nicholas had finally been confronted with the worst: the Duma had lost control of the situation in Petrograd, and troops guarding the city, including even the elite Imperial Guards, were deserting and joining the revolutionaries. Distraught at news of this treachery and anxious about his sick children and his family's safety, Nicholas sent word that he would return to Tsarskoe immediately. At 5 a.m. the following morning he boarded his train at Stavka, confident that he could restore order in the capital. 'Thoughts always together. Glorious Weather. Hope are feeling well and quiet. Many troops sent from front. Fondest Love, Nicky,' he telegraphed.[66] All being well, he would arrive back at Tsarskoe Selo by the early morning of the 14th.

But 100 miles from Petrograd, his train was stopped at Malaya Vishera. The revolutionaries had taken Gatchina and Luga further up the line. He would have to turn back. Arriving at Pskov, HQ of the Northern Army, Nicholas was informed by its commander, General Ruzsky, that the situation in Petrograd was now desperate. After further communication from Prime Minister Rodzianko, Nicholas had to concede: 'My abdication is necessary.'[67] Soon afterwards Alexander Guchkov, Minister of War in the Provisional Government, and Duma deputy Vasily Shulgin arrived at Pskov to ensure that Nicholas did not change his mind and to oversee his signing of the abdication manifesto.* No one, however, had anticipated what happened next: Nicholas declared that he was unable to concede to constitutional government and, in so doing, abandon his divine right to rule as God willed it; he therefore had decided to abdicate not just for himself, but for his son as well. Everyone had been expecting Alexey to take the throne under a regency of Grand Duke Mikhail Alexandrovich. Nicholas had made the decision knowing that his haemophiliac son had little chance of surviving beyond his teens, but also because Alexey's accession would have required him and Alexandra, as former monarchs, to go into exile. Nicholas would not, and could not, countenance being separated from his son. The throne therefore passed to his younger brother Mikhail. Yet Mikhail was only too aware of the poisoned chalice being offered to him and a day later, having taken Rodzianko's advice, declined. Like his sensible relative, King Haakon, Mikhail declared that he 'would not accept the throne unless called to it by the voice of the people expressed in a constituent assembly'. Nicholas's abdication thus left the way clear for the Duma, of which Rodzianko was president, to grasp the status of supreme authority in Russia.[68]

It is one of the great ironies of the Nicholas and Alexandra story that the momentous decision to abdicate, when it came, was made by Nicholas in complete isolation from the wife who for the past twenty-three years had done her utmost to oversee his every crucial political decision. Had she been with him, Alexandra would have fought this to her last breath. But to

---

* German Foreign Ministry documents contain an intelligence report from Ulrich von Brockdorff-Rantzau, German ambassador to Denmark, suggesting that Nicholas was threatened harm might come to his family if he did not sign the abdication. Certainly he was extremely anxious about his wife and sick children, and his only thought was to get back to them as soon as possible.

Nicholas, given the breakdown of law and order in the capital and the desperate situation in Russia at large, it seemed the best and only thing he could do – an act of self-sacrifice to stem the tide of revolution. In so doing he hoped it would save the Imperial Army from a crisis created by the division between monarchists and revolutionaries, save the Allied effort from collapse, and save Russia itself from civil war.

True to his conscience, Nicholas II had acted 'as God places it in my soul', thus fulfilling his duty as a devout Russian Orthodox believer. The abdication was like 'a great unburdening of the spirit'. He was prepared to give up 'not just his throne, but also his life for Russia'.[69] The heartfelt loyalty expressed in the abdication manifesto, in which he insisted that 'the welfare of Russia must come above all else', made no impression, however, on Russia's new men: 'we laughed at the naïve anachronism of the text,' recalled Bolshevik Nikolay Sukhanov, 'the act of abdication was a worthless scrap of paper which might have a literary, but certainly no political, interest for us.'[70]

At 1 a.m. the following morning, the 16th, Nicholas II, the last Tsar of Russia, boarded the imperial train for the last time and set out under close escort on his journey into captivity. He was deeply melancholy at the thought of what lay ahead. 'There is treason, and cowardice, and deceit all around,' he noted in his diary.[71]

But the worst of it was only just beginning. The race to save the Romanovs from themselves had failed; could they now be saved from the revenge of the revolution?

Chapter 3

'Alicky Is the Cause of It All and Nicky Has Been Weak'

In his study at Buckingham Palace on Tuesday, 13 March 1917, King George V noted in his diary with horror that the inevitable had finally happened: 'Bad news from Russia, practically a revolution has broken out in Petrograd.' 'Some of the Guards regiments have mutinied and killed their officers,' he went on with alarm, but one thing at least was a mercy: 'this rising is against the Govt, not against the war'.[1] The King's initial reaction is, in the political scheme of things, a logical one. Nicky had been overthrown, tsarism was at an end and there was nothing more he could do about that. His primary concern, as monarch, had to be the Allied campaign on the Western and Eastern Fronts. At all costs Russia must be kept in the war. Political exigencies came first, even in this, the King's first comment about his cousin's fall from power.

He was, nevertheless, in despair at the collapse of Nicholas's throne after twenty-three years, especially after all his own and his royal relatives' attempts to warn them had gone unheeded. He had no doubt at all where the blame lay: 'I fear Alicky is the cause of it all and Nicky has been weak.' His wife, Queen Mary, had little to say on the matter, merely noting in her diary that Grand Duchess George (sister of King Constantine of Greece) had come to tea and that they had 'discussed the surprising events in Russia'.[2]

Over in Berlin, Willy the Kaiser was cock-a-hoop. It also happened to be the Silver Jubilee of his cousin Ernie, Grand Duke of

Hesse. He could not resist enjoying a degree of *Schadenfreude* over the abdication, and made a telephone call to inform Ernie that his sister Alexandra had been deposed, adding, without a word of sympathy, 'happy anniversary', before he slammed the phone down.[3]

Historical accounts of the fall of the Romanovs in March 1917 have, till now, revolved around the response of King George V, but in fact documents in AVPRI, the Archive of Foreign Policy of the Russian Empire – an institution notoriously difficult to access, and which contains the papers of Russian diplomats in Europe for the period prior to the revolution – reveal that other players took an interest from the very first. The earliest messages of support sent to Nicholas in Russia did not in fact come from King George, as has always been assumed, but from one of his less conspicuous and less likely royal cousins: King Alfonso XIII of Spain.

On 14 March the Russian ambassador to Madrid, Prince Ivan Kudashev, received an unexpected visitor.* It was King Alfonso of Spain's private secretary, the Marquis de Torres de Mendoza, who passed on a message 'in the name of the warmest feelings of friendship towards the emperor and his deepest sympathies with Russia', expressing Alfonso's grave concern for the welfare of the Imperial Family, in light of the recent disturbances in Petrograd. Torres asked Kudashev to confirm the news and send Alfonso's commiserations to Nicholas. The following day Alfonso sent Torres to the Russian ambassador again, to reiterate his concern over the situation in the capital.[4]

Until now, Alfonso and the Spanish royals had figured very little in the lives of the Romanov family, although theirs was a blood tie through Alfonso's wife Ena, who was Alexandra's cousin. As monarch of a neutral country, the thirty-one-year-old Spanish king had since 1914 been working tirelessly for the welfare of prisoners of war on both sides, and his first impulse on behalf

---

* Kudashev had been appointed shortly before the revolution and was removed soon afterwards, replaced by Anatoly Neklyudov.

of the Romanovs was humanitarian. However, Alfonso perhaps had more reason than other royals to show sympathy for Nicholas and Alexandra, because Ena, like Alexandra, was a carrier – from their shared grandmother Queen Victoria – of the fatal haemophilia gene. Her marriage to Alfonso had been blighted by the birth of two haemophiliac sons: the heir, Alfonso, in 1907 and Gonzalo in 1914.

It is more likely, however, that Alfonso's instinct for the preservation of thrones was the impulse behind this gesture of solidarity for a fellow monarch, in the spirit of gallantry of the *Rey Caballero* (Knightly King) in which he viewed his own monarchy. There is no doubt that of all the European royals, Alfonso appreciated the seriousness of Nicholas and Alexandra's position. For he too had been living with the threat of revolutionary violence for years and had already survived several assassination attempts, including one on his wedding day in 1906 when a Catalan anarchist threw a bomb and killed thirty people. In 1917 Alfonso himself was facing the increasing threat of insurgency from Spanish republican and anarchist groups.[5]

In Copenhagen the Danish king had also greeted the revolution and Nicholas's abdication with considerable horror: 'the tsaritsa's family has removed my family from the throne,' he told his Prime Minister, in a reference to Alexandra's German ancestry and his cousin Nicholas's Danish descent. Even in 1917, among her close relatives Alexandra was still perceived as a pro-German intriguer against the Russian state. Such was King Christian's anxiety that he sent instructions to Harald Scavenius, his ambassador in Petrograd, to report back in detail on the Imperial Family's situation and find out about the possibility of them leaving Russia. At this very early stage the Danish government made the logical assumption that both the Danish Dowager Empress (who was his aunt) and the Imperial Family would be given political asylum by King Christian.[6] This also seemed to be the initial expectation in Russia, as British nurse Dorothy Seymour confirmed in her Petrograd diary: 'Rumour has it that the (imperial) family is to go to Denmark almost at once.'[7]

After signing his abdication manifesto at Pskov and attempting once more to head back to his wife and children at Tsarskoe Selo, Nicholas had asked to be allowed to travel to Stavka to say farewell to the army and the officers of his entourage. His train arrived at Mogilev at 8.20 p.m. on 16 March and, in one of their final private conversations, Nicholas's ADC, Anatoly Mordvinov, asked the Tsar what he intended to do now. 'I shall live as a completely private person,' he said. 'I think we shall go to Livadia – for Alexey's health.' 'It is essential too for my sick daughters.' Or perhaps, he added somewhat fancifully, they might be able to go to the monastery at Kostroma, 215 miles south-west of Moscow, where the Romanov dynasty had been founded in 1613. Mordvinov could not disguise his alarm: 'your majesty, you must go abroad as quickly as possible,' he urged, 'even Crimea is not safe in the present situation.' 'No, not for anything!' was the reply. Nicholas was adamant: 'I do not want to leave Russia, I love her too much.'[8]

Back in Petrograd, the question of what would happen next to the former Tsar and his family was also being addressed. At a meeting of the Cabinet of Ministers of the newly formed Provisional Government, Foreign Minister Pavel Milyukov made an announcement on their future. It was essential that they be removed beyond the bounds of the Russian state, for political reasons and their own safety. This measure, Milyukov argued, was justifiable for all members of the House of Romanov, but in the first instance his government considered it absolutely essential for Nicholas II and his brother Grand Duke Mikhail and their families. Meanwhile their places of residence would be put under guard and their freedom restricted. Their secure containment was a matter of urgency.[9]

In London, however, where news of the abdication had just been announced, 'government circles were preoccupied with one thing only: the potential weakening of Russia's military strength', as the Russian ambassador to London, Konstantin Nabokov, recalled in his memoirs. Even the British Labour movement, while busy congratulating the Russian working classes for overturning the old order, was nevertheless urging their continuing support in the war and warning that 'any remission of effort means disaster'.[10] British Foreign Secretary Arthur Balfour made clear the government's anxieties about a republic being established in Russia, now that Nicholas had abdicated on behalf of his son, and worried that in the face of extremist pressure 'a disgraceful peace will be patched up with Germany'. With this in mind, the Foreign Office was quick to make clear to Sir George Buchanan in Petrograd how he should conduct matters with the new government: 'All your influence should be thrown into the scale against any Administration which is not resolved to fight to a finish.'[11]

At Stavka, his role in the war now over, Nicholas sat down on 17 March and composed a note in pencil, in which he laid out four major demands about the future of his family and those in the entourage who remained with them:

1) That I may proceed unimpeded to Tsarskoe Selo with the persons accompanying me.
2) That [we] may reside in safety at Tsarskoe Selo until the children's recovery, with those same persons.
3) That [we] may proceed unimpeded to Romanov-on-the-Murman [Murmansk] with the same persons.
4) That we may return to Russia at the end of the war to settle in the Crimea – in Livadia.[12]

That evening, the document was telegraphed to the Prime Minister of the Provisional Government, Prince Lvov, by Nicholas's Commander in Chief, General Alexeev. While being extremely reluctant to leave his country at all, Nicholas had realised that he might have to agree to evacuation out of Russia for the duration of the war, on the promise of being allowed back when it was all over. But thereafter he set his heart on being able to live in quiet obscurity in the place that he and his family loved most – their home on the shores of the Black Sea at Livadia. It was a naïve hope and Nicholas did not know that when Alexeev transcribed his draft into a telegram to the Provisional Government, he omitted the fourth demand, knowing full well that the response to it would be an emphatic 'No'.[13] The Romanovs would never be allowed to live in Crimea; the continuing presence of the former Imperial Family in Russia was something the new government would not countenance. Wherever the Imperial Family went, it had to be out of Russia and well away from any attempt at a counter-revolution. Even now the government was fearful of an officers' uprising at Stavka in support of the former Tsar.

For the time being, Nicholas's cousin King George was silent. No one in Britain was entirely sure where the Tsar was at present, but one thing was certain: there 'seemed to be no hope of keeping the Emperor on the throne,' reported Buchanan. The immediate preoccupation, in telegrams between him and London, remained how to keep the Russian people onside in the war and, more importantly, get crucial munitions production in Russia, which had stalled during the revolution, back on track. On the day of the abdication, Sir George had urged that British Labour leaders send messages of support backing the Provisional Government, as 'advice from England at present carries great weight'. The Foreign Office responded with a message on 16 March that 'Organized Labour in Great Britain' was 'watching with the deepest sympathy the efforts of the Russian people to deliver themselves from [the] power of reactionary elements which are impeding their advance to victory'. The 'despotism of Germany must be overthrown'; any 'remission of effort means disaster to comrades in trenches and to our common hopes of social regeneration'.[14]

As yet, no ultimate destination of exile for the Romanovs was mentioned. Although Sir George Buchanan had a meeting with Milyukov of the Provisional Government in the company of the French and Italian ambassadors on the afternoon of the 17th, the discussions covered a wide range of issues. Milyukov, who was clearly under a great deal of strain, confirmed that his priority was to ensure, like them, that Russia continued 'ruthlessly prosecuting the war to victory'. But to do so required concessions and the need to remove any threat of counter-revolution – in other words, the Imperial Family. With this in mind, Buchanan asked 'what the Emperor was going to do'? Milyukov was vague; the Tsar's position 'was a precarious one as all the faults committed by the late Government were laid to his charge'. But was His Majesty's life in danger, asked Buchanan? No, Milyukov responded; but 'he would like to see him leave the country as soon as possible'.[15] The Provisional Government was in such a precarious situation that ambassador Paléologue wired the French Foreign Office to inform them that it was seriously considering 'expulsing [sic] the entire Imperial Family from Russia'.[16] Such was Paléologue's concern that later on the 17th he went over to the British embassy to see his colleague Buchanan. Over tea and in the company of Buchanan's wife, Lady Georgina, all three discussed the dangers to the Imperial Family at Tsarskoe Selo and the need for an urgent evacuation:

> They thought that a British cruiser should be sent to fetch the fallen Sovereign on the Murman Coast. It would not be suitable for a French boat to assume this task, as the Arctic Ocean was comprised in the zone of the British naval operations.[17]

Over at Mogilev, General Alexeev was becoming extremely anxious about the delay in receiving a response from the Provisional Government to the Tsar's telegram. On 18 March he sent another, urging permission for Nicholas's train to leave Stavka as soon as possible for Tsarskoe Selo. By now the complexities of what to do with the former Tsar had begun to unravel for the Provisional Government. Three days on from the abdication, and much to its consternation, it had still heard nothing from King George. As Russia's main ally, everyone was now looking to him for a solution. On 18 March, Milyukov therefore sent a pre-emptive telegram to the British government, expressly asking that they offer asylum to the former Tsar and his family.

Oblivious to all the toing and froing behind the scenes, Nicholas was meanwhile spending time with his mother Dagmar, who at his request had travelled up by train from Kiev the previous day to see him. She arrived with her son-in-law Sandro. Dagmar had sat there 'sobbing aloud, while [Nicky] stood motionless, looking at his feet and, of course, smoking,' recalled Sandro, who thought that his brother-in-law's uncanny calmness 'showed his firm belief in the righteousness of his decision'.[18] For the next three days Dagmar and Nicholas walked together, wept together, dined, went to church and shut themselves away in private conversation. Reassuring news came of Alexandra and the children on the 19th: Olga, Tatiana and Alexey were now recovering from the measles; Anastasia, who had also succumbed, was still running a fever; and, sadly, Maria had now been laid low by the illness too and was suffering the complications of pneumonia.[19]

That same morning of 19th March, Dagmar sent for Major-General Hanbury-Williams, one of the Allied commanders at Stavka, and they had a long conversation about Nicholas's future. Both felt that he should leave Russia immediately, straight from Stavka, under British military protection, but 'the crux of the situation and the difficulty' was that there was no way Nicholas would go anywhere without Alexandra and the children.[20] Like Milyukov, Hanbury-Williams had already seized the initiative and telegraphed his government about 'possible plans to send the tsar to England', but Dagmar was 'alarmed by the question of the sea voyage', given the German submarine blockade, and preferred Denmark as an option, which was a lot nearer.[21] But even a protracted rail journey to an ice-free port, as Sandro pointed out, would be risky. Hanbury-Williams assured them that together with his fellow Allied generals, Maurice Janin and Louis de Ryckel, he was willing to escort the Tsar's train back to Tsarskoe Selo and beyond, to ensure his safety. 'We have been his guests for over a year and have received much kindness from him.'[22] Nicholas was touched by the offer, but told Hanbury-Williams that 'he hoped that he would not have to leave Russia'. He still clung to the idea of being allowed to go to Crimea.[23]

It was not until that Monday, 19 March, that General Alexeev finally received a response from the Provisional Government agreeing to Nicholas's three requests. Once he had returned to

Tsarskoe Selo, and his children had recovered from the measles, the family would then be granted 'unhindered passage' north to the port of Murmansk.[24] The government's agreement to these demands had been thought necessary, it was later revealed, in order to win Nicholas's confidence and ensure his swift and compliant departure from Stavka. Nicholas now had a long conversation with Hanbury-Williams and reluctantly conceded that if he really had to leave the country, he would rather go to England than anywhere else.[25] Hanbury-Williams and Buchanan had both been urging the British government to take in the Romanovs, but the Foreign Office was still instructing Buchanan to act with caution: 'As regards future movements of the Emperor we would of course be glad to see him leave Russia, if only in the interests of his personal safety.' But, Sir George was informed, 'no invitation has, however, been sent to His Majesty to come to England, and it seems very doubtful whether such a course would be desirable'.[26] The British government's position continued to be one of extreme reticence to do anything.

In conversation with Buchanan later that day, however, Milyukov continued to press for a commitment from the British and asked 'whether I knew if arrangements were being made for His Majesty to go to England'. The following day came further requests for Buchanan to emphasise the urgency of the matter, for the Provisional Government had now declared its hand by publicly stating its 'intention of sending Nicholas II abroad' – a fact confirmed by Minister of Justice Alexander Kerensky at a meeting that day at the Moscow Soviet of Workers' and Soldiers' Deputies. Angry workers' meetings in Petrograd's factories were already demanding retribution against 'the deposed Nicholas II, the bloodstained'; 'We have no guarantee that this vampire will not make new attempts to enter the arena of our lives,' proclaimed one resolution. Other workers were calling for the arrest of all members of the House of Romanov. Abdication was not enough; regicide was in the air.[27] By 20 March Hanbury-Williams was filled with alarm: 'Anarchism is showing itself already,' he noted in his diary, 'and it will be lucky if the Imperial Family can be got away somewhere in safety.'[28]

In response to calls for Nicholas's imprisonment and even his execution, Alexander Kerensky insisted that the government had taken responsibility for the personal safety of the Tsar and his family and it would honour that obligation to the letter. 'After the briefest of delays and under his personal supervision they would all be transferred to Murmansk from where they would sail for England.'[29] But was a ship on its way? asked a harassed Sir George Buchanan in yet another urgent telegram to London on the 20th. Foreign Minister Milyukov was now 'positively pressing for the tsar's departure and was taking it for granted that Britain would send a ship to pick him up'.[30]

But still no official invitation came; the British Cabinet was clearly dragging its feet. The best it could suggest, in response to Milyukov's and Buchanan's frantic messages, was that Denmark or Switzerland might be a better place of refuge for the Imperial Family.[31] It was a lacklustre suggestion, Denmark never being a realistic option for the Allies, as it was far too close to Germany. Such proximity would pose 'a serious danger of His Imperial Majesty becoming a focus of intrigue of Germany'.[32] There were other political considerations to bear in mind as well: David Lloyd George had only recently congratulated the Russian people on a revolution that had been 'the greatest service' they had 'yet made to the cause for which the Allied peoples have been fighting since August, 1914'.[33] 'A little strong,' thought King George when he saw this, though it turned out the wording had been on the advice of the Russian ambassador to London, Nabokov.[34]

By now Milyukov was seriously concerned that his government would not be able to protect the Tsar if the revolutionaries marched from Petrograd out to Tsarskoe Selo, and this time he asked the straight question: would 'the King and HM's government ... at once offer asylum in England?'[35] He had confided to French ambassador Paléologue that he wanted to see them go 'mainly in order to spare them the sorrows of imprisonment and trial, which would greatly increase the difficulties of the Government'.[36] The Tsar's continuing presence in Russia was a destabilising influence; his departure would 'strengthen the Russian Government and help matters settle down'.[37] Milyukov also hoped that the British would ensure that Nicholas would 'abstain from interfering in Russian politics while on English soil'.[38] In Russia or out of Russia, the former Imperial Family had fast become a headache for him and his colleagues and they desperately wanted rid of them.

Before leaving Stavka on 21 March, and now having being told that he was under formal arrest, a pale and drained Nicholas composed a final order to his troops, trusting in their abiding love of and loyalty to Russia and their commitment to carrying on the fight on the Eastern Front. He then said a restrained farewell to his officers, in particular the loyal Cossacks of the Tsar's escort. It had seemed as though 'those around him had been far more upset than he,' as one officer recalled, but Nicholas later confided in his diary: 'my heart was almost breaking'.[39] He then had lunch with his mother, during which he reiterated how much he would prefer to remain in Russia. She, however, had been begging him not to delay, once he got back to Tsarskoe Selo – but to travel out of Russia immediately, even though the children were still sick.[40] Mother and son sat together in her train, until at 4.30 p.m. came the 'terrible painful parting', as Dagmar later recalled. A quarter of an hour later, Nicholas – wearing his simple khaki tunic 'with the cross of St George in its buttonhole' – stood at the window of his carriage as his train pulled away. 'His expression,' recalled Sandro, was 'infinitely sad' as the train headed off, 'a stream of smoke on the horizon', away from a windy and frosty Mogilev on its journey back to Tsarskoe Selo. On the train shortly afterwards he informed his companions: 'Did you know? I've been deprived of my freedom.' His matter-of-fact delivery reminded one of them of that famous 'Rien!' in the diary of Louis XVI on the day the Bastille fell.[41]

Dagmar's plea that Nicholas make haste to get out of Russia was of course futile, for it was already too late. As a prisoner of the Provisional Government, he no longer had any control over his onward journey. At Tsarskoe Selo on the morning of the 21st, General Kornilov (Commander in Chief of the Petrograd

Garrison) had arrived to inform Alexandra that she and her family were also under arrest. It was, he explained, for their own safety, as well as to put paid to rumours of any attempt there might be to restore the monarchy.[42] (Evidence has since made it clear that the Provisional Government almost certainly put Nicholas and Alexandra under arrest in order to placate the belligerent Petrograd Soviet, which might even then have usurped control of the Imperial Family's fate, had they not done so.) It was left to Kornilov to reassure Alexandra that 'As soon as the health of the children allowed it, the Emperor's family would be sent to Murmansk where a British cruiser would await them and take them to England', an assumption for which the government had as yet received no confirmation.[43] Meanwhile, with all entrances except one securely locked, the Alexander Palace was cut off and heavily guarded.

When an exhausted Nicholas finally arrived back at the Alexander Palace at 11.30 a.m. on 22 March, he and his family began their new life as prisoners, little knowing that two days previously a message of support from cousin George had been sent to Stavka, only to arrive after Nicholas had left. With his government still prevaricating, King George had taken it upon himself to despatch a personal and private message, addressed to Nicholas, as Tsar and Emperor, c/o Major General Hanbury Williams, as follows:

> Events of last week have deeply distressed me. My thoughts are constantly with you and I shall always remain your true and devoted friend as you know I have been in the past.[44]

At last, a week after the abdication, a brief but non-committal token of support had arrived from England, although not the expected concrete offer of help, which was a disappointment, given George's professed deep attachment to Nicky. But at least it was confirmation that Nicholas had not been forgotten. The telegram was forwarded from Stavka to Sir George Buchanan in Petrograd, who, receiving it on the 24th and unable to hand it over to the Tsar, who was now a prisoner at Tsarskoe Selo, delivered it to Foreign Minister Milyukov, asking him to pass it on.[45]

This single relatively innocuous telegram has been the source of considerable misunderstanding and blatant misinterpretation over the years. Many subsequent memoirists, including French ambassador Maurice Paléologue, seem to have been under the misapprehension that it contained an offer of asylum, which it patently did not. The King was not in a position to take that kind of executive decision. The misinterpretation was, however, widely disseminated, and without investigation, perhaps leading in part to King George later being made the scapegoat for the failure to get the Romanovs out of Russia. Equally, it has often been claimed that Sir George Buchanan decided not to hand the telegram over, but this was not the case either. It was the Provisional Government that had second thoughts about giving it to its intended recipient. Milyukov had informed Buchanan that they would not pass it on to the Tsar, first because it was addressed to 'The Emperor' and Nicholas no longer enjoyed that title, and second because its contents, however innocently expressed, might be misinterpreted 'as a further argument for the detention of the Imperial Family, and probably augment the severity of [the Tsar's] imprisonment'. Sir George protested, but was told that it was 'impossible to deliver the telegram' because it could be used as evidence 'of a British plot to rescue the Tsar'.[46]

The knock-on effect from this one small independent act by King George was extraordinary. When, on 8 April, the British Cabinet finally heard about the telegram, they asked to see it; the King refused. It was 'purely a personal one', his private secretary Lord Stamfordham told them, and he 'does not feel disposed to communicate its text'. Indeed, George was already regretting that any reference to it had been made in an official Foreign Office telegram. If his personal message to Nicholas had not yet been delivered, then the King now wished Buchanan not to hand it over.[47]

King George was clearly rattled. The unexpected fuss that his telegram had aroused is recorded in notes of a telephone conversation between Hanbury-Williams and British Foreign Office official Harry Verney. Overlooked till now, this handwritten note can be found in the National Archives file FO 800/205 marked 'Russia and Siberia'. Observing that Buchanan should not have made an 'official question' of this personal matter in his telegrams to the FO, it also notes: 'The fact that the whole of the Government here seem to have been much intrigued by this natural and harmless telegram has rather annoyed H.[is] M.[ajesty].'[48] It might have seemed a storm in a teacup to some, but the official response to the King's telegram had a clear consequence in his subsequent reticence about engaging further in the Romanov matter.

George V was already treading on eggshells. So much so that he did not resend this much-needed gesture of sympathy to his cousin. He had been made only too clearly aware of just how politically sensitive any independent support that he might show the ex-Tsar would be. The British could not risk compromising Russia's new Provisional Government – their wartime ally. All the British Cabinet felt able to do, at this stage of what was already an extremely delicate diplomatic and political crisis, was to authorise Buchanan's suggestion that he make a more general humanitarian appeal to the Provisional Government that 'any violence [done to the] Emperor' would have a 'deplorable effect' and would 'alienate His Majesty's Government's sympathy for [the] present regime'.[49]

At the British Embassy on Petrograd's Palace Embankment on the evening of 21 March, Sir George Buchanan had a visitor. Duke Alexander of Leuchtenberg, a close friend of the Imperial Family, had come specially, as Buchanan's daughter Meriel later recalled, 'to implore my father to take immediate action to get the Emperor and his wife and children out of Russia'. 'They stood in the gravest danger,' he insisted, 'and if they were not soon removed to England it would be too late to get them away, too late to save them from possible disaster.'[50]

The next morning, after another anxious meeting with Milyukov, Sir George telegraphed London yet again 'urging the necessity of a quick action'.[51] He had good reason to keep pushing his government, for 'the extremists ha[d] been exciting opinion against His Majesty'. 'I entirely agree that the Emperor should leave before the agitation has time to grow, and I earnestly trust that, in spite of the obvious objections, I may be authorized without delay to offer His Majesty asylum in England.'[52] That day a gloomy Milyukov had told him that time was running out: 'It's the last chance of securing these poor unfortunates' freedom and perhaps of saving their lives,' he had said.[53] 'I have put things very strongly,' Sir George told his daughter that evening, 'I think they will have to take action.'[54]

From Stavka, Major-General Hanbury-Williams was also exerting pressure. General Alexeev was keeping him up to date on events in Petrograd, now that the Romanovs were prisoners at Tsarskoe Selo, and begged him to telegraph at once:

> to request that H.M. Government should make strongest possible representation that absolute safe conduct should be given to whole Imperial Family to ROMANOFF [Murmansk] and to England as soon as possible. He fears for safety of their persons if such action is not taken at earliest possible moment.[55]

Hanbury-Williams could only hope 'that all steps possible can be immediately taken'.[56] But 'personally and privately' he considered the Provisional Government's 'condition regarding Emperor's going to United Kingdom unfair and an insult to him'. At the least, the former monarch should be allowed to stay in Russia, as he wished, and under their protection.[57]

It was not until 22 March, at a meeting held at Downing Street, that Prime Minister David Lloyd George finally sat down with Lord Stamfordham, the King's private secretary, to discuss the plight of the Imperial Family. After being joined later in their discussions by the Chancellor of the Exchequer, Andrew Bonar Law, and Lord Hardinge, Permanent Under-Secretary at the Foreign Office, they concluded that the British government, like it or not, had an obligation 'to invite the tsar and empress to take up residence in this country', in the interests of their 'personal safety' and as a gesture of solidarity to a wartime ally. Milyukov's request 'could not be refused'.[58] But *not refusing* a request is not the same thing as making a free and unprompted offer. And there were provisos: Milyukov's government would need to offer assurances on how 'His Imperial Majesty' would be supported financially, so that he would have 'sufficient means to enable him to live here with suitable dignity'.[59]

These reservations were communicated to Petrograd by their ambassador in London, Konstantin Nabokov, after a 'friendly and private' conversation later that day with Hardinge, who had emphasised that the Tsar's stay in England presented 'great difficulties'. His government, he told Nabokov, was concerned about the possibility of 'undesirable agitation' that might be brought into the UK by the Tsar's presence there, and that it was down to the Provisional Government to exercise strict control over those coming and going from Russia during the Imperial Family's stay, to prevent 'intrigue and agitation for a restoration of the monarchy'.[60]

At this point, of course, no one had any idea how sizeable an entourage the former sovereigns would wish to bring with them. Where would they live, and who would pay for it? Perhaps one of the royal residences could be made over to them? But Sandringham, Windsor and Buckingham Palace were all in regular use by the royal family, and Osborne House had become a convalescent home for injured officers. Balmoral was the only privately owned royal residence that could possibly serve, but Stamfordham insisted that it was not suitable in winter.[61] (When Nicholas and Alexandra had visited Queen Victoria there in 1896, their Russian entourage had all complained of how miserably cold the castle was.) As for the Romanovs' financial ability to support themselves, Milyukov agreed that his government would make 'a liberal allowance' to this effect, but 'begged that the fact that the Provisional Government had taken the initiative in the matter should not be published'.[62] In reality, as the Tsar had confided to the former Grand Marshal of the Court, Count Benckendorff, after his return to Tsarskoe, he no longer had any financial resources in England; 'all the monies he had deposited there had been sent to Russia' (to help the war effort) and 'if he went to England he would have to fall back on the charity of his relatives'.[63]

Milyukov was becoming increasingly nervous, as British officials noted, fearing that in 'pressing for the asylum issue for the ex-Emperor in England' he had gone 'beyond the wishes of some of his colleagues'.[64] Be that as it may, late in the afternoon of 22 March, Buchanan in Petrograd was informed by Lord Hardinge that the British government had agreed to his request to receive the Tsar and his family. On 23 March – the day that the ambassadors of France, Italy and Britain announced their governments' formal recognition of the new regime in Russia – the British offer was finally made. But contrary to Milyukov's request to Buchanan, David Lloyd George's government insisted that any public announcement about this offer of sanctuary must make it absolutely clear that it had been made not by them, but specifically *at the request of the Russians*.[65]

In Madrid, where he had been monitoring events in Russia closely, King Alfonso was equally fearful that time was running out and had asked Russian ambassador Kudashev to come and see him. A telegram quickly winged its way to Milyukov in Petrograd:

> Urgent and Highly Confidential. Having just returned today from Andalusia, the King summoned me. His Highness is very concerned about the fate of the Imperial Family, but also, by the same token, fears that the continuing presence in Russia of His Majesty, having renounced the throne, might inflame revolution and a great deal of bloodshed. Although our conversation was a private one, and the King asked me not to report it, I consider it my duty nevertheless to warn you that the Spanish ambassador [in Petrograd] will be urged to appeal to the Provisional Government concerning the future fate of the Imperial Family. The gist is unknown to me, but the King stresses the fact that events in Russia impact upon Spain. There are already signs of revolutionary ferment

in working districts. In Barcelona there have been disturbances involving casualties that they are trying to conceal.[66]

Having finally reached a deal with the British to send the Romanovs out of Russia, the Provisional Government saw no need to pay much attention to King Alfonso's appeals for 'guarantees of the future fate of the Tsar' and discounted them as 'superfluous'.[67] But it is clear from this message that the Spanish king's survival instinct had now kicked in. He was worrying not just about the safety of the Romanovs, but about how their remaining in Russia would affect his own throne, in the light of extremist republican and anarchist sympathy for the Russian Revolution. As one newspaper presciently noted on the situation in Russia: 'What affects one throne may react on another. History shows that all important revolutions in one country have shaken the position of rulers in others.'[68]

One wonders, even at this early stage, whether such thoughts might already have been in the mind of King George. England had once been the favourite place of refuge for banished monarchs, especially French ones like Charles X, Louis-Philippe and Louis-Napoleon, who had all taken advantage of British hospitality when they lost their thrones during the previous century. But the international repercussions of the Russian Revolution went far deeper, and already an outburst of popular left-wing sympathy for the revolutionary cause was spreading in Europe, as King Alfonso was discovering. Does this perhaps explain the puzzling absence of appeals from King George for the British government to take action on behalf of his cousins, even though his mother, the Dowager Queen Alexandra, was already lobbying the Foreign Office for news of her sister Dagmar? As a constitutional monarch, King George had no power to order his government to act, which begs this question: had Milyukov, backed up by urgent and repeated representations from Buchanan and Hanbury-Williams, not persisted in his request for the British to take in the Romanovs, would King George and his government ever have seized the initiative and offered to do so?

Eight days after Nicholas's abdication and at the end of what had seemed like an agonisingly long wait, a formal communication from British ambassador Buchanan was received at the Russian Foreign Ministry:

Monsieur le Ministre,

Referring to the conversation which I had the honour to have with Your Excellency on Monday last, I have the honour to state that the King and His Majesty's Government are happy to offer asylum to the late Emperor and Empress, and trust that their late Majesties will take advantage of it for the duration of the war.[69]

'Alas I fear it is too late,' sighed Milyukov when Buchanan's letter finally arrived.[70] Russia's Foreign Minister had good reason to think this, for he knew full well that a far more belligerent political force had already swung into action to ensure that the Romanov family would encounter great difficulty in getting out of Russia, whoever offered them a refuge.

For days Sir George Buchanan had been pressing his government to make a decision, warning that 'the power of the Soviet was growing daily'.[71] He was right to do so, for it would be the Petrograd Soviet of Workers' and Soldiers' Deputies that ultimately controlled the fate of the Imperial Family in the spring of 1917 – and not the Provisional Government.

Chapter 4

'Every Day the King Is
Becoming More Concerned'

Within days of the revolution, the former members of the old Imperial State Duma in Petrograd had scrambled to pull together some kind of caretaker government. It was hoped this would be sufficient to impose order until elections to a Constituent Assembly later in the year could be organised. But instead this so-called Provisional Government had found itself increasingly in conflict with a rival political body – the Petrograd Soviet. This council of militant revolutionary workers and soldiers had come together to press for the declaration of a republic and nothing less than the establishment of a new socialist state, controlled by the people and for the people. Many of the members of the Soviet held sway over the workers in key sections of Petrograd's industry, its postal and telegraph services and the strategically crucial railways. One further essential in the balance of power was also increasingly under their control: the army. Until October 1917, when Lenin's Bolsheviks finally took over, the country would be governed by the dual powers of the regional and city Soviets, often in direct conflict with the Provisional Government.

While the Provisional Government under Prince Lvov, with its mix of old monarchist landowning and bourgeois elements, might have wished to see the former Tsar allowed to depart from Russia with his life and some dignity intact, the hardliners in the Petrograd Soviet had no intention of letting Nicholas II walk quietly away from the wreckage of the old corrupt tsarist system that he had headed. There was a price to pay for centuries of imperial despotism. On 19 March 1917, as soon as the Soviet got word that the Provisional Government was planning to send the Romanovs abroad, an urgent meeting of its Executive Committee was called. So alarmed were the Soviet's deputies by rumours that a special train was preparing to take the family out of Russia that they sent troops to occupy all railway stations, as well as telegraphing along the lines, instructing stationmasters and railway workers 'that the Romanovs and their train must be detained wherever they were found'.[1] The Petrograd Soviet had in fact sent out messages to get the Tsar's train stopped on its way back from Stavka, and for him to be arrested immediately after the abdication, but their telegrams had not arrived until after Nicholas had arrived at Tsarskoe Selo.[2]

'It was obvious we could not let the Romanovs go abroad and seek their fate elsewhere and await their moment,' recalled Soviet Executive Committee member Nikolay Sukhanov; nor could they be allowed to return to the 'historical arena'. The committee 'acknowledged very quickly and unanimously that the Soviet must take the Romanov question into its own hands', and they were prepared to do so 'even if this should threaten a break with the Provisional Government'.[3] Its members were convinced that the Romanovs had vast reserves of wealth safely hidden in foreign banks; why should they be sent abroad so that they could draw on their 'millions' to fund a counter-revolution, asked the new official newspaper, the Bolshevik-run *Pravda*. 'No! the Romanovs must not be allowed abroad. That would be a state crime; a betrayal of the nation.'[4] There was the question too of political security: 'the Emperor knows too many state secrets'; he had to be isolated, and ideally locked up in the Peter and Paul Fortress or sent to the revolutionary stronghold at Kronstadt.[5] On 22 March, Sergey Maslovsky, a commissar of the Petrograd Soviet, was sent out to Tsarskoe to 'gain control over the situation' – in other words, to take Nicholas to the fortress, where he would be incarcerated in the dreaded Trubetskoy Bastion.[6] Maslovsky arrived at the Alexander Palace with three commandeered armoured cars bristling with men and machine guns. En route he had brandished his pistol and vowed to 'arrest Nicholas Romanov and bring him back to Petrograd, dead or alive'. He was prepared to 'liquidate the matter here in Tsarskoye' if necessary, he bragged. When they arrived at the palace, he and the Bolshevik commissar Alexey Tarasov-Rodionov tried to incite the guards to hand over 'Niko-lashka', in case it was decided to 'spirit him abroad and then later set him on your necks again'. When the officers of the guard assured him that the former Tsar was a captive and was going nowhere, Maslovsky relented. Having been allowed to see Nicholas from a distance in a corridor, to verify that he was actually there, Maslovsky was briskly seen off by Colonel Evgeniy Kobylinsky, commander of the external guard at Tsarskoe Selo.[7]

That evening, Nikolay Chkheidze, the Menshevik chair of the Soviet, reported that the Provisional Government had capitulated to pressure 'not to allow the former tsar and his family to leave Tsarskoe Selo without the explicit agreement of the Executive Committee', which had by now resolved to 'immediately take extraordinary measures' if any attempt was made to do so.[8] To ensure that the government kept to its word, the Soviet set up its own network of watchers to confirm that the Imperial Family remained locked up at the Alexander Palace.[9] French ambassador Maurice Paléologue noted that they had also 'posted "revolution-ary" guards at Tsarskoe Selo and on the roads leading from it, to prevent any surreptitious abduction of the sovereigns' by the Provisional Government or anyone else.[10]

So the night before Foreign Minister Milyukov even received the British offer of asylum, his government had already been placed in an impossible position: how could it hope to effect the safe evacuation out of Russia of the Imperial Family, when the Petrograd Soviet was already doing all it could to stop that from happening and was demanding Nicholas's trial and execution?

The British offer, when it came the following morning, was thus virtually redundant – yet another ineffectual piece of paper that has gone down in history as promising much, but delivering nothing. Why did Milyukov continue the charade of discussing an evacuation that he knew was logistically impossible, and would otherwise end violently? The issue of the Romanov evacuation was already – within a week of the abdication – an entirely academic one. Yet the controversy and recrimination over who was responsible for the ensuing embarrassing debacle would continue for decades.

With the Soviet doing all it could to wrest control of the fate of the Romanov family from the government, the Provisional Government was forced to act. Alexander Kerensky, a Socialist Revolutionary who also had a position in the Petrograd Soviet, was now tasked, as the new Justice Minister, with overseeing the Imperial Family's protection at the Alexander Palace until some kind of arrangement could be made for their future. 'We regarded any display of revengefulness as unworthy of Free Russia,' Kerensky later recalled. The arrest of the Tsar and Tsaritsa and their family had been, he insisted, a protective and not a punitive measure, and he relied on Colonel Kobylinsky – who would soon be made commandant of the Alexander Palace garrison – to ensure that the family were fairly treated and that there were no breaches in security.[11] In the meantime, in order to calm the volatile situation, and with the approval of Sir George Buchanan, the Provisional Government assured the Petrograd Soviet that it had not as yet informed Nicholas of the British offer. In a private meeting with Milyukov, Buchanan agreed that two important things had to be dealt with before they informed the Tsar and his wife of any arrangements: the government needed to 'overcome the opposition of the Soviet, and ... their Majesties could not in any case start till their children got better'.[12] There were now 300 soldiers guarding the outer perimeter of the palace; all the telephones and the telegraph machine were out of bounds; and all incoming and outgoing mail was subject to close scrutiny. Recreation outside, in a closed-off part of the park, was strictly regulated. Those of the Imperial Family's entourage who had not accepted the Provisional Government's offer to leave were now prisoners with them.[13]

Thus, while Kerensky and Milyukov trod a difficult path keeping the Petrograd Soviet onside by assuring them that they were not going to allow the Romanovs to leave Russia, they were, simultaneously, juggling talks with England about precisely that. At Tsarskoe Selo, no one in the imperial entourage could get a straight answer about what was going on; the former monarchs were kept in the dark about where they would eventually go, though they had come to the conclusion that perhaps Norway might be a better option; it would be good for Alexey's health, as Alexandra had mentioned to her lady-in-waiting Baroness Buxhoeveden.[14] This much at least filtered out to the Western press, desperate for any reliable news of the Imperial Family. According to a 'Copenhagen telegram', 'the ex-Tsar has asked permission for his son to go to Norway, in order to be restored to health'. An article in the *Liverpool Echo* on 29 March, entitled 'Ex-Tsar's Future Home', engaged in intense speculation about whether the Imperial Family were to come to England, noting that a report had arrived 'from a well-informed quarter' pointing to the 'probability of the Russian royal family ultimately making their home in Denmark.'[15]

And then, a day later, the first warning sign of a change in British official sentiment was sounded. Almost from the moment his government had expressed its disapproval of his private telegram to the Tsar, King George had been in an agony of doubt about the whole issue of the Romanov asylum, and on Thursday, 30 March, he instructed Lord Stamfordham to write to the Foreign Secretary:

My dear Balfour,

The King has been thinking much about the Government's proposal that the Emperor Nicholas and his Family should come to England.

As you are doubtless aware the King has a strong personal friendship for the Emperor, and therefore would be glad to do anything to help him in this crisis. But His Majesty cannot help doubting, not only on account of the dangers of the voyage, but *on general grounds of expediency* [my italics], whether it is advisable that the Imperial Family should take up their residence in this country.[16]

The British government pondered this message for three days before responding. It had never encouraged the idea of asylum in England, hoping that Denmark or even Switzerland might step in, but nevertheless it had done the honourable thing under pressure from Milyukov and had issued an official invitation. While it fully appreciated that the King was now having second thoughts, this put David Lloyd George in a very tricky position. The following day, Stamfordham was therefore informed that the government 'do not think, unless the position changes, that it is now possible to withdraw the invitation which has been sent, and they therefore trust that the King will consent to adhere to the original invitation'. As a constitutional monarch, George had no choice but to capitulate. A brief response came the following day from Stamfordham informing Balfour that the King 'must regard the matter as settled, unless the Russian Government should come to any fresh decision on the subject'.[17]

But what exactly were the 'general grounds of expediency' that were by now so exercising King George? In a nutshell, it was fear of inflaming the radical left-wing sentiment for the revolution and against the Imperial Family that was gathering ground in Britain as that doing its damnedest in Petrograd to stop them ever leaving. Already what had been initiated as a seemingly straightforward humanitarian exercise was being loaded with political overtones, which were not just anti-monarchical and potentially damaging to the Allied war effort, but were forcing the King into an uncomfortable, and very personal, moral dilemma.

King George's reign had, since the outbreak of war in 1914, already witnessed a darkening atmosphere of strikes and industrial unrest, fuelled by the growth of support for socialism and the rise of the Labour Party. Socialism had brought with it the much-feared spectre of republicanism, and King George was only too acutely aware that his government's priority was to hold the

Home Front together all the time there was a war going on. He dreaded the onrush of a class war in Britain mimicking that in Russia; his cousin Nicholas's fall from power posed a serious conflict of interests over which he dithered and agonised as he tried to balance his private familial sympathies with his duty as head of the nation.

The voice of dissent was gathering outside his door. On 31 March at London's Royal Albert Hall a rally had been held to 'rejoice' the advent of the Russian Revolution, chaired by republican Labour politician George Lansbury. This was no meeting of a handful of left-wing extremists; the Hall was packed to the rafters with 12,000 people, with a further 5,000 outside unable to get in.[18] Although the Albert Hall meeting had not been openly hostile to the King, in its celebration of revolution and a newly free Russia it had provided a huge boost to working-class confidence in its own growing political muscle. On the lookout for warnings of public hostility, the King's private secretary, Lord Stamfordham, was now vigorously stoking the fires of George's anxiety by feeding him a stream of negative press cuttings about the question of the Tsar coming to England.

Day after day Stamfordham scoured the newspapers for any criticism of the King or signs of a growing anti-monarchical movement, pasting the cuttings into a file marked 'Unrest in the Country'. One passage in particular was heavily marked up in red ink for the King's attention: it came from an article published on 5 April by Independent Labour Party leader Henry Hyndman, entitled 'The Need for a British Republic'. Published in *Justice – The Organ of Social Democracy*, which was soon to become the official weekly newspaper of the Labour Party, the article reminded readers that the British royal family was 'essentially German'* and called for a British republic, remarking that 'If the

---

* There is no doubt that this and other insinuations about the royal family's possible pro-German sympathies, made even by eminent writers such as H. G. Wells, prompted the change of the family's name from Saxe-Coburg-Gotha to Windsor on 17 July 1917, in order to help defuse such accusations.

King and Queen have invited their discrowned Russian cousins to come here, they are misinterpreting entirely the feelings of us common Englishmen.'[19]

The article went on to warn of a desire for a post-war republic in Britain. On the same day, the King had received a warning letter from a friend, the Bishop of Chelmsford, that there was 'a suspicion among the public that the Tsar [was] backed by this country'; other letters to the King, both solicited and unsolicited, were arriving, expressing serious concern about the rise of the Labour Party and the extent to which it was stirring up social unrest.[20] Fear of the mob was widespread. Perhaps the government had not given sufficient consideration to all this, before conceding to Milyukov's request to give sanctuary to the Tsar? Nor had the government taken account of the fact that the British people had not forgotten the brutality with which the 1905 Revolution in Russia had been suppressed. Stamfordham was scrupulous, if not obsessive, in ensuring that every disturbing piece of evidence was placed before the monarch: 'There is no socialist newspaper, no libellous rag, that is not read and marked and shown to the King if they contain any criticism, friendly or unfriendly to His Majesty and the Royal Family,' he stated.[21] His systematic assault on the King's already fragile confidence in the matter would soon have its desired effect.

At the Alexander Palace at Tsarskoe Selo meanwhile, Alexander Kerensky had made his first official visit to the incarcerated Romanovs on 3 April, arriving ostentatiously in one of the numerous luxury motor cars confiscated from the Imperial Garage. On being introduced to Nicholas, he grandly informed him that one of his first acts as Justice Minister had been to abolish the death penalty. But was this perhaps less out of general altruism than to defuse the anticipated pressure for Nicholas's trial and execution? Kerensky was certainly being put upon to retain the death penalty for 'leaders of the old regime'.[22]

When asked by Nicholas, Kerensky was unable to give any definitive answer to the question of his departure from Russia, but told him he still hoped to arrange it. He was disconcerted by the Tsar's strangely passive and detached manner so soon after the tumultuous events he had gone through; there was a profound sense of loneliness, desolation even, about him. 'He did not wish to fight for power, and it simply fell from his hands'; Nicholas's retirement into civilian obscurity had 'brought him nothing but relief'. Having been freed from hours at his desk signing 'those everlasting documents', he seemed truly content with his life reading, walking, chopping wood and gardening with his children. It was Alexandra 'who felt keenly the loss of her authority and could not resign herself to her new status'; her negative and hostile attitude dragged everyone down.[23] Kerensky later confided to a friend that, like many others, he had pre-judged Nicholas unfairly. Indeed, he had been so struck by the former Tsar's dignified demeanour that during their meeting he had found himself calling him 'Your Royal Highness' instead of just plain Nikolay Alexandrovich.[24]

During the first few days of April, unaware of all the machinations going on behind the scenes regarding his evacuation, Nicholas noted that he had begun to start sorting through his things, 'put[ting] aside everything that I want to take with me, if we have to go to England'.[25] When one of her captors suggested to Alexandra that maybe she should hurry things along and 'write to the English queen to beg her to help her and the children', she gave him short shrift: 'I don't need to beg anyone's help after all we have been through, except the Lord God's,' she snapped. 'I have nothing to write to the English queen about.'[26]

During his visit, Kerensky had informed the family's physician, Dr Evgeniy Botkin, that the Danish queen had telegraphed the Provisional Government from Copenhagen 'to enquire about the health of the former Empress'. This passing comment has always been assumed to be an enquiry about the Tsaritsa Alexandra, but surely not. Why should the Danes suddenly be interested in German-born Alexandra's health? It was her children who were sick. Was it not a request about the health of the Dowager Empress Dagmar, King Christian's aunt, who had by now returned to Kiev, and news of whom had been intermittent?* *In a similar vein, Kerensky was heard to say during his visit that 'the English queen' was also asking about the health of the Empress. Again, this seems to be a misinterpretation, based on the loose use of 'Queen' and 'Empress' in such brief telegrams. In light of the kerfuffle about her husband's recent private telegram to Nicholas, the last thing Queen Mary would have done is send a private telegram asking about the Tsaritsa. No, the telegram was from Alexandra, the Queen Mother, urgently seeking news of her sister, the Dowager Empress Dagmar.*[27]

At this crucial juncture in the Romanov asylum negotiations, the Queen Mother was indeed becoming something of a thorn in the side for the British government. 'Mother dear' was badgering her son George on a regular basis 'about Russia, and Nicky', as she 'was very much upset about it all'. Although the King had had a private meeting with the exiled Grand Duke Mikhail Mikhailovich† about 'the idea of poor Nicky coming to England', without his knowledge telegrams had also been arriving at the British embassy in Petrograd from his mother, who was 'most anxious for news', not having heard from Dagmar 'for some days'.[28] The Queen Mother was begging Sir George Buchanan to sidestep officialdom and forward letters to Dagmar in Kiev, as were other members of the royal family with relatives in Russia – all of whom were finding it impossible to get news – but he regretted that he could not do so 'until I obtain permission from the Government'.

---

* Dagmar, who suffered from stomach trouble, had been living in Kiev since May 1916, where she had been undertaking Red Cross and other wartime hospital work. This almost certainly saved her from arrest and incarceration at Tsarskoe Selo with the rest of the Imperial Family, had she still been resident in Petrograd.

† Grand Duke Mikhail Mikhailovich, or Miche-Miche as he was known in the family, had been banished from Russia by Alexander III for contracting a morganatic marriage to Countess Sophie von Merenberg in 1891. He had settled in England in 1900, where he later leased Kenwood House on Hampstead Heath.

In a message to the Foreign Office on 4 April, Buchanan confided that these private interventions were causing him a lot of problems: 'I hear that two telegrams sent by Queen Alexandra have been held up. One was quite harmless but the other I fear was rather compromising in its language. It is useless for Her Majesty to telegraph at present.'[29] There was good reason to fear such telegrams falling into the wrong hands: the Russians were intercepting and reading all British telegrams sent '*en clair*', and possibly ciphered diplomatic ones too, having a long tradition of code-breaking established under the old tsarist secret police, the Okhrana.

In the Russia and Siberia FO 800/205 file there is a previously uncited but revealing exchange between Queen Alexandra's private secretary Sir Arthur Davidson and Foreign Secretary Arthur Balfour. Its contents illustrate how once again – and only days after King George's unofficial telegram of support to Nicholas had so alarmed them – the British government was getting extremely irritated about the royals sending private messages to Russia behind its back.

Sir Arthur Davidson explained the problems to Balfour:

> It is hoped H.M. will not send any more telegrams as their continuance may very easily lead to the most serious results which it is imperative should be avoided. Queen Alexandra is however very averse to taking advice except from the Fountain Head of knowledge [i.e. her son King George] and I am afraid that any caution will have little or no effect unless it is supplemented by something from a very much more authoritative source.
>
> Could you therefore send me … a short memorandum showing that owing to the transition state through which Russia is now passing, the situation is most delicate and may very easily become most dangerous.[30]

Balfour responded promptly with an official memorandum for Davidson to approve and pass on to the King and his mother:

The Government are very apprehensive lest it should be thought that influence is being exerted from England in order to restore the Imperial regime. If the revolutionary Committee [the Soviet] were able to produce any evidence that such was the case the [Provisional] Government would be greatly weakened and the whole question of the alliance and of the continuance of the war by Russia might be endangered. The safety also of the whole Imperial Family depends in a great measure on the strictest and most careful avoidance of any form of interference or expression of opinion from England, especially from the King, the Queen and Queen Alexandra. Even the simplest messages of sympathy may easily be distorted into political views or actions.[31]

It was Good Friday, 6 April, but the deepening crisis over the Romanov asylum offer was keeping everyone at their desks, both at Windsor and in Westminster. The King, no doubt having perused the latest updates in the 'Unrest in the Country' file, had barely had breakfast that morning before sending for Stamfordham. Soon a letter was winging its way to Balfour at the Foreign Office:

Every day the king is becoming more concerned about the question of the Emperor and Empress coming to this country.

His Majesty receives letters from people of all classes of life, known or unknown to him, saying how much the matter is being discussed, not only in clubs but by working men, and that Labour Members of the House of Commons are expressing adverse opinions to the proposal.

As you know from the first the King has thought the presence of the Imperial Family (especially the Empress) in this country would raise all sort of difficulties, and I feel sure that you appreciate how awkward it will be for our Royal Family who are closely connected with both the Emperor and Empress ...

The King desires me to ask you whether after consulting the Prime Minister, Sir George Buchanan should not be communicated with a view to approaching the Russian Government to make some other place for the future residence of their Imperial Majesties.[32]

Six hours later another note arrived from Stamfordham; by this time King George's anxiety levels were so high that he was positively *begging* Balfour to:

represent to the Prime Minister that from all he hears and reads in the press, the residence in this country of the ex-Emperor and Empress would be strongly resented by the public, and would undoubtedly compromise the position of the King and Queen from whom it would generally be assumed the invitation had emanated.[33]

King George had clearly read the Hyndman article from the previous week's issue of *Justice*, for he was now panicking about its suggestion that the invitation to the Tsar 'has come from Their Majesties'. This time Stamfordham did not beat about the bush:

Buchanan ought to be instructed to tell Miliukoff that the opposition to the Emperor and Empress coming here is so strong that we must be allowed to withdraw from the consent previously given to the Russian Government's proposal.[34]

Arthur Balfour had no option but to act on this, and that evening he sent off a note to Lloyd George about the need for contingency plans: 'I think we may have to suggest Spain or the South of France as a more suitable residence than England for the Czar.'[35]

One of the first-ever studies of the murder of the Romanovs, published in Paris in 1931, was written by émigré Russian historian Sergey

Melgunov. In his Sudba Imperatora Nikolaya II posle otrecheniya (The Fate of Emperor Nicholas II after the Abdication) *Melgunov quoted a British newspaper article,, which in the most uncompromising terms made patently clear the level of official opposition already gathering towards the Romanovs coming to England.*[36] *However, he wrongly attributed the article to the* Daily Telegraph *and gave no date, so it has never, till now, been verified. From the tone, it was clear that it had to be an editorial, as it was entitled 'A Respectful Protest'. The* Daily Telegraph *for the crucial period is not digitised, and a long search on microfilm failed to locate it. And so I sat down at my desk one Sunday morning to make a speculative search in the British Newspaper Archive online. I entered the keywords 'respectful protest' and a few other possible combinations – and, suddenly, there it was.*

The reference to the Daily Telegraph *was wrong; the article was published in a London evening newspaper,* The Globe. *The timing behind this editorial – 5 April 1917 – is crucial; its political significance only too plain to see.*

A Respectful Protest

We most sincerely hope that if there really is any idea of inviting the ex-Tsar and his Consort to make their home in England it will be abandoned. It is necessary to speak very plainly on this matter. To offer an asylum to the Imperial Family in this country would be deeply and justly resented by the Russians who have been compelled to organise a great revolution mainly because so long as the ex-Tsar remained on the throne, they were continually being betrayed by those who are our enemies as well as theirs. We regret to be obliged to speak in strong terms of an exalted lady nearly allied to our own Royal House, but it is impossible to blink [*sic*] the fact that the ex-Tsaritsa was the centre, if not the actual originator of the pro-German intrigues which inflicted the gravest disaster upon our Allies, and were very nearly successful in beguiling them into a premature and dishonourable peace. The Consort of the Russian Tsar, she yet could never forget that she was a German Princess, and wrecked the dynasty of the Romanoffs by attempts to betray the country of her adoption to the country of her birth. The English people will not endure that she shall be given a refuge in England, from which to resume her dangerous activities, and no pity for fallen greatness will induce them to countenance a step so suicidal. We speak plainly because we must, and because the danger is great and imminent. The British Throne itself would be imperilled if this thing were done.[37]

There was a very good reason for this damning, if not libellous piece appearing in *The Globe*. The newspaper was Conservative in its political leanings and occasionally published ministerial communications; its target audience was the educated classes. In 1917 it was controlled by the industrial magnate Max Aitken, who as owner of the *Daily Express* had the previous year been a key player in the downfall of Asquith's Liberal government. He was also a leading supporter of David Lloyd George's new coalition ministry, which was now in power. Lloyd George rewarded Aitken with a peerage for his support, and he took the title Baron Beaverbrook.

It is a curious thing that this most rabid character assassination of the Tsaritsa does not appear amid the numerous cuttings in the 'Unrest in the Country File' presented to King George by Lord Stamfordham. Perhaps its subversive tone was deemed too strong for the King's sensitive ears – Alexandra being his cousin after all. But it makes clear, by acting as an indirect mouthpiece for David Lloyd George, that the British government's position over the Romanov asylum was, despite the display of superficial good intent, entirely negative. Which makes it even more poignant that the one and only positive, well-intentioned message of support from his British cousin and ally, King George, had never reached Nicholas.

Over in Russia, Sir George Buchanan was still in discussion with Kerensky about a possible departure date for the Imperial Family.

Kerensky had told him that he would be visiting the Tsar at Tsarskoe Selo the next day, but that:

> he did not think the Emperor would be able to leave for England for another month. It would be difficult to allow him to go until examination of documents seized had been completed and he hoped that I would not press Government to hasten his departure. I said I had no intention of doing so though we were naturally anxious that every precaution should be taken for His Majesty's safety.[38]

Kerensky hinted that these were potentially incriminating documents showing the Tsaritsa's 'pro-German sympathies' and her involvement in a plot to bring about a separate peace with Germany. As a result, Nicholas and Alexandra were temporarily separated at Tsarskoe Selo and were only allowed to share meals together while the investigation was ongoing.

What is so striking about this despatch from Buchanan is that it was sent to Balfour on 9 April, three days after the King and his government had begun back-pedalling, at a point when the British resolve to get the Imperial Family out of Russia was already falling apart. Why had Buchanan not been informed sooner? An obscurely published but crucial letter written that very same day by Stamfordham's deputy – assistant private secretary Sir Clive Wigram – is damning in its candid assessment of the situation:

> You have probably heard rumours of the Emperor and Empress of Russia, together with many Grand Dukes, coming to England to find asylum here. Of course the King has been accused of trying to work this for his royal friends. As a matter of fact His Majesty has been opposed to this proposal from the start, and has begged his ministers to knock it on the head. I do not expect that these Russian royalties will come, but if they do their presence here will be due to the War Cabinet and not to His Majesty.[39]

On 10 April, the King was so adamant that his feelings be made abundantly clear to his government that Lord Stamfordham, armed with his file of cuttings, travelled from Windsor Castle, where the royal family were spending Easter, to 10 Downing Street for a face-to-face meeting with David Lloyd George. During the meeting Stamfordham fiercely defended George's position, and 'tried to impress upon him [Lloyd George] the King's strong opinion that the Emperor and Empress of Russia should not come to this country'. The situation since the King's first expression of support, he argued, had changed dramatically: public opinion here had become 'stoutly opposed to the idea'; he emphasised again that the King was daily receiving messages, 'anonymous and otherwise, from persons unknown to him as well as from his friends, inveighing against an arrangement, which, say what the Government may, *will be put down entirely to the King* [my italics]'.[40]

As defender of the King's honour, this wasn't good enough for Stamfordham: 'Even if the Government publicly stated that they took the responsibility for T.I.M.'s [Their Imperial Majesties] coming here the PEOPLE would reply that this was done to screen the King.' Such loading of personal responsibility for the entire exercise on George's shoulders was more than he could tolerate – or, for that matter, risk. 'His Majesty's Government,' insisted Stamfordham once more, 'must withdraw the consent previously given.'[41] Lloyd George agreed that perhaps the South of France might be a better place for the Romanovs; he said he would raise the matter with the French president, Alexandre Ribot, in a forthcoming meeting; his Foreign Secretary, Balfour, would also solicit the opinion of Francis Bertie, British ambassador to France.

Stamfordham was somewhat surprised to discover, at a meeting with Balfour immediately afterwards, that Sir George Buchanan was still '[taking] it for granted that the Emperor and Empress were coming to England, and that it was a question of delay with regard to certain matters that had not been cleared up, which prevented an early start'. Shouldn't the ambassador have 'been informed that the whole question was being reconsidered, and that our previous Agreement could no longer be held as binding?' he asked. Balfour agreed that a telegram would be sent to Buchanan in Petrograd forthwith.

In her later memoirs, Buchanan's daughter Meriel claims to have vividly remembered the moment an urgent telegram was received at the British embassy in Petrograd. '"I have bad news from England," her father said, and his voice sounded flat and lifeless, "They refuse to let the Emperor come over."'[42] 'It was the 10th April,' she claimed, but this cannot be so.[43] I searched long and hard for this much-quoted communication of the 10th. But I could find no Foreign Office telegram to Sir George in Petrograd on that date in the official files, although there is one about the Queen Mother's letters to Dagmar. The telegram to Buchanan instructing him about the change of heart was sent to Petrograd at 4 p.m. on 13 April, marked 'Personal and Most Confidential'. It probably did not arrive till the following morning – the 14th.*

Approved by Lord Hardinge and David Lloyd George, the telegram outlined the government's serious concerns:

There are indications that a considerable anti-monarchical movement is developing here, including personal attacks upon the King ... It is thought that, if the Emperor comes here, it may dangerously increase this movement. It is also worth consideration whether the presence of the Emperor here might not weaken us in our dealings with the new Russian Government ... Please let me have your views and in the meantime *say nothing further* [my italics] to the Russian Government on the subject unless they themselves raise the question.[44]

---

* One has to conclude that Meriel Buchanan's recall is faulty, writing many years after the event; a few lines down on the same page she misdates another important document in this story. Kerensky also appears to muddle or conflate dates in this sequence.

Sir George was deeply upset about the government's change of heart, but by 15 April was beginning to regretfully accept the wisdom of the decision made in London, having recently become more fully aware of the wider political ramifications. Only the previous day he had welcomed two British Labour MPs to Petrograd, Will Thorne and James O'Grady. In private conversation Thorne had advised him that 'if we were to offer His Majesty asylum in England, consequences might be very serious'; no doubt a veiled threat of left-wing unrest. But what if the initiative came from the Provisional Government rather than being an invitation from the British? asked Buchanan hopefully. Thorne replied that 'we must not allow him to stop in England under any circumstances so long as the war lasted'.[45] In Moscow soon afterwards, a Labour Party delegate was even more candid at a dinner given for the British colony there: 'People are saying that the Tsar is going to England. Let me tell you at once, that this is not true. If he is not good enough for Russia, he is not good enough for us.'[46]

Nevertheless, although the official British initiative to give asylum to the Romanovs had now withered away, Sir George Buchanan was still searching for an alternative solution. Why could the Provisional Government not let the Tsar 'go, as I believed he wished, to Livadia?' he asked Prince Lvov. He would have thought it 'would be quite easy to isolate him there as well as to provide for his protection'. 'The risk of the journey would be too great,' Buchanan was told; Lvov's government was still hoping for England. But by now the ambassador was also worrying about the reaction of the 'extreme Left Parties' to such an eventuality. 'If only the French Government would consent,' he telegraphed to London, 'it would be far better from our point of view. Perhaps it would be well to sound them on the subject?'[47]

Lord Cecil, the Under-Secretary of State for Foreign Affairs, confirmed that an approach had already been made to France.[48] A private letter from Lord Hardinge had meanwhile been sent to the British ambassador in Paris, Francis Bertie, backed up by a personal message from Stamfordham on the King's behalf. The British government found itself in 'a situation of grave embarrassment'. The King would not like to show the Tsar 'the cold shoulder', Hardinge explained, but could the French step in and save the situation?[49]

Alas, all hopes of a resolution were quickly dashed. Not only were the French indifferent to the fate of the Romanovs, they were actively hostile. Many in the French political establishment had been delighted at the overthrow of the Tsar, seeing in it close parallels with the French Revolution of 1789; and, like the British, the French Left sent socialist delegates to Russia in April to congratulate the new government. French Prime Minister Raymond Poincaré worried, as the British did, about the effect that the revolution would have on the Russian war effort.[50] It came as no surprise, therefore, when Francis Bertie wrote to Balfour that he thought it was 'a mercy that the idea has been dropped':

> I do not think the ex-Emperor and his family would be welcome in France. The Empress is not only a Boche by birth but in sentiment. She did all she could to bring about an understanding with Germany. She is regarded as a criminal or a criminal lunatic and the ex-Emperor as a criminal from his weakness and submission to her prompting.[51]

With so much violent hostility towards Alexandra being expressed in diplomatic circles, it is obvious that Nicholas and Alexandra were a political hot potato that nobody wished to handle. By the end of April, barely six weeks after the revolution had toppled them from power, the former Emperor and Empress of Russia were *personae non gratae* across Europe. 'We are looking round for a refuge for them,' Lord Hardinge told Bertie in Paris, 'but do not see where they would be welcome. I can quite understand that the French do not want them any more than we do, but the position here would be much more difficult than in France.'[52]

Over in Russia, the Imperial Family and the Provisional Government continued to wait for news of an evacuation, not knowing that the British offer was already dead in the water and that the former Tsar and Tsaritsa were pariahs in the eyes of the rest of Europe. Nevertheless, persistent rumours over the last 100 years suggest that perhaps the British had in fact put tentative evacuation plans in place in the very first days after the revolution.

Chapter 5

'Port Romanoff by the
Murmansk Railway'

At the end of March 1917, Swiss tutor Pierre Gilliard, held captive with the Romanovs at the Alexander Palace, noted a gathering sense of uncertainty about the hoped-for evacuation to England: 'The days passed and our departure was always being postponed.' He had already become aware that the Provisional Government was running up against the intransigence of the Petrograd Soviet in arranging things and that its 'authority was slipping away from it'. 'Yet we were only a few hours by railways from the Finnish frontier,' he noted plaintively, 'and the necessity of passing through Petrograd was the only serious obstacle ... If the authorities had acted resolutely and secretly it would not have been difficult to get the Imperial Family to one of the Finnish ports and thus to some foreign country.'[1]

Gilliard's conclusion was of course entirely logical; but the reality was far more complex. After the February Revolution, Finland – which had till then been a Grand Duchy of the Russian Empire – had gained semi-autonomous status and its own parliament, and might have offered the Romanovs, had they got that far, a degree of protection on their way out of Russia. But any suggested evacuation plans from Petrograd in March or April 1917, after the British offer was initially made, all fall at the first hurdle: the logistics of getting the family out of Tsarskoe Selo. The winter weather, the distance, the sick children, the state of the railways and who controlled them all had a crucial part to play. And this is not to mention the ominous presence of the Petrograd Soviet, which was already policing the Romanovs' every move.

When asked his opinion by the War Office in March 1917 about an evacuation, the British military attaché in Russia, Brigadier-General Waters, rather glibly observed that if the 'moderates' had acted quickly enough – and before the Petrograd Soviet got the upper hand – 'a fast torpedo boat and a few bags of British sovereigns' could have got the family out across the Gulf of Finland. But it had to be done 'within a fortnight'.[2] Waters was certainly right about the timing: the only realistic window of opportunity for a successful evacuation of the Imperial Family was in fact even tighter than his rough estimate. It amounted to the six days from the abdication on the 15th to the Provisional Government voting on 20 March that 'the deposed Emperor and his consort be regarded as deprived of their liberty' – and certainly before the Petrograd Soviet sent its bully boys to Tsarskoe Selo to ensure that the family did not leave.[3]

Had Nicholas gone straight back to Tsarskoe Selo after his abdication, instead of diverting to Stavka to see the army and his mother, he could have been back by 16 March – that is, if his train had not been stopped before it even got there.[4]*

Waters's suggestion of the Romanovs making a hasty exit via the shores of the Gulf of Finland (their summer dacha at Peterhof could have been the base for this) – and out via the Baltic to England – certainly would have been the quickest route, but they would have needed to avoid their own Russian minefields, laid there against Germans submarines. In March, however, much of the Gulf would have been iced up; and the Baltic beyond was patrolled by murderous German warships and submarines that

---

* So desperate were members of the entourage Count Benckendorff and Elizaveta Naryshkina, the former Mistress of the Robes, to see the Tsar and Tsaritsa escape possible Bolshevik reprisals that they urged them to flee Russia immediately, offering to take care of the sick children and to escort them abroad later to join their parents.

were deliberately positioned to confine British and Russian vessels to the Gulf.[5]

It is clear that days before the official British offer, and indeed even *before* Nicholas had arrived back from Stavka, such was the anxiety of the Provisional Government to get the Romanovs out of Russia that it had already begun exploring the logistics of how it could be done. In their later memoirs, Kerensky and Milyukov emphasised how they were expecting the family's arrest at Tsarskoe Selo to be merely temporary (a necessary placatory measure to the Petrograd Soviet), pending their departure abroad. So confident were they that they would be able to effect this that in a speech made to the Moscow Soviet on 20 March, Kerensky had publicly committed to personally escorting the family to Murmansk.[6] And later that same day, as he reiterated in an article published in 1932, 'we had firmly settled the Tsar's departure, and had fixed the itinerary of his journey abroad.'[7]

When the British offer arrived on 23 March, according to Meriel Buchanan, her father immediately went to see Milyukov to 'make the necessary arrangements'. 'It was agreed,' she wrote, 'that the Emperor should go to Port Romanoff by the Murmansk railway ... and a British cruiser was to meet them and conduct them to England.'[8] This much of a tentative plan is confirmed in an undated 'List of measures to be taken in connection with proposed departure abroad of Nicholas II', drawn up by a key figure in this story, Count Benckendorff. Its priorities were:

1. Journey abroad via Romanov on the Murman or through Tornio [the Finnish border crossing with Sweden] in view of the desire for a stop in Norway for the treatment of the children.
2. Count Benckendorff to be charged with liaising with a representative of the Provisional Government in discussing issues connected with the journey.

Other points in this document enumerated the protection of the Imperial Family's personal effects and furniture left behind at the Alexander Palace, the preservation of the contents of Dagmar's Anichkov Palace in Petrograd and of the other Romanov properties at Peterhof and Livadia. The document also insisted on payment of the pensions of the former Imperial Family's servants being guaranteed.[9] It is clear from the tone that initial hopes were for an orderly evacuation of the family. Any kind of covert, dramatic 'rescue' from Tsarskoe Selo in this context is nonsensical.

At this point we must ask the question that has puzzled many: was a British ship actually, specifically sent in March 1917 shortly after the British offer was made? There is not a single document to be found anywhere, in either the Foreign Office or War Office archives or in the logbook of political signals from Petrograd, referring to this. There is, however, a document in the secret archive of the Russian Foreign Minister at AVPRI that confirms the sense of extreme urgency. This aide-memoire of their conversation (rather than an official memorandum), handed by Sir George Buchanan to Milyukov on 24 March, stressed 'the utmost urgency being given by the king's government to the safe evacuation to England in the shortest possible time of the former emperor and the members of his family'.[10] So any tentative plans by Sir George and Milyukov, if there were some, appear to have been discussed entirely off the record.

There are two possible scenarios with regard to evacuating the Romanovs from Russia at this time: the first is the Murmansk option.[11] Indeed, Murmansk as the point of exit has been the repeated mantra of most books on the Romanovs since the 1920s, but without any serious exploration being undertaken of the logistics involved. One wonders whether the viability of a Murmansk evacuation was properly investigated, even in March 1917. How realistic was it in fact to get the Imperial Family to a British destroyer bound for England at that time, given the German submarine war and the volatile political situation in Russia? What possible chance was there that any train carrying them would even get beyond Petrograd? The realities of the Murmansk proposal soon fall apart when one analyses the details. Any train taking the Romanovs out would have had to travel into Petrograd from the station at Tsarskoe Selo, east via Petrozavodsk on the newly constructed Vologda–Petrograd railway line and then north via Zvanka to Romanov-on-the-Murman (renamed Murmansk on 16 April 1917).

The town of Romanov had been created on the Kola Peninsula of the Russian Arctic coast in 1915 as an important wartime supply point into Russia from England, via its nearby ice-free port on the Barents Sea. In early 1917 it was a mere cluster of huts, docks and railway sidings. But it would later become a major base for the Allied Intervention and the White Army during the civil war of 1917–22. The idea of a British submarine or destroyer, with nothing better to do, waiting expectantly for the Romanovs at Murmansk in the spring of 1917 is a fantasy. Although Murmansk was an ice-free port, the sea route to it at that time would have been extremely dangerous, with a great deal of ice in the water. In addition, submarines were not able to submerge for very long distances, having in the main to travel on the surface with a cruiser as escort, and German submarines had already sunk several ships in the area of Murmansk. It was also, at this time of the year, pitch-black for most of the day and night. In early 1917 the only vessels known to have been at Murmansk were an old battleship, a cruiser (which was stationed there regularly) and six armed trawlers. The British Admiralty *did* send two submarines on war operations to Murmansk from Scapa Flow, but they did not arrive until 27 April.[12]

Any suggestion of the port at Archangel as another possible evacuation point at this time of year is even less credible. Although it lies nearly 1,000 miles south-east of Murmansk, at the entrance to the White Sea, the ice there was twelve-foot thick in March/ April; the weather was bitter and the port, with its vast expanse of unbroken ice, looked at times like the North Pole, only being ice-free between mid-May and early November. Even then, as the ice receded it tended to pile up in the narrow neck of the White Sea where it flowed into the Arctic, often impeding navigation in and out of Archangel until well into June.[13] However, according to a secret telegram sent to Ambassador Nabokov in London, an evacuation from Archangel was preferred, as soon as the first sailings became possible in mid-May.[14]

In the winter of 1917 a journey of 846 miles north from Tsarskoe Selo to Murmansk would have been extremely difficult – particularly for five children still weakened by their recent bout of measles – even in the best of circumstances. The railway line was a single-track one, with no proper rail bed (a contingency in wartime to ensure that if there were any accidents, the rails could be pulled up to bypass the site) and it had been laid in a hurry, mainly by prisoners of war, to link the supply route with the capital. A passenger train would have taken up to six days to get there; only munitions trains, which took priority, could do it faster. At any point during the long, arduous journey, a train carrying the Imperial Family could have been stopped dead, simply by belligerent railway workers pulling up the tracks ahead of it or, worse, could have been attacked by Red Guards itching to lay hands on the former Tsar and Tsaritsa and impose their own rough justice on them. The family would have been sitting ducks for the entire duration of the journey.

However, that is not the end of the Murmansk/Archangel scenario. Murmansk will reappear in our story in early 1918.

There is, meanwhile, a second, more practical and entirely feasible Scandinavian route out of Russia that could have been explored, and which was suggested in the Benckendorff memo – and that is the route *through Tornio*. This would have involved taking the Imperial Family by rail through Petrograd and then north across the Karelian Isthmus, to the Finnish border forty-two miles away at the River Sestra. From there, the train would have travelled past the Russian border station at Beloostrov and headed west and then north on the slow single-track line to the British-controlled crossing point with neutral Sweden at Haparanda/Tornio, a rail journey in all of 744 miles, and 200 miles longer than the shortest direct route. The situation in Finland was less volatile than in Russia and a train might have had a chance of getting through to the Swedish border. From there, with the connivance of the neutral Swedes, the family could have been taken by an undercover British military escort across Sweden to Norway (the two countries, having been in a political union till 1905, must have had cross-country links) to an evacuation point by sea at Bergen.

In Lord Stamfordham's record of the 22 March meeting that he had with David Lloyd George, the King's private secretary noted that the Provisional Government 'wished the Emperor to go to Romanov because he would be in their keeping until he was safe on board an English ship, *whereas if he travelled to Bergen he would be free as soon as he crossed the Russian frontier* [my italics]'.[15] The Bergen option, had it been pursued, might well have been the only viable way of getting the Romanovs from Scandinavia to England in those first crucial days. For in early March, shortly before Nicholas abdicated, the British Admiralty had inaugurated a new, weekly fast steamship service from Bergen across to Aberdeen – a secure port into which only British vessels were allowed – to facilitate the safer and more efficient transport of diplomatic bags and military and diplomatic personnel to and from Russia. This had been prompted by delays experienced in getting crucial Secret Intelligence Service material from Petrograd to England by the normal boats operating out of Norway. It would have offered the perfect route out of Russia for special incognito travellers such as the Romanovs, as the boat itself was armed and the British Consulate at Bergen strictly controlled access to it. The British Military Control officer based in Petrograd, who was in charge of the Bergen operation, was SIS agent Major Stephen Alley (who will reappear later in this story); and the landing point at Aberdeen had its own permanent Port Control Officer – who was a member of MI5, the British Security Service.[16]

Perhaps it is a coincidence, but another version of a British evacuation plan told to Simon Sebag Montefiore by Prince Michael of Kent was the possibility of bringing the family to the naval base at Scapa Flow in the Orkneys, and from there to house them temporarily at Balmoral.[17] This indeed would have been the route taken by a British cruiser coming from Murmansk – but it seems illogical when Aberdeen is only forty-seven miles away from Balmoral along a straight road. Would this not have made the Bergen–Aberdeen scenario a far better option?

There is no way of knowing whether the Bergen option was ever considered, although it seems too obvious an alternative not to have been, at the very least, entertained. If so, any consideration of it went entirely undocumented or was discussed via a set of back-channels. Uncensored SIS material was certainly getting through to England from Russia, which never appeared in the Foreign Office registers, and the Admiralty had its own telegraphic address and ships' radios.

These are the best tentative scenarios for any Romanov evacuation – a plan that was aborted no sooner than it was mooted. The Romanovs' departure from Tsarskoe Selo in April 1917 'proved impossible ... for internal reasons', as Kerensky himself admitted later.[18] Put simply, any evacuation – no matter the willingness of the parties involved – was stymied by the distance that would have to be covered, along railway lines largely controlled by hostile Bolshevik revolutionaries. Even the relatively short journey of fifteen miles from Tsarskoe to Petrograd might have proved too dangerous, given that the government was 'not yet complete master of the administrative machine', as Kerensky euphemistically put it. The 'railways, in particular,' he conceded, 'were very much at the free disposal of all kinds of Unions and Soviets'. The admission has been there, in print since 1935, for all to see: 'there would have been a strike the moment the Tsar was entrained for Murmansk [or anywhere else for that matter], and the train would never have left the station'.[19]

And yet for the last 100 years the vast majority of commentators on the failed Romanov asylum have contented themselves with an oversimplified view of the situation, based on little or no in-depth examination of the circumstances, choosing instead to make King George V the target of their wrath and the repository of all blame. The King may have been a moral coward, but in terms of personally effecting the Romanovs' physical removal from Russia and their safe journey to England in the spring of 1917, he had absolutely no power. Nor did anyone else. It was Minister of War Alexander Guchkov who best summed it up: 'the only way to send the Emperor abroad was to do so unexpectedly, and, as far as possible secretly'.[20]

There was also, of course, the more romantic alternative of rescue by loyal Russian monarchists. In the story of the Romanov captivity there is a great deal of intrigue and mystification on this score, but few published details are to be found other than in the White Russian émigré press of the 1920s and 1930s. Evidence shows, however, that the Tsaritsa's close friends, Anna Vyrubova and Lili Dehn, who had been banished from the Alexander Palace by Kerensky on 3 April for being too close to her, over the following months conspired with various nebulous monarchist groups to hatch a rescue plan.[21] Thanks to a reasonably sympathetic regime inside the palace under the commandant Evgeniy Kobylinsky, Alexandra had been able to smuggle letters, with the coded names of recipients, out to Vyrubova and Dehn via another former lady-in-waiting, Rita Khitrovo. At that time Khitrovo was working as a volunteer nurse in one of the Tsarskoe Selo hospitals, and Kobylinsky had allowed her to come to the palace regularly to pick up and deliver letters.

In May 1917, German intelligence reported to the Chancellor, Theobald von Bethmann-Hollweg, in Berlin that there were widespread hopes in Russian monarchist circles that Grand Duke Nikolay Nikolaevich, the Tsar's uncle and former Commander in Chief of the army, 'possessed the resolution to place himself at the head of a counter-revolution'; but he had been put under house arrest in Crimea, where he was closely guarded and living under threat of a court martial. Nevertheless, such rumours 'preoccupy and worry the minds of the St Petersburg [sic] government circles, as indeed those of the actual government, if not the "second power"— the Petrograd Soviet'.[22] By June, further reports from a 'most reliable' source were arriving in Berlin that 'a strong monarchist conspiracy exists in Moscow' and even named various 'pretenders to the crown', including Rasputin's murderer, Prince Felix Yusupov, and his father, Count Sumarokov-Elston.[23] Many of the potential monarchist conspirators were officers who had served in either the Tsar or Tsaritsa's own regiments or had been treated as war wounded in the hospital patronised by Alexandra, her daughters and other aristocrats at Tsarskoe Selo.

In around June 1917 various of these monarchist officers, anxious that the Imperial Family had still not been taken out of Russia to safety, began trying to come up with a viable plan for springing them from captivity. Their efforts to keep watch on the situation at the Alexander Palace had begun shortly after the revolution, when Cornet Sergey Markov, an officer in Alexandra's Crimean Cavalry regiment, had managed to get into the palace to see her, just prior to Nicholas's return from Pskov. When Lili Dehn was sent to receive him, Alexandra being unwell, Markov announced his undying loyalty: 'I've fought my way through the mob in order to see the Empress, and assure her of my devotion. The assassins wanted to tear off my epaulettes with HER cypher. I told them that the Empress had given them to me, and that it was her right alone to deprive me of them.'[24] When Lili Dehn was sent away from Tsarskoe Selo, the devoted Markov (who in sources, for reasons soon apparent, is referred to as Little Markov) visited her. In the meantime she had received a smuggled letter confirming the Tsaritsa's intransigence with regard to the idea of being 'saved from this monstrous position' in which she and her family found themselves, and fleeing abroad. 'He would be a scoundrel who would leave his country at such a fateful time,' she had written. 'They can do what they like with us; they can throw us into the Fortress of SS. Peter and Paul, but we will not leave Russia in any circumstances.'[25] Alexandra's reluctance to capitulate and leave Russia was perhaps also a reflection of her stubborn determination that she and Nicholas might one day be able to reclaim the throne – not for themselves, but for their beloved son.

This did not deter Little Markov from recruiting a dozen or so loyal officers at his base at Novogeorgievsk, in Kherson province, southern Russia, to plan a rescue mission, complete with 'special secret code, covering addresses, false names, and words with secret meanings'.[26] It was at this point that he met another Markov, Nikolay Evgenevich (known as Markov II, for the sake of clarity), to whom he was loosely related. A former Duma deputy and an influential figure in monarchist circles, Markov II was a leading member of a right-wing organisation known as the 'Union of the Russian People' – founded in 1905 and sanctioned by Nicholas for its defence of 'Tsar, Faith and Motherland' – which was plotting an uprising and had 'made it its mission to protect and free the imprisoned Imperial Family'. Despite the organisation being hounded since the revolution, with some of its members arrested and killed, Markov II had managed to lie low, establishing underground links with groups of officers in the south and elsewhere who would eventually rally counter-revolutionary forces against the Bolsheviks. The Union had even infiltrated Bolshevik ranks with their own people, in the hope of gleaning information on the government's plans for the Imperial Family.[27] With this in mind, Markov II and other monarchists were already in touch with Lili Dehn, holding secret meetings in the relative safety of a dacha at Kellomäki (Komarova) across the border in Finland. As a result of these meetings, Dehn had passed on a secret message to Alexandra that the monarchists were utterly devoted to the cause and could be counted on to offer effective help.[28]

Both Markovs agreed that the situation the family were facing at Tsarskoe Selo was becoming increasingly dangerous: the Palace Guard was volatile and untrustworthy, the town 'packed with demoralized soldiers' who might march on the palace at any time. They concluded that the Tsar and Tsaritsa should be 'removed, if necessary by force, for their own safety'.[29] They discussed forming 'a group of thirty officers, prepared to dare all', to include the twelve loyal officers that Little Markov had already recruited in the south. Little Markov had it all worked out: the group would disguise themselves in civilian clothes and carry false papers for themselves and the seven members of the Imperial Family.

Armed with guns and grenades, and after secretly informing the Imperial Family in advance of the exact day and time, they would launch a 'sham attack' on the Palace. Markov thought it would be easy enough to pick off the external guards 'with the help of air-guns with poisoned darts', before 'forcing their way into the palace'. All Nicholas need do was don civilian clothes and shave off his beard, 'to make it certain that no one would recognize him'.[30] The liberators would then create a large diversionary explosion using grenades, giving them time to spirit the family out to several waiting cars, 'with trustworthy drivers' gunning their engines in the side streets. Having installed the fugitive Romanovs in a prearranged safe house, they would then arrange their exit through Finland and Sweden. If the Romanovs refused to leave Russia, they would hide them – separately – 'in the remote villages of North Russia, where one could be certain that no spy would track them down, and where they could tranquilly await the future course of events'.[31]

Such is the stuff of *Boy's Own Paper* fantasy, so disarming in its naïveté; Markov II quickly dismissed Little Markov's idea as 'quite impossible'; they had 'no right to expose Their Majesties to such a risk'. He was in the process of planning things 'quite differently', he said enigmatically, but failed to elaborate. Under the unlikely cover name of 'Aunt Ivetta', he had, through Lili Dehn, made contact with Nicholas via a concealed note in a box of cigarettes, in which he had solicited the Tsar's permission to serve him and his family's interests in any way he could. Would the Tsar give his group his blessing by sending an icon, he asked? In response, Nicholas had smuggled out an icon of St Nicholas the Wonder-worker to Lili Dehn, bearing his own and Alexandra's initials.[32]

Little Markov's hare-brained scheme does, however, have some interesting parallels with an equally audacious, though more cred-ible, rescue plot conjured up around the same time by a British officer then in Russia: Oliver Locker-Lampson. In command of the Royal Naval Armoured Car Squadron that had been sent to assist its Russian allies on the Eastern Front, Lampson had met Nicholas at Army HQ at Mogilev and had been in Petrograd when the revolution broke in March. He had noted how often the Tsar was to be seen outside in the Alexander Park digging the vegetable garden, cutting wood or chatting with his guards: 'It appeared to be so easy to rescue him that I decided it should be done.'[33] He planned to use an insider at the Alexander Palace, one of the servants whom he had recruited – code name Vladimir – who had learned to cut hair and shave in order to be instated as the Tsar's barber. Lampson bribed key members of the guards inside the palace with vodka, cigarettes and tins of British bully beef. While they were otherwise drunk or distracted, the plan was that Vladimir would smuggle in Lampson's orderly, Tovell (who was the same size as the Tsar), have the Tsar shave off his beard and then dress him in the British khaki uniform that Tovell had on under his own clothes. He'd then walk out under the noses of the guards, leaving Vladimir wearing a false beard and cloak to take the Tsar's place. Outside, Locker Lampson – pretending to be an orderly – would meet Nicholas, who would then be taken away in a field ambulance. From there he would be sent by military train to Archangel and smuggled out to Britain by sea. In the event, when word of the plan reached Nicholas, he 'absolutely refused to be rescued unless his wife and family could be saved also'. It confirms that at no stage would the Tsar ever have agreed to be separated from his family in order to save his own skin. If nothing else, it proved him to be, in Lampson's eyes, 'a true king and a true man'.[34]

Although Markov II was adamant that there should be no attempt at a forced rescue while the family were at Tsarskoe Selo, which would clearly be against the Tsar's will, by the autumn he and Little Markov would be bound up in another ongoing plot to rescue the Imperial Family. But in May 1917, as the former Mistress of the Robes, Elizaveta Naryshkina, noted in her diary, 'a monarchist response is impossible right now: there are neither leaders, nor organization; torrents of blood would flow in vain. Later – yes.'[35]

Chapter 6

'I Shall Not Be Happy till They Are Safely out of Russia'

When King George expressed his grave anxieties in early April 1917 about welcoming his Russian cousins to England, the best anyone could hope for was that the political situation would ease; the Romanov evacuation would then be rearranged when 'a more favourable psychological moment could be chosen'. The British government was determined to maintain radio silence on the matter, although its dogged ambassador Sir George Buchanan continued to lobby unofficially for the family, as a matter of personal honour. An atmosphere of stealth now crept into any official correspondence about the Romanovs; they had rapidly become a problem that everyone in the British Cabinet hoped would quietly go away, and instructions were sent round 'to keep an eye on anything that may be put into the War Cabinet minutes likely to hurt the King's feelings'.[1]

While the French had made it clear to Lord Hardinge that the 'Ex emperor and family [are] not welcome in France', King Alfonso of Spain had continued to ask for news, fearful that the Imperial Family might be murdered.[2] The British ambassador to Madrid, Sir Arthur Hardinge (who clearly had not been disabused of the fact), had been reassured that the Romanovs would 'find refuge in England'. All British diplomats other than Buchanan seem to have been kept carefully out of the loop concerning what was actually going on, while an increasingly frustrated

Buchanan repeatedly insisted to his wife and daughter, 'I shall not be happy till they are safely out of Russia.'[3]

Although the British War Cabinet did discuss the possibility of Spain as an alternative destination, the threat there from left-wing activists made them fearful that 'there might be constant plots' against the Imperial Family. Nevertheless, it might still have been considered a better option than Britain, but 'only in the event of Spain joining the Allies'.[4] Spain might have been neutral in the war, but Madrid at this time was a hotbed of international espionage and the Germans there were monitoring the situation closely. Their ambassador, Prince Maximilian von Ratibor, had reported on Alfonso's intercession, informing Berlin that the Provisional Government's response had been that 'great difficulties are to be expected from the soldiers and peasant committees'. The question of the Romanovs, Ratibor also noted, 'is being viewed with considerable pessimism in Britain'.[5]

By the end of April it would have taken considerable effort to find out anything at all about the well-being, let alone the state of mind, of the captives at Tsarskoe Selo. 'The confinement of our unhappy sovereigns has become so rigorous,' wrote Nicholas's uncle, Grand Duke Pavel Alexandrovich, still resident at his home at Tsarskoe Selo not far from the Alexander Palace, that even he had to admit, 'we know practically nothing of what they are thinking and doing'.[6] Kerensky observed that the ordinary 'man on the street' in Russia had ceased to show any interest in the Romanovs. Nor could any foreign journalists in the city get a fix on what was happening to the former monarch, as American Bessie Beatty recalled: 'I discovered with surprise that the Tsar's name was seldom mentioned. He ceased to count for anything. A month after the first revolutionary attack, he was as completely forgotten as if he had never lived.'[7] 'No news from Russia of our dear ones,' wrote Prince Louis of Battenberg disconsolately in England in May. 'It is terrible and really all A[un]t Alix's fault.'[8]

With the Romanovs settling into an acceptance of the limitations placed on their lives as prisoners, things on the diplomatic front seemed to have gone very quiet. However, the issue of what to do with the Romanovs had never been absent from the Provisional Government's agenda. Lacking the power to facilitate an exit, Justice Minister Kerensky was still hedging his bets. When asked once more by the Tsar about the family being able to go to Livadia, in order for the children to recover their health, Kerensky had said it was 'quite impossible for the moment' but, according to Pierre Gilliard, he seemed to agree that Crimea was now a better option. Once more the family were given false hope.[9] For the time being, Kerensky seemed to have won the confidence of the Tsar and even of the Tsaritsa, as Count Benckendorff noticed, particularly after he withdrew the ban on them associating, which he had been forced to impose a month previously.[10] Not having been officially informed of the British change of heart, the government still patiently awaited news of the arrival of a mythical destroyer to take the Imperial Family to safety and hoped that the problem would soon be off their hands.

Then, in early May, the issue resurfaced when the highly sympathetic Foreign Minister, Milyukov, was forced to resign over his discussions with the Allies on Russian territorial annexations to be made after the war was over (the widespread demand in post-revolutionary Russia being for 'peace without annexations'). Just days before, Milyukov – who had hoped for the eventual establishment of a constitutional monarchy, with Alexey as Tsar and Grand Duke Mikhail as regent when the war was over – once more asked the question of Buchanan: was a British cruiser coming to take the Romanovs to safety *pro tem*? Sir George replied 'with some embarrassment', Milyukov recalled in his later memoirs, 'that his government "no longer insists" on its invitation'.[11] Milyukov was very clear about this: 'I reproduce the term "insist" deliberately. It does not signify that the initiative in this question had come from the English government. The initiative was ours, the Provisional Government's. The term "insist" was used in the sense given it in diplomatic language.'[12]

★

The key phrase 'His Majesty's Government does not insist' — albeit in several variant forms — has been widely quoted as signalling the final British rejection of providing asylum for the Romanovs. Many sources repeat Kerensky's claim that it came in a 'semi-official Foreign Office statement' of 10 April that was published in the newspapers.[13] *But despite an extensive search, I was unable to locate such a document anywhere in Foreign Office or Cabinet records. Nor did I find it, as Kerensky states, in the British press at the time, with either that or even variant wording. It is in fact highly unlikely that the British government would have made any such definitive public statement with regard to an issue as politically sensitive as this, and one about which it was clearly determined to maintain a low profile. Indeed, Sir George Buchanan had been specifically instructed to 'say nothing further' on the subject, which underlines as erroneous the suggestion that the British government made such a public pronouncement. It didn't; but the myth that it did has been endlessly repeated, unchallenged.*[14]

Despite Sir George having admitted to Milyukov privately that his government was not pursuing (rather than *actively withdrawing*) its original offer, in the middle of May Milyukov's successor at the Russian Foreign Ministry, Mikhail Tereshchenko, 'revived negotiations with the British ambassador Sir George Buchanan on the subject of the transfer of the Imperial Family to England'. And so the charade continued, as once more the options of an exit via Murmansk, or perhaps via Finland, Sweden and Norway, and from there across the North Sea to England, were discussed, although Tereshchenko warned that his government could not guarantee the family would get out 'safe and sound'.[15]

Oblivious to the unravelling controversies about their future, the Romanov family were making the most of the spring weather, using their two daily periods of recreation within a fenced-in area of the park to plant and maintain a vegetable garden, watched by a sickly Alexandra, who spent most of her time in a rolling chair, sewing or knitting. Nicholas, always desperate for vigorous exercise and missing the freedom to go for long walks, had thrown his pent-up energies into shovelling the lingering snow, breaking the ice on the canals and, when the spring came, cutting down dead trees and chopping logs with the help of his children. Evenings were cheered up when he read aloud to the family from favourite detective and adventure stories such as *The Hound of the Baskervilles* and *The Count of Monte Cristo*. He was, he noted in his diary, 'much more with my dear family than in normal years', and for him that was all that mattered.

He recorded all this daily trivia punctiliously in his diary, showing little or no reaction to the regular and petty humiliations to which the family were subjected by guards brandishing fixed bayonets.[16] He tried hard to be polite and friendly with them, though such efforts largely received a hostile response. According to a report on the family in the press, Nicholas had 'recognized the hopelessness of his situation and submitted to his fate'; the only thing he found difficult was 'having no news of dear Mama', but he was 'indifferent as to the rest'.[17] 'He does not yet realize that he will not be allowed to go as he had hoped to Livadia, but the loss of his Throne does not seem to have depressed him,' Buchanan reported to London. His wife, however, 'feels the humiliation of her present position deeply'.[18] Alexandra had made no attempt to disguise her bitterness at the loss of power; unable to reconcile herself to their changed situation, she still believed that Russia 'could not exist without a tsar'. Elizaveta Naryshkina noted in her diary how steadfastly the Tsaritsa clung to hopes of a counter-revolution.[19]

At last recovered from the measles, the children had resumed their lessons, with their tutors, parents and members of the entourage rallying round to create a regular timetable and share in their tuition. It was important to Nicholas and Alexandra to restore a degree of normality to their children's imprisonment.[20] When May brought a bursting into bloom of the wonderful lilac bushes in the park, they all breathed in the glorious aroma with delight, and took pleasure in the first fruits of their kitchen garden. The warmth of summer soothed anxieties for a while, but days were frequently marred by aggressive and often abusive comments from their guards, and an awareness of crowds of the curious trying to grab sight of them through the palace fence.

These, however, were as nothing – had they known it – compared to the calls being made by extremist elements for more draconian punishments to be meted out on Nicholas and Alexandra, such as this one:

In view of the incongruity of the conditions under which the former Tsar and former Tsarinas [i.e. Alexandra and Dagmar] are living and the weight of their guilt before the people, and in view of the obvious danger of their further remaining under such conditions, which afford them an opportunity for contact with sympathizing circles, the Congress of the Delegates from the Front resolved … to present the Executive Committee of the Soviets of Workers' and Soldiers' Deputies with an unequivocal demand to transfer the former Tsar and both formers Tsarinas to the Peter and Paul Fortress.[21]

By the end of May, as American photojournalist Donald Thompson confirmed, demands for retribution against the Romanovs were mounting:

The clamor for putting the Ex-Czar in the Peter and Paul Fortress is growing daily. Where formerly only a few of the soldiers and anarchists wanted it, now it is being heard everywhere. Lenine [sic] demands that the ex-Czar should be transferred to Kronstadt or sent to the Siberian mines. The sailors stationed at Helsingfors have demanded that Nicholas be given to them; they say they will take him to Petrograd and keep him until he is placed on trial, and that if their demand is rejected, they will bring warships and force it. They say this must be Russia's last revolution and that the only way to make it the last is to imprison the ex-Czar. Thousands of handbills are being thrown broadcast from automobiles in Petrograd saying, 'Try him at once, Nicholas II'.[22]

As early as April, rumours had been swirling on this subject among the Romanovs' royal relatives in Europe. The King and

Queen of Sweden had got wind from their envoy in Petrograd, General Edvard Brändström, that the 'Czar and Czarina in person had been interned in the Peter & Paul Fortress'. 'His Majesty fears that the royal couple could be murdered or executed,' Ratibor, the German ambassador to Madrid, reported to Berlin, 'the situation according to other (British) sources of information is frightful and the most terrible things are to be expected daily.' The main charges of treason, he noted, were levelled against the Empress, and she faced 'the full severity of the law'.[23]

King George had obviously heard similar worrying press reports, for on 4 June he noted in his diary: 'I fear that if poor Nicky goes into the fortress of St Peter and St Paul he will not come out alive.'[24] An article headed 'Calls for Revenge' had recently been published in *Izvestiya*, the mouthpiece of the Petrograd Soviet, reporting on a resolution passed in the Soviet for the transfer of Nicholas to the radical stronghold at Kronstadt. 'We would like to note that all these resolutions are permeated by one and the same mood – a dissatisfaction with the extremely mild treatment on the part of the victorious revolution of the person who was the bitterest enemy of the people.'[25] The Spanish ambassador to Petrograd nervously reported in cipher to Madrid on the 'ultra-radical political programme' of the Kronstadters, who refused to recognise the authority of the Provisional Government, demanding that 'Emperor Nicholas II, his wife and their children are handed to the city of Kronstadt, under threat, or else, they will attack Petrograd'.[26]

This increase in calls for the trial and imprisonment of Nicholas and Alexandra stemmed from a growing concern that their continued presence near the city posed a threat to the new revolutionary order. They were a reminder of the hated past and of a defunct tsarist regime that the revolution had destroyed. How they were dealt with could tip the delicate balance of the Provisional Government's power, and it found itself in a cleft stick. To keep the Romanovs at Tsarskoe might incite an attack on the palace by mobs from the city; but then again, to send them abroad might also galvanise the monarchist element, which was even now gathering in Tsarskoe Selo and elsewhere to rally around them and attempt to restore the monarchy. In a word, moving the Romanovs anywhere out of Russia might destabilise a very delicate political situation – and the government, of which Kerensky had become Minister of War in May, now of all times needed to keep the country on an even keel, for it was about to launch a major military push on the Eastern Front.[27]

In June, three months of British prevarication finally came to its inevitable, ignominious end when an extremely emotional Sir George Buchanan, 'with tears in his eyes', arrived at the Russian Foreign Ministry to see the new Foreign Minister, Mikhail Tereshchenko. Buchanan had at last received a categorical rejection from London. Tereshchenko's recall concurs entirely with Kerensky's concerning how distressed Sir George had been to receive 'the British government's final refusal to give refuge to the former Emperor of Russia'.[28] Kerensky later wrote that he never saw the letter in which the news came, but was told the gist. But he could say 'quite definitely' that 'this refusal was due exclusively to considerations of internal British politics'.

Until now we have only had Kerensky's say-so on the final British rejection of asylum for the Romanovs, and no record of the transmission of this directive to Buchanan has turned up in Foreign Office or other British sources. But it did not come from Lloyd George or from Foreign Secretary Balfour: it came from none other than Lord Hardinge, Permanent Under-Secretary of State for Foreign Affairs and a key decision-maker in the issue. I discovered a reference to this crucial document in the papers of Nicolas de Basily, a senior Russian diplomat and minister, held at the Hoover Institution in California.* These papers include a number of folders of eyewitness testimony relating to the Romanovs and the asylum

---

* After a long diplomatic career, including service as secretary of the Russian embassy in Paris in 1908–11, de Basily joined the Imperial Chancellery and in 1916 was appointed its director. Based with the Tsar at Imperial Army HQ at Mogilev, he drafted Nicholas's abdication manifesto.

question, gathered by de Basily in exile in the 1920s and 1930s. Buried amongst them is a four-page statement in French made by Mikhail Tereshchenko to de Basily in Paris in April 1934. The letter to Sir George Buchanan was in fact not an official typed and ciphered despatch, but a personal, handwritten letter from Hardinge, who signed it 'Charlie'. The fact that it was transmitted privately and not via official channels (there being no copy of it in the FO files) suggests that 'Charlie' felt the time had come to personally disabuse Sir George, once and for all, of any hopes he still clung to that a Romanov rescue was possible.

The contents of the Hardinge letter made such a strong impression on Tereshchenko, when Sir George showed it to him, that although Tereshchenko was not able to memorise it word-for-word, he retained a very precise recall of its heavily ironic tone and repeated it to de Basily in his imperfect English thus:

How can the 'Provisional Government' expect that His Majesty can be put before the problem of giving asile [exile] to his Cousin, when the only way to explain the present strange policy of the Provisional Government is that it seeks to impress on the world's public opinion, that it endeavours to re-establish in Russia a national Russian policy, as against the pro-German tendency of the former Tsar. You cannot expect the members of His Majesty's Government to put the King's feelings of affection towards his cousin to such a test.[29]*

In his own account, Kerensky confirmed that the content of the letter received by Buchanan inferred that the British Prime Minister could hardly advise King George to 'offer hospitality to

---

* The original was probably lost when Sir George destroyed all his personal papers and diaries after writing his memoirs in 1921, perhaps aware of their potentially damning content on the discreditable British role in the Romanov asylum.

people whose pro-German sympathies were well known'.[30] Tereshchenko agreed: the final British refusal was a damning admission of the still-persisting British mistrust of the Tsar and Tsaritsa as German sympathisers. To receive them in Britain, in time of war against Germany, was something the government was no longer willing to risk. This final rejection appears to have been passed on to Sir George without any further reference back to the King himself. In London, Lloyd George was privately relieved. He was, he admitted in a note to Hardinge, glad that the 'idea of asylum was dropped as it would have been used by Germans'.[31] Indeed, it had also been made clear to Sir George by now that such was the deepening official intransigence in the matter, London would refuse to take in *any* members of the Russian Imperial Family until after the war was over. After months of lobbying on behalf of the former Tsar, Sir George Buchanan was finally forced to capitulate. The elusive 'English mirage' (as White Russians in exile later came to refer to the aborted British asylum offer) vanished over the horizon.[32]

What now for the Romanovs, still prisoners at Tsarskoe Selo and still hoping for a resolution? When Kerensky arrived at the Alexander Palace soon afterwards to fulfil his 'thankless task of telling the former Tsar of this new development', Nicholas 'took the news calmly and expressed his wish to go to the Crimea instead'.[33]

One of the most dispiriting aspects of the Romanov asylum issue in 1917 is a total lack of coordination between the various interested parties who might, had they acted in unison, have collectively been able to effect the family's safe evacuation from Russia. Although the governments of Germany and Britain were enemies in the war, it is clear that the Danish royal family were willing to facilitate a solution with their cooperation. Certainly Harald Scavenius, the Danish ambassador in Petrograd, working in tandem with his cousin Erik, who was Danish Foreign Minister, had been called upon to approach the Germans and obtain from them a promise that their submarines would not attack any British ship taking the Romanovs out on a white flag.[34] With the current war footing between Entente and Allied forces, all Germany could do would be to undertake not to stand in the way of any evacuation. Tereshchenko's subsequent secret request to the Kaiser received a highly stilted but official answer, sent via the Danes, a few days later:

> The Imperial government considers it a duty to guarantee that not a single naval unit of the German military-naval fleet would venture to make an attack on any kind of vessel, on the deck of which the Russian Emperor and His Family are being conveyed.[35]

With this undertaking, the Germans had thus, effectively, fulfilled their obligation to assist the Russian monarch on humanitarian grounds.[36] Unfortunately, the historian faces yet another closed door in trying to uncover documentation on Danish initiatives. According to information given to me by Danish scholar Bernadette Preben Hansen, who has been engaged in an exhaustive study of Harald Scavenius, the Danish Royal Archives for this period are 'hermetically closed' to historical research. She tells me that although there are many hints about a desire to get the Romanovs out of Russia to be found in the archives of the Danish Foreign Ministry and in the records of the Danish Embassy in Petrograd, there has as yet been no systematic, scholarly study of any of these sources. When authors Anthony Summers and Tom Mangold applied for access to the Danish Royal Archives during their research for the 1987 second edition of their book File on the Tsar, *they were given short shrift. Word came back from the Danish queen that 'It is a family matter, and nobody else's business.'[37] Other Romanov scholars have confirmed similar experiences to me, when trying to access material on the Danish royals at this time. There is also surprisingly little, if any, obvious material on British relations with Denmark and the Danish Crown in the British Foreign Office files at the National Archives during this period, and nothing referring directly to the Romanovs.*

But what about the other Scandinavian monarchs?

On 29 May, British envoy to the King of Sweden, Sir Esmé Howard, reported that the Russian ambassador, Anatoly Neklyudov, had suggested to him that if the family's lives were in danger, 'it might be possible to get them off in a British submarine when they could be met by Swedish destroyers and brought to Sweden in safety. He said he was sure that the King of Sweden would do everything in his power to secure their safety.' Neklyudov had apparently begged Major-General Hanbury-Williams to 'submit this plan to The King, when he returned to London'. But Hanbury-Williams and Howard had agreed that it was 'quite impracticable', not to mention 'most impolitic and inopportune from many points of view'. It all boiled down to the same old problem:

> The Russian Imperial Family, if they come to Sweden, would almost certainly become the centre of German intrigue. Only in [the] case of Russia's falling into the hands of the extreme Anarchist party [i.e. the Bolsheviks] who are willing to treat with Germany anyhow, does it seem to me that such an arrangement would no longer be open to any objections, and it would then probably be too late to do anything, even if it is not too late already.[38]

Whether or not the King of Sweden ever had any thoughts of sending a ship remains a mystery, although in 1987 Summers and Mangold claimed that 'British official papers show that King Gustav of Sweden ... offered a Swedish submarine for a proposed naval operation to take the Romanovs to safety.'[39] They further state that in response to this, Lord Hardinge at the FO noted on a file that this Swedish initiative was a typical example of the 'Trust of Kings' – or, as King Edward VII had referred to it, 'The Kings' Trade Union' – the closed world of royal freemasonry that operated independently of governments. Unfortunately, the Swedish Royal Archives are no more open to scrutiny than the Danish ones. The Swedish king, Gustav, was coping with his own internal crisis in 1917, during which time three successive governments fell as a result of rationing and famine brought on by the Allied blockade. Gustav found himself facing hunger demonstrations and worker unrest, encouraged by left-wing sympathy for events in Russia, and, like King George and King Alfonso, had begun to fear for the safety of his own throne, so much so that it is said he had his suitcases packed and ready, should revolution break out and it be necessary for him to flee.

In the midst of continuing rumours of attempts at diplomatic intervention, ambassador Neklyudov once more found himself drawn into the Romanov issue when at the end of June 1917 he arrived in Madrid to take up a new appointment to Spain. On 2 July he processed in a gilded coach, complete with liveried postilions, to the Royal Palace at the Escorial for a lavish reception at which he was to present his credentials to the King. After approaching Alfonso, who sat resplendent on the throne flanked by life-sized gilded lions, Neklyudov discovered that all the grandees of the Spanish court had turned out to witness 'a Muscovite revolutionary' being presented to the King, but were somewhat disappointed to see the ambassador of the Provisional Government dressed in traditional, heavily embroidered imperial garb.[40] After Neklyudov had read out his speech in which, among other things, he lauded the King's humanitarian work for Russian prisoners of war, Alfonso seemed eager to have a private word and drew him aside, out of earshot of the surrounding dignitaries:

> Monsieur, in your speech you were good enough to allude to the help we have been able to render to your prisoners. Allow me to tell you of the deep interest I take in the fate of other 'Russian prisoners'. I allude to His Majesty the former Emperor Nicholas II and his family. I come to beg you, Monsieur, to transmit to your Government my fervent prayers for their liberation.[41]

Who was the official head of the Provisional Government, asked Alfonso? He wanted to ensure that his appeal went to the most senior person. President of the Council of Ministers, Prince Lvov, Neklyudov responded. He was a man who, despite the overthrow of the tsarist regime, he assured the King, still held great feelings of sympathy and loyalty towards the Tsar. Neklyudov would not hesitate to 'transmit to my Government the words that Your Majesty has just spoken'. 'You can be assured,' he continued, 'that while the present government is in power, not a hair will fall from the former tsar's head.' But he also warned Alfonso that although it was indeed the Provisional Government's one wish to 'allow the Emperor and his family to leave for foreign parts; if it does not do so, it is on account of the extreme elements'.[42] Moreover, any attempts at intercession by foreign governments, or special pleading on behalf of the Imperial Family, would only inflame an already difficult situation. For this reason Neklyudov did not recommend an official petition by the Spanish king to the government; he would instead convey Alfonso's words to Prince Lvov, not by official telegram, but by private letter.[43] True to his word, Neklyudovwrote to Prince Lvov on 3 July, communicating the King's personal and heartfelt plea for the government to ensure the safety of the 'first citizen of Russia, now overthrown and incarcerated', and of his family also.[44]

Once again, King Alfonso was the only European royal to make any kind of direct, impassioned appeal on behalf of the Romanovs. But Neklyudov had been right to express the need for caution: for if the truth be known, even the Provisional Government was now changing its position and was not inclined, for reasons of *realpolitik*, to push the issue of asylum any more. For by the summer of 1917 the government was facing not just looming catastrophe on the Eastern Front, but also a serious challenge from the Bolsheviks, who had been gaining ground since the return to Russia of their leader, Lenin, in early April.

In Petrograd on 16 July, disturbances erupted among groups of disgruntled workers and soldiers eager to foment public discontent in the wake of the failure of the latest Russian offensive in the war. After coming out onto the streets, they encouraged others to go on strike and join in their demonstrations, in the hope that this would trigger a second revolution and the Petrograd Soviet's takeover of government. The protests soon turned ugly and degenerated into armed clashes. There was talk of the insurgents heading for Tsarskoe Selo with armoured cars 'and tear[ing] away from the Provisional Government the Emperor and all his family'.[45]

The Bolsheviks in the Soviet, however, although now in the majority, had not been prepared for this sudden turn of events, and their leaders were hesitant about whether it was the opportune moment to seize power. The threat of insurrection fizzled out and instead several of the Bolshevik leaders, including Trotsky, were rounded up and put in jail, while Lenin fled to the safety of Finland. The Bolsheviks were further discredited when the Provisional Government produced evidence that Lenin and his colleagues had been in collusion with the Germans and were receiving financial assistance from them.

On 20 July, the day the violence in Petrograd subsided, a weary Prince Lvov – who had increasingly found himself at odds with his own government, let alone the Petrograd Soviet – stood down as Prime Minister. Kerensky succeeded him and assumed full control of the fate of the Romanovs. With the Bolsheviks for the time being in retreat, the Provisional Government had the upper hand, including better control of the railways. For all too brief a time, an opportunity presented itself for getting the Romanovs if not out of Russia, then at the least – in the words of Hanbury-Williams – 'as far as possible from the seat of ever-lasting trouble – Petrograd'.[46]

With the Imperial Family's continuing presence there, 'Tsarskoe Selo was becoming the tender spot of the body politic', admitted Kerensky, and he had to move quickly. On Sunday, 24 July, he drove out to the Alexander Palace and informed Nicholas that the family needed to be moved south to a quieter, more remote location, 'due to the proximity of Tsarskoe Selo to the restless capital'.[47] He was vague about where exactly he was thinking of sending them, but it was evident that he feared that sooner or later there might be an attack on the palace and an attempt to take Nicholas and Alexandra away to prison, or worse. His decision to evacuate was prompted not just by the recent disturbances in the city, but also by a growing awareness of the activities of 'amateur monarchist plotters', whom Kerensky noted had been sending the Tsaritsa 'mysterious little notes' hinting at 'prompt liberation'. 'Inexperience and childish simplicity were intertwined with mockery and treachery,' he recalled; the garrison at Tsarskoe had 'become unsettled by talk of conspiracies, of attempts to free the Tsar'. Word was reaching him, too, about growing right-wing anti-government resentment in the army. Kerensky needed to act.[48]

Crimea, free from the problems of ice and German submarines, was the easiest southerly exit point by sea and might have seemed the most logical stopover for an evacuation now. It was also, of course, where – since the abdication – Nicholas had hoped the family might be allowed to live, in preference to any departure for England. In fact it was the last place Kerensky would send him; the monarchists had a strong base in Crimea and the surrounding area, where they controlled their own telegraph and telephone communications and were actively circulating propaganda favouring the restoration of the monarchy.[49] Several other members of the 'fallen dynasty' had by now gathered in Crimea, including Dagmar and Nicholas's two sisters, and were already creating a security problem for the government, in view of the presence in the peninsula of the highly belligerent sailors of the Black Sea fleet that was based there.

Having rejected the idea of sending the Romanovs to Grand Duke Mikhail's estate at Brasovo in the southern Russian province of Orel, Kerensky opted for somewhere more out of the way. Still, taking the Romanovs to such a place would not be easy, if the train carrying them had to travel through 'central provinces with their dense population' or industrial towns or regions where there had been violent peasant disturbances against the tsarist regime.[50] Tobolsk in Western Siberia was therefore chosen; Kerensky had heard tell of it and knew something of its location. It was 'an out-and-out backwater' that could be reached at this time of year from the north not by railway but by river, and 'without crossing any thickly populated districts'; in winter it was totally ice-bound on all sides. It had a 'very small garrison, no industrial proletariat, and a population which was prosperous and contented, not to say old-fashioned'. It also, fortuitously, had 'a very passable Governor's Residence … where the Imperial Family could live with some measure of comfort'.[51] The choice of a Siberian location also held symbolic significance that would not go unnoticed by the Russian public, as Kerensky well knew. Sending the former Tsar to the place of transportation and exile to which so many dissidents were condemned under the old regime was an act of poetic social justice that might 'earn him a dividend' later, when he needed it.[52]

Kerensky sent two trusted officials on a secret recce of Tobolsk. When they returned in mid-July confirming its suitability, plans were set in motion for the family's transfer, without any further discussion with the government and no public announcement. Privately, Kerensky told Count Benckendorff that he hoped, when elections for the Constituent Assembly were held in November and a stable government was installed, that the Romanovs might be allowed to return to Tsarskoe Selo, or leave Russia for a country of their choice via the Trans-Siberian Railway to Vladivostok and across to Japan.[53]

On 25 July, Foreign Minister Tereshchenko met Sir George Buchanan to inform him of the family's imminent transfer. 'I expressed hope that when he was in Siberia the emperor's freedom would not be so restricted as at Tsarskoe Selo and that he would be allowed to go out driving,' Buchanan informed London. 'In spite of many faults which he had committed and his weak character [the] Emperor was not a criminal and deserved to be treated with as much consideration as possible.' Tereshchenko confirmed that this would be the case, and that the Tsar would be allowed to choose 'those whom he wished to accompany him and he would have a very comfortable house with large garden. Whether he would be able to drive out would depend a good deal on [the] state of public feeling in Tobolsk.'[54]

The last family wedding attended by Queen Victoria, Coburg 1894. Victoria, centre, with her eldest daughter the Dowager Empress of Prussia. Left, the Young Kaiser, Wilhelm II, and immediately behind him Tsarevich Nicholas of Russia and his fiancée Princess Alexandra of Hesse and By Rhine.

Nine reigning European monarchs at the 1910 funeral of King Edward VII. Back, L–R: Haakon VII of Norway; Ferdinand of the Bulgarians; Manuel II of Portugal; Wilhelm II of Germany; George I of Greece and Albert I of the Belgians. Front, L–R: Alfonso XIII of Spain; George V of the United Kingdom and Frederick VIII of Denmark.

Above: The five Hesse siblings at the Coburg wedding. Front, L–R: Irene (later Princess Henry of Prussia); Ella; the bride, Victoria Melita and Grand Duke Sergey, Ella's husband. Back, L–R: Nicholas; Alexandra; Victoria (soon to be Marchioness of Milford Haven) and the groom, Ernst.

Right: The British Royal Family. King George V stands behind his daughter Mary, with Queen Mary holding John, and in front his brothers, L–R: George; Henry; David (Edward VIII) and Albert (George VI).

Above: The Danish princesses Dagmar (left) and Alexandra (right), now Empress Maria Feodorovna of Russia and Queen Alexandra of Great Britain, with Dagmar's husband – and Nicholas's father – Tsar Alexander III, centre.

Left: The royal cousins Georgy and Nicky enjoyed close and cordial family relations in the pre-war years. Their uncanny resemblance prompted people to refer to them as 'the heavenly twins'.

Above: Like the British royals, the Russian Imperial Family preferred family life at home in Tsarskoe Selo, 15 miles from St Petersburg. Here they are seen on the steps of the baroque Catherine Palace, but they lived at the more modest Alexander Palace next door.

Left: King Haakon, formerly Prince Carl of Denmark, accepted the vacant throne of Norway in 1905. Married to his and Nicholas II's cousin Maud, he was one of several royal relatives who urged Nicholas to initiate political reform in the run up to the revolution.

Nicholas after his abdication, now under house arrest, with Alexandra in the Alexander Park at Tsarskoe Selo, Spring 1917.

In Spring 1917 all the children fell seriously ill with measles. Maria, seen here recovering with her father beside her, developed pleurisy and nearly died.

Two of the Romanov daughters, Tatiana and Anastasia, pushing a water barrel in the Alexander Park. During their captivity at Tsarskoe Selo, the family were able to plant a vegetable garden.

Tsarevich Alexey helping to clear snow in the Alexander Park, 1917. At Army HQ and in captivity, Alexey wore military uniform like his father. In 1916 he had been promoted to Lance Corporal and is seen here proudly displaying his Order of St George.

The four Romanov sisters – Anastasia, Tatiana, Olga and Maria – had all been losing their hair as a result of the measles and in June 1917 decided to shave their heads. Alexey did likewise, in solidarity.

Lord Stamfordham (Sir Arthur Bigge) enjoyed a unique position of influence over King George V as his Private Secretary and played a key role in persuading him to change his mind about the Romanov asylum.

British ambassador in Petrograd, Sir George Buchanan, did his utmost to effect an early evacuation of the Romanov family after the February Revolution 1917.

British prime minister, David Lloyd George, headed the coalition government of 1916–22 that offered temporary asylum to the Romanovs in March 1917.

Russian liberal politician Pavel Milyukov, first foreign minister in the Provisional Government, was the driving force in securing the British asylum offer of 23 March 1917.

Left: Alexander Kerensky, justice minister in the Provisional Government, supervised the Romanovs' captivity at the Alexander Palace. As prime minister, he organized the family's removal to Tobolsk in August 1917.

Below: The Russian port at Murmansk (Romanov-on-Murman), July 1918. In 1917 it became a major British military supply base and was proposed as a temporary staging post for the Romanovs, should they be evacuated by sea.

Left: This American supply ship on the frozen White Sea at Archangel in 1919 had cut through 15 feet of ice to reach port, demonstrating how difficult a Romanov evacuation out of Russia by sea, even in May, would have been.

It was at this late juncture that somebody else stepped forward to plea for the Imperial Family's release. Till now, his efforts have remained entirely unsung. His name was Petr Botkin and he was the former Imperial Russian ambassador to Portugal. He had very good reason to be anxious about the fate of the family, for he was the brother of Dr Evgeniy Botkin, their devoted physician, who had opted to travel with them to Tobolsk. Full of righteous good intent, Petr Botkin chose to address his appeals to the French government, unaware that it had already made it abundantly clear to the British that it had no interest whatsoever in helping the Romanovs.

On 25 July, Botkin wrote privately, and without the sanction of his government, to a diplomatic colleague, Baron de Berckheim, French Chargé d'Affaires at the Berlin embassy, on the 'question that at present preoccupies very many Russians: the danger threatening the emperor in captivity' – which had become more urgent in view of the recent disturbances in July. Botkin might have been a servant of the Provisional Government, but he admitted candidly that despite its best intentions, it simply was not capable of protecting the Imperial Family against danger. Therefore, in view of the 'feelings of sympathy and loyalty which the government of the French Republic had always shown toward His Majesty the Emperor Nicholas II, a devoted ally of France', might it not be more effective, he asked, for 'some kind of collective effort by the great powers, Russia's allies' to be made in helping the Provisional Government deal with a problem that was 'difficult to resolve on its own initiative?' Perhaps the king of a neutral country such as Denmark could help evacuate them from Russia? A Danish cruiser could be sent to the Gulf of Finland and the family could be boarded from Peterhof. Botkin was putting himself at the disposal of the French government in order to do whatever was necessary to rescue the Emperor and 'save the history of our times from catastrophe, the consequences of which would be most perilous'.[55]

No reply came, not even the courtesy of an acknowledgement. Undaunted, on 5 August Botkin wrote again and with an even greater sense of urgency, this time to Jules Cambon, Head of the Political Section of the French Foreign Ministry. With polite insistence he suggested that France, as Russia's long-standing ally, should 'take the initiative in the freeing of the emperor from prison'. In somewhat recriminatory tones, Botkin also reminded Cambon that France had recently 'hurried to greet the Russian revolution, closing her eyes to the past, but that the past had not died and might, one day, rise up before her as a living reproach'. The French had recently sent a socialist delegation to Petrograd to welcome the new revolutionary state, but what had they done 'to relieve the fate of the unfortunate Monarch to whom France is, all the same, in some way indebted?'

Botkin knew there was no time to be lost. He waited for France to respond and make 'a beautiful and generous gesture that would go down in history'. Unfortunately, France was not in the business of 'generous gestures' any more than Britain was, with regard to the Romanovs right now. Botkin did not receive a reply.[56]

At Tsarskoe Selo, the Tsar himself was still in the dark about the precise location of his family's future place of exile. He had spent his time, since hearing that they would be moved, calmly sticking photographs in his albums, sorting out his books and, with Alexandra, putting together the things they wanted to take with them. The children were spending more and more time outside, working on the vegetable garden and taking great delight in eating their own home-grown produce for the very first time. But the weather was so hot and they all missed the cool of the Baltic and sailing round the Finnish skerries on the *Shtandart*, or swimming in the Black Sea at the Livadia Palace in Crimea, where they spent most summers.

It was not till 10 August, in his inscrutable, matter-of-fact style, that Nicholas recorded how that morning after breakfast they had 'found out from Count Benckendorff that we are not being sent to Crimea but to a distant provincial town, three or four days' travel east. But where exactly they won't tell us and even the commandant doesn't know,' adding with a sigh, 'and there we were still counting on a long stay in Livadia!' The family knew that east meant one thing – Siberia. With their characteristic passive air of acceptance, they prepared to travel many hundreds of miles from Tsarskoe into the Russian interior, no doubt privately dreading the unfamiliar location, the cold of winters there and the distance from friends and relatives. The sun of Crimea was in their blood; the snowy wastes of Siberia were entirely alien to them.

Four days later, on 14 August, Sir George Buchanan was able to confirm to King George that 'The Emperor and his family attended by small suite left for Tobolsk this morning' and that Tereshchenko had assured him 'every care had been taken to provide for their comfort and protection on their journey', adding that 'the Emperor, he said, was quite cheerful'. Indeed, Nicholas had been grateful: 'I have no fear. We trust you,' he had told Kerensky on hearing the news of their destination. 'If you say that we must move, it must be so … We trust you.'[57]

For all those who had had some passing concern for Russia's Imperial Family, but had faltered when it came to making any serious offer of help, it was a comforting gesture of acceptance on Nicholas's part. There was no cause for alarm, they all told themselves; the Romanovs would be safe out in the no man's land of Siberia. As French ambassador Paléologue observed, for now 'The Great War that persistently kept rolling on in the West was more than enough to satisfy everyone's curiosity.'[58] British officialdom would instead turn its attention to the plight of the Dowager, under house arrest in Crimea. How could the Russian government, Sir George told Tereshchenko, 'act so harshly towards a lady of her age, who was generally beloved' (whereas, one supposes, Nicholas and Alexandra were not)? Such 'unnecessarily harsh treatment of a near relative of the King would make a very bad impression in England.'[59] The Queen Mother was alarmed that her sister was being 'kept like a criminal'; once again she bombarded Buchanan for news. Clearly, when it came to the Russian royals, there was one level of concern for Dagmar and another for Nicholas and Alexandra – not to mention their children.

★

On the night of 14 August 1917, Georgiy Lukomsky, recently appointed commissioner in charge of the preservation of the Tsarskoe Selo palaces by Kerensky's government, found himself one of the very few witnesses to the departure of the Russian Imperial Family from their home of twenty-three years. For days beforehand Lukomsky had been at the palace assessing its contents and how best they could be maintained as a museum after the family's departure.

Together with Kerensky and Baron Steinheil, the political administrator of the Alexander Palace, Lukomsky watched the family wait patiently that final night. As instructed, their bags were ready for them to leave at midnight on the 13th, but after many hours' wait, still no convoy of cars had come to take them to the station. Kerensky was in a highly nervous state, recalled Lukomsky, pacing up and down and constantly making telephone calls to try to find out what was going on. Indeed, such was his level of agitation that he seemed unable to control his impatience at the delay. The Romanovs meanwhile stayed calm, the four sisters struggling with their longing to sleep, the Tsarevich dressed in khaki and playing on the parquet floor. At 5 a.m. the cars finally arrived and Lukomsky watched as the Tsar, with a touching expression of calm that he had maintained throughout, supported the Tsaritsa, swathed in a cape of black silk, as they descended the steps.[60] As they did so, the soldiers outside unexpectedly formed an impromptu guard of honour and greeted them with the traditional 'Good morning, little father'. Lukomsky watched the dawn break over the Alexander Park as the convoy of cars drove off; he later wrote that as he watched the Romanovs leave, he could not help thinking of the French Revolution and that fateful night in June 1791 when King Louis XVI and his family had fled from the Tuileries to Varennes to seek support for a counter-revolution.

After the sixteen rooms of the Romanov apartments were vacated, Lukomsky went inside and took photographs of the interiors. He was struck by how much they seemed to embody the spirit of the family, and the former monarch especially. For in this grand palace, designed by the great architect Giacomo Quarenghi for Catherine the Great, the Imperial Family had lived in a modest bourgeois style that was decidedly limited in its aesthetic taste. 'All the tsar's personal effects were left in perfect order,' Lukomsky told a reporter in 1928:

In his study were twenty-six photograph albums cataloguing his reign that he had methodically classified and patiently assembled – an inestimable source for future study. In a symbolic gesture he had left on his desk a newly edited collection of his addresses and speeches; alongside this volume I found a richly encrusted revolver with his imperial insignia, and a watch on a gold chain, which he had cast off shortly before his departure, declaring to Baron Steinhel *'eto ne moe, eto prinadlezhit narodu'* – 'It isn't mine, it belongs to the people.'

In contrast, recalled Lukomsky, the Empress's apartments were 'prey to an incredible muddle of jewel boxes that had been emptied and thrown into a pile'.[61] Once he had made his inspection, Lukomsky sealed all the rooms: the final symbolic severance of the old tsarist order from the new socialist Russia. He was dismayed that things could not have been different: 'At that time,' he said in 1928, 'had a few resolute men suddenly appeared, nothing could have stood in their way and, I believe, the Imperial Family would have been saved and the world, perhaps, doomed to other destinies.'[62]

Chapter 7

'The Smell of a Dumas Novel'

Two days before they left their home at the Alexander Palace, the Romanovs were instructed to pack warm clothes. The cook accompanying them was told to assemble five days' supply of food. The family did not, of course, depart Tsarskoe Selo alone and unassisted, but with a considerable entourage of thirty-nine servants – chambermaids, cooks and footmen – as well as their physician Dr Evgeniy Botkin, the children's tutor Pierre Gilliard (with Sydney Gibbes, Baroness Buxhoeveden and Dr Botkin's children following later with additional servants), the Tsaritsa's personal ladies-in-waiting, Anastasia Hendrikova and Ekaterina Schneider, and two of Nicholas's equerries, Count Ilya Tatishchev and Prince Vasily Dolgorukov. Two trains transported them and an escort of around 300 soldiers of the 1st, 3rd and 4th Rifle Brigade, armed with machine guns and headed by Kobylinsky, the palace commandant, now charged with supervising the family's safe transfer to Tobolsk.

But two of the family's longest-serving and most devoted courtiers, Elizaveta Naryshkina and Count Pavel Benckendorff, were forced to stay behind due to age and infirmity. It was a great wrench for Benckendorff in particular, but over the months to come he would prove a crucial link with the family. Thanks to his contact with Tobolsk, via letters from his stepson Prince Dolgorukov, he was able to pass on news about the family's welfare. Benckendorff was also an important source of news about the family for the Dowager in Crimea, to whom he wrote a letter over several days, 2–8 August 1917, telling her that the last hours at Tsarskoe had been 'horribly painful'. 'The Emperor is bearing up as well as possible in these awful circumstances,' he told Dagmar. 'However he has changed physically and has become nervous. He has been trying to tire himself out as much as possible by doing physical work, which has brought relief to his state of mind.' The Empress, however, was 'full of illusions' about what the future held. Benckendorff's major concern, though, was for Olga Nikolaevna, the eldest and most impressionable daughter, who in his opinion was 'in a worryingly melancholic state. She has lost weight and cannot hold back her tears.'[1] Of all the Romanov children, Olga had suffered the most, emotionally, since her father's abdication and seemed to be finding the dramatic change in circumstances painful and difficult to come to terms with. She had in particular been grief-stricken at the violent hatred targeted at her parents when, to her, all they had ever done was love Russia and wish the best for her and her people.

The three-day train ride to Siberia turned out to be surprisingly comfortable for the Romanovs, who travelled in a first-class carriage of the International Wagons-Lits Company and had morning coffee, lunch, tea and dinner served as punctiliously as though they had been back home at the Alexander Palace. Every day the train stopped so that the family could take an hour's recreation. The final stage of the journey was completed by steamer up the River Tura from the railway terminal at Tyumen. They arrived in Tobolsk at six in the evening of 19 August to a curious and respectful crowd – the local population being largely sympathetic – who were waiting on the quayside to catch a glimpse of them, and who later sent them sweets, eggs and other food in short supply.[2]

In 1917 Tobolsk was a town of 21,000 inhabitants and the commercial centre of a huge province that extended for half a million square miles – an area nearly eight times the size of Great Britain, yet 'a mere flea-bite in Asiatic-Russia', in the words of one visitor.[3] A large proportion of that land was marshy and very sparsely inhabited; the town itself was 'a picture of stagnant desolation, even in summer', at which time it was plagued by swarms of mosquitoes. Much of the city's trade came in on the Tobol and Irtysh rivers, but the Irtysh was only ice-free for about 200 days of the year. The city itself was built on the high right bank of the river, looking out over the mouth of the River Tobol, and was dominated by a kremlin built by Swedish prisoners of war captured at the Battle of Poltava in 1709.

While the Romanovs remained on board the steamer, Nicholas's equerries Dolgorukov and Tatishchev went in an advance party with Kobylinsky and a representative of the Provisional Government to check out the state of the house, which was located in the centre of town on the main Freedom Street. The sight of it filled them with dismay: 'a dirty, boarded up, stinking house of 13 rooms, with some furniture and with dreadful toilets and bathrooms,' wrote Dolgorukov in his first letter to Benckendorff on 27 August.[4] In the attic there were five rooms for the servants, but the rest of the entourage – himself, Tatishchev, Hendrikova, Botkin, Schneider, other servants, officers of the guard and the commandant Kobylinsky – were lodged in a rented house across the street. It was fairly spacious but similarly unkempt and had no furniture, which they had to go out and buy for themselves. But at least those housed there, unlike the Imperial Family, had permission to move about fairly freely in the town, making it possible for local monarchists to make contact and, through them, send messages of support to the family, and gifts of money and other necessities.

On leaving Tsarskoe Selo, Kobylinsky had been instructed by Kerensky: 'Don't forget that this is the former emperor. Neither he nor his family should experience any deprivation'. And certainly the commandant did his best to ensure that the Romanovs had a degree of comfort and freedom of movement within the large fenced-in yard attached to the house, as well as occasional walks beyond to attend church.[5] Their guards too were a great deal more friendly and courteous than those at Tsarskoe and, from their rooms on the first floor, and the small balcony on which they were allowed to sit, the family could see the ordinary people of Tobolsk passing by on the street outside, who often stopped and waved and even crossed themselves.

For loyal monarchists gathering in the Tobolsk area and keeping watch on the Governor's House, the period from August to November 1917 was undoubtedly the opportune time to try and spring the captives from their prison. Siberia then was still relatively 'quiet' politically and, with his removal there, Citizen Romanov (as the papers now referred to him) and his family had receded even further from the public consciousness. Kobylinsky was sympathetic, and would not have resisted a forced abduction of the family; security was lax and the exercise yard where the Romanovs spent a great deal of time was relatively easy for a group of determined monarchists to storm. Indeed, some of the family's own guards, from the former 4th Imperial Rifles, even suggested to Nicholas that the best time for an escape would be when they were on duty.[6]

Logically speaking, the best exit route for any group hoping to rescue the Romanovs from Tobolsk would have been the one Kerensky had hoped to follow through on later – taking them out of Russia from Tyumen on the Trans-Siberian Railway to Vladivostok on the east coast, and from there putting them on a boat for Japan and eventually the USA. But such plans were vastly outside the scope of local monarchists in Tobolsk, for whom the only viable option that seems to have been discussed was to hide the Romanovs within Russia, in the hope of at least protecting them from harm until the political situation changed.

By the autumn of 1917 there was no shortage of willing, idealistic officer-rescuers from the former Imperial Russian Army eager to wear the badge of honour for mounting a rescue. Unfortunately, most of what has been written about their plots to save the Romanovs is the stuff of insubstantial and largely speculative myth, a mixed bag of often confused and inconsistent accounts by those who supposedly took part, often recalled many years later in exile. Few of these accounts concur and many contradict each other; the majority, infuriatingly, refer to people involved by their initial only. In the main they serve merely to confuse any historian trying to make sense of them. Sadly, however, these plans were all doomed to failure: what the monarchists shared in enthusiasm was outweighed by internal rivalries and an inability to keep their schemes to themselves. As World War I expert Phil Tomaselli put it to me in one of our many conversations:

> Any plot with a single Russian involved will leak; one with two Russians will leak shortly; one with more than two Russians has already leaked. One with 70 Russians is handicapped from day one.

For now, let us return to Little Markov, who in Petrograd in August 1917, under instructions from Markov II, was busy making contact with monarchist cells. He reckoned that by this time there were around fifty such groups, some of them holed up in the Astoria Hotel, where they had clandestine meetings with Lili Dehn, formerly of Alexandra's entourage. Markov II meanwhile held secret meetings with others, in the offices of a commercial company on the Nevsky Prospekt. They were all 'inspired by the same sentiments', noted Little Markov, but got themselves in an 'incredible muddle' and seemed incapable of coming together into one well-organised direction. The problem, as he noted, was that they were all deeply suspicious of each other and had no organisational skills. Nor, at this stage, did they have the one crucial essential: sufficient money to fund their various plans. 'The young officers were enthusiastic about all the mystery-mongering, the passwords, signs, and other paraphernalia of conspiracy,' he recalled, 'but had no idea of the technical side of such activities.'[7] In the meantime, Lili Dehn had become aware that she was being watched by the authorities and decided to move to her mother's home in southern Russia to keep a lower profile. Little Markov travelled with her to Beletskovka in southern Ukraine. During their journey they discovered that 'the whole of the south was honeycombed with monarchist groups'.[8] There was much talk of counter-revolution among them, but as yet no one to marshal any of these groups into a cohesive force.

A typical example of 'an enthusiastic display of loyalty without sense', in the words of Alexander Kerensky, came in August 1917 when one of the Imperial Family's closest friends, twenty-two-year-old Rita Khitrovo, took it upon herself to travel to Tobolsk.[9] Acting entirely independently and without consultation with other Romanov supporters, she arrived there with a pillow stuffed with gifts and a bundle of fifteen or so letters for the Imperial Family.[10] Such had been her thoughtlessness and lack of discretion about the trip that word had soon reached Kerensky. Alerted to her departure and paranoid that she was involved in a plot to free the Romanovs, he had her arrested and searched by Kobylinsky as soon as she arrived in Tobolsk.

Khitrovo's motive for travelling to see the Imperial Family had been one of foolish devotion rather than anything counter-revolutionary, but it put the authorities on their guard for other plots. She was immediately put on a train back to Moscow, where she was interrogated and eventually released. Khitrovo was, however, able to pass on valuable details of the family's greatly straitened living conditions at the Governor's House – prompting a frenzy of fund-raising on their behalf back in Petrograd and Moscow. But in Tobolsk her 'thoughtless visit' did nothing to help the Romanovs, instead having 'the effect of a heavy stone falling upon the still surface of the prisoners' lives'.[11] Thankfully, Kobylinsky deemed the letters she had brought harmless and they were at least passed on to the family. But as a direct result of this incident a new Socialist Revolutionary commissar, Vasily Pankratov, and his assistant Alexander Nikolsky were sent from Moscow to take charge of the captives, with Kobylinsky being sidelined to command the 337 troops guarding them.

Unlike the more sympathetic Kobylinsky, Pankratov was a hardened and trusted revolutionary who had spent fourteen years incarcerated in the notorious Shlisselburg Fortress for the murder of a policeman, and then another twenty-seven years in internal Siberian exile. Arriving on 14 September, he had been extremely reluctant to take up his appointment, but as a dedicated servant of the revolution he carried out his instructions to the letter and with a strong sense of moral rectitude.[12] Nevertheless, though he might have seemed 'a fanatic imbued with humanitarian principles' to tutor Pierre Gilliard, as revolutionaries went, Pankratov was a decent and fair man; he wished no harm to the Imperial Family and was vigilant about their security. He was polite and got on well with the Tsar and his children and earned their respect.[13] Indeed, such was his even-handedness that some of the more militant guards in the detachment at the Governor's House formed their own Soldiers' Committee and began insisting that Pankratov, and Kobylinsky as well, take a much tougher line with their charges.

At the beginning of November 1917, the Bolshevik takeover of power from the Provisional Government in Petrograd brought with it growing anxieties about how the new draconian socialist regime would impact on the Romanovs in Tobolsk. Nicholas was distraught at the news when it finally reached him two weeks later. He had abdicated for the sake of Russia, but his country had not been united by his act of sacrifice; instead it was now riven with even greater violence and discord. Alexandra, meanwhile, was becoming increasingly impatient and anxious, sending word to Dehn and Vyrubova asking, 'what was Markov II doing, and how far had the work for the liberation of Their Majesties really advanced?'[14] By now Little Markov and Dehn had returned to Petrograd to find their group was still trying to collect money to fund sending officers to Tobolsk to mount a rescue. Markov II had recruited 150 people, so he claimed, with everyone becoming increasingly concerned that 'the position of the Emperor and Empress seemed to ... be dangerous, even critical.'[15]

Another important figure had meanwhile also entered the frame: Archbishop Germogen. This well-known spiritual leader and monarchist, who had been influential in Rasputin's rise to a position of influence over the Romanov family, was now based in Tobolsk. Although he had, in the end, turned against Rasputin, Hermogen had remained loyal to the Imperial Family and was lobbying locally for support and funds. He was also in secret communication with the Dowager in Crimea and with monarchists in Petrograd and elsewhere who were organising for a counter-revolution. More importantly, Hermogen had control of a network of monasteries in Western Siberia that might have provided ideal hiding places for the family, once liberated.[16] Acting as a conduit for letters being passed to the family in the Governor's House, Hermogen had, however, aroused much suspicion among the local Soviets. It was under his auspices, and with the assistance of Father Alexey Vasiliev – the priest he had appointed to the church where the Romanovs were occasionally allowed to attend services – that one of the most mysterious plotters now emerged.

Lieutenant Boris Solovev, formerly of the 2nd Machine Gun Regiment, was a leader of the 'Rasputin circle' of Petrograd-based monarchists. Aged twenty-seven, he was 'tall and fair, with a toothbrush moustache' and penetrating grey-green eyes.[17] The son of the treasurer of the Holy Synod, after studying in Berlin he had briefly flirted with theosophy and spent time at Madame Blavatsky's commune in India. In 1915 his interest in the occult drew him to Anna Vyrubova's circle of Rasputin admirers, where he had met Rasputin's daughter Maria, in whose direction Rasputin himself deliberately steered him. Solovev proposed to her several times, but Maria rejected him, until finally agreeing in September 1917 to marry him.[18] Solovev's motives in this are questionable. Many would later allege that he married Maria as an act of cynical self-advancement in order to gain the Empress's confidence as an associate of the two people (family aside) who had been closest to her – Rasputin and Vyrubova.[19] From such an advantageous position he was able, so it seemed, to convince Alexandra that, guided by Rasputin's all-powerful spirit, he was there to ensure not just the Imperial Family's financial support and safety, but also its ultimate liberation.

In October, Solovev had heard that the family were having a difficult time in captivity and were running out of money. Alexandra had been sending messages to Anna Vyrubova, pleading for financial help and other basic commodities. When the family had left for Tobolsk, Count Benckendorff, as Grand Marshal of the Imperial Court, had entrusted Kobylinsky with a large sum of money to cover the family's household expenses, food, servants' salaries and doctors' fees. But these funds had also had to be drawn on by Kobylinsky, to pay the men guarding the family; by November, Prince Dolgorukov was writing to his stepfather in alarm that the money had run out and the Romanovs were piling up debts.[20] Economies had to be made and several servants were let go; many members of the entourage were already covering their own subsistence costs, but even so the Romanovs were living in severely straitened circumstances. Benckendorff had been soliciting donations far and wide – in Moscow and even abroad – on their behalf.[21] The French and British ambassadors, Noulens and Buchanan, had been approached by another group for financial support and had politely declined, but in France the Marquis de la Guiche and other monarchists were also collecting money.[22] As too was Boris Solovev, who had found a major donor in Kiev-based banker and sugar manufacturer Karol Yaroshinsky, for whom Solovev had in the past worked as an assistant. Yaroshinsky had stocks and shares in numerous banks and railroad companies, as well as agricultural investments in Ukraine, and was well known to the Romanov family, having been a benefactor of the hospitals at Tsarskoe Selo set up under the patronage of Nicholas and Alexandra's younger daughters Anastasia and Maria. Accounts vary, but he is said to have stumped up around 175,000 gold rubles (worth more than $3 million/£2,175,000 today), which Anna Vyrubova passed on to Solovev to deliver to the family in Tobolsk, in his guise as a 'fully accredited representative of various monarchist organisations, which trusted him because of Vyrubova's recommendation'.[23]

In Tobolsk in November 1917, Solovev handed over the money, as well as letters for the family, to Father Vasiliev. Some of these gifts were smuggled into the Governor's House by two maids, Anna Romanova (no relation) and Anna Utkina; others went astray. The two women had travelled to Tobolsk separately from the Imperial Family and were able to do this, as they lived independently.[24] In response, Alexandra expressed her gratitude for Yaroshinsky's financial support in a coded letter to Vyrubova: 'Really it is touching that even now we are not forgotten ... God bless him.'[25] By now she had also received word about '300' monarchist rescuers gathering in the area, supposedly under Solovev's auspices, which he referred to as the Brotherhood of St John of Tobolsk. As an expression of their loyalty to the Tsaritsa, they had adopted as their calling card the Buddhist sign of the left-facing sauwastika, which had long been Alexandra's favourite good-luck symbol.[26] Ever watchful for signs from above, Alexandra put her trust in Solovev and his gallant knights: 'I pray tirelessly to the Lord and put my hopes in Him alone,' she wrote to him. 'You talk of a miracle, but it isn't a miracle that the Lord has sent you here to us.'[27]

Investing all her hopes in this promised rescue, Alexandra was also providing another valuable source of funding: her hidden cache of jewels, *objets d'art* and other precious family items – ornamental swords, gold- and jewel-encrusted medals and orders, and so on – that she had brought with her from Tsarskoe Selo. The difficulty was turning such items into hard cash. Some of these jewels were smuggled out by the maids Utkina and Romanova to Bishop Hermogen and Father Vasiliev; others were passed on to Solovev to be converted into money and were never seen again. A large collection of gold and diamond jewellery was taken to the Mother Superior of the nearby Ivanovsky convent by the Tsar's valet Chemodurov and was hidden there for many years.* Other jewels and valuable items were dispersed for safe-keeping among members of the entourage, as the only insurance policy for the Romanovs' future lives in exile, should they escape Russia.

---

* In 1933, this hidden collection of Romanov jewels weighing eight kilograms was finally discovered by the Soviets and listed as 154 individual items, appraised at 3,270,793 rubles then – a modern-day equivalent of many millions. And this was only a portion of the jewels that Alexandra had taken with her from Tsarskoe Selo.

By the beginning of 1918, however, the situation in Tobolsk began to change dramatically. For a while the local government had resisted the slow encroachment of Soviet power in their district, but after news of the second revolution in November filtered through to the guards of the detachment at the Governor's House, some of the more militant among them had become increasingly hostile towards the Romanov family. Kobylinsky was having difficulty keeping them under control: they were more and more disruptive, complaining that the Romanovs had better food and more comfortable beds than they did and demanding an increase in wages. When a consignment of six crates of wine arrived for the family from Tsarskoe Selo, in a rage they demanded it be poured into the River Irtysh. Their own Soldiers' Committee continued to insist on a much stricter regime at the Governor's House. In so doing they effectively usurped power from Kobylinsky, and even the more authoritarian commandant Pankratov.

Pankratov had hoped that elections to a new Constituent Assembly promised in December might restore order to the political situation, but his hopes were in vain. The proceedings to elect the assembly had no sooner begun than Lenin closed them down on 19 January, when the Bolsheviks failed to gain sufficient seats. With his position undermined, friction between the commandant and the ever more militant Soldiers' Committee forced Pankratov's resignation at the end of January.[28] From now on, the regime around the family tightened, as the attitude of the more politicised guards became ever more belligerent and intimidating. They demanded that all guards and officers no longer wear epaulettes, a rule extended to Nicholas and Alexey, who still took pride in wearing their army tunics and who were upset at having to kowtow to it. Kobylinsky noted with alarm how those men who had served under him, when completing their term of duty, were replaced by much more aggressive new recruits from Petrograd; these guards were 'a pack of blackguardly-looking young men', in the view of Pierre Gilliard.[29]

★

In the meantime, on 20 January 1918, Boris Solovev had set off for Siberia once more, with another 10,000 rubles ($173,000/£125,000 equivalent today) from Yaroshinsky and a suitcase full of chocolate, perfume, underclothing and winter clothes for the Imperial Family from their friends in the capital, and three packets of letters passed on by Vyrubova. At Tobolsk the gifts were again smuggled into the Governor's House by the maids. Alexandra, believing that Solovev had been sent by the ghost of Rasputin, in response smuggled out an icon as a gift for him.[30] Shortly afterwards Solovev established a base for his rescue 'conspiracy' at Tyumen. Here, jealous of rival groups arriving from Petrograd and Moscow who might try to exploit the funds raised for the Imperial Family, Solovev 'established a kind of toll-gate for all persons trying to visit Tobolsk with the object of seeing the Romanovs'.[31] He insisted that 'our people' were primed and ready for a rescue – with plants at the local telegraph office, in the Tobolsk militia and the police.[32] There were, he told his supporters, eight former revolutionary regiments that had come over to the cause, and who 'had occupied every approach to Tobolsk, so that it was complete encircled'. He even had, he claimed, 'several trusted men within the house of detention itself' and 'mines had been laid under every bridge within reach of the town, so that it could be isolated at a moment's notice'. When the moment to strike came, this loyal chain of men would pass the Romanovs safely from one group to another. Solovev announced there was no need for further supporters to be sent from Moscow and Petrograd, 'because every new face increased the risk of arousing suspicions'. 'Money was all he asked for' and, needless to say, 'the money was forthcoming'.[33] All they needed now was the right weather and the right opportunity to storm the house.

Predictably, Solovev's promised rescue never materialised. Many in the White Russian émigré community, particularly supporters of Little Markov, subsequently blamed him for the failure of a mission to free the Romanovs. But was there actually ever any concrete mission at all? The whole Solovev escapade is still viewed as something of a 'pseudo-conspiracy', and Solovev himself is frequently condemned as an adventurer and opportunist intent on siphoning off money from the rescue fund. Much of the money collected in Petrograd had been forwarded to Tobolsk by the naïve and trusting Dehn and Vyrubova, some of which Solovev may have pocketed. Other monies and goods passed by him to Father Vasiliev also disappeared, and it is even claimed that the two men quarrelled over their share-out. The later inquiry into the Romanov murders by investigator Nikolay Sokolov suggested that of the 175,000 rubles he had received from Yaroshinsky, Solovev had passed on only 35,000 to the Romanovs.[34]

Solovev has also been labelled a covert Bolshevik and double agent, who 'headed off' Markov's emissaries and 'even handed over at least two of them to the Bolshevik authorities'.[35] There are even unfounded claims that he was a German spy. Whatever his true motives were, he remains an enigma in this story. Nevertheless, accounts of a more credible rescue plot by Russian monarchists, in existence at around the same time, are to be found buried in obscure émigré literature produced in the 1920s, which have never before been discussed.

At the end of 1917 another monarchist group entirely independent of Solovev's Rasputin circle centred itself around Prince Vladimir Trubetskoy, his cousins Princes Alexander and Sergey Trubetskoy and officers of the Sumsky Hussars. The Sumskys were an elite Cossack regiment from Sumy in southern Russia. One of the oldest Imperial Russian Hussar regiments, founded in 1651, its officers were drawn from the nobility and very wealthy families. In December a member of the group, Captain Viktor Sokolov, joined forces with two fellow officers – the Raevsky brothers – who adopted the absurd, giveaway pseudonyms of Kirillov and Mefodiev* when sent on a recce of Tobolsk. They

---

* Viktor Sokolov is not to be confused with the better-known Nikolay Sokolov, a lawyer who in 1919 was appointed by the White commander Alexander Kolchak to investigate the Romanov murders. The Greek brothers Kirill and Methodius were famous Russian theologians and missionaries, venerated in the Orthodox Church as apostles.

reported back that there was considerable monarchist sympathy in the area, which even extended to some of the Tsar's captors. It was suggested that the best time for a rescue would be on a Sunday when the Imperial Family were allowed out to church, with a guard detachment of only twenty men. The group planned to secrete themselves in the church, behind the iconostasis, and then attack the guards when the Romanovs arrived for the service. Much like Little Markov's rescue plot from the Alexander Palace, the idea seemed absurdly fanciful; it had 'the smell of a Dumas novel', as Sokolov himself admitted, and it was not long before he and the Raevsky brothers were arrested by the militia and interrogated by the local Soviet.[36]

Nevertheless, as Sokolov later described, several officers from the Sumy regiment travelled to Tobolsk to check out the guard situation at the Governor's House and to make contact with local monarchists. They were, however, deeply disappointed to discover that these supposed 'monarchists' turned out to be about thirty inexperienced teenage 'boy scouts', and although the local population was largely indifferent, the garrison guarding the Romanovs was huge. Nevertheless, through Father Vasiliev they sent word to Nicholas, who agreed to an escape, but only if the family took their loyal servants as well – a demand that immediately hamstrung any hope of an efficient rescue.[37]

The whole plan was, in any event, scuppered when on 19 December a deacon at the Church of the Ascension inadvertently read the old prayers for the Imperial Family and the 'Mnogoletie' (Many Years) – the traditional salute to the Tsar – was sung.[38] In retribution for this prayer for the prolongation of the Emperor's life, the soldiers guarding the family had a meeting and imposed an immediate clampdown on the family's attendance at church.[39] The only option left, as Sokolov recalled, was to try and spring Nicholas at night from the Governor's House, when half the guards would be asleep – something that Nicholas of course would never have agreed to.

The plan had to be revised: a new version was devised by a monarchist named Polyansky, a Moscow-based barrister who apparently had the moral and material support of several eminent state officials as well as, so he claimed, the French ambassador Noulens. His plan was that a detachment of lower-ranking midshipmen (*gardemariny*) would go to Tobolsk brandishing bogus orders instructing them to take over the guard of the family at the Governor's House.[40] If the resident guards objected, they would take the house by force. Alexandra and the girls would be sent out by rail to the coast and then across the Pacific to Japan. Nicholas, who they knew adamantly refused to leave Russia and part with Alexey, would be hidden somewhere in the country with his son. Together they would be taken incognito on horseback to the Troitsk monastery in the Orenberg region that was controlled by loyal Cossacks – the Tsar with his beard shaved off, posing as French tutor to Alexey as a boy from a rich family.

At this point, any historian would be prompted to ask immediately the obvious question: had the group actually stopped to think whether Nicholas and Alexandra would agree to being separated in this dramatic way? Had they managed to sound them out about their hare-brained plan? If they had done so, and had entered into any kind of serious forward planning of the details, they could have spared themselves a lot of wasted effort.

Nevertheless a circle of ten conspirators fixed on a departure date of 10 January 1918, travelling to Tobolsk in two separate groups in disguise and under false names, and by different routes. One group, led by Prince Alexander Trubetskoy, travelled via Vyatka (now Kirov), Ekaterinburg, Perm and Chelyabinsk; the other, headed by Captain Mikhail Lopukhin, via Orenburg and Ufa.[41] During their seven exhausting days on the train from Moscow to Chelyabinsk the first group discovered, to their dismay, that the railroads were in a state of utter chaos; the stations along the route were policed by Red Guards and any trains heading east were frequently attacked. When they arrived at Chelyabinsk they learned that the monastery at Troitsk, eighty-seven miles away, held by the White general Dutov, where they had been hoping to hide Nicholas and Alexey, had been taken by the Bolsheviks on 25 December. They had no option but to send a coded telegram to Moscow: 'The prices have changed; the deal cannot take place.'[42]

Undaunted, the conspirators fell back on the idea of making a sudden attack on the Governor's House, if they could first disable the telegraph and post offices. In preparation they sought out a network of safe places – Old Believer monasteries deep in Siberia – where the family could be hidden, should the opportunity to free them arise. This time they planned to take the Romanovs out to Yalutorovsk (in Tyumen district), then on horseback sixty-eight miles south-west to the town of Kurgan, using bridlepaths on the southern branch of the Siberian road. It would take two days to cover the distance, travelling in secret by night, and would need twenty-three changes of horse – not to mention considerable logistical organisation.[43] Such a difficult and complicated mission, further endangered by the presence of marauding Bolsheviks in the area, was simply beyond anyone's capabilities, let alone a group of poorly organised monarchists. As things turned out, some of the officers involved were rounded up and arrested, leaving those hiding in Tobolsk in serious danger. Then a message came from Moscow that the 'task of freeing the Imperial Family was unrealizable and their mission was considered to be at an end'.[44] Looking back on it many years later in exile, Trubetskoy was still of the opinion that, given more favourable circumstances, it would have been perfectly feasible to rescue the Imperial Family:

Liberating them and getting them out of Tobolsk was not the most difficult part of the mission. The main difficulty was in how to hide and protect them once rescued. A much more solid organization was needed in order to do this, greater preparatory work, better intelligence, and – the main thing – money, money, and more money. Nothing else was lacking in those ready to carry out the plan.[45]

Another ill-conceived plan to save the Romanovs had ended in abject failure, yet the dogged Little Markov remained determined to help the 'tsar's abandoned family', this time via a group to which Markov II and Count Benckendorff were affiliated, known as the Pravyi Tsentr (Right Centre), which was plotting to restore the monarchy.[46] One of the group, Captain Nikolay Sedov, had been sent on alone to Tyumen in September the previous year to keep an eye on the situation, there being insufficient funds at the time to send anyone else, but they had lost touch with him.[47] Little Markov was dismayed by Markov II's inefficiency. There simply wasn't enough money to 'take any serious measures for the liberation of the Imperial Family', yet here was Markov II with high-flown plans about a major insurrection and the overthrow of the Bolsheviks, and bragging that he had 'more than a hundred officers at his disposal, all supplied with the necessary papers and ready to start at any moment'.[48]

On 10 March 1918, Little Markov arrived with letters, books and other gifts for the Romanovs, under instructions from Markov II, who told him he was convinced 'that we shall be able to establish ourselves in Tobol'sk'.[49] 'Do not forget that you won't be long alone,' he confided; 'other officers will follow you, one after another.'[50] When Little Markov handed the parcel of gifts to Father Vasiliev, he was told that the family's position was 'growing worse every day', as the Bolsheviks in the area were 'devoting increasing attention' to them and a new detachment of much tougher guards had been sent out from Petrograd to guard them.[51] At his lodgings, Little Markov wrote a letter to the Tsaritsa assuring her that 'Tante Ivette' [Markov II's code name] 'was working feverishly, everything was going like clockwork and the day of their release would soon be here'. A day later he received a small icon to wear around his neck and a prayer book inscribed by Alexandra, 'To little M. with my blessing'. She signed it 'Chief', as head of his regiment.[52] Yet, worried for Little Markov's safety, Alexandra begged him to go to Pokrovskoe and join Solovev, who was staying at Rasputin's house there.[53]

Before he left, Little Markov was grateful to be able to catch sight of the Imperial Family standing at the windows of their rooms on the second floor of the Governor's House. He dared to stop and linger long enough on the street below for them to recognise him and smile; Alexandra noted in her diary that she had seen him.[54] Little Markov was overjoyed: 'I had seen the Imperial Family again, and kept my oath. But, at the same time, I was desperately anxious about Their Majesties' hopeless position.' At dawn the following morning, as his sledge drove through the forest towards Pokrovskoe, he encountered two troikas full of swarthy men in leather, armed to the teeth with rifles and machine guns. It was an ominous sign: 'The Bolsheviks were reaching out their bloodstained hands to Tobolsk.'[55] Little Markov hurried to send word to Vyrubova, Dehn and other supporters in Petrograd that 'help must be sent to Their Majesties with all speed'.[56]

Making sense of the extremely fragmentary, often conflicting, and poorly written accounts of monarchist attempts to free the Romanovs is an uphill struggle in any study of the last days of the Imperial Family, and it was one of the greatest bugbears in my research. Frustrated by a lack of reliable, concrete information, in April 2017, while in New York, I visited the Bakhmeteff Archive in the hope that an obscure typescript I had located in its online catalogue might prove useful. It was worth the effort. Alexander Ievreinov's till now overlooked 'Poezdka v Tobolsk' (Journey to Tobolsk) has brought to light not just a valuable account of the situation in Tobolsk in the spring of 1918, but a considerably more coherent account of some of the rescue plans.

During the time Little Markov was out in Siberia on his fruitless quest, he does not seem to have been aware that another member of Markov II's Petrograd group – the economist and former senator Mikhail Tugan-Baranovsky – had sent out his own emissaries to Tobolsk. One of them, Alexander Ievreinov, was a Colonel of the Lifeguard Jaeger regiment and came from a Kursk family with distinguished military service to the tsars. In disguise and using false names and passports, Ievreinov and his fellow officer Tunoshensky set off, posing as brother merchants on business, to try and make contact with the Tsar and pass on messages of support. Count Benckendorff was also privy to the plan, but had reservations that Ievreinov's mission might easily be uncovered and might expose the Romanovs to more harm for little gain.[57]

Arriving in Tobolsk in March 1918, Ievreinov quickly discovered through the local clergy that the best way he could hope to make contact was via one or other of the family's physicians – Dr Botkin or Dr Derevenko, who lived in the Kornilov House across the road from the Governor's House – as they had been allowed greater freedom of movement in order to continue in medical practice and offer help to the sick in Tobolsk. Importantly, they were the only members of the entourage who were not searched when going in and out of the Governor's House.[58] Feigning a serious throat infection, Ievreinov went to see Botkin at his daily surgery, but it was difficult to talk as the room was full of people. He made an excuse to return later in private, when he revealed his true identity and the reason for his mission. Reassured, Botkin took him into his confidence. Ievreinov managed to maintain the phoney illness cover so well that Botkin was able to make several visits to him in his rooms, where they discussed the Imperial Family's difficult situation.[59]

During their conversations Botkin revealed how the family was living inside the Governor's House. Mindful of their money difficulties, the Tsar was extremely economical, to the point where, with matches now being so hard to get hold of and very expensive, if someone else in the room was smoking he would light his cigarette from theirs rather than waste a match. The local people were constantly asking Botkin to smuggle in gifts of sugar, pies and jam, which he did inside his large English overcoat, though he worried that the jam might leak out of the pockets and give him away. Botkin also made clear, during his visits to Ievreinov, something that would be a significant factor in the latter part of this story: while Nicholas and Alexandra supported an internal Russian rescue of some kind, 'their Majesties utterly refused to be the subject of any political moves to help them – in particular any discussions on their behalf with the Germans'.[60]

'Unfortunately, people such as you are very rare of late,' a weary Botkin told Ievreinov. It was so difficult to trust anyone, and

Nicholas and Alexandra would be grateful to hear any news from Ievreinov of their friends in the capital and to know there were a few experienced and loyal people looking out for them here in Tobolsk.[61] The leader of the monarchists – presumably Markov II – with whom they had had contact, Botkin told him, had seemed to 'lack any authority', despite his energy and devotion. Ievreinov too had come to the conclusion that Romanov supporters in Petrograd were hopelessly disorganised and had no effective overall leader to unite them in their efforts. They concentrated too much on the political and not the practical side of things, such as cultivating the key support of Kobylinsky, whom Dr Botkin assured Ievreinov was 'heart and soul devoted to the Imperial Family, to the last drop of his blood'. Ievreinov concluded that, with Kobylinsky's cooperation, it would be relatively easy to get the Romanovs away from the Governor's House on a day when the men of his guard were in a good mood.[62]

But where could they take them? Ievreinov pondered the options for many days. It was 132 miles to the nearest railway station: that was too far and would expose the family to too much danger; they had to be taken somewhere inland, the Semipalatinsk region, for example – an area of remote steppe on the border with Kazakhstan – or perhaps eastwards.* To take them west into European Russia was out of the question.[63] Either way, it had to be done on horseback: Ievreinov found himself encountering precisely the same logistical problems as those that had defeated the Trubetskoy/Sokolov group. Such a journey would require the help of Kirghiz tribesmen and would need a great deal of time and resources, a knowledge of local dialects and bridlepaths and a whole chain of stopping-off points. To make matters even more difficult, this route could not be undertaken in March, for this was just as the heavy spring rains began, making the roads impassable with deep mud. A rescue on

---

* Romanov historian Victor Alexandrov suggested that 'a convoy protected by a hundred resolute cavalrymen stood a reasonable chance of reaching northern Turkestan, a region of Moslem tribes hostile to the Revolution'.

horseback could only be carried out in the autumn.[64] But could a sickly tsarevich and his equally sick mother endure such a journey? No one seems to have asked the question. Whichever way you looked at it, every possible factor conspired to defeat this latest rescue plan.

Dr Botkin's son Gleb, who was living with his father at the Kornilov House in Tobolsk, later wrote that he was convinced Kobylinsky had been hoping to get the family away to safety not long after their arrival in Tobolsk. Looking at the options, he had thought the only viable escape route to be north, on the road through Berezov (Berezovo) to Obdorsk (now Salekhard) and then 'on one of the Norwegian schooners which come to Obdorsk' to the Arctic Ocean beyond. He had held out hopes to flee with the family before Pankratov arrived, taking with them a protective convoy of thirty loyal men from the guard. By the time the Bolsheviks were able to respond, the convoy would be too far ahead for anyone to catch them; and if they did, their firearms would be virtually unusable in the freezing conditions. Once the thaw came, the dirt roads beyond Berezov would be impassable. But like all other would-be rescuers, Kobylinsky had needed funds to set this plan in train; and the monarchists, whom Botkin thought 'incapable of sensible action', had refused to help him, mistrusting his motives. They were, Botkin concluded, 'utterly futile chatter-boxes' and had missed a golden opportunity offered by Kobylinsky, who in his view was utterly loyal to the Romanovs.[65]

There was really only one viable option, as far as Alexander Ievreinov was concerned: a route by water out of Tobolsk, as soon as the ice-bound rivers were navigable again. In a quiet backwater of the Irtysh not far from Tobolsk, out of the water for the winter, stood a screw-driven schooner, suitable – according to those in the know – for sea and even ocean sailing.[66]* This schooner was much faster than the ordinary paddle-driven

---

* An article published in a Soviet journal in 1956 also mentioned the schooner, naming it as the *Svyataya Mariya*, and said it was reported to have been British in origin.

steamships that plied the River Irtysh. To take possession of it would be easy; one of the members of the organisation could navigate – perhaps a former merchant sailor who was familiar with the northern river routes. The plan would also involve disabling telegraph stations along the Ob and at the coast, which might have sent out a warning. When the waterways were free of ice, the Romanovs could be taken north by river to the Arctic Ocean and from there across to Archangel. But to pass through the upper reaches of the Irtysh and Ob was only possible from the beginning of June, when the ice had melted. With this suggestion in mind, Ievreinov sent his fellow officer Tunoshensky urgently back to Petrograd to consult with their monarchist leaders.[67]

At last we have the first serious discussion in Russian – by someone directly involved in the monarchist campaign to free the Romanovs – of a mooted rescue by river from Tobolsk. Alexander Ievreinov was not in fact alone in considering this option. For it is one that has long circulated, in the usual frustratingly fragmented form, in sources on the fate of the Romanovs. Evidence suggests that a plan for a river rescue was indeed discussed even earlier in 1918. It did not, however, come from Russian monarchists, but from a Norwegian shipper named Jonas Lied – and with the unofficial involvement of the British.

Chapter 8

'Please Don't Mention My Name!'

During the winter of 1917–18 the safety of the Romanovs, to all intents and purposes, appeared to have been taken care of by the Provisional Government. Being shut away in Western Siberia, with the snow encircling the town and the rivers leading in and out of it frozen solid, ensured the family's remoteness. It seemed they could come to no harm – for the present at least. A last brief blip of interest in his cousins' welfare had been expressed by King George on 5 August 1917, when he had asked Stamfordham to send a note to the Cabinet enquiring whether the 'removal of the Emperor and Empress from Tsarskoe Selo … as having been decided upon by the Provisional Government, has been carried into effect'. Sir George Buchanan was not sure; 'the matter has been kept such a profound secret,' he responded, 'that even [the] Minister for Foreign Affairs whom I questioned on the subject a week ago could not give me a positive answer'.[1] He did not in fact receive official confirmation that the family had left for Tobolsk until the actual day of their departure – 14 August.[2]

From here on, the FO file Russia and Siberia 800/205, as well as the Royal Archives, is silent on the Imperial Family until a brief flurry of interest the following May. The British Crown and government would appear to have totally disengaged from the problem, turning their occasional attention instead to the plight of Dagmar in Crimea (as did King

Christian of Denmark), but only because the Queen Mother continued to be constantly at the Foreign Office's back, demanding news of her.

If the British government had had its way at this juncture, the whole sorry plight of the Romanovs in Russia would have been left in abeyance. The record appears to fall silent. What can we infer from that?

In their 1976 book The File on the Tsar, *Summers and Mangold argued that this 'gap in the files' for the period 'right up till July 1918' was 'extraordinary, and highly improbable' – their conclusion being that official documents relating to the Romanovs had been weeded out or destroyed.[3] Contrary to what they say, there was in fact a revival of British interest in early May 1918, as we shall see, but nevertheless this claim is something I pondered long and hard as I sifted through the evidence. While we have no way ever of knowing what documents (if any) might have passed via the back-channels of the Secret Intelligence Service, there is perhaps an obvious and logical explanation. Might it not have been a simple case of official complacency – of 'out of sight, out of mind'? The war was still raging and, now that the Bolsheviks had seized power, the Allies were far more preoccupied with preserving the Eastern Front and keeping Russia in the fight against Germany. Worries about the Imperial Family came a very poor second to this. For now, at least, the Romanovs seemed to be well out of trouble in the relatively quiet backwaters of Western Siberia.*

The Imperial Family may for now have been removed well away from the hotbed of trouble in Petrograd, but far away in Tobolsk the Romanovs were longing for word that they had not been forgotten. By the end of 1917 they were clearly feeling cut off from their loved ones. As Olga explained to a friend, Zinaida Tolstaya: 'Tobolsk is a corner lost when the river freezes, the only communication with the rest of the world is the road to Tyumen: over 200 versts [132 miles]. News reaches us with a great delay.'[4]

For months, in their often innocent-sounding letters and post-cards sent from the Governor's House to friends and relatives outside, the family had been sending a paper trail of intelligence about the house in which they were held, its grounds, the location of their rooms and even the disposition of their guards. The four Romanov sisters had described how often they were outside in the yard or sunning themselves on the balcony or on the roof of the greenhouse; how they could see the public passing by and thus how visible, if not accessible, the family actually were, given the restrictions placed upon them.

Anastasia in particular had been quite open to her friend Katya Zborovskaya when sending photographs: 'Here is the space where we walk. We often sit on this balcony; it is very nice. One of the windows that looks to this side is of Papa's office. Our windows look to the other side; there is a street there.' And again: 'I am sending you the view of the Governor's House. This is the balcony where we sit often and for a long time. Our windows face the street, which is in the corner behind the trees. The windows on the balcony that are the closest to the street are the windows of our big living room.'⁵ These were clearly covert messages that Anastasia knew Katya would pass on to her brother Viktor, a close friend of the Imperial Family and an officer of the former Cossack Escort that had loyally protected them at Tsarskoe Selo. Many of the Escort, including Viktor, had now gone over to the Whites and were holding out with monarchist groups in the south.

Such feelings were no doubt the impetus behind a letter from Alexandra to Margaret Jackson, her English governess from her childhood days in Hesse. She had kept in touch with 'Madgie', now living in retirement at a Home for Governesses in London's Regent's Park, but had not heard from her for some time. In the letter, written to Alexandra's dictation by Sydney Gibbes – in the hope that, coming from an innocuous tutor, it would avoid suspicion – she sent details of the location of the rooms inside the house, and of the family's daily routine. On the surface this might have seemed like idle chit-chat, but it was clearly designed as useful intelligence for any possible rescue attempt:

Our House or rather Houses, for there are two, one on one side of the street and one on the other, are the best in town; that in which the Household proper lives is entirely isolated and possesses a small garden besides a piece of the roadway which has been railed in to make a recreation ground. The other house which is almost exactly opposite, is occupied by Government officials and contains quarters for the Suite.[6]

Even more emphatic was the question that followed, in barely disguised code, which Madgie would surely immediately recognise: 'I hear that David is back from France, how are his mother and father?'[7] This reference to David, Prince of Wales (the future Edward VIII) and his parents, King George and Queen Mary, very pointedly indicated that the contents of this letter were intended for the royal family. It was a faint but plaintive cry for help.

Gibbes kept a draft of the letter, which was sent from Tobolsk to the British embassy on 15 December, and then from Petrograd by diplomatic bag via the Foreign Office to England. But did it ever arrive? No reply or acknowledgement was received in Tobolsk, nor does the original letter itself survive. Did Madgie pass it on to the royal family? If so, there is no record of it in the Royal Archives. As it turns out, this is highly unlikely. For Miss Margaret Hardcastle Jackson died on 28 January 1918. Even if she did receive the letter, she was almost certainly too old and frail to deal with it, for one of the causes of her death recorded on the certificate was 'senility'.[8]

While the letter to Miss Jackson sadly never served its intended purpose, word on the Romanovs does, however, briefly resurface in a document that I found during research for this book. The allusion in itself contradicts the assertion by Summers and Mangold that there was no reference to the Romanovs in the official record at this time. The circumstances in which they are mentioned are significant, but perhaps not for the right or hoped-for reasons.

In December 1917, at the invitation of the British Foreign Office, the experienced journalist Robert Wilton, who after serving as Russia correspondent of *The Times* since 1903 had returned to London in September, submitted a confidential report to the government. Headed 'Russia Still the Greatest Factor in the War. German Plans – The Need of Urgent Measures', much of the report was taken up with economic issues. The British were by now greatly preoccupied with the threat that Allied military stores might be confiscated by the Bolsheviks as the revolution spread north, but also that the German advance in south-western Russia would lead to them seizing control of the crucial grain-growing areas and the route to Crimea through the oil-rich Caucasus to the Black Sea. Wilton warned that if the Germans 'took forcible possession of the country', they might restore the Romanovs to a puppet monarchy – 'a possibility that is by no means excluded even under Bolshevik auspices'.[9]

By now there was widespread rumour that the Bolsheviks were intriguing with the Germans for a separate peace deal. In a five-point list of recommendations, Wilton urged that an Allied inter-vention force be prepared to go into Russia via the Far East to offer support to anti-Bolshevik groups of Cossacks, Siberians and Ukrainians, as well as into Archangel in the north to protect British military supplies there. His fifth and final point, however, was perhaps the most significant in terms of this story and he emphasised its importance by underlining it:

> 5. Secret and expeditious measures should be taken to prevent the Bolsheviks from capturing the ex-Tsar and his family or any of the Romanovs.[10]

'Will the Allies realize the importance of the issues at stake,' asked Wilton in conclusion, 'and proceed without loss of time to take the necessary action?'[11] But the Imperial Family were already captives, surely? Yes, but up till now of a fairly benign Provisional Government that had wished, however ineptly, to protect them. With the recent usurpation of power by Lenin and his hardliners, the British had been following their peace negotiations with Germany through intercepted telegrams from Russian military and naval advisers at the talks, forwarded by British attachés in Petrograd. A different kind of concern had taken over: that the Bolsheviks, now gaining a foothold in Siberia, would seize control of the prisoners at Tobolsk and use them as political pawns in a game of power play with the Germans over a separate peace deal.

There is no follow-through in official Foreign Office documents to shed light on how, and if, Wilton's recommendation for 'secret measures' was actively pursued with regard to the Romanovs. But during the winter of 1917–18 evidence suggests that there were tentative plans to shelter the family at Murmansk.[12] Under the protection of the Allies already established there, the Romanovs would, once liberated from Tobolsk, wait at the port till an opportune time came to get them out by sea to either Britain or Scandinavia. The project to construct a house to accommodate them is confirmed in a telegram from the British consul at Archangel to the Hudson's Bay Company (HBC) offices at Bishopsgate on 9 October. The house was to be assembled first in Archangel, as the telegram explicitly states, the consul confirming that he had 'placed order for immediate construction of house which we intend shipping to Murmansk with last steamer for erection in ground allotted to us by Government'. But time was against them and the consul explained that he had had 'to act promptly as otherwise no possibility of getting house ready in time and now only under great pressure'.[13] Telegrams from London followed, confirming that furniture and supplies would be sent by the Admiralty to equip the house, but there is no mention of the Romanovs.[14] At this stage, because of a chronic shortage of accommodation at Murmansk for British officials, it seems that the eight-roomed house was to be temporarily made over to the use of HBC staff and British military there. But on 2 November a telegram came from Archangel saying that the furniture and stores for the house would not be needed: 'unlikely that under existing conditions *will erect house this season* [my italics]'. A telegram went back saying that the supplies had already been ordered and urging that 'every effort should be made to complete house before end of November'. A sum of 50,000 rubles had been set aside for the purpose.[15]

Here the record breaks off. But there is one crucial piece of surviving evidence. On 10 August 1918 − note the date − the house's original purpose was confirmed, albeit retrospectively, in a Royal Navy telegram found in Admiralty records. Addressed to the senior naval officer at Murmansk and sent by Francis Cromie, the British naval attaché in Petrograd, it states:

Following received via Christiania [now Oslo] from Naval Attaché Petrograd for SNO Murmansk begins:

I have received from Mr Browd on behalf of the Murmansk Scientific Industrial Co[mpan]y the offer of the building *to be erected* on the Dived Company's land near the British Consulate Murmansk *formerly intended for the late Czar* and now offered for occupation by General Poole or Admiral Kemp. Buildings complete with heating Light [sic] utensils etc. and now in charge of Kambulin Engineer erecting them. [my italics][16]

According to an account submitted to the HBC by the Russian contractor P. S. Kuznetsov, it would appear that around mid-November 1917 work had indeed begun on the wooden house, which was cut and prefabricated at Solombala sawmill outside Archangel, after which it was dismantled, shipped in sections across the Dvina estuary to Khabarka Island opposite and stacked in storage there.[17] This was done under the supervision of Henry Armitstead,* the Hudson's Bay Company agent based at Archangel, and from there the sections were to be shipped to Murmansk.[18]

---

* The Armitsteads were English immigrants to Latvia who had arrived from Yorkshire in 1812 and built their wealth on the flax trade there. Henry was related through his grandfather to George Armitstead, Mayor of Riga 1901−12, who had built the city up into 'the Paris of the North' and entertained Nicholas II on his three-day visit there in 1910.

The location chosen for the house was the best Murmansk had to offer; the British consulate next to it, although wooden and single-storey, had been built to look as 'imposing' as a construction of squared logs could. The house for the Romanovs would be 'in close proximity to branch offices of several Petrograd banks, and close also, to Government buildings and to the Cathedral', according to a description of the town at the time, and would be of even better quality.[19] But it was never built in time for the Romanovs – should they have been spirited away from Siberia – to to use it. The telegram of 10 August 1918 clearly shows that the sections were yet to be sent over and assembled.

This does not, however, take away from the fact that there might have been a tentative British plan to get the Romanovs out of Tobolsk and on to the safety of Murmansk that winter. And there was one man who was best placed to help effect it. Norwegian businessman and adventurer Jonas Marius Lied had an unrivalled knowledge of the White and Kara Seas and the Siberian river systems that were crucial to the undertaking of such a mission. Born in Solsnes in 1881, 'a tall, lean redoubtable figure with a high brow and firm lips and chin', Lied was, according to a friend, the kind of man 'who could break his way through social ice, in fact a human ice-breaker, but also the most remarkable businessman that Scandinavia has produced'.[20] As a young man, Lied had gained wide experience working for engineering companies in Europe. In 1910 he turned his sights on the business potential of Russia, spending the next two years travelling there and learning the language, before founding the Siberian Steamship, Manufacturing & Trading Company in Christiania in 1912, with branches in Krasnoyarsk, St Petersburg and Archangel.[21] Such became his long association with Russia that Lied was 'mentally even more devoted to Russia than to his native land'.[22]

His objective was to bring to fruition centuries of ambition by navigators to exploit the commercial potential of the Kara Sea passage and develop a trade route in minerals and timber between Western Europe and Siberia. His venture would make use of the Yenisey and Ob, two of the great rivers that intersect the Siberian land mass, flowing from the southern Russo-Chinese border down to the Kara Sea and from there into the Arctic Ocean. At that time there were no routes via rail or road that covered these vast distances, and the river routes could only be exploited during the short, ice-free season between July and September.[23]

In order to better acquaint himself with the geography of Siberia, in 1913 Lied explored the Yenisey on a chartered steamer with the famous Norwegian explorer Fridtjof Nansen, thus pioneering the opening up of the route upriver from southern Siberia. By 1914 Lied had been appointed Norwegian consul at Krasnoyarsk by King Haakon and had established a state-of-the-art sawmill at Malaklovo on the Yenisey. One of the Russian grand dukes happily arranged the Russian citizenship that Lied needed in order to enter the Russian steamship business and buy shares in the riverboat fleets on the Ob and Yenisey. In 1915 the Tsar elevated Lied's citizenship to honorary and hereditary status, 'in recognition of his successful leadership of a convoy of cargo ships and river steamboats from Hamburg through the North Sea to Siberia at the outbreak of World War I'.[24] By 1916 his Siberian Company held the majority of shares for all boats operating on the Yenisey, and control of forty-nine riverboats on the Ob and 140 barges.[25]

Lied was in Petrograd when the Bolsheviks seized power in October 1917. He met Lenin and Trotsky in the hope of striking a business deal with the new government and, having a flat in Petrograd where he had amassed a considerable art collection, travelled back and forth in an attempt to hang on to his Russian company or at the least sell up and get the profits out of the country.[26] Lied was therefore pleased to receive an invitation on 26 February 1918 to go to London to 'discuss the possibility of leading an expedition to the Kara Sea during the forthcoming summer'. It came just after he had resigned as managing director of the Siberian Trading Company, which would soon fall victim to the Bolshevik nationalisation of foreign businesses in Russia.

The invitation had come from Henry Armitstead, the Hudson's Bay official involved in the construction of the putative Murmansk House, who had met Lied during 1916 on business trips to northern Russia. Armitstead had been in conversation with HBC's accountant about the continuing viability of trade with Siberia and whether there was sufficient demand for its hemp, flax and linseed. They had agreed that Lied's opinion on the matter was important and that 'Something might be built upon his experiences and upon the organization which he possesses.'[27]

In response, Lied wasted no time in taking the fast British boat from Bergen to Aberdeen. Arriving in London on 4 March, he was met and installed in the comfort of a suite at the swish Savoy Hotel by Colonel Frederick Browning. This came as something of a surprise, for Browning was no ordinary army officer; he was in fact number two to Mansfield Cumming, head of MI1(c), the foreign division of the Secret Intelligence Service (now MI6), which had already been taking an interest in Lied.[28]

According to Lied's diary, held in the Norwegian Maritime Museum in Oslo, he had several meetings at the Savoy Hotel with Armitstead and his superior, Charles Sale, to discuss the Kara Sea expedition.[29] A whole string of further encounters – with senior government ministers – followed over the next few days. The names are recorded in Lied's diary: William Mitchell-Thomson, director of the Restriction of Enemy Supplies (whose significance will become apparent later in this chapter); Foreign Secretary Arthur Balfour; and Lord Robert Cecil, Parliamentary Under-Secretary of State for Foreign Affairs. Lied was also invited to dinner with Armitstead at the home of Sir Reginald Hall, director of British naval intelligence. This roster of pre-eminent military and political officials suggests that the utmost importance was being placed on their private discussions with Lied; but at this point none of them had revealed to Lied exactly why they were paying so much solicitous attention to him. 'What is all this about?' he asked his diary on 8 March.[30]

★

Till now a huge amount of wishful thinking has been invested in this scenario – first by Summers and Mangold, and then by Shay McNeal in The Secret Plot to Save the Tsar *– followed by everyone else who has drawn on these two sources as gospel on the subject and repeated the story without questioning it. The assumption has always been that Lied was called to London specifically to discuss a Romanov rescue plan. But this is not so. We have here a classic chicken-and-egg situation. It was British self-interest in wartime that prompted the invitation. Lied's expertise was being drawn on during these meetings first and foremost with a view to a* secret economic mission *to protect and promote British trade interests in Siberia.*[31]

This expedition did in fact set out in late June 1918, involving Henry Armitstead, British industrialist Leslie Urquhart and others, under instructions from SIS chief Mansfield Cumming.[32] It is confirmed in a Commercial Russia file FO368/1970 held in the National Archives and headed 'Supplies from Central Siberia: Regarding proposal of Siberian Trading Co for expedition to Kara Sea', which talks of the expedition 'tapping the area between Tobolsk and Krasnoyarsk … for our own requirements'. Documents in this file for March–May 1918 refer to the Hudson's Bay Company, Armitstead and Lied – but not as putative Romanov rescuers. The mission (under the umbrella of the department for the Restriction of Enemy Supplies) was to be composed of four 3,000-ton steamers taking 'salt, nails, clothing, sheet iron and carpenters tools' to be 'unloaded at the mouths of the rivers Yenisei and Obi', where the return Siberian cargoes – of flax, hemp, linseed oil, butter and hides that had been brought down in barges from Krasnoyarsk and Tobolsk – would be loaded. These commodities (of which hemp and flax,* essential for war industries, were in short supply) were abundant in Siberia, but could

---

* There were serious economic reasons for the Lied flax- and hemp-purchasing mission in this regard. Pre-war Russia had provided 80 per cent of British supplies of flax, and stocks were running seriously low in 1918.

only be got out via the waterways, as the railways in northern Russia were 'in total disorganisation'.[33] But to bring them out of Siberia would have to be agreed with the Russians.

Enter Jonas Lied. British intelligence was already well aware of his valuable Russian experience; he was 'understood to be on good terms with the Bolshevik regime, and would therefore perhaps stand a fair chance of securing good relations with the Soviets' on their behalf. After extensive consultation, Hudson's Bay Company director Charles Sale advised that such an expedition 'would involve much risk and high cost', but that 'Mr Lied, who is now in London on a very brief stay [i.e. his March 1918 visit] ... has expressed his willingness to carry out such transactions in co-operation with the Hudson's Bay Company.'[34]

It is only at this point that the much-discussed Romanov connection, about which there has been so much subsequent speculation, begins to fall into place.

During his discussions with British officials, as he later described in his 1943 memoir *Return to Happiness*, Lied says that he 'became possessed of another idea' that perhaps could be achieved as part of this expedition: to 'rescue the tsar and his family from Siberia'.[35] The Kara Sea mission would involve taking boats to and from Tobolsk – why not try to help the beleaguered Imperial Family while they were at it?

To an experienced navigator such as Lied, the best way of getting the family out would be by his river steamer, based at Nakhodka at the mouth of the Ob, which also served Tobolsk. 'It should not have been beyond the power of Tsarist sympathisers to organize the escape of the Tsar and his family down the rivers to the Arctic and thence to Western Europe,' he argued. It would be their task to liberate the family from their Tobolsk prison in the first phase of the operation. Indeed, a river rescue had been mooted by Alexander Ievreinov the previous autumn; and Markov II also later claimed to have a skipper ready and waiting to take the Tobolsk schooner *Svyataya Mariya* up the Ob (though whether his plan was in any way connected with Ievre-inov's is unknown). But in reality it would have required a highly experienced navigator such as Lied to oversee the family's escape via the Irtysh at Tobolsk, downriver to the mouth of the Ob and out to the Kara Sea.[36]

Nearly two weeks after his arrival in London, and after he had been vetted carefully by this assortment of key officials and had discussed his idea of the Romanov rescue with them, Lied was invited to a meeting. On 20 March he met Sir Francis Barker, director of the famous engineering and armaments firm Vickers, which had 'made millions out of imperial Russia' during the war. Vickers, Lied suggested, could provide the final essential link in the plan – a 'fast motor launch' to get the Romanovs out from the Kara Sea and presumably across to the safe house at Murmansk.[37]

Such a rescue, north and then out via the Arctic, could only be effected once the ice had melted – at the earliest, late June 1918, which would of course tie in with the Kara Sea mission planned for July. Sir Francis Barker, as Lied recalled, thought his idea 'feasible', though 'daring and certainly most romantic', but put the dampener on any official involvement by Vickers. There was also the problem, as always, of obtaining financial support for the project, even though Lied had received the offer of funding of £500 from a Norwegian friend named Hagen.* Vickers, Barker told him, 'would not wish its name to be in any way associated with the adventure'. Instead he put him in touch with the Tsar's cousin, Grand Duke Mikhail Mikhailovich, who lived at Cambridge Gate near Regent's Park, as 'the man you ought to meet'.[38] While the Grand Duke in turn offered Lied his 'courtly attentiveness' during their meeting and wished him all the best with his scheme, he referred to Nicholas somewhat disparagingly as 'the little man' and, like Barker at Vickers, was

---

* Possibly the ski manufacturer L. H. Hagen, who had supplied skis to Lied's friend Fridtjof Nansen for his expeditions.

adamant about one thing: 'on no account must his name ever be mentioned in connection with the proposed exploit'. Lied found this kneejerk British reticence extremely frustrating: 'Well, if his name was not to be mentioned, whose name was? It was characteristic of the whole reaction to my plan: "Please don't mention my name!"'[39]

> As a Norwegian, the revolution was not my funeral. Even my scheme to save the Emperor was non political. Its inspiration was partly the call of the Kara Sea, and partly, I admit, a sense of gratitude to the imperial house for the sympathetic way it had helped me to establish the Siberian business.[40]

Lied felt a certain loyalty to the Tsar, whom he had found 'extremely warm and friendly' when he had met him at Tsarskoe Selo before the revolution; and the Romanovs were, after all, relatives of the Norwegian king, Haakon.[41]

Official British War Cabinet, Admiralty and FO papers are all, predictably, absolutely silent on Lied's Romanov rescue scheme. Not a word survives, if there ever was one on the record, of the discussions that took place with him in March 1918 about getting the Romanovs out of Tobolsk. And the situation is not helped by there being some discrepancies between the Lied manuscript diary and the much later account in his published memoirs.[42] Summers and Mangold spent many years trying to get to a British 'Naval Intelligence dossier on a mission to bring the family out' that might back up the Lied plan. Its existence was confirmed to them in 1974 by the then Under-Secretary of State, Sir Anthony Royle. But 'He could not reveal its contents, he said, because he was bound by the Official Secrets Act.'[43] Does that file still exist somewhere in the National Archives?

A close examination of all available Scandinavian and English sources indicates that the whole story of the supposed Lied Romanov rescue has been repeatedly misinterpreted. That is not to say, however, that the British did not briefly toy with the idea, before dismissing it as foolhardy. The desire of all those concerned to be 'kept out of it' clearly implies that the initiative had not come from them, but from Lied. In the face of their lukewarm response, he placed the idea in abeyance after leaving London on 30 March. What is more, Lied would seem to have felt obliged to conceal the details when he published a very anodyne version of the story in *Return to Happiness* twenty-five years later. This is reinforced by the fact that the memoirs describe a meeting Lied had with Sir George Buchanan after the October Revolution in which they appeared to discuss 'the future of large British undertakings' in Russia, such as the British petroleum industry in the North Caucasus and mining enterprises in the Urals, but puzzlingly it makes no mention of the one subject for so long close to Sir George's heart – the welfare of the Romanov family.[44]

According to Summers and Mangold, Jonas Lied did in fact later confide the true story of his rescue plan to an English friend, Ralph Hewins, who for many years had been a specialist Scandinavian newspaper correspondent and is best known for his biography of the Norwegian traitor, Quisling. In private conversation, Lied told Hewins that:

> he was asked by Metropolitan-Vickers … to berth a British boat at his sawmill depot [this must be Maklakovo] at the mouth of the Yenisey and to transport the Imperial Family from Tobolsk downriver in one of his cargoboats. The plan was feasible. The torpedo boat [i.e. a British RN or a Vickers one sent specially] was to take a course far north into the Arctic, through Novaya Zemlya, so as to avoid wartime minefields and possible Bolshevik pursuit.[45]

As Wilhelm Wilkens, Jonas Lied's nephew, confirmed to me in an email, 'I remember that my uncle (he died in 1969) told me that neither the monarch, nor the British government were interested in saving the tsar's family. I think that was from political reasons.'[46] In fact ahead of the London meetings, the Hudson's Bay Company had already expressed doubts about Lied's abilities to head the economic mission, being of the mind that he was 'inclined to minimize the difficulties and exaggerate the possibilities', and concluding that 'it will be necessary to regard both Mr Lied and his organization as instruments rather than as the controlling element'.[47]

The faulty and often second- or third-hand recall of crucial events many years after they happened is a persistent problem that all historians have to deal with on a regular basis. There are a number of them in the Romanov story, in particular an assortment of claims about either a Russian monarchist or a British Secret Service rescue plan, backed – or even instigated – by King George V himself. The possibility of such a mission is something I had frequently discussed with my World War I and Intelligence Services expert adviser, Phil Tomaselli. We had, despondently, picked over what little evidence there was and agreed that while the Lied/Murmansk plan was viable, there was little or nothing in official records to back it up, let alone tie it to a clear British initiative.

But then a few clues came my way, as things often do in historical research, via an unsolicited email from a reader.

I don't know where to start really … I have just watched the wonderful documentary films about the Romanovs,[*] and wondered if you would be interested in some additional material concerning their last days, and a planned British rescue mission, all of which I can authenticate … It was my maternal grandfather who was actually responsible … for a very well planned British escape. His full name was Stephen Berthold Gordon-Smith.

My informant went on to describe how his grandfather had been involved in an operation:

---

[*] A reference to the two-part BBC2 documentary *Russia's Lost Princesses*, based on my book *Four Sisters* and first transmitted in 2015.

with the necessary connivance of a lot of minor local Russian people … bribing people, such as … domestic staff to help prepare necessary supplies, clothes, food and valuables for transport, organizing overland transport via carriages & sleighs & arranging drivers and their reindeer or horse Staging Posts, for all the various parts of the route to Archangel, plus the coordinated arrangements of a British submarine to be standing by, fully crewed and briefed, at the appointed date, in the only ice-free port Arkhangelsk.[48]

There was talk too of 'a seaplane' being involved in the rescue, but all this rather confused information had been passed down to my informant at a two-generation remove, and no doubt elaborated on in the process. Through no fault of his own, the version that he in turn handed on to me was, to say the least, muddled and full of loopholes.[49] But might there be a grain of truth in it?

Could there really have been a British plan to get the Romanovs from Tobolsk to Archangel overland? Surely not; it is clear that this was something even the monarchists inside Russia had abandoned as logistically impossible. The Lied plan by river was much more efficient. The only supporting material my informant could give me was a 1980s newspaper cutting and some typed notes from his step-grandmother – Gordon-Smith's widow, Patricia Eykyn – that she had made for the family:

In 1917 Steven [sic] was sent to Russia ostensibly with the British Military Mission, Victor Warrender (now Lord Bruntisfield) and Bruce Lockhart* were in the same party, but the real reason Steven was sent was to bring The Imperial Family

---

* Lockhart, who until the autumn of 1917 had been consul-general in Moscow, travelled back to Russia on an Admiralty boat on 12 January 1918 via Stockholm and Tornio. If Warrender and Gordon-Smith did indeed travel out together, there is curiously no record of passports being issued to either of them for Russia, although there is one for Lockhart.

to England. He not only knew the Imperial Family, but could easily pass as a Russian. There was a British submarine standing by at Archangel. And then the word came from London 'Abandon operation return via Stockholm' … and so, as Steven has told me so often, he did what he will regret to his dying day. He obeyed orders. No one other than Steven will ever know all the details and the whole truth.[50]

Stephen's grandson confirmed that the diaries and letters referring to this mission had been kept by Stephen's daughter – his mother, Joy – and that his sister and Patricia, the second wife, had both seen them. And yes, 'the diaries and letters showed there was definitely a rescue plan that Steven was involved in'.[51]

'But where are those diaries and letters now?' I asked, with a sense of mounting excitement.

The response, when it came, was the one all historians dread hearing: 'Joy burnt it all.' When Patricia Eykyn remarried, 'out of discretion to her new husband' she passed on all her former husband Stephen's letters and diaries to their daughter, Joy. But Joy, sadly, destroyed all Gordon-Smith's papers, including this precious evidence.[52]

Such bitter disappointments are legion in historical research.

The newspaper cutting provided to back up the Gordon-Smith story comes from the *Mail on Sunday* for 20 November 1988, entitled 'The King Could Have Saved the Tsar'. In it Patricia Eykyn confirmed that 'though he never told me many details', the 'real reason' her husband was sent to Russia 'was to *bring* [my italics] the Tsar and his family to England' – perhaps suggesting a role as escort. But there is a fly in the ointment: when asked by the *Mail* about his role in this alleged mission, Lord Bruntis-field denied all knowledge of it, adding however that 'if influential people in Britain had seriously attempted to get the Tsar out, I am pretty sure they would have succeeded'.[53]

Studying these two flimsy accounts of Gordon-Smith's alleged mission, and setting aside the obvious discrepancies, he would appear, at the very least, to have had all the right credentials. At this time the British SIS mission in Russia numbered only about ten personnel and consisted mainly of desk officers and security personnel validating travel documents and watching border crossings; it is logical therefore that highly experienced military men such as Gordon-Smith, based in northern Russia, would be called upon as back-up.[54]

Stephen Berthold Smith (without the Gordon, which was added during World War I to avoid confusion with so many war-dead named Smith) was born in Russia in 1890 to a wealthy English grain exporter who had married a Russian and settled in Taganrog. The family had been extremely well connected, and during his childhood he had met several members of the Imperial Family. He was bilingual and also spoke fluent French and German. After studying at Cambridge he enlisted with the 8th South Staffordshire regiment on the outbreak of World War I, but was invalided out with trench foot in 1915. 'I can't march, but I can fly,' he said defiantly, and joined the Royal Flying Corps. He soon got his wings and in around November 1916, no doubt due in part to his language skills, he was seconded to the Russian Air Force.[55] He was sent with a group of airmen to assemble and test British aircraft transported by sea to the Russians via Archangel and from there by rail to Moscow. Based at the flying school of the Moscow Imperial Aeronautical Society, the RFC team trained Russian pilots and mechanics, and in March 1917 Gordon-Smith was awarded the Order of St Stanislav, third grade, for his 'achievements in preparing the aircraft and aeronautic equipment from Britain'.[56] In June 1917, the RFC team was sent to the south-western front in Galicia. It was attached to the XIth Army during Kerensky's summer offensive, but by the autumn the collapse of discipline in the Russian army in the wake of the Bolshevik Revolution prompted a decision to bring the British pilots home. Gordon-Smith was back in England by the beginning of 1918, but soon afterwards was reposted to the British Supply Mission to Russia (known as Rusplycom) based at Archangel.

Setting aside the impossibility of any attempted airborne rescue of the Romanovs from Tsarskoe Selo in 1917 – when Gordon-Smith was with the RFC in southern Russia (though the myth persists that the RFC were in some way involved in such a plan) – his rescue mission only makes sense if we look at it in terms not of 1917, but of the spring of 1918 when he was sent back to Russia. This chimes with the fact that Robert Bruce Lockhart, with whom he travelled there, was till January 1918 back in England before he returned to Russia as head of an unofficial British mission to the new Bolshevik government in Moscow. Was it a coincidence that Victor Warrender, who travelled with them, was also returning to Russia to rejoin the staff of the British Supply Mission? And how do we explain the award to Warrender of the Military Cross, gazetted on 3 June 1918 at the age of just eighteen? This was presented to him personally by King George V in a Birthday Honours Ceremony at Windsor, 'for distinguished services rendered in connection with Military Operations in Russia' – yet his Medal Card at the National Archives bears no mention of his Russia service.[57]*

From his base at Archangel, Gordon-Smith could have been called on to travel across to the Gulf of Ob to take part in a rescue mission based on the Lied plan. But the distance was considerable: 1,400 miles or so. By sledge it would have taken weeks, and no British aircraft – if there were any based at Archangel at that time – was capable of flying that far without numerous stops. Be that as it may, from the Gulf of Ob the Romanovs would presumably have been boarded onto a British torpedo boat (perhaps one of those operating in the North Sea Patrol Flotillas in the Kara Sea area) sent specially for them. Unless, of course, Vickers had been persuaded to offer one of their own boats after all. These boats operated at a top speed of twenty-six

---

* It is a matter of considerable regret that it has proved impossible to uncover any kind of paper trail on the role of Warrender, aka Lord Bruntisfield, in this story, despite Patricia Eykyn's conviction that he was indeed involved.

knots and were the next fastest to the bigger destroyers, but far more manoeuvrable, so they were ideal for a rescue at speed. Alternatively, Gordon-Smith might have been designated to lead a reception party sent to look after the Romanovs, once installed at the safe house at Murmansk. The mention of supplies and transport, and the bribing of household staff by his grandson, might well make sense in this context.

The fact remains that Rusplycom, to which Gordon-Smith was seconded in 1918, and which was overseen in London by Mitchell-Thompson (whom Lied had been taken to meet in March), was by now increasingly involved in secret work. This involved preventing British military, industrial and food supplies already stockpiled in the northern Russian ports of Archangel and Murmansk from falling into the hands of the advancing Germans (or the Bolsheviks, who by February were beginning to gain a foothold in the area). By this time, Rusplycom probably had the biggest viable group of British personnel based in or near Russia, with the exception of the Royal Navy's submarine flotilla and its Armoured Car Division. With British relations with the unpredictable and devious Bolsheviks becoming strained, the work of Rusplycom's personnel in Russia became increasingly clandestine (some of them eventually joining the SIS).[58]

Nevertheless, in the spring of 1918, much as we would like it to be otherwise, British officialdom was not preoccupied with a Romanov rescue. It was far more concerned with the bigger commercial, financial and industrial objectives of opening up the Russian markets after the Bolshevik takeover. And their efforts were intensified when, on 3 March 1918 – the very day that Jonas Lied arrived in London for his series of meetings – after three and a half months of diplomatic wrangling at Brest-Litovsk, Trotsky signed a peace treaty with Germany. In so doing he pulled Russia out of the war and ceded great swathes of Russian territory in the Baltic, Ukraine and Caucasus to the Germans. The very real prospect of German dominance over a still-fractured Russia, further weakened by the spread of civil war, brought a new and serious turn to the situation. If Russian troops were pulled from the Eastern Front, the Germans could redirect their own army there to the war on the Western Front.

On 10 March the Bolshevik government moved the capital back to Moscow. Most foreign diplomats decamped soon afterwards for the safety of Vologda, leaving the British embassy in Petrograd with only a skeleton staff. With an ailing Sir George Buchanan sent home to England at the beginning of January (and not replaced as ambassador), who was there left in Russia to speak for the Romanovs via official British channels? Robert Wilton's warning of the previous December became even more telling: 'It is evident from the overtures made on their behalf by the Germans at Brest-Litovsk that the enemy intend to make use of [the former Imperial Family].' Many of the Russian monarchists were pro-German and fiercely anti-Bolshevik and would have supported German intervention in Russia and the restoration of a puppet monarchy.[59] But what exactly were the motives behind these German 'overtures' now being made on behalf of the Romanovs?

Chapter 9

'I Would Rather Die in Russia than Be Saved by the Germans'

When writing about his time in Russia, in retirement in the 1930s, the former French ambassador to Petrograd, Maurice Paléologue, never had any doubts as to who had been best placed to effect the safe evacuation of the Romanovs from Russia at the beginning of 1918. In his study of the two deposed emperors, *Guillaume II et Nicolas II*, published in Paris in 1935, he asserted that:

> One solitary person was capable of saving the tsar, the tsarina and their children: and that was Wilhelm. He had the means and, more than any other sovereign, he had the duty, as no other sovereign was as closely linked to the house of Romanov by such direct and intimate ties. Was he not the godfather of Alexey the Tsarevich?[1]

In support of his argument Paléologue cited a long-overlooked open letter written to Wilhelm by General Maxim Leontiev, commander of the Vyborg regiment – of which Wilhelm was honorary Commander in Chief – that had been published in Paris in 1918. Leontiev had been present during the Kaiser's meeting with the Romanovs on board the *Shtandart* at the Baltic harbour of Paldiski in Estonia in 1912, where Wilhelm had played the benevolent uncle, showering the Romanov children with gifts. In his letter Leontiev reminded Wilhelm of the affection he had shown at that time to his godson Alexey:

Do you remember how on that very first day of your arrival, when you were sitting at table on the *Shtandart* next to the Empress, a playful and vivacious little boy rushed into the dining room, and on seeing such a large gathering of unfamiliar people shyly clutched onto his mother. You beckoned him to you, sat him on your knee, joked with him and stroked his head.[2]

And how attentive the Tsar's four young daughters had all been towards Wilhelm; and how all five children had hung on his every word. 'Were they not right,' Leontiev asked, 'to see in you a guest and a friend, not only of Russia, as you then tried to present yourself, but also a true friend of their own family?' Leontiev proceeded to berate Wilhelm about his many failings as a professed friend of Russia, but what concerned him most of all was this question: 'What did you do to protect this family? ... Why did you not come to their aid? One word from your ambassador, Mirbach, to put pressure on the Bolshevik government would have been sufficient. You could have saved them and you didn't!"[3]

It has long been claimed that there was a special, secret clause in the Treaty of Brest-Litovsk, under which the Romanovs would be set free by the Bolsheviks and allowed to leave Russia. To date no evidence has emerged, however, to support this, or Robert Wilton's claim that the Germans made any 'overtures' on their behalf during the Brest-Litovsk negotiations. The German historian Kurt Jagow fiercely rebutted Paléologue's assertion that Germany could have included such a clause. They would hardly have risked intervening on behalf of the sovereign of an enemy state who had just been deposed, he argued, 'while simultaneously negotiating for a peace with his deposers'. 'The monarchist question was like a red rag for the Bolshevists'; why would Germany risk such a move, when Nicholas's own allies had failed to help him?[4] Certainly hopes were raised, after the failure of the British to act in the spring of 1917, that Russia's peace with Germany would ensure that the Romanovs were brought to safety. By the spring of 1918 the Russian monarchists had certainly come to the conclusion that the only hope for saving the family lay in making an appeal to the Kaiser. Indeed, many of them had been, and remained, pro-German before and during the war.

For Lenin, the decision finally to capitulate to the Kaiser had been a grudgingly pragmatic one: the Russian fight on the Eastern Front had collapsed and the Germans were advancing on Russia with frightening ease. Without a peace deal his government would be finished.[5] Wilhelm was equally pragmatic: he had no affection for the Bolsheviks, whom he despised as 'robber chieftains', and found dealing with them extremely distasteful. They were all 'swine' and 'Jew boys' in his eyes and he made no attempt to conceal his utter, rabid contempt.[6] But he had to work with them in order to achieve the German domination of Russia that he aspired to and his dream of the eventual division of the old empire into 'four "Tsardoms": the Ukraine, eastern Caucasus, Siberia and Rump Russia', all of which would serve German industrial and economic interests.[7] Supporting the Bolsheviks, and in so doing enabling the spread of German influence south through the oil-rich Caucasus and Russia's vast grain-growing areas, was infinitely preferable to helping the Whites in a restoration of the monarchy.[8] Yet how different things might have been if in the spring of 1918 the Germans had pursued Supreme Commander General Ludendorff's plan to go all out for an overthrow of the Bolsheviks and enlist the support of the Cossacks and other White and monarchist groups in introducing, as Robert Wilton wrote, a 'more agreeable form of government'.[9] Instead, Lenin's Soviet government was allowed a valuable breathing space in which to consolidate its control, a fact that eventually sealed the fate of the Romanovs.

Nicholas and Alexandra would have been horrified, had they known of the hopes raised in Russia that the Germans would save them. The Brest-Litovsk Treaty was, for them, a wicked betrayal of their beloved country, which would reduce it to a client state of the German Empire. 'To think that *they* called Her Majesty a traitress!' Nicholas exclaimed. 'Who is the real traitor?'[10] Well might Nicholas mourn, for the treaty initiated a brutal dismemberment of the Russia over which he and his Romanov forefathers had ruled for 300 years. In many respects Russia had been 'almost reduced to the old frontiers of Muscovy under Ivan III'.[11] For a soldier of honour such as he, this triumph for Prussian militarism was a shameful abandonment of his wartime allies. It was a 'disgrace for Russia' amounting to suicide, tutor Gilliard heard him say, 'and it would not save the Bolsheviks from ruin'.[12]

Alexandra felt exactly the same. In captivity she had never ceased to rail against her cousin Wilhelm and his 'petty nature', with the utmost venom.[13] 'I never thought he could sink down as far as coming to terms with the Bolsheviks,' she exclaimed. 'What a disgrace!'[14] All thought of being offered protection by the Germans was abhorrent to her. When Prince Dolgorukov read out a newspaper article alleging that the treaty had this secret clause guaranteeing the safety of the family, Alexandra was heard to say in French (so that their captors would not understand), 'I would rather die in Russia than be saved by the Germans!'[15]

Many years later Pierre Gilliard recalled that 'The Treaty of Brest-Litovsk had been a blow from which the Emperor had never recovered.' Russia, for Nicholas, represented 'above all the *muzhik* [the Russian peasant] and the army ... Before and after his abdication he had had one solitary preoccupation: the future of his country; one solitary hope: the victory of Russia's armies.' For the first time Gilliard heard Nicholas expressing regret that he had allowed himself to be persuaded to abdicate:

> Brest-Litovsk had so profoundly affected and depressed him that his health was greatly undermined by it. He aged considerably after this. We all noticed it at Tobolsk: his complexion became pallid, there were large bags under his eyes and his beard went very grey.[16]

During his darkest days in captivity Nicholas had continued to hold out hope for Russia. But now all seemed lost. Brest-Litovsk marked the point at which he fell into a deep depression and a fatalistic acceptance of whatever life threw at him thereafter.

This was accompanied by a stronger resistance – if not dread – in both him and Alexandra to the idea of leaving Russia at all: 'more than anything they feared being sent away somewhere abroad' (i.e. Germany), recalled Klavdiya Bitner, the girls' tutor at Tobolsk.[17] In conversation with Commandant Pankratov earlier that year, one of the Romanov sisters had commented that there was talk in the papers that the new Constituent Assembly, when established, would 'send us all abroad'. She had been disturbed by this suggestion: 'It would be better if they sent us someplace else in Siberia but not abroad,' she said. Pankratov was surprised: 'You don't want to leave Russia?' 'It's best if we stay in Russia,' Tatiana had replied. 'Let them send us deeper into Siberia.'[18]

After Brest-Litovsk there was a significant shift regarding the diplomatic efforts being undertaken to protect the Romanovs or get them out of Russia, as well as a change of internal Russian policy in relation to their future. The struggle between the government in Moscow and some of the militant regional Soviets deepened, as the latter began trying to dictate how the Romanovs should be dealt with. On 4 March, 'In response to concern that Nicholas would become the puppet of the Germans', the regional committee of the Soviet of the Kolomensk district of the Moscow region was the first of numerous hardline groups to send in demands for official state retribution to be carried out against the Imperial Family. In their telegram they 'unanimously' demanded the 'prompt annihilation of the entire family and relatives of the former tsar' in order to pre-empt any attempt by 'the German and Russian bourgeoisie' to re-establish a tsarist regime.[19]

In this heightened atmosphere, concerns for the family were once more being raised abroad. On 12 March, King Christian of Denmark received such alarming reports from Harald Scavenius, his ambassador in Petrograd, that he felt he must renew his appeals to Wilhelm to 'intercede in the fate of the deposed monarch and his family'. Their safety was seriously threatened, he telegraphed, as well as that of Nicholas's Danish mother and her daughters Olga and Xenia and son-in-law Sandro in Crimea, who were now suffering considerable 'want and hardship' as well as being 'completely at the mercy of the capriciousness of swarming gangs of sailors'.[20] The Germans were the only power with any influence over the Soviets, and Christian urged the Kaiser to do something.

We have no access to Scavenius's private reports to King Christian, as the Danish Royal Archives are off-limits, but the fact that intelligence had reached Scavenius in Petrograd on the plight of the Romanovs in Tobolsk and Crimea is confirmed by a letter written by Scavenius's secretary, Esther Aksel-Hansen, to her family:

> The Imperial Family is suffering a great deal. It looks like they are close to starving and are being molested in all sorts of ways without any sort of protection. It would be amazing if they were to come out of it all alive.[21]

There was good reason for this heightened sense of alarm: Nicholas's brother Mikhail, who had been planning his escape out of Russia via Finland, had recently been arrested at Gatchina and sent to Perm, 600 miles west of Tobolsk. At the Governor's House in Tobolsk the guards were 'in a very vicious mood'. No one could 'predict the fate that may befall the Tsar and Tsarina, as well as the children'. 'I am turning to you,' King Christian told Wilhelm, 'in case it might be possible for you to do something for the improvement and safety of the possible fate of persons who are so close to me.'[22]

In response to Christian's telegram, on 15 March Wilhelm assured him that his message had 'made a profound impression' on him:

> I completely understand that the future fate of the Imperial Family that is so close to you fills you with the greatest anxiety. Despite all the affronts and great harm that my fatherland and I have suffered from this once friendly quarter, I cannot withhold my purely humanitarian concern for the Imperial Family, and were it in my power, I would willingly

do my part to ensure that the Imperial Family is granted a secure and dignified lot.[23]

But like his cousin George, the British king, Wilhelm could not be prompted to act purely out of family feeling. 'Immediate assistance,' he said was 'impossible in the present circumstances'. Why? For precisely the same reasons that had influenced the change in the British position: undemocratic political interference in the government of another country. Any direct intervention made by Wilhelm would 'be misconstrued by the Russian government' and 'could possibly be interpreted as meaning our intention was to bring about the reinstatement of the Czar'. Wilhelm was sorry, but 'for that reason, I can unfortunately see no possibility of offering assistance'. The best option, he concluded, would be for the 'Nordic kingdoms collectively to approach the Russian government. As neutral powers, it would be much more likely for them to be believed to be solely acting from humanitarian motives rather than pursuing any political interests.'[24]

The German envoy to Copenhagen, Count Ulrich von Brockdorff-Rantzau, passed the Kaiser's telegraphed response to the King two days later. Christian was surprisingly accepting: he thanked Wilhelm for the 'human understanding' he had shown for 'the fate of my unhappy relatives … from the bottom of his heart'. 'I am convinced,' he told the Kaiser, 'that regarding this matter you would always be prepared to do *everything in your power*, but I also understand the important reasons that at present prevent you from undertaking anything in this matter.' He would, meanwhile, do his best to take up Wilhelm's suggestion.[25]

It has to be emphasised that Christian's primary concern was still his aunt in Crimea, and although his efforts for the Imperial Family in Tobolsk might have been put on hold after Wilhelm's reassurance, those for Dagmar continued. In April, Christian and Prince Valdemar sent a secret telegram to Scavenius in Petrograd asking him to try and organise the urgent evacuation of Dagmar and her other Romanov relatives, now incarcerated together at a villa at Djulber, across the Black Sea from Yalta, to Constanza in Romania, and 60,000 rubles were set aside for this purpose.[26] Behind the scenes there had been no let-up in Harald Scavenius's efforts on behalf of the various members of the Romanov family. In Petrograd he had acted swiftly after Grand Duke Mikhail's arrest, to arrange the secret evacuation of his seven-year-old son George to safety. Scavenius was closely involved in humanitarian work with POWs and managed to smuggle young George and his English nanny, Miss Neame, onto a train repatriating German prisoners of war to Germany, now that hostilities had ceased. Posing as mother and son on false passports, and accompanied by a Danish officer, on 25 April they left Petrograd by train and reached the safety of the Danish embassy in Berlin. The Kaiser was fully aware of the rescue and turned a blind eye to the fact that Miss Neame was an enemy alien, allowing her and George to be taken on to Copenhagen. In 1919, after staying for some time at the Danish royal family's Sorgenfri Palace, George settled in England.[27]

Since the end of 1917 the Bolsheviks had been aware of rumours – probably circulated by Boris Solovev and Father Vasiliev – about the mythical '300 officers' at Tobolsk who were plotting to free the Romanov family. It had no doubt prompted the arrest of Mikhail, and a closer guard over the Romanovs held in Crimea and Tobolsk. Wild talk was circulating in Petrograd that Nicholas – and even some of his family – had made their escape from the Governor's House. In response, the Council of People's Commissars had, as early as 29 January 1918, minuted the transfer of Nicholas back to Petrograd for trial, as a topic for urgent discussion.[28]

People's Commissar of Justice, Isaac Steinberg, recalled that three weeks later – when the Germans had resumed their advance on Russia after the Brest-Litovsk talks had temporarily stalled – the subject was raised again. On 20 February 'Representatives of the Peasant Congress appeared at a session of the Commissars,' he wrote, 'and introduced a motion demanding that the czarist family be brought back from Tobolsk ... for public trial', arguing that such an act would be a morale-booster at this time of a renewed German threat.[29] It would be Steinberg's task to 'plan and stage this grandiose spectacle of right and retribution', but he argued vigorously against the idea:

> The monarchy was no longer a live issue with the people, and … a trial of the former Czar – however solemn and theatrical – would add neither joy nor courage … I warned that the Czar's long transport from Siberia might tempt the lynch-justice of fanatics or self-styled revolutionaries.[30]

All eyes in the room turned to Lenin, who – to Steinberg's surprise – agreed, saying that he 'doubted the timeliness of such a trial, that the masses were too preoccupied with other concerns, and that it would be well to postpone the matter'. Nevertheless, Steinberg was instructed to prepare the 'pertinent documents for future use'. That night, however, 'the issue was waived' and he was ordered, 'Do not pre-assign a place for the trial of Nicholas Romanov as yet.' Days later, Steinberg, as a member of the Socialist Revolutionary party who opposed the Brest-Litovsk Treaty, resigned in protest at his government's capitulation to Germany.[31]

In Tobolsk, persistent talk of monarchist plots continued to unsettle the local Soviet, prompting a flurry of telegrams to the Council of People's Commissars about their concerns. In response to the heightened danger of an attempted escape, and seeing monarchist conspiracies everywhere, hardline Bolsheviks were gathering in the town in anticipation of taking matters into their own hands.[32] Such were their fears of an escape that militant groups of local workers were monitoring all road and river routes out of Tobolsk – north downriver to Obdorsk, and south-east through Ishim and Tyumen province. Other workers had come out from Ekaterinburg to bar the roads from Tobolsk to Tyumen. At the village of Goloputovskoe, a cell of officers plotting to help the Romanovs were uncovered and summarily killed. All over the Tobolsk region rival bands of Bolshevik loyalists were lurking in an effort to winkle out potential monarchist liberators.[33] There was even talk in the Tobolsk Soviet of transferring the Romanovs and their entourage 'up the "mountain" to the prison' – the notorious Prison Castle inside the Kremlin on the hilltop over-looking the city, which had been used for incarcerating political prisoners under tsarism – and preparations were made to take them there.[34] With recent lapses in vigilance by the guards at the Governor's House, it is not surprising things came to a head. A telegram was sent to Lenin in Moscow by the Western Siberian Soviet about the security there, insisting that the present guard had become hostile and unmanageable. They were disloyal and should be replaced by Red Army guards sent by their own Soviet from Omsk. Extremists in the Ural Regional Soviet were equally eager to take control of the Imperial Family and transfer them to their own stronghold at Ekaterinburg – at that time 'perhaps the most vehemently Bolshevik spot in Russia'.[35]

On 23 March the prisoners at the Governor's House on Freedom Street were greeted by the one thing they had all been dreading: 'A detachment of over a hundred Red Guards has arrived from Omsk,' Pierre Gilliard noted in his diary. 'They are the first Maximalist [Bolshevik] soldiers to take up garrison duty at Tobolsk.' It was a bleak moment for everyone: 'Our last chance of escape has been snatched from us.'[36] The commissar accom-panying this new contingent insisted on inspecting the Governor's House, and on 30th he ordered that all the members of the entourage living in the Kornilov House across the street – bar the two doctors, Derevenko and Botkin – move in with the family, so that they could keep a better eye on them all. More alarming, however, was the announcement, under orders from Moscow, that four of the entourage – Tatishchev, Dolgorukov and the two ladies-in-waiting, Anastasia Hendrikova and Ekaterina Schneider – were now under arrest, along with the family, no doubt on suspicion of passing messages in and out and of col-luding with the monarchists.[37] Numerous other petty restrictions were being enforced at the house: the family's recreation periods outside in the yard were shortened and the servants were no longer allowed to move freely around the town. Worse, with the last of Kobylinsky's more sympathetic contingent of guards being sent away at the end of their term of duty – some of whom came to the Romanovs secretly in their rooms to say goodbye – the prisoners were increasingly deprived of what little moral support they had from their captors.

Soon a group of 400 Red Guards from Ekaterinburg arrived in town, intent on gaining supremacy over the Omsk contingent and control of the Governor's House. They proceeded to terrorise the locals and intimidate the guards at the house.[38] Nicholas noted in his diary on 10 April: 'By nightfall the guard had been doubled, the patrols reinforced and sentries posted in the street. There was talk of some passing danger for us in this house and the need to move to the archbishop's house on the hill.'[39] Tension was riding high throughout the city, particularly now that the local Soviet had been taken over by the Bolsheviks, following elections in April. By the middle of the month, the situation was so volatile that there was a danger of armed clashes breaking out between these aggressive rival groups. Fearing that monarchists would try to liberate the Imperial Family, they were repeatedly demanding that they should assume custody of the Romanovs.[40]

Meanwhile, in Moscow on 1 April a decision was made to deal with the rivalry between the Omsk and Ekaterinburg Red Guards by sending a supplementary detachment of 200 men to Tobolsk, specially selected by the Central Executive Committee 'to increase the watch over the prisoners ... reinforce the guards, and, should the possibility arise, to immediately transport all the arrested to Moscow'.[41] It was signed by Yakov Sverdlov, who, as Lenin's right-hand man, was now taking executive control of the Romanovs. Sverdlov, who had worked as a political agitator in the Urals during the 1905 Revolution, liaised directly with the Bolsheviks of Ekaterinburg and Omsk, informing them about the 'Special Purpose Detachment' that Moscow was now sending to secure the 'transfer of all the arrested'. However, in the space of five days the Central Executive Committee changed its mind about a transfer to Moscow, and Sverdlov sent word that the family was to be sent 'to the Urals' for the time being. This may well have been a response to pressure from the Ekaterinburg and Omsk militants who, mistrustful that a transfer to Moscow might lead to the Romanovs being allowed into exile, were insistent that they remain in the Urals, where they could keep an eye on them.[42]

Sverdlov was adamant, however, in choosing his own man to command the special detachment about to be sent from Moscow. His party name was Vasily Yakovlev, though his real name was Konstantin Myachin, and he had grown up at Ufa in Western Siberia. From 1905 he had become well known to Sverdlov and Lenin as a party worker, and his loyalty and ruthlessness were undoubted: 'Starting with my first speech, bullet and a soaped rope dogged my heels,' Yakovlev wrote in his later biographical notes.[43] Under constant threat of arrest for his seditious activities, involving expropriations, terror, sabotage and murder, he fled Russia in 1909 and lived in Brussels, before moving to Canada. He returned to Russia after the February Revolution and resumed his work for the party in the Urals, based in his home town, and came to know Tobolsk and Ekaterinburg well. On returning to Moscow in early 1918 he became the Bolshevik commissar responsible for the telegraph and telephone stations and was a founder member of the Cheka (Secret Police).[44] In the spring of 1918, and now promoted to the Central Executive Committee, Yakovlev was unexpectedly called in to see Sverdlov. Trusting implicitly to Yakovlev as a dedicated party man, Sverdlov informed him that he would be left entirely to his own initiative, but must deliver the Romanovs alive to their ultimate destination, whatever location was finally decided upon.[45]

A Central Executive Committee memorandum of 6 April confirmed the decision to transfer 'all those under arrest' to the Urals, and in an additional handwritten directive to Alexander Beloborodov, chair of the Ural Regional Soviet, on 9 April, Sverdlov sent confirmation that it was Yakovlev's task to 'settle [Nicholas] in Yekaterinburg for now'.[46] This was a provisional arrangement, pending an eventual transfer of Nicholas to Moscow for a public trial, but Sverdlov did not make that explicit at the time. For now, Yakovlev was to personally deliver Nicholas and his family to either Beloborodov or Filipp Goloshchekin, the regional military commissar for the Urals (who was a close personal friend and fellow Bolshevik, he and Sverdlov having been in exile together in Siberia). This temporary measure had been intended to remove the Romanovs from the reach of the monarchists, by placing them in a location that was fiercely Bolshevik and that would provide a far more secure prison.[47] Sverdlov sent instructions that the Ekaterinburg Bolsheviks, in collaboration with the local Cheka, were to offer Yakovlev their full cooperation. 'Decide for yourselves whether to place him [Nicholas] in prison or to outfit some mansion,' he wrote. 'Do not take him anywhere outside Yekaterinburg without our direct order.'[48] But Sverdlov had clearly underestimated the long-held determination of the rival renegade elements from Ekaterinburg and Omsk to be the arbiters of the fate of the Tsar, and the problems this would create for Yakovlev.

A pall of gloom descended over the Governor's House when the ominous news was delivered on 22 April that a 'commissary with extraordinary powers' had just arrived in town with his own special detachment of soldiers to take charge of the prisoners. His arrival, wrote Gilliard, was 'felt to be an evil portent, vague but real'.[49] Alexander Ievreinov, who was still living undercover in Tobolsk, found out from an informant that Yakovlev had been ordered to fulfil his mission within the next three weeks. There was also much talk that the Tsar would be taken away, on the orders of the Germans, and the monarchy restored.[50]

Yakovlev, who made his first visit to the Governor's House on 25 April, arriving 'dressed in a sailor's uniform and armed to the teeth', was a striking, fine-featured man of thirty-two with jet-black hair and a thin stylish moustache. Kobylinsky remembered him later as 'taller than average, thin, but strong and muscular'. 'He gave one the impression of being very energetic.' He also appeared well educated – cultured even, according to Dr Botkin – and spoke French.[51] Less endearing was his subordinate Alexander Avdeev, a thuggish commissar from Ekaterinburg who had formerly worked as a locksmith. Kobylinsky found him 'dirty and uncouth', and the family would come to loathe him for his boorishness.[52]

Throughout his dealings with Nicholas the new commissar was extremely polite, to the point of being respectful; 'he talked to the Emperor standing all the time at attention and actually addressed him several times as "Your Majesty",' Dr Botkin noted.[53] Yakovlev showed Kobylinsky 'all his papers, mandates and secret instructions' signed by Lenin and Sverdlov, and announced that he would be taking Nicholas away at 4 a.m. on 27 April but, despite repeated requests for clarification, he insisted that he did not yet know their ultimate destination; he would be informed en route.[54]

Yakovlev's original orders had been to remove the whole family from Tobolsk, but on 11 April, before his arrival, Alexey had had a serious attack of pain and bleeding – the result of a strained groin – and had been confined to bed for days on end. It was such a disappointment, after he had been well for so long: it was the worst attack he had experienced since a near-fatal one at Spala in Poland in 1912.[55] As soon as he saw how seriously ill the boy was, Yakovlev realised that it would be impossible to transfer him until the spring, when he could go by river rather than the arduous journey overland on barely passable roads, and he informed Moscow. On 24 April word came back on the telegraph from Sverdlov: Yakovlev was to remove the Tsar with immediate effect. Yakovlev knew that he needed to do so quickly, without further inflaming the rival claims for control by the Omsk and Ekaterinburg contingents. And it was made all the more pressing by the onset of the spring thaw causing the road from Tobolsk to the railway at Tyumen to be heavy going.[56]

Nicholas's response, when told that he alone was to be taken away, was one of horror; his first thought was that he was to be taken to Moscow and there compelled by the Bolshevik government – at Germany's behest – to sign the Brest-Litovsk Treaty. 'I'll see my hand cut off ... before I do it,' he exclaimed.[57] 'Perhaps they are taking him out of the country!' Alexandra exclaimed with alarm, to which Nicholas responded despairingly, 'Oh, God forbid! Anything except to be sent abroad!'[58] He and Alexandra remained convinced that the ultimate destination was Moscow, a conviction that was encouraged by Kobylinsky.

'Be calm,' Yakovlev entreated, 'I am responsible with my life for your safety. If you do not want to go alone, you can take with you any people you wish.'[59] It took all the persuasive powers of Kobylinsky to convince the family that they could not resist Yakovlev's demands. For many hours they debated who should go, and who should stay with the sick Alexey. Alexandra was distraught at the suggestion that she and Nicholas be separated; her maternal instincts had always been to remain with her sick boy, but this time her fears for her husband were far greater. Anxious that Nicholas might be browbeaten without her, after much agonising she opted to travel with him. The four sisters, always so protective of their mother, were insistent that one of them should travel with her as companion. It was agreed that Maria should go, while the capable Tatiana should be left to hold things together at the Governor's House. Olga, sadly, was in poor health; and the youngest, Anastasia, was needed to keep up morale. The hope was that in about three weeks' time they would follow on from Tobolsk with Alexey, when he was better.[60]

Those last few days of April 1918 had been the bleakest time yet endured by the Romanov family and their entourage in their fourteen months of captivity: 'We are all in a state of mental anguish,' wrote Pierre Gilliard on 24 April:

We feel we are forgotten by everyone, abandoned to our own resources and at the mercy of this man [Yakovlev]. Is it possible that no one will raise a finger to save the Imperial Family? Where are those who have remained loyal to the Czar? Why do they delay?[61]

As Nicholas, Alexandra and their daughter Maria packed to leave, it would seem that their monarchist rescuers had failed them. What now, as they prepared for incarceration in a new, unknown and far more forbidding environment?

Since the beginning of 1918, Russian monarchists had in fact renewed their efforts to come to the aid of the Romanovs, notably the Pravyi Tsentr (Right Centre) group of former tsarist officials, industrialists and politicians, in which Markov II was involved. It was led by former Agriculture Minister, Alexander Krivoshein, and a former Prime Minister, Alexander Trepov, and they had been closely monitoring the situation in Tobolsk. Many of the group had wanted to establish a constitutional monarchy after the revolution in February 1917, and after Brest-Litovsk still hoped to enlist German support for a restoration. At a meeting in January with another Right Centre member, Dmitri Neidgart, Count Benckendorff had expressed his concern at the lack of news from Tobolsk.

Early that year, a member of the group, Vladimir Shtein, had been selected to travel to Tobolsk to find out details of the Romanovs' current 'moral and material needs'.[62] He had managed to make contact with Tatishchev and Dolgorukov and returned with discouraging news that the family was suffering intimidation from their guards and serious food and money shortages.[63] On hearing the news in Moscow, the group rallied round and soon sent Shtein back to Tobolsk at the end of February with 250,000 rubles, which he managed to hand over to Tatishchev and Dolgorukov. In return, the Romanovs sent their thanks and small gifts of hand-sewn amulets made by Alexandra and the girls.[64] Because the situation for the family was becoming far more perilous, the group decided to send their own people permanently out to Tobolsk to keep an eye on things. But no sooner had two officers arrived there than Shtein, who was still in the town, sent word back that the Tsar and his family were to be taken away. It came in the form of a cryptic telegram, under the guise of discussion of Alexey's illness:

Doctors have demanded urgent journey to a health resort in the south. We are greatly perturbed by this demand. We consider the journey undesirable. Please send advice. Situation extremely difficult.[65]

Unaware as yet of the arrival of Yakovlev and his secret mission, the Right Centre in Moscow was both alarmed and baffled by the message, for they could not understand the reason for this sudden need for the Romanovs to leave Tobolsk. In response the group advised, 'Unfortunately we have no information to explain the reasons for such a demand. Not knowing the patient's situation and circumstances, it is very difficult for us to give a precise opinion, but we advise the journey is postponed if possible, and that you should only submit as a last resort, on the categorical insistence of the doctors.'[66]

Greatly alarmed by this unwelcome news, the monarchists had no other recourse than to appeal once more to 'the only power capable of easing the situation in which the family found itself and averting the danger that threatened them – the German embassy'.[67] Shortly before this second telegram was sent, full diplomatic relations between Russia and Germany had been restored, with Count Wilhelm von Mirbach, who had already been in Russia for some time, taking up his appointment as the new German ambassador to the Soviet government in Moscow on 23 April. At the same time his counterpart, Adolph Joffe, had arrived as Soviet ambassador to Berlin.

It was only now that the German position on the Romanovs finally became clear.[68]

No sooner was Mirbach installed than he received a request for a meeting from members of the Right Centre. The austere and formal Mirbach, an old-school diplomat from a family of devoted servants of the Hohenzollern Kaisers, seemed very aloof. At first he would have nothing to do with the Right Centre, refusing to engage with what he deemed the counter-revolutionary underground, but finally he agreed to receive Dmitri Neidgart. The meeting was brief and frosty, and inconclusive. 'Be calm,' Mirbach kept on insisting. 'We Germans have the situation well in hand and the Imperial Family is under our protection. We know what we are doing, and when the time comes, the Imperial German Government will take the necessary measures.'[69] Mirbach promised that he would put pressure on the Bolsheviks; he would not just ask, but would 'demand' that they improve the situation in which the Romanovs were being held.[70]

At this point the Right Centre did not yet know that Nicholas and Alexandra had already left Tobolsk. Soon afterwards, another telegram arrived from the monarchists: 'Had to submit to the doctors.'[71] Neidgart went straight back to Mirbach, who, as he later recalled, had placated him with further reassurances that he had not just 'demanded' that the Bolsheviks ensure the well-being of the prisoners, but that he had 'accompanied his demand with a warning'. Neidgart by this stage felt he had nothing to lose by taking matters to a more personal level. 'How did he [Mirbach] wish to be seen in Moscow?' he asked, 'as a dictator, an ambassador, or as a hostage to the Bolsheviks?'[72]

Having discussed the situation with Alexander Trepov, Neidgart then decided to enlist the help of Count Benckendorff in writing a more personal letter to Mirbach, appealing for German help in protecting the Imperial Family.[73] There was good reason for this choice: Benckendorff was of German extraction; he had known Mirbach before the war, and his sister was a close friend of Mirbach's sister. Neidgart and Trepov travelled to Petrograd to see Benckendorff, who was now living on the Millionnaya, and together they agreed the contents of the letter. Describing it later to investigator Sokolov, Trepov emphasised that they were careful that it was not pleading and contained no political overtones, emphasising instead the purely humanitarian impulse behind their request and their devotion to the Imperial Family.

In the letter, Benckendorff reminded Mirbach that 'in the present circumstances in Russia, only the Germans were capable of taking effective measures to achieve the wished-for conclusion. For this reason if they were able to save the life of the Sovereign and his family, then they should do so out of a sense of honour.'

Benckendorff asked also that the letter should be 'brought to the personal notice of Wilhelm II so that the responsibility should be entirely his, should the Russian Imperial Family perish, because it would be the Germans – the only people who could save them – who had failed to take immediate and drastic measures'.[74] Returning to Moscow, Neidgart delivered the letter to the German embassy. Relations between the Right Centre monarchists and the Germans eased thereafter; Count Benckendorff was confident that the letter would be acted upon and that the group should be 'completely reassured'.[75]

Not only had Benckendorff appealed directly to Mirbach, but now he also turned to the Swedes. He went to see their Moscow envoy, General Edvard Brändström, who in turn described the situation that the Imperial Family was enduring to King Gustav on 27 April as 'desperate'. Gustav immediately summoned Albert von Kienlin, the German-legation secretary in Stockholm, to express his concern. 'The royal personages were exposed to the derogatory treatment of the Red Guards and were suffering all kinds of hardship,' he told him, and 'because of the royal heir's repeated attacks of illness [these] were even harder to endure'.[76]

Kienlin reported on Brändström's appeal to the Swedish king in a telegram to Berlin on 7 May, adding that Mirbach had declined Brändström's request for him to intervene in Moscow, saying it was too diplomatically sensitive an issue. This suggests that Mirbach's reassurances to the Right Centre monarchists had been hollow and were intended only to deflect their repeated calls for action. King Gustav had therefore instructed Kienlin to ask the Kaiser to 'help work towards an improvement of the situation of the Czar and his family *through Joffe* [the new Soviet ambassador to Berlin] and pointed out that the King of England once took a similar step with the Kerensky government'. Kienlin concluded his telegram by remarking that King Gustav was 'intending to have similar ideas broached via Brändström with the Russian representative Vorovsky' in Stockholm.[77]

When this despatch reached Berlin, Kaiser Wilhelm, who had an inordinate fondness for adding his own outraged interjections on all German Foreign Ministry documents submitted for his scrutiny, inserted his own cynical, dismissive comments in the margin. With regard to the Jewish Soviet ambassador Adolph Joffe, he added that it *'would never cross my mind to have anything to do with the swine'*; and to the remark about King Gustav's appeals to Vatslav Vorovsky, he observed that this *'will be of no use at all'*. He also noted that any direct requests to the Soviets to improve the Tsar's situation would be *without success*; he was clearly convinced that such attempts were futile.[78]

However, the Kaiser was not without personal concern for one particular relative in Russia, which had already been transmitted to Mirbach. Alexander Krivoshein was told that during a private meeting with Count Dmitri Obolensky, another monarchist who had appealed to him, Mirbach had confided: 'In essence, the fate of the Russian tsar depends entirely on the Russian people. Our sole preoccupation now is the safety of the German princesses in Russia.'[79]

By 'German princesses' Mirbach was referring not just to the Tsaritsa Alexandra and her sister Ella (Grand Duchess Elizabeth), both princesses of Hesse, but also to Grand Duchess Vladimir, who was a princess of Mecklenburg, and Grand Duchess Konstantin, a princess of Altenburg. The Tsar's daughters were also considered to be German princesses through their mother. At a meeting with Commissars Lev Karakhan and Karl Radek on 10 May, marking the first official German intervention in the matter with the Soviets, Mirbach had been assured that 'the German princesses will be treated with every consideration' and 'would not be subjected to unnecessary petty annoyances or threats to their lives'.[80] But they made very clear that the fate of the Tsar (and probably his male heir, Alexey, by implication) was a political matter in which the Germans should not interfere.[81]

In this expression of concern for the German-born princesses still in Russia, Mirbach finally gave official voice to behind-the-scenes efforts that the Kaiser had made not long after the revolution the previous year, to secure the safety of his long-lost love, Ella. In April 1917 he had sent a message to her via Swedish envoy

Brändström, begging her to leave Russia at once and offering her safe passage to Germany. Brändström had called on Ella at the Kaiser's express wish, at her convent in Moscow, warning of the dangers of the anticipated Bolshevik takeover to come. As Ella's close friend and former mistress of the robes, Countess Olsufieva, recalled:

> The Swedish Minister, representing a neutral power was received by her, and urged her to follow the Emperor's advice. She listened attentively, and answered that she, too, believed that terrible times were at hand, but that she would share the fate of her adopted country, and would not leave her spiritual family, the Sisters of the Community. Then she rose and concluded the audience.[82]

Inevitably, news that the monarchists were busy lobbying the Germans in Moscow during April and May filtered back to London from the kings of the neutral countries, Gustav and Christian. But no new British ambassador had been sent to Petrograd since the return to England of Sir George Buchanan. Instead, it was the British consul Arthur Woodhouse, still at his post there after the majority of the embassy staff had left the city, who received the news that the Romanovs were now in serious difficulty, if not danger.

On 26 April 1918 the British Foreign Office ledger of 'Telegrams Received from Russia' noted a brief precis of an incoming signal from Consul Woodhouse. Headed 'Ex Imperial Family', it read:

> Ct Benckendorff has received pitiful account of condition of; asks that Mr Lockhart may be instructed to suggest modification of treatment.[83]

Robert Bruce Lockhart, recently returned to Moscow and now the most senior British diplomat in Russia, was to investigate the situation. Does this suggest that British officialdom was about to stir and do something, finally, to help the Romanovs, after turning an indifferent eye to them for so many months? When we went in search of the full text of the original 'Woodhouse Telegram' – as Phil Tomaselli and I came to refer to it – it was missing from the TNA file FO 371/3329, where it should have been located at sub-section 78031. We resisted jumping to the conclusion that the document had been redacted or destroyed, and began a determined search instead.

In the meantime, in Siberia in April 1918, Nicholas, Alexandra and Maria had set off on a very uncertain and frightening journey to Ekaterinburg, in the charge of an enigmatic Bolshevik commissar, to whom we must now return.

Chapter 10

'The Baggage Will Be in Utter Danger at All Times'

In the entire Romanov story there is no more enigmatic, elusive figure than Vasily Yakovlev. Debate has never ceased on his motives and whether or not he tried to subvert his mission and save the Romanovs. Whose side was Yakovlev really on? Was he a true and dedicated revolutionary, a loyal Bolshevik who followed to the letter his orders from Sverdlov? Or was he a secret monarchist who took matters into his own hands in order to try and get the Romanovs to safety? There has even been a third option, suggested by Victor Alexandrov and Summers and Mangold, among others, that he was a British agent sent on a dangerous rescue mission.[1]

In the light of the greater availability of documentary evidence from Russia, this last suggestion now seems absurd. There are, however, still some who persist in claiming that Yakovlev was a double agent working for the German High Command, who had come to take the Romanovs out to a German-occupied area of Russia and from there to safety. It is further alleged that this was all at the insistence of Count Mirbach, the German ambassador in Moscow. This has been a favoured argument in Russia since the Sokolov investigation into the Romanov murders published in 1925, perpetuated in the accounts of Bulygin, Kerensky, Melgunov and others. But according to the German historian and archivist Kurt Jagow, who made a close study of official German papers relating to the Romanov matter, the story is a 'fantasy', 'based solely on circumstantial evidence, which does not stand up to closer examination'.[2] There is simply no documentary trace of a serious German attempt to rescue the Romanovs in 1918, let alone one involving a high-level Bolshevik commissar at the behest of Mirbach.

Over the years the amount of speculation about, and mystification of, Yakovlev's role – much of it based on little or no hard evidence – has served only to unnecessarily overcomplicate the story of what happened after Nicholas, Alexandra and Maria left the Governor's House in the early morning of 26 April 1918. At this point, the Bolshevik government had not yet made a final decision about what they were going to do with them. But one thing had already been made clear: it was Yakovlev's task to ensure that they did not fall into the hands of one or other group of renegade Urals hardliners, out to wrest control of the Imperial Family and administer their own summary rough justice.

There has been considerable debate about whether Lenin wanted to use the Romanovs in a ransom trade-off between the British and the Germans – the figure of £500,000 has been much bandied about – involving mediation by the shadowy figure of the British spy Sidney Reilly. Reilly, the archetypal daredevil spook, seems to pop up with alarming regularity in various undercover plots involving Russia in World War I, but any claims that he had a role in such a mission were efficiently demolished by Andrew Cook in his biography of Reilly, *Ace of Spies*, in 2004.[3] As evidence here has already shown, neither the Germans nor the British were interested in getting their hands dirty in such a deal. They both had much more pressing military, economic and political interests than to be sidelined at this time by the emotive issue of the Romanovs. And neither side would have funded or masterminded a rescue of them that would bring accusations of interfering in Russian internal politics.

The simplest and most logical view – indeed, the only one that we can consider unless more evidence comes to light – is to take Yakovlev's mission literally, and to strip it of all the conflicting and confusing mythology that has been attached to it since 1918. In the run-up to the Romanov centenary in 2018, the State Archive of the Russian Federation (GARF) made available online for the first time a whole range of original Russian documents connected with the Romanov story. When one examines this primary evidence (some of which has already been translated and published), what emerges from the exchanges between Yakovlev in Siberia and Sverdlov in Moscow is in fact no mysterious subterfuge, but the extent to which Yakovlev in fact did his utmost to act according to instructions. It was his job to keep the 'baggage' safe and deliver it to Sverdlov's chosen people – the Ural Regional Soviet (URS).[4]

At 4 a.m. on the morning of 26 April a convoy of nineteen miserable-looking horse-drawn, springless tarantasses, and several carts full of luggage, set off on a journey of 155 miles south-west to Tyumen. It was an arduous journey, through wind, mud and rain along heavily rutted roads. It involved numerous changes of horses, delays to repair broken wheels and the dangerous crossing of the Irtysh and Tobol rivers, swollen with the thaw and spring rains.

Nobody in the convoy, other than Yakovlev, knew exactly where they were heading, beyond the railway station at Tyumen. But it is clear that he was proceeding on the expectation that the route and destination – Ekaterinburg – might have to be altered, depending on the rapidly changing situation in the region.[5] Yakovlev had every intention of fulfilling Sverdlov's directive to the letter, but already had doubts as to whether he could successfully do so. Detachments of Red Guards from Ekaterinburg were already on his tail, intent on attacking the convoy before it even got to the railway station at Tyumen.[6]

As far as Yakovlev was concerned, all these renegade groups were 'brigands'. The following morning he telegraphed Filipp Goloshchekin, military commissar of the Ural Regional Soviet, who should nominally have been in control of them, warning that they were little more than armed thugs who 'have only the single wish of destroying that baggage for which I was sent', before he could hand it over to Beloborodov and the URS.[7] He anxiously double-checked with Sverdlov whether he should continue on the 'old route' to Ekaterinburg as previously agreed, thinking it already too dangerous to stick to the plan of taking the Romanovs there.[8] He was right to be concerned; such was the single-mindedness of the Ekaterinburg Bolsheviks about overriding any orders from the URS and killing Nicholas en route that they had even covertly warned Yakovlev, before he left Tobolsk, not to sit next to the Tsar in the tarantass in case of attack. But Yakovlev had ignored the warning, 'in keeping with my goal of delivering everything intact', he informed Sverdlov.[9]

Eventually a reply came from Sverdlov agreeing about the danger of heading straight to Ekaterinburg at present; once on the train, Yakovlev should now divert instead south-east to Omsk and await further instructions when he got there. When the convoy arrived safely at Tyumen on 27th, with 'a squadron on horseback form[ing] a chain' around them, it was 9.15 p.m. Exhausted from their journey, Nicholas, Alexandra and Maria were hugely relieved to board the dirty sleeping compartment on the train that awaited them and fall into bed.[10]

Before they left Tyumen the next morning Yakovlev again warned Sverdlov that the Ekaterinburgers, with the exception of military commissar Goloshchekin, had only one desire: 'to finish off the baggage at all costs'; sooner or later the train would be ambushed. Having got Sverdlov to agree to the diversion to Omsk, he now offered an alternative contingency measure: to take the Romanovs on the southern loop out of Omsk back west to Simsky Gorny, a mining district on the River Sim in the province of Chelyabinsk, an area that Yakovlev knew well from his teenage years in Ufa.[11] 'There are good places in the mountains,' he explained in a telegraph to Sverdlov, 'that are exactly and purposely suited for this'; from a comment he made to his deputy Avdeev, it would seem he had in mind holing up with his charges somewhere at the vast Ust-Katav tram factory in the foothills of the Ural Mountains.[12] In order to underline that there was no intended subterfuge in this proposal – though many have since read it as such – Yakovlev reiterated that his suggestion was as much to prevent the Romanovs being rescued en route by right-wing monarchists as it was to protect them from the murderous Ekaterinburgers. 'I offer my services as the permanent commissar for guarding the baggage right up to the end,' he insisted.[13]

It did not take long for the Ekaterinburgers in pursuit of Yakovlev's convoy, and closely monitoring its progress, to notice when his train diverted east to Omsk instead of travelling on the preordained route west to Ekaterinburg. Any train heading to Omsk could pick up the junction there with the Trans-Siberian Railway and head on east, all the way to Vladivostok. Alternatively it could head back west on the southern loop of the Trans-Siberian, bypassing Ekaterinburg, all the way to Moscow.[14] When they heard this, the leaders of the Ural Regional Soviet smelled a plot to deny them the promised custody of the Romanovs. But if indeed there was a plot to stymie them, it was not one between Yakovlev and other mythical Romanov rescuers, but was in fact based on secret instructions from Sverdlov. On 28 April, in response to paranoid accusations of subterfuge telegraphed to him by the URS, Sverdlov sent instructions to the Omsk Soviet insisting: 'Follow only our orders [and] no one else's. I place full responsibility on you; conspiracy is necessary.'[15]

As Yakovlev and his charges headed for Omsk with an escort of 100 men, he insisted to Avdeev that taking the Romanovs there was the only guarantee of complete fulfilment of Sverdlov's orders. The Romanovs themselves were deeply disturbed when they noticed this change of route: 'Where will they take us after Omsk,' Nicholas noted in his diary, 'to Moscow or Vladivostok?'[16] Alexandra overheard the guards saying that the local Soviet in Omsk was now panicking that the train was going to take them out to the coast and on a boat to Japan.[17]

Having failed to intercept the convoy on its journey to Tyumen, Yakovlev's pursuers had now commandeered their own train and were in hot pursuit. Word had reached Yakovlev of plots to blow up his train near a railway bridge at Poklevskaya (now Talitsa). Local Soviets along the route had, apparently, been ordered to use extreme measures to stop the train and to ignore any official documents that Yakovlev was carrying.[18] As Yakovlev's journey with the Romanovs became ever more unpredictable, the chair of the URS was denouncing him to Sverdlov in Moscow: Yakovlev's behaviour, said Alexander Beloborodov, had been condemned by the URS as an 'outright betrayal of the revolution'. They were convinced that he was trying to 'transport the tsar [beyond] the bounds of the revolutionary Urals for reasons unknown'. It was the duty of all 'revolutionary organizations' in the area to 'stop the former tsar's train', arrest Yakovlev and his detachment and turn 'Nicholas Romanov' over to the regional Soviet in Ekaterinburg.[19]

After two days on the train and still with no safe destination in sight, Nicholas, Alexandra and Maria were now in great peril. Sverdlov had to act swiftly in order to bring the URS to heel, or Yakovlev's prisoners would perish at the hands of this renegade mob. On 29 April Sverdlov telegraphed the URS, reiterating in no uncertain terms: 'Everything done by Yakovlev … is in direct fulfilment of an order I have given … Undertake absolutely nothing without our agreement. Yakovlev is to be trusted completely. Once again, no interference.'[20]

Sverdlov was by now alarmed at the escalating situation. Fearing that Yakovlev's mission might end in a bloodbath and the deaths of his valuable charges, Sverdlov reluctantly ordered Yakovlev to turn the train round and head back to Tyumen. From there he was to continue his journey, as per the original plans, west to Ekaterinburg. Sverdlov reassured him that he had 'reached an understanding [with the] Uralites', who had 'guaranteed that they will be personally responsible for the actions of the regional men' and were now guaranteeing Nicholas's safety. 'Without question I submit to all orders from the center,' responded the loyal Bolshevik on the 29th. 'I will deliver the baggage wherever you say.'[21] But he emphasised that the danger was 'entirely well founded'. Yakovlev still recommended that he take his charges to Simsky Gorny, from where they could then travel on to Moscow rather than the hotbed of Ekaterinburg. 'The baggage will be in utter danger at all times' if he headed there, Yakovlev warned, adding that, once delivered, 'I doubt that you will be able to drag it out of there.' He was putting this warning on the record one last time, he added, to absolve himself and his deputy Avdeev 'from any moral responsibility for the future consequences'.[22] And with that, Yakovlev headed back north to Tyumen and then west to Ekaterinburg.

At 8 a.m. on 30 April 1918 Nicholas, Alexandra and Maria, and their small entourage, arrived at Ekaterinburg railway station to be greeted by a hostile crowd, who had been warned of their imminent arrival and were shouting for Nicholas to be brought out. 'Show us this bloodsucker,' they screamed. In response, Yakovlev told them he would 'show them machine guns' if they did not disperse. He was forced to take the train out to the goods station on the outskirts of the city to unload his prisoners, where they were handed over to Alexander Beloborodov and the members of his Ural Regional Soviet.[23] Finally, at 3 in the afternoon, the three prisoners were driven in an open motor car to their new place of incarceration – the Ipatiev House on Voznesensky Prospekt. It was, remarked Yakovlev later, extremely modest in comparison with the Governor's House at Tobolsk, 'which could have been a country palace by the size of its rooms and hall'. The new house was much smaller, the view from it blocked by a high wooden palisade, and very heavily guarded. Tobolsk might have been a place of tolerable house arrest, but Ekaterinburg was clearly going to be a prison. As they entered the courtyard gates it was the last sight that the former Tsar and Tsaritsa and their daughter Maria would have of the world outside, and it of them.

How ironic it is that it was neither the British nor the Provisional Government, nor even the Russian monarchists, but a man who appeared to be a punctilious Bolshevik commissar, who had saved three of the Romanov family from being murdered in April. Vasily Yakovlev undoubtedly acted decisively to keep them safe. He risked his own life, certainly not through any love of the former Tsar or any pro-monarchist sentiments, but out of a sense of political honour and duty. While he had never had any intention of spiriting the Romanovs away, one must concede that he had behaved impeccably and had fulfilled his orders to keep the Romanovs alive at all costs.[24]*

There is, of course, small comfort in Yakovlev's delaying of the inevitable. He bought Nicholas, Alexandra and Maria a few more weeks. During that time, until they were joyfully reunited with the rest of the family, only a few precious letters written by Maria and her mother got through to Tobolsk. Tatiana, Olga and Anastasia were intensely relieved when they finally received word from them. The agony of separation is only too painfully apparent: 'We miss our quiet and peaceful life in Tobolsk,' Maria told her sisters in a plaintive note of 10 May. They had all been contented with their life there and had made the most of it. But everything about the new house in Ekaterinburg seemed ominous and uncertain; the guards were more oppressive than ever and had searched all their belongings, confiscating what little money they had. 'It is difficult to write anything pleasant, for there is little of that kind here,' Maria wrote five days later. But there were always consolations, she added, trying to be positive: 'on the other hand, God does not abandon us, the sun shines and the birds sing. This morning we heard the dawn chorus. That was the only pleasant and agreeable event.' In response, messages of love and support

---

* Yakovlev's subsequent behaviour suggests, however, a growing ambivalence in his loyalties and a creeping disenchantment with the Bolsheviks. After serving as a commander on the Ural–Orenburg front in the Russian civil war, in the autumn of 1918 Yakovlev defected to anti-Bolshevik forces. He did so, he later claimed, because as a populist he was sickened by the savagery of the Bolshevik oppression of the peasantry, its raids on their lands and the famine that followed. In early 1919 he fled across the border to Manchuria, where he resumed his revolutionary work. Repenting his political sins in 1928 and denying that he was a counter-revolutionary, he made the grave error of returning from Harbin to Stalinist Russia; after spending five years in the Gulag, he was eventually rearrested and shot in 1928.

eventually arrived from Tobolsk: 'May Our Lord protect you, my dear beloved Mama and all of you,' Olga wrote to Alexandra, 'I kiss Papa, you and M. many times over. I clasp you in my arms and love you.'[25]

The Romanovs had been conveniently forgotten for near on nine months when, just as they were being taken away to Ekaterinburg, almost 3,000 miles away in London there was at last a sudden brief spurt of activity on their behalf. It was prompted by the arrival of that important telegram from British consul Arthur Woodhouse – sent from Petrograd on 26 April, but not received till 1 May.

From the moment my colleague Phil Tomaselli found the short entry in the incoming telegrams ledger and went in search of the actual 'Woodhouse Telegram' that appeared to have gone missing from the relevant file, we had been baffled as to why no other Romanov books had mentioned it till now. Phil has many years' experience working in World War I records at the National Archives and put the telegram's absence down to the vagaries of their faulty filing and indexing system. No conspiracy here; just plain bureaucratic inefficiency. He finally found the full text of that elusive telegram during one of his 'periodic trawls through mounds of paperwork', as he put it, not where it should have been in FO 371/3329/78031, but in FO 371/3938/22804.

Count Benkendorf lately Grand Court Marshal called yesterday afternoon Thursday begs me to telegraph following: he has received information privately that present condition of the ex-Imperial Family at Tobolsk is pitiful in the extreme. They are being persecuted in every way. He solicits your intercession on their behalf and trusts you will instruct Mr Lockhart to suggest modification of treatment of exiles especially as regards liberty within bounds. The young Prince is again in ill-health.[26]

The telegram was, of course, circulated to the King. On 3 May a short private note on headed paper was delivered to the Foreign Office, as follows:

Lord Cromer* has telephoned to say that The King is much distressed at the news contained in Mr Woodhouse's telegram No. 142, and hopes that the Foreign Office will telegraph without delay to Mr Lockhart instructing him to take up the matter with M. Trotsky and <u>insist</u> on better treatment.[27]

So what happened next? Did the head of the British mission to Moscow, Robert Bruce Lockhart,† make any representations to Trotsky about the Romanovs? If so, what did he report back to London? Predictably, the record is silent. There is nothing in Lockhart's memoirs or diaries, or any mention in those of Trotsky, or on the official Foreign Office record. But one can infer a great deal from the scribbled official notes appended to the front cover of file FO 371/3329/78031, added as each official who read it passed it on to the next.

In tiny, barely readable handwriting, a note on the front of the file observes: 'I fear intercession for the ex-Imperial Family will not do us much good with the Bolsheviks, and it is very unlikely to do them any good either … If known it is considered necessary to do something Mr Lockhart had better be given discretion as to what form the representations should take.'[28]‡

An urgent cipher telegram was therefore sent by Foreign Secretary Balfour to Lockhart in Moscow at 10.30 p.m. that same day, reiterating the King's concern at the news, but also adding a dampener:

---

* Roland Thomas Baring, 2nd Lord Cromer, was George V's assistant private secretary, subordinate to Stamfordham, 1916–20.

† Lockhart's position after his return to Russia in January 1918 was unofficial, as the first British envoy to the Bolsheviks. The ambassadorial position remained vacant until 1924; from 1917 to that date Britain had no ambassador in place.

‡ The comment is initialled 'EHC' and was almost certainly made by Edward Hallett Carr, who was then a fairly low-ranking FO official, having joined the service straight from Cambridge in 1916. He went on to become a distinguished historian and specialist on Russia, writing three volumes on *The Bolshevik Revolution*.

I entertain grave misgivings whether any representations you will make would not do more harm than good to these unhappy victims. But it is impossible for us here to form any opinion worth having on this point: and I must leave it to your tact and discretion to do what is in your power to diminish the hardships of their confinement.

In closing, Balfour for once expressed real apprehension about the family:

... If it were generally believed here that they were the victims of unnecessary cruelty the impression produced would be most painful.[29]

After the Lockhart telegram was sent, another observation was added at the very bottom of the file cover:

In view of the King's wishes [my italics] I think we must instruct Mr Lockhart to bring the matter before Mr Trotsky. We must be careful not to give away the source of our information.[30]

As there appears to be no official follow-up to this suggestion, one must assume that the British government in the end opted to let sleeping dogs lie. In Petrograd, meanwhile, the Danish ambassador Scavenius had taken a much tougher line in response to this news of the treatment of the Romanovs. Soviet ambassador Joffe's assurances to Berlin that 'nothing untoward would befall the Imperial Family' were worthless. Indeed, his statements in response to requests about the Imperial Family – in Tobolsk and in Crimea – had been 'full of exceptional cynicism', in Scavenius's opinion. In Crimea the Dowager and her family were practically starving and at the mercy of their sailor guards, who so far at least had 'not taken it into their heads to kill her', he wrote in a despatch to Copenhagen. 'Mr Joffe knows just as well as I,' Scavenius reported, 'that if such an idea had seized the guards, not a single soul could have prevented it happening.'[31]

Scavenius then went on to describe the situation being endured by the Imperial Family at Ekaterinburg, in their new and much more cramped conditions, in a residence 'surrounded by high palisades that completely block both house and windows up to the first floor':

> The windows that are not blocked by the palisades have been pasted over with newspaper. Their Majesties are thus living in the semi-darkness and without any ventilation, as they are not allowed to open the windows.

Their access to the outside, and to exercise, was severely curtailed; the food – mainly *kasha* [buckwheat porridge] and cabbage soup – was barely edible and served in dirty tin dishes; and they were often forced to eat with their guards. 'It is evident that the goal is to break Their Majesties down both physically and mentally, and this will have a disastrous effect.'[32]

This, concluded Scavenius – and one can hear the outrage in his words – 'is what Mr Joffe calls good and reasonable treatment'. The German government was clearly unaware of the truth of the conditions in which the Romanovs were living. Scavenius now urged that the Danish Foreign Minister ask King Christian to make a direct approach to the Kaiser:

> If there is a desire to save Their Majesties, then it is absolutely necessary to take steps to do so quickly. I have felt compelled to write this report, since I cannot take responsibility for not having informed those persons who are perhaps able to do something about the actual, unvarnished truth of the situation.[33]

The Danes might now have been raising serious concerns about the plight of the Romanovs, but what about King George? He had personally expressed his anxiety for his Russian relatives, albeit briefly, once before – after the abdication in March 1917. But how deep was his 'distress' now, and what was he prepared to do for them?

When investigating the possibility of the King having initiated some kind of last-ditch rescue plan in the spring of 1918, Summers and Mangold hit a wall that has continued to firmly bar the way to historians. It is clear from the comments on the cover of TNA 371/3329/78031 that the British government did not wish to be dragged into any overt intercession on behalf of the family, and was reluctant even to ask Lockhart to make representations to the Soviet government.

Throughout 1917, until the Bolsheviks seized power in October, there had appeared to be no direct threat to the Imperial Family. It was not until 20 May 1918 that the British government received confirmation from Consul Woodhouse in Petrograd – forwarding a telegram of the 10th from Thomas Preston, British consul in Ekaterinburg – that the Tsar had been brought to the town. 'He is living in a private house a few doors from the Consulate,' Preston confirmed:

Many rumours are current as to the reason of his arrival here, one, which is widely circulated, being that he is being held for a ransom by the local Bolsheviks against the Central People's Commissaries, or in order to enable the former to exercise pressure on the latter ...

The report to which most credence can be attached is that the ex-Emperor has been brought here in view of the fact that the Ural district, especially Ekaterinburg, is at the present time the most solid stronghold of Bolshevism in Russia.[34]

This report from the horse's mouth must surely have set alarm bells ringing in Britain about the heightened threat to the safety of the Imperial Family. But in the face of government intransigence, any possible talk of a rescue operation could only have taken place privately between the King and SIS agents, presumably without even the Prime Minister's knowledge. As Summers and Mangold reported in 1971 – in response to an original TV documentary that they made on the subject – any records of this 'were unlikely to be found in the sort of archives which became available to the public'.[35] It seems highly unlikely that, having officially refused to save the Imperial Family in June 1917, the British government in some way secretly colluded in an underground attempt to 'recoup the loss' a year later.[36]

The problem with seeking evidence of such a move is that what little we have to go on is linked to bogus claims of one or all of the Romanov family's miraculous survival. In order to argue their case, denialists and conspiracy theorists have come up with an assortment of scenarios involving eleventh-hour rescue from the Ipatiev House, and mysterious trains with their blinds down heading north-west to Perm, but without any solid evidence to back them up. Nevertheless, might King George have been so conscience-stricken as to act independently and make a private request for something to be done? He knew full well that he could not interfere in another government's business, but he was, as head of the armed services, in regular contact with the War Office and members of the Secret Service, and it is quite plausible that at some point he might, at the very least, have asked their advice.

Such a meeting was in fact alleged in the diaries of a now utterly discredited fantasist, an army officer named Colonel Richard Meinertzhagen. In a note in his diary for August 1918, he described an alleged conversation that he had had earlier in the summer with the King and Lord Trenchard, Chief of the Air Staff, at Buckingham Palace.[37] During it, Meinertzhagen claimed that King George had said 'he was devoted to the Tsar and could anything be done about rescuing them by air as he feared the whole family would be murdered'.[38] With his limited technical knowledge, it is not improbable that the King might have asked Trenchard about the possibility of an air rescue; but the logic of such a mission rescuing – one by one – all seven members of the Romanov family is absurd. The best aircraft on offer at the time by the RFC (two-seater fighter or reconnaissance aircraft, such as the Sopwith 1½ Strutter) had a maximum flying distance of about 300 miles before they would need to land and refuel.[39] Murmansk was 1,844 miles from Ekaterinburg, and Archangel considerably closer, at 1,162. To cover that kind of distance, any plane based with Allied forces there would have needed a vast, coordinated system of fuel dumps at strategic points along the route. The only feasible alternative could have been a shorter flight to the White Russian lines in the east, but this too would have required a network of White agents and personnel to facilitate it.

In a *Mystery Files* programme for National Geographic in 2010, Prince Michael of Kent claimed that when Air Commodore Peregrine Fellowes (who was appointed ADC to King George in 1926) was a pilot in the Royal Naval Air Service, he had been involved in 'an attempt made by aircraft' to rescue the Romanovs. Fellowes, he asserted, was 'given the opportunity to plan an escape and would have flown in and landed nearby and got them out'. Peregrine Forbes Morant Fellowes was indeed a pioneer pilot of considerable courage and daring during World War I. He qualified as a pilot in the Royal Naval Air Service in August 1915, and in April 1917 was appointed Squadron Commander of 2 Squadron at Saint-Pol-sur-Mer, Dunkirk and was based there until November. But there is no indication of him being stationed in, or even near, Russia at any time. There is nothing in his service record either to suggest that he would have chosen to fly anything other than a single-engined aircraft – and certainly nothing like a Handley Page Type O/400 biplane, used by the RNAS and capable of carrying a passenger.

The myth of Peregrine Fellowes's role goes back, sadly, to the untrustworthy Meinertzhagen. According to the author Julian Fellowes, his father was told back in the 1970s, when interviewed by Summers and Mangold, that Meinertzhagen had claimed that 'the pilot of the aircraft in this scheme was my great uncle'.[40] Puzzlingly, Summers and Mangold did not feature the Meinertzhagen claim until the third edition of *File on the*

Tsar in 2002, by which time nobody was taking Meinertzhagen seriously; nor did they mention Fellowes's supposed involvement. The story was, however, fashioned to suit the narrative of Michael Occleshaw's *Romanov Conspiracies* in 1993, when he accessed the original Meinertzhagen diaries at Rhodes House Library, Oxford, in order to claim that Grand Duchess Tatiana escaped the slaughter at the Ipatiev House, spirited away by a plane that had – quite preposterously – landed nearby. In the end the Meinertzhagen rescue plan, in so far as it remotely relates to Lieutenant Colonel Fellowes in 1918 – by which time he held a senior enough rank to take charge of some kind of secret 'aerial extraction unit' – has one enormous gaping hole. In May 1918 (when this last-ditch mission was supposedly being talked of) he was a prisoner of war, having been shot down by the Germans over Zeebrugge.

There are other reasons to doubt Richard Meinertzhagen as a reliable witness. Far from being involved, as he claimed, in developing British intelligence in Russia during World War I, prior to 1918 he had in fact been based in East Africa and then Palestine.* He had no proven on-the-ground knowledge of Russia and seems a most unlikely candidate for such a mission, particularly as in 1918 he was yet to retrospectively create his supposed career as a dashing and daring intelligence officer.[41] His undoubted forging, at a later date, of what are supposed to be contemporary diaries was conclusively proved in Brian Garfield's 2007 book *The Meinertzhagen Mystery – The Life and Legend of a Colossal Fraud.* Garfield here provides compelling evidence that Meinertzhagen was often not where he claimed to be and had a habit of stealing other people's exploits as his own. Did he do so here, with regard to the Romanovs?

---

* Meinertzhagen may well have met Fellowes in the Middle East, when the latter was posted to the Royal Flying Corps Command there in 1920. He may well have spun a yarn from information on the RFC gleaned retrospectively from him.

Not a shred of reliable evidence on this or any other meeting between the King and the SIS about a rescue plan has ever surfaced from the Royal Archives. In the case of the National Archives, this is not to say that documents might not once have existed, or still lurk there, overlooked or misfiled. Searches undertaken for this book have yielded, for example, the Woodhouse Telegram, not previously listed or cited, which was sitting in a file waiting to be discovered, despite repeated assurances made over the years by the TNA that 'nothing has been withheld'.[42]

When we strip away all the false trails and improbabilities, we are left with only one tenuous scenario relating to the Ekaterinburg period. This revolves around a secret British mission planned by forty-two-year-old Major Stephen Alley of MI1(c) – undoubtedly one of the best SIS operatives in Russia at the time. It appears to have involved, at the least, an initial recce of the Ipatiev House, its location and guards, in order to assess the potential for a rescue.

The dapper, moustachioed Stephen Alley was born in Moscow in 1876, son of a British engineer working for the Russian railways, and was a fluent Russian speaker. After university and training as an engineer he worked for the family firm in London, before returning to Russia in 1910. In 1914 he was recruited by Mansfield Cumming of the SIS as an assistant military attaché at the Petrograd embassy, as part of the Intelligence Mission later headed by Lieutenant Colonel Samuel Hoare. In 1916 he was made British Military Control Officer in Petrograd, working on counter-intelligence. Alley and a fellow agent from the Petrograd Station, Oswald Rayner, have since been implicated in the murder of Rasputin at the Yusupov Palace in December that year. Whether or not they played a part in his demise, Alley was certainly aware of the murder plot, and well in with members of the old tsarist regime (he had actually been born in a house owned by the Yusupovs in Moscow and had worked with the Provisional Government's secret service). In view of this, he was quietly removed from Petrograd after the Bolshevik takeover in October 1917.[43] His on-the-ground knowledge of Russia was, however, too valuable not to exploit, and in March 1918 he was sent to Murmansk as Senior Naval Intelligence Officer, where he remained until approximately August 1918.[44]

In Russia, Alley ran an extensive spy network and may have also been connected with an American National Intelligence Department operation running Russian agents into Siberia. A file in the National Archives indicates that the British were certainly intercepting telegrams between the local Soviets, including Ekaterinburg, and Moscow, and Alley would have been in a position to receive ciphered information about the Romanov family in the city.[45] In 2006, a television documentary, *Three Kings at War*, for Channel 4 showed for the first time Alley's personal notebook and a sketch map of the crossroads by the Ipatiev House, to which historian Andrew Cook had been granted access by the Alley family. The assumption has always been that Alley himself made the trip, but given his key role at Murmansk in control of numerous agents in Russia, it is far more likely that these observations were passed back to him by another agent whom he had sent on ahead.[46] The sketch map shown could in fact quite easily have been made by Alley from examination of a good 1900s map of the city that was then in existence. He would not have needed to go there to draw it.

Whoever it was who sent information back to Alley (and whether indeed any British agent at all was specifically sent to Ekaterinburg), that person would most likely have holed up at the British consulate not far from the Ipatiev House, or possibly even in Thomas Preston's own home, in order to spy on the comings and goings there. The Ipatiev House was located at 49 Voznesensky Prospekt; the British consulate was further down at no. 27, but Preston's house was much closer, 'some four houses away', at either 46 or 44.[47] Or perhaps Preston himself provided the information via an internal ciphered message to Murmansk? He had after all been living in Ekaterinburg since 1913 and knew the city better than anyone.

Wherever Alley – or his agent – was based in Ekaterinburg, the evidence in his notebook is scanty, suggesting the vantage point was very limited. Finding somewhere high enough that would allow sight of the house and the garden where the family walked, over and beyond the two high palisades surrounding it, would have been extremely difficult. It was bristling with machine-gun posts and had a rota of fifty or so heavily armed guards – stationed outside the gates, between the two palisades, and also within the house itself. The building was impregnable to anything but a highly organised military attack; and, even then, the family were held in upstairs rooms accessible only by a single staircase. In the event of an attack, their captors could have killed them all before help had reached them.

Nevertheless, on 24 May, ahead of this recce, Alley had written to MI1C headquarters to discuss the possible rescue and delivery of the seven 'valuables' (a promotion for the Romanovs from Yakovlev's 'baggage') back to Murmansk. He would need a grant of £1,000 a month to fund the surveillance by four officers, he said, and specifically named the SIS men whom he wished to enlist for the mission: Second Lieutenant G. Hill (possibly George Edward Hill), Lieutenant John Hitching, Lieutenant Ernest Michelson and Lieutenant Commander Malcolm MacLaren, the last of whom was already on his staff at Murmansk. 'These officers should clearly understand [the] nature of employment,' he added, 'which may require them to pass as civilians.'[48] Alley chose well: all four men spoke fluent Russian and knew the country like any native. Hitching, like Alley, had spent much of his early life in Russia; Hill's family had traded with Russia since the eighteenth century; and Michelson had lived in Russia since the 1890s and had done undercover sabotage and intelligence work in Finland; MacLaren had been born on an oil claim near the Caspian Sea, was married to a Russian and could pass as one.[49]

At this point one must ask the question: had the original Jonas Lied rescue plan via the Arctic been reconsidered, even though the house in Murmansk had still not been erected to receive the family? For Henry Armitstead was once again back in the frame as the important link-man in Archangel, having already been primed for the British economic mission to Siberia discussed with Lied. As Alley noted:

I have made it clear to Armitstead, in no uncertain terms, that his role is strictly liaison and that he must leave all arrangements for the journey to Murmansk to us. We are responsible for securing and delivering the valuables, he is responsible for their safe passage out of Russia.[50]

Comments in Alley's notebook suggest his plan was that the Romanovs should be taken *by train* to Murmansk, and from there on a British ship to England. But bearing in mind the hair-raising experiences only recently encountered by Yakovlev during a much shorter rail journey with the family, this would have exposed them to constant danger and certain attack. Alley's knowledge of the Russian railway system might have influenced his choice, but the added complication of getting the Romanovs north from Ekaterinburg, rather than from Tobolsk, makes Lied's original river plan seem a much better bet. Archangel as the ultimate venue – again as per the original Lied plan – would have been nearer and thus quicker to reach, although by June 1918 the British and Americans had landed an intervention force at Murmansk and had control of the port. A Royal Navy cruiser could, theoretically, have been waiting for the Romanovs there in June/July 1918.

Of the undercover British officers who can actually be placed firmly in Ekaterinburg, the only one who can be identified is someone not on Alley's list: Captain Kenelm Digby-Jones. His presence in Ekaterinburg on 'special duty' is confirmed in British consul Thomas Preston's memoirs *Before the Curtain*; his service record is extant and certainly supports the fact that he was on a mission there in July 1918 on behalf of the commander of Allied forces in Northern Russia, Major General Poole.[51] Fortuitously Digby-Jones's War Office file contains detailed timings of his movements. He left Murmansk on about 3 June, travelling via Vologda to Archangel. On 10 July he carried on south from Archangel to Ekaterinburg via Vyatka and Perm – a circuitous route through Bolshevik-controlled territory, and some of it on horseback by road and track, in order to avoid arrest. But Digby-Jones did not arrive in Ekaterinburg until 16 July.[52]

The timing does not fit the Alley scenario, but it does show that the overland journey from Archangel alone was about five days, thus indicating the enormous difficulties faced in getting one person, let alone seven Romanovs, out to safety. It would almost certainly preclude Alley giving up that amount of time to go to Ekaterinburg himself, particularly as on 29 May he stated that he was 'short of staff'. A ciphered FO telegram confirms that the nature of Digby-Jones's mission was primarily to make contact with the Czech Legions, who were advancing along the Trans-Siberian Railway from the east, and pass on secret despatches for their leaders that they should 'occupy Perm and Viatka, and join up with Allied forces at Vologda'.[53] But Digby-Jones died of complications brought on by Spanish flu at Chelyabinsk in September 1918, and yet again the door slams shut: we have nothing more to go on.[54]

If we take a more rational look at the possible presence of British agents in Ekaterinburg in the summer of 1918, it is likely, as with the Lied mission, that there has been a degree of misinterpretation. There was a very good reason for Allied spies to be there – indeed, the city was swarming with them, especially American and French ones – in the run-up to its seizure by the Whites and Czechs at the end of July.[55] In mid-May 1918 a German 'Red Cross mission' had arrived in Ekaterinburg, ostensibly undertaking humanitarian work with POWs. *Times* correspondent Robert Wilton confirmed that their ranks included undercover agents, sent to ascertain details on how the Romanovs were living and being treated at the Ipatiev House. But most of the agents watching the city had other objectives: the Urals region was rich in mineral deposits and the Russian mint was based in Ekaterinburg. A major platinum refinery had been established there in 1914, at a time when Russia was providing 90 per cent of the world's supply.[56]

The Bolsheviks, who had nationalised all the mines in 1917, knew that the city was likely to fall to the counter-revolutionaries and for weeks had been busily moving out consignments of minerals and gemstones by rail to Perm and on to Moscow.[57]* Thomas Preston, who had mined for gold in Siberia in his youth, had been specifically reappointed British consul to the city in 1913 so that he could monitor the Urals mining industry, in particular platinum production, to the War Office. In 1918 he was sending back regular reports on this and was attempting to procure platinum for the British Ministry of Munitions.[58] There were thus plenty of other reasons – both military and economic – for British agents to be on clandestine missions in Ekaterinburg in June–July 1918, to which the possible rescue of the Romanovs was (much like the Jonas Lied mission) only a possible adjunct.

Whatever the truth of the matter, it would appear that Stephen Alley quickly concluded that any attempt to storm the Ipatiev House would be madness – a suicide mission. But there is no report to confirm this in the official files, if he did indeed put anything in writing. He was recalled to London soon afterwards, maintained his intelligence links and worked in MI5 from 1939 until his retirement in 1957. Bound by the Official Secrets Act, Alley never spoke of his mission to Ekaterinburg, nor did he ever reveal anything of his secret exploits in Russia to his wife Beatrice; he was 'a real clam', she said.[59] Many years later she confided to Anthony Summers that 'when she asked her husband what he did, he would say, "Sometimes I will go away for a night and sometimes for a year, and I won't be able to tell you where I am, but I'm working for the king." She thought he was going for dirty weekends.'[60]

Alley's elusive personality is but one of the many obstacles in this story. Was this eleventh-hour rescue plan devised at the explicit

---

* Francis Lindley, formerly a counsellor at the Petrograd embassy, who was now based at the Archangel consulate, reported that by the beginning of August the Bolsheviks had shipped out 36,000 pounds of gold and 7,200 pounds of platinum. In all, four billion rubles-worth of platinum, gold, stores and money was taken away during the Bolshevik tenure.

request of King George without his government's knowledge? Or was it an offshoot of another secret government objective? There is no evidence to show it ever got beyond Alley's sketchy notes, but if such a foolhardy mission had been initiated – and then botched – it would by necessity have had to be hushed up, in order to spare the King and his government any embarrassment. Romanov writer Michael Occleshaw argues that in this situation the Royal Archives would have had to be 'weeded of any incriminating evidence', to save the King from being accused of 'wilfully gambling with his relatives' lives'. A member of the Alley family interviewed in 2006 said that word in the family was that the mission 'was actually aborted because it wasn't possible to achieve it'. But at what point this happened we shall never know.[61] Certainly it was the view of Thomas Preston that 'to have attempted anything in the nature of their escape would have been madness and fraught with great danger to the Royal family themselves'. There were 'ten thousand Red soldiers in the town and Bolshevik spies at every corner and in every house'.[62]

By the summer of 1918 the difficulties of obtaining news of the Romanovs, made worse by the fact that they were no longer allowed to send and receive letters, had greatly heightened not just their sense of abandonment, but also the anguish of their relatives who were desperate for news of them. Yet, from a distance, one member of King George's extended family in England had by now become so deeply concerned about the fate of the family – particularly the Romanov children – as to take independent action on their behalf.

Chapter 11

'Await the Whistle around Midnight'

On 23 May 1918 – the very day that Olga, Tatiana, Anastasia and Alexey were finally brought from Tobolsk to join their parents and sister at the Ipatiev House – their aunt Victoria wrote an impassioned letter to British Foreign Secretary Arthur Balfour. As Alexandra and Ella's sister, and one who knew the Romanov family intimately, Victoria Milford Haven made perhaps the most logical suggestion yet. Writing from her home at East Cowes on the Isle of Wight, as any mother would, she prioritised the welfare of the innocent Romanov children. What is telling, though, is the manner in which she opened her letter: 'I must apologize for troubling you with my private anxieties and wishes at a time when you are so heavily burdened with work,' she wrote in her large and emphatic hand, 'but I know of no one else to turn to.'[1]

'No one else to turn to'? What about her cousin, King George? Does this despairing comment in itself speak volumes about the King's utter impotence – both practical and political – in effecting any kind of assistance to his beleaguered Romanov relatives at this desperate time?

Victoria went on to explain her concern at the lack of news about her sisters and her other relatives in Russia. What little she knew came from the papers, and that was 'of a nature to cause me grave anxiety'. At this stage all she had ascertained was that Nicholas, Alexandra and Maria had been taken to Ekaterinburg, and the other children seemingly abandoned in Tobolsk. 'As long as the family were all together and sharing the same fate I felt this is what they would wish,' she continued, with an insight few others in the family shared. But now she 'dread[ed] to think of the grief their separation must have been to them all', particularly Alexandra. It seemed as though her sister's children were now 'left without a single relation to take care of them'.[2] Victoria had clearly thought through the ramifications of the appeal she was now making; 'the boy', she conceded, 'is a political asset which no party in Russia will allow to be taken out of its hands or to leave the country'.

But the girls (except perhaps the eldest)* can be of no value and importance as hostages to a Russian government nor be an embarrassment to any other government in whose country they might reside. I desire greatly, if it be possible to try and have these girls, the youngest of whom are 19 and 17 years old only, put under my charge.[3]

What harm could there be, Victoria asked, in the three other sisters being allowed a refuge in this 'out-of-the-way little Isle of Wight', where they could live 'a simple private life with me who am myself politically quite unimportant'. She and her husband would undertake to keep them there 'in quiet obscurity, out of touch with all Russians'. Might arrangements not be possible for the girls to be sent out of Russia into her care? It was, she emphasised, 'the only thing I can do which might be a small comfort to their poor mother, my sister, under present circumstances'.[4] Victoria went on to suggest that her proposal could be

---

* When he was seriously ill with typhoid in 1901 Nicholas had instructed ministers to see whether it would be possible for his eldest daughter Olga to join the Regency Council for Alexey, if he, Nicholas, should die and Alexey come to the throne. The implication here is that Victoria sensed that Olga was therefore of more political significance than her sisters and thus would not be released by the Russian government.

mediated by Germany; she was sure that her sister Irene (Princess Henry of Prussia) was equally concerned about 'the fate of these young girls'. Could the British government make an approach now, 'without loss of time'?[5]

Balfour took Victoria Milford Haven's plea seriously enough to note on 25 May that he would 'like the question considered officially'.[6] There is no record of the Cabinet discussion, but five days later he drafted his response:

> I regret that from all the enquiries I have made privately from those best acquainted with present conditions in Russia, the difficulties in the way of such a proposal seem to me at this moment almost insuperable.[7]

Once again, the handwritten notes added on the front cover of the file containing this correspondence underline British officialdom's rigid adherence to a political line adopted more than a year previously. The decision, which appears to have been minuted on 28 May, did not take note of the recent move to Ekaterinburg:

> I fear that, even were there no objection on general grounds, we could not get the Imperial children away. Trotsky might conceivably be prevailed on to give his secret consent, but, even so, that would only be the first difficulty surmounted. To entrust them to a Bolshevist escort would be unsafe and we should accordingly have to send British officers to fetch them at Tobolsk and take them to Vladivostok. The mission would immediately become known and we should be suspected of some Czarist conspiracy – when local antagonism would probably endanger the lives of everybody concerned.[8]

If this indeed was the British government's position, then its tone makes it all the more likely that the Stephen Alley rescue plan was completely off the record and unofficial. Thoughts of a

'Czarist conspiracy' seemed to be a British obsession, but right now, in the final weeks, some kind of improbable but gallant last-ditch monarchist rescue was in fact all that was left to the Romanovs.

Sometimes material turns up in the most unexpected of places. One such discovery I made during research for this book was a till-now-unknown and uncatalogued typescript memoir by British consul Thomas Preston, entitled 'The Vigil'. I found it in the archive of American journalist Isaac Don Levine, held at Emory University, Atlanta. How Levine came to have this copy, which is not among Preston's papers at Leeds University, I have no idea, but he must have met Preston at some point, possibly during his visit to Russia in 1919, and discussed their mutual interest in the Romanovs. 'The Vigil' is a valuable and powerful account of what the terrible days of June and July 1918 were like for the inhabitants of Ekaterinburg.

By the summer of 1918, with the spread of the civil war into Siberia and an increase in counter-revolutionary activity in the area, Ekaterinburg was enduring a reign of Bolshevik terror during which thousands were being brutally murdered. In this 'maelstrom of lawlessness', Preston recorded the frequent vengeful acts of cold-blooded murder being wreaked by bands of fanatical Red Guards. There were something like 10,000 soldiers roaming the town, looking for trouble, their numbers recently boosted by the arrival of 500 vicious Kronstadt sailors, who immediately proceeded to terrorise the population.[9] Preston later recalled the fear under which everyone was living:

> Lorries containing terrorist police and firing squads made nightly house to house visits, taking their victims from their beds. They then drove them to the outskirts of town, and, having forced them to dig their own graves, they either machine-gunned them or bayoneted them to death, according to the caprice of the drunken firing squad whose duty it was to put an end to them. The only crime of the

victims was that as 'bourgeoisie' they were 'enemies of the people'.[10]

Preston recalled that during that summer of 1918 he was able, from time to time, to send ciphered reports about the Russian Imperial Family via undercover messengers of the Anglo-American expeditionary force that was now based at Archangel. He used an English–Russian dictionary to create his rather crude cipher, which mercifully the Bolsheviks who intercepted his messages never figured out – 'Perhaps they didn't approve of bourgeois dictionaries.'[11]

The Romanovs themselves could only guess at what might be going on in the city, but outside on Voznesensky Prospekt – the main road to the railway station – they could hear the gunshots, the shouts and the rattle of artillery and lorries and troops constantly passing by and must have had a strong sense of gathering danger. They were, of course, unaware that on 20 May, Alexandra's sister Ella, who had been briefly held, separately from the family, in Ekaterinburg, had been sent on to Alapaevsk ninety-three miles away and incarcerated there with Grand Duke Sergey Mikhailovich, the three brothers (Princes Ioann, Konstantin and Igor Konstantinovich) and Prince Vladimir Pavlovich Paley. The Ural Regional Soviet (URS) had no doubt concluded that keeping so many members of the Romanov family conveniently together in one city, Ekaterinburg, was too much of a liability, inviting rescue plots and counter-revolutionary conspiracies. Two weeks later, Nicholas's brother, Grand Duke Mikhail, and his personal secretary Brian Johnson, who had been held in Perm since March, were taken away from their hotel and disappeared. On 13 June, they were driven out to the forest nearby and murdered in secret by the local Cheka.

Such was the dangerous situation for all civilians in Ekaterinburg by the summer of 1918 that even the Allied consuls were not immune to the threat of summary execution. The Ekaterinburg Bolsheviks regarded them as enemies, and it was becoming increasingly dangerous for Thomas Preston to continue his determined and almost daily representations to the URS about the welfare of the Romanovs. As Dean of the city's Consular Corps, he had been most vigorous in his appeals, as too, so he said, had been the French consul, Commandant Giné.* At the beginning of June, word reached Preston that large forces of Czechs and Cossacks were approaching Ekaterinburg and 'were marching to liberate us from our persecutors'; a message came through from the Czechs telling all foreign residents 'to keep our national flags flying on our houses so that they might avoid hitting us with their artillery fire'.[12]

Help was at hand for the besieged city – but would it arrive in time to save the Romanovs? It would seem that, once again, what remaining hopes there were fell back on the Russian monarchists to mount some kind of daring rescue. It was noticed that 'from the first days of the Romanovs' transfer to Ekaterinburg there began to flock in monarchists in great number, beginning with half-crazy ladies, countesses and baronesses of every caliber and ending with nuns, clergy and representatives of foreign Powers'.[13] One resident recalled how people would make their way up to the Ipatiev House every day, despite severe warnings that they should not do so. 'They gathered in small huddles, whispering, gazing anxiously at the high fence and sighing until they were dispersed by shots from a hefty Red Guard with a rifle in his hands.' Commandant of the Ipatiev House, Avdeev, remarked that some of them even brought cameras and tried to take photographs.[14]

Thomas Preston found some of these do-gooders a decided nuisance: they were 'a tiny clique', but constantly pestered him for news. They seemed intent, one way or another, on engineering hare-brained plots to liberate the family, turning up at the Ipatiev House with messages and letters for the family or trying to make direct contact with them.[15] It seems likely that Alexey's personal physician, Dr Vladimir Derevenko – who was living

---

* Sadly, not a shred of information has come to light about Giné or any efforts he may have made on behalf of the Romanovs.

in town and was occasionally allowed into the house to treat the sick boy, as a special concession – may have tried to smuggle in letters, but his visits were closely monitored, making handover extremely difficult; 'the commissar never leaves my side,' he said.[16] Nevertheless, Derevenko is claimed to have liaised with a man named Ivan Sidorov (formerly one of Nicholas's ADCs) who was sent to Ekaterinburg in May by a friend of the Romanov family to offer gifts of food.[17] According to a contemporary account, notes from well-wishers were variously passed on to the family 'in loaves of bread, on parcels and wrapping paper'. One monarchist officer later claimed to investigator Sokolov that Derevenko had provided him with a sketch plan of the family's rooms. At the very least, whether or not he was able to transmit correspondence, the doctor would have been the one person capable of providing important updates on the conditions in which the Romanovs were living and the state of their morale.[18]

A lone royal visitor to Ekaterinburg at this dangerous time was Princess Helena of Serbia, who came in June on her way back to Petrograd, having been forced to leave Alapaevsk where her husband Prince Ioann Konstantinovich was imprisoned with Ella and the other princes. Helena had gone straight to the URS, demanding permission to see her relative Nicholas. She also appealed to Thomas Preston, but he had long since concluded that direct appeals to the URS only antagonised and could make matters much worse.[19] Nevertheless, Helena made her way up to the Ipatiev House in early July, to be confronted by 'machine guns, trucks and armed men, all Red Guards' posted outside. 'My heart was sick,' she recalled, but nevertheless she had the courage to ask to see the commandant and demand that she be allowed to visit the family. 'Moscow does not permit them any visitors,' Avdeev told her. He promised he would pass on a message. Later that evening a commissar arrived at her hotel to inform Helena that 'The ex-Emperor and ex-Empress thank you for your visit and your interest in [them]. They are in want of nothing.'[20] The following morning, 9 July, Helena was arrested and a couple of weeks later sent by train to prison in Perm.*

The Bolsheviks guarding the Romanovs were now highly suspicious of anyone showing concern for their captives, paranoid that conspiracies to liberate them were afoot all over the city. When Prince Dolgorukov had arrived on the train with Nicholas, Alexandra and Maria at the beginning of May, he had been summarily arrested and searched and was found to be carrying weapons, as well as maps of Siberia, indicating the route of a planned river escape – perhaps the same plans described by Ievreinov that the Tobolsk monarchists had been entertaining.[21] Around the same time, Commandant Avdeev had also confiscated a rough diagram of their rooms on the upper storey that Nicholas had tried to smuggle out. He had hidden it inside the lining of the envelope of a letter that Maria had been allowed to send to her siblings still in Tobolsk.[22]

Having been responsible for running the household at Tobolsk, Dolgorukov was also found to have on him a large amount of money – 80,000 rubles – which was, of course, confiscated.[23] These were no doubt funds smuggled to him by the monarchists in contact with his stepfather, Benckendorff, in Petrograd.[24] Already in poor health, Dolgorukov was hauled off to Ekaterinburg jail, from where he sent a plaintive letter to Benckendorff:

> I sit here not knowing why I have been arrested. I've written an appeal to the Regional Soviet, begging them to release me and allow me to go home to my sick mother in Petrograd. I hope with my whole heart that I will see you again soon and embrace you. Don't frighten poor mama about my arrest, she is old and you must take care of her. Tell her only that, God willing, I will see her again soon.[25]

---

* Helena languished in jail in Perm for five months before Norwegian diplomats located her and arranged for her transfer to the Kremlin in Moscow. She was eventually allowed to leave Russia for Sweden and join her mother and children there.

Not long afterwards Dolgorukov was joined in jail by Nicholas's ADC, Count Ilya Tatishchev, who was refused entry to the Ipatiev House when he arrived with the other children at the end of May, perhaps also suspected of trying to contact the monarchists. From prison, Dolgorukov managed to send out 'several pencil-written notes' to Thomas Preston, 'imploring [him] to intervene on behalf of the royal family', but to which Preston did not respond, for fear of further compromising Dolgorukov.[26] He and Tatishchev were never heard of again; it was not until the 1990s that it was confirmed that they had been shot by the Cheka – on 10 July.[27]

Had they known it, revolutionary sentiment in Ekaterinburg was mounting against the Imperial Family. The local papers were full of strident letters demanding Nicholas's execution. It was frequently talked of in workers' meetings; other revolutionary groups, such as the Socialist Revolutionaries, accused the URS of inconsistency in their 'preservation' of the Romanovs 'in the service of imperialism'.[28] The Anarchists went further and, according to Avdeev, tried to push through a resolution that the 'former tsar be immediately executed and that within 24 hours all the others under arrest be liquidated'.[29] There was talk that the Anarchists might attack the Ipatiev House, and Avdeev warned the Romanovs that they might be moved at short notice – probably to Moscow.[30] When the Moscow newspapers ran a story that Nicholas had 'already been killed at some railway stop outside Yekaterinburg', on 12 June Reingold Berzin, the commander of the Northern Ural-Siberian Front, was sent to check the security arrangements at the Ipatiev House.

Official rebuttals of the various murder rumours were published in *Izvestiya* on 25 and 28 June, at around the time that Nicholas and Alexandra had been receiving a series of secret messages from would-be monarchist rescuers hiding out in the city.[31]

Or so they seemed to be …

In December 1919 the American journalist Isaac Don Levine pulled off a sensational scoop in the Chicago Daily News *when, on arriving back from a visit to Soviet Russia, he published four letters, written in French, that had supposedly been smuggled into the Imperial Family at the Ipatiev House in June/July 1918, outlining plans by monarchists hiding in the city to rescue them.** *Published under the heading 'Last Efforts to Save Czar and His Family', the letters (which had first been published in the newspaper* Vechernye izvestiya *in Moscow in April), to which Levine was given exclusive access in the Soviet Archives, caused a considerable international stir. But in the century since publication their authenticity has been much disputed. Were they indeed bona-fide proof of a desperate last-minute attempt to save the Romanovs or – as historians have now concluded – a cruel deception? Were 'The Officer Letters', as they came to be called, in fact a cynical act, spun out to raise the family's hopes and win their confidence, which could ultimately be used as proof of the need to prevent their escape by killing them?*

The first letter, written in French and undated, was probably smuggled into the Ipatiev House around 19 or 20 June, inside the cork of a wide-necked bottle of cream brought to the house for the family. Deliveries of milk, cream, eggs and other foodstuffs by nuns from the nearby Novo-Tikhvinsky Convent were a new and most welcome concession, to which Avdeev had agreed on 18 June.†

Whenever the nuns took gifts to the Ipatiev House they were obliged to hand them over in a basket at the door; they were never allowed in to present them personally and thus protect these smuggled messages from interception. Avdeev and his guards

---

* This was in fact not Levine's only Romanov scoop. A year later the Soviets again gave him unique access to their archives to publish *Letters from the Kaiser to the Czar*, in a further PR drive to discredit both former monarchs.

† It is important to emphasise that the Romanovs, although on rations, were far better fed than the vast majority of the population of Ekaterinburg. No evidence has come to light to substantiate allegations in some émigré memoirs that they were badly treated and starved in the Ipatiev House, or that Avdeev was deliberately cruel to them.

often helped themselves to much of the food when it arrived, and he clearly checked the contents of the basket before passing it on. Although something of a boor, he was on the alert for subterfuge and, having found the letter hidden in the cork, 'turned it over to Comrade Goloshchekin'.[32]

It is certainly the case that both the nuns of the convent and the officers of the academy were being very carefully watched by the Cheka, and reports were being sent back to Sverdlov in Moscow. Indeed, at the end of May, Sverdlov had sent specific instructions to Goloshchekin: 'Increase guard at Ekaterinburg ... Take particular note of the Academy.'[33] With these instructions in mind, Goloshchekin may well have decided to play the 'officer letter', when it was intercepted, to the government's own advantage. It was decided to copy it out and pass the copy on to the Romanovs. A series of further notes were also fashioned, in French and in the same hand, in order to flush out the family's response to a rescue bid.[34] These letters were composed by Petr Voikov (a Urals commissar who had studied at Geneva University and spoke French), with input from Goloshchekin and Beloborodov. But Voikov had terrible handwriting, and so Isay Rodzinsky, one of the more literate guards, copied them out in red ink.[35]

The first letter immediately raised the family's morale, for it opened by announcing that 'Friends are no longer sleeping and hope that the hour so long awaited has come.' The Whites and the Czech legions were about fifty miles away; Ekaterinburg would soon fall, and the family was instructed to 'be attentive to any movement from the outside; wait and hope'.[36] They were asked to make a drawing of the location of their bedrooms and of the furniture in them. What hour did they go to bed, the letter asked? 'One of you must not sleep between 2.00 and 3.00 on all the following nights.' It was signed 'One who is ready to die for you. An Officer of the Russian Army.'[37]

A response in French to this letter, written some time over the next two to three days, was added at the bottom of the crumpled page. It appears to be Olga Nikolaevna's handwriting, probably to Nicholas's dictation, and had the family's bedtime of 11.30 inserted in the margin alongside the original question. It warned that all their windows facing the street were 'glued shut and painted white'; worse, Alexey was 'still sick and in bed and cannot walk at all' – 'every jolt causes him pain'. This immediate impediment to any rescue plan was further complicated by the fact that Olga also added – at the end of the letter – 'No risk whatsoever must be taken without being <u>absolutely certain</u> of the result. We are almost always under close observation.'[38]

Although the removal of the Romanovs from Tobolsk to Ekaterinburg had been a major blow for the Russian monarchists, by the time this first letter was received there was a considerable gathering of former tsarist officers in the city. Some of them had followed the family from Tobolsk and were in hiding; others were based at the Nikolaevsky Military Academy of the General Staff, which had been evacuated to Ekaterinburg from Petrograd in March 1918. Composed of more than 300 students and thirty-six members of staff, it was an obvious breeding ground for pro-tsarist conspiracy and the Academy had already aroused considerable suspicion at the URS. As a result, Beloborodov had telegraphed his displeasure to Trotsky, who in July ordered the college to be transferred to Kazan.[39]

There has been talk in White Russian sources published since 1918 of various secret cabals of loyal officers based at the Military Academy who were, in one way or another, plotting some kind of rescue of the Romanovs. Among these shadowy figures is Captain Dmitri Malinovsky, sent from Petrograd to the Academy by an unnamed underground group, who there recruited a team of twelve fellow officers to 'gather information and make preparations for the "removal" of the family'.[40] He seems to have made contact with Dr Derevenko, as well as the nuns – whose Novo-Tikhvinsky Convent was located not far from the Academy. It may well be that this first, genuine letter – though intercepted and rewritten – was smuggled in from the Malinovsky group, though there is no evidence at all to prove it was from them. In any event, Malinovsky* appears to have quickly abandoned his mission, later telling Sokolov that his group never received any help or financial support: 'What could be done without funds?' he asked. It was the same old complaint. The only help they were able to offer the Imperial Family was to 'send in some *kulich* [sweet Easter bread] and sugar; nothing else was possible'.[41]

Although the Romanovs had already expressed a degree of reluctance about agreeing to any reckless rescue plan, bearing in mind Alexey's fragile physical state, the 'officer letters' seem to have drawn them into the trap that was being set. It is perhaps no coincidence that on 22 June, after the family's reply to the first letter, the windows in Nicholas and Alexandra's bedroom were inspected, and the following day one of the double windows was removed and a small ventilation window was opened, perhaps in order to facilitate this cat-and-mouse game.

About two days later, on 25 June, a second letter in French arrived, reassuring the Romanovs that 'we hope to succeed without taking any risk' and that they should somehow contrive to unseal one of their windows in preparation for their daring escape. 'The fact that the little tsarevich cannot walk complicates matters, but we have taken that into account,' it said. The family must ensure that he was asleep for one or two hours before the escape and, if need be, they should give him something to sedate him. It was a vague letter, with no details on how this rescue was to be effected logistically, ending merely with the reassurance that 'no attempt will be made without being absolutely sure of the result. Before God, before history, and before our conscience, we give you this solemn promise.'[42] This final exhortation seems to have convinced the Romanovs sufficiently to compose a reply that same day, written by Olga in blue ink on the blank half of the page, describing the windows and the location of their guards – who moved freely in and around all their rooms at all times – and

---

* Malinovsky and other officers from the Academy initiated the very first investigations into the murder of the Romanovs in August 1918.

of the machine guns within the house. Another fifty guards were billeted in a house across the street, they warned.

The family, however, had more pressing concerns: 'Do not forget that we have the doctor, a maid, 2 men, and a little boy who is a cook with us. It would be ignoble of us … to leave them alone after they have followed us voluntarily into exile.' They also expressed concern about two trunks stored in an out-building containing all of Nicholas's diaries and letters (which, if the family fled and left them behind, could of course be highly compromising politically, if they fell into the wrong hands). Yet by the end of the letter they conceded:

Doctor Botkin begs you not to think about him and the other men [Trupp the valet and Kharitonov the cook], so that your task will not be more difficult. Count on the seven of us and the woman [their maid Anna Demidova]. May God help you; you can count on our sangfroid.[43]

Despite this, the Romanovs remained extremely preoccupied by what might happen to the people who would be left behind. What becomes most glaringly apparent, from all the details they provided in this letter, is how closely watched they were, day in and day out, and how well guarded the house was. Yet the flabby response to this, which arrived the following day, brushed aside the many difficulties and was once again extremely vague about how this escape plan would be carried out.

'Do not worry about the fifty or so men who are in a little house across from your window,' it began dismissively, referring to the nearby house where the guards lived, 'they will not be dangerous when it comes time to act.'[44] When the signal came from their rescuers, the family were to 'close and barricade with furniture' the door separating the entrance to their rooms from the guards, and were to climb out through the window on a rope that they were somehow to improvise themselves. Signed 'An officer', this third letter, when looked at objectively, carries no conviction. Perhaps they already had their suspicions, for

Nicholas and Alexandra were by now very alarmed. They had done as instructed in the previous letter: on the night of 26–27 June they had moved Alexey into their bedroom and 'kept vigil, dressed', as Nicholas noted in his diary. 'But the signal never came.'[45] They had all found the 'waiting and uncertainty … most excruciating' and were totally unnerved. Later on the 27th they responded most emphatically:

> We do not want to, nor can we, escape. We can only be carried off by force, just as it was force that was used to carry us from Tobolsk. Thus do not count on any active help from us.[46]

Their guards were kind to them, they said, and 'we do not want them to suffer because of us, nor you for us; in the name of God, avoid bloodshed above all'. It was, moreover, impossible for them to escape via the only unsealed window in Nicholas and Alexandra's room. They had heard the sentries under their window being told to be even more vigilant, in case any of them should attempt to make signals at the window, and there was a machine gun in the courtyard immediately below. There really was only one solution: 'If you watch us, you can always come and save us in the event of real and imminent danger.'[47]

There was a pause in the correspondence after this highly reluctant response from the Romanovs. A fourth letter was finally smuggled in some time after 4 July, when a new commandant, Yakov Yurovsky, and a change of guards arrived. Their arrival inaugurated a much tougher regime at the house, which included the banning of milk and cream bottles being brought in for the family.[48] The fourth letter's awkward phrasing (indeed, the marked absence of any kind of deferential forms of address in any of the notes, which one might have expected from a loyal monarchist), in addition to a couple of spelling mistakes, mark it as a final, half-hearted attempt at luring the Romanovs into a positive response. But it was as woolly and evasive over the details as letter three had been: 'We are a group of officers in the Russian army who have not lost consciousness of our duty before Tsar and Country,' it insisted. But they were not prepared to tell the family 'in detail about ourselves for reasons that you can understand'. It did, however, assure them that their two loyal friends 'D and T'– a reference surely to Dolgorukov and Tatishchev – 'who are already safe, know us'. It is this detail that betrays the lie. The two men had been thrown into jail, as the Bolsheviks well knew. The absurdity of this provocative letter is also exposed in its final crude reassurances:

> The moment has come. We must act. Rest assured that the machine gun downstairs will not be dangerous. As for the commandant, we will know how to take him away. Await the whistle around midnight. That will be the signal.[49]

Until Russian historian Lyudmila Lykova's article on the subject was published in *Otechestvennye arkhivy* in 2006, it had been thought that the correspondence ended here. But there was in fact one final, brief, anguished response, added by the Romanovs on the bottom corner of the small envelope containing letter four, which for decades had been overlooked. Barely discernible in faint pencil, it read simply: 'Surveillance of us is constantly increasing, especially because of the window.'[50] This fact alone belies claims that the Romanovs were in some way involved in the covert signalling of messages to supporters outside, or throwing notes through the window into the street. When Anastasia had tried to sneak a look outside, a guard had immediately shot at and narrowly missed her. Nor could a hidden observer nearby see over the two palisades into the garden and signal to Nicholas whenever he saw him there.[51]

By the time the Romanovs capitulated to the impossibility of their situation in early July, not wishing any blood to be shed on their behalf, many of the monarchist plotters based at the Academy seem to have dispersed. Some were joining the counter-revolution, hoping that the city's imminent seizure by the Czechs and Whites would effect a speedy and more effective liberation of the Romanovs. Others who had travelled out from Moscow and Petrograd, or had been left behind at Tobolsk, had tried and failed to get to Ekaterinburg and had been rounded up and arrested en route. One such was Captain Paul Bulygin, who had been sent to Ekaterinburg by a group known as the National Centre, following the announcement of Nicholas's execution in early June, to check if this was true. On discovering it was not, Bulygin had become involved in a plan to rescue the family when (as he was misinformed) they were to be moved from Ekaterinburg to Kotelnich, near Vyatka.[52] The rumour turned out to be deliberate Bolshevik disinformation intended to throw would-be rescuers off the scent, and Bulygin was arrested in Ekaterinburg in early July. Markov II seems also to have had his own separate plans, based around a small group, including Sedov, who had earlier been sent to Tobolsk; but – like everyone else – by June he had had to concede that he had no effective means of mounting any kind of rescue.[53] A sense of frustration and resignation ruled among the old guard, and even the Tsaritsa's loyal cornet, Little Markov, was now admitting defeat. 'All those on whom we could rely who had been to Ekaterinburg agreed that a forcible abduction of the Tsar and his Family was out of the question.' Quite apart from the risk to all involved, 'money was not available to bring an adequate number of trustworthy men to Ekaterinburg'.[54]

Attempts by Russian historians to unravel the truth of monarchist plans to rescue the Romanovs have, till now, been plagued by so much confusion, misinformation, rumour and contradiction that piecing together the true scenario is an impossible task. Mikhail Diterikhs, the White Russian general who supervised Sokolov's investigation in 1919, took a highly sceptical view of the many claims he heard about monarchist plots. 'It is possible that in reality none of them were part of any organized group and that no such groups in fact ever existed; they only existed by word of mouth,' he concluded in 1922. 'These officers were distinguished by their braggadocio and their arrogance; they sounded off about their activities wherever they could; they shouted from practically every rooftop, opened up to the first person they met, ignoring the fact that they might be overheard by Soviet agents and foreign powers.'[55]

The distinguished Urals historian, Professor Ivan Plotnikov, after many years of research in the local archives, uncovered no feasible plans in Ekaterinburg. But there was, however, one story circulating in émigré literature, involving '37 officers' at the Military Academy who had been 'ready for everything' in order to 'save the dynasty'. It was a plan that may in some way be connected with a more detailed one that finally surfaced in 1923.[56]

It comes, not via Russian sources, but from the American journalist Isaac Don Levine. During a visit to Moscow that year, he was staying at the Hotel Savoy when he was introduced to a twenty-five-year-old student at the technological institute named Gorshkov, who turned out to be the brother-in-law of a former imperial officer, Colonel Rustam-Bek (also known as Boris Tageev), whom Levine had already met in the USA. Levine and Gorshkov struck up a friendship, and one day Gorshkov called him and asked if they might meet, for he had a 'confidential story' he wished to tell him.[57] At their meeting, Gorshkov handed to him 'a neat manuscript of some eight legal-size sheets of paper' and an accurately drawn map of Voznesensky Prospekt and the square opposite the Ipatiev House, which described a plan hatched by officers at the Military Academy to rescue the Romanovs. With the help of the British journalist Arthur Ransome, with whom he travelled by train out of Russia, Levine managed to hide the manuscript when the Soviet guards came to check their luggage at the border. In the safety of Berlin he translated the document and sent it to New York, where the article was published that August.[58]

This is the story that it told.

In the summer of 1918, Gorshkov, who had been born in Ekaterinburg – the son of a geologist and prospector in the Urals – was a cadet at the Military Academy. On 24 June, he had joined a conspiracy to rescue the Romanovs. It was led by Major General Vladimir Golitsyn, who at that time was based with anti-Bolshevik

Nikolay Markov, right-winger and former Duma member known as 'Markov II', was closely involved in plots to liberate the Romanovs from captivity.

Cornet Sergey Markov from the Tsaritsa's Crimean Cavalry, known as 'Little Markov'. Devoted to the Imperial family he collaborated with Markov II and other monarchists to try and rescue the Romanovs, but his plans came to nothing.

English tutor Sydney Gibbes took this previously unseen view of the inner courtyard of the Governor's House at Tobolsk. The Romanovs were held here from August 1917 to the end of April 1918.

The courtyard at the Governor's House, in which the Romanovs and their entourage were allowed regular periods of exercise and from where they could at least still see the outside world.

At Tobolsk the four sisters happily shared a room, sleeping on modest camp beds. They crammed it with their favourite icons, photographs and knick-knacks, but despite the large white-tiled stove the room was bitterly cold during the Siberian winter.

Above: Alexandra's sitting room at the Governor's House, Tobolsk. Beyond the parted curtains can be seen the ballroom, converted into a chapel by the family, where they had placed a portable iconostasis brought with them from Tsarskoe Selo.

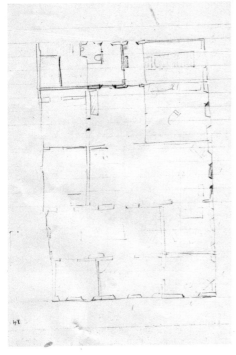

Left: In December 1917, Sydney Gibbes wrote a letter at Alexandra's dictation to her old governess in England, Miss Jackson, describing the family's daily life at Tobolsk and enclosing a room plan – a desperate thinly veiled plea for help.

The Romanov children's three favourite tutors, Spring 1917. L–R: Swiss national Pierre Gilliard taught French; Petr Petrov taught Russian literature and language; Sydney Gibbes taught English. Gibbes and Gilliard were both with the family at Tobolsk but were refused permission to join them in Ekaterinburg.

Prince Vasily Dolgorukov had been with Nicholas at Army HQ and joined him in Tobolsk. He passed on valuable information about the family's well-being but was arrested and later shot.

A more familiar image of the Tobolsk captivity, but a rare one in that it shows all the family together – on the greenhouse roof – bar Alexandra, who rarely went outside.

Count Benckendorff, Grand Marshal and Master of Ceremonies of the Russian Court, served as an important link with the monarchists in Petrograd. He passed on news from his stepson, Dolgorukov, about the conditions endured by the Romanovs in Tobolsk.

Kaiser Wilhelm II had a difficult relationship with Nicholas and Alexandra. Nevertheless, in 1917 he agreed to the idea of a British ship being allowed to evacuate the Romanovs by sea under a white flag. By Spring 1918 he had become the last hope for those seeking the family's rescue.

The Norwegian shipper and navigator Jonas Lied, who had extensive business connnections in Siberia, was the person best-placed to get the Romanovs out of Tobolsk. Yet his 1918 plan for a rescue downriver to the Kara Sea was greeted with indifference by the British.

The mysterious Vasily Yakovlev, aka Konstantin Myachin, was a tough-minded Bolshevik commissar tasked with escorting Nicholas, Alexandra and Maria safely to Ekaterinburg ahead of the rest of the family at the end of April 1918.

Major Stephen Alley, of the British Secret Service, who ran agents out of his base at Murmansk. In May 1918 he mooted a possible rescue of the Romanovs from Ekaterinburg.

Left: King Alfonso XIII of Spain. Probably the furthest removed of all Nicholas and Alexandra's royal relatives, and yet the one who made the greatest efforts to secure their release.

Left: A secret shot snatched by Sydney Gibbes of the tarantasses waiting outside the Governor's House to take Nicholas, Alexandra, Maria and their luggage away to a new Siberian location. The rest of the family would join them in Ekaterinburg on 24 May 1918.

Right: A contemporary postcard of Ekaterinburg showing the Ipatiev House (bottom left) located on Voznesensky Prospekt, and in the background the River Iset.

Below: The Romanov family were held at the Ipatiev House from 30 April until their murder on the night of 16/17 July 1918.

Above: The last photograph of Alexey and Olga. Taken by Sydney Gibbes on the steamer *Rus* en route from Tobolsk to join their parents and sister Maria in Ekaterinburg, May 1918.

Below: This chilling photograph taken inside the Ipatiev House shows the twenty-three steps down which the Romanov family were led before being taken out across the yard to the basement room where they were killed.

Left: After months of being out of the news and almost forgotten by the world outside, the Romanovs make front page headlines when their murders were finally announced, here in the *Daily Mirror* for 13 September 1918.

forces in the Urals, and Prince Riza-Kuli-Mirza, a Caucasian Muslim, formerly of the Imperial Cossack Escort, who had followed the Imperial Family in secret to Ekaterinburg.

Rumours had been circulating that, in view of the threat from the Czechs, the Bolsheviks were going to try and move the Romanovs away from the city; the plot in which Gorshkov was involved sought to rescue them and hide them somewhere in the Urals until the Czechs arrived. The group was composed of some of the monarchist officers who had travelled on from Tobolsk: Colonel Berens, Major Gorev and a 'Lieutenant X'; and four officers from the Military Academy: Captains Sumarokov, Dobrovolsky, Burov and a Lieutenant M.[59] Kuli-Mirza apparently planned the mission in great detail. He, Golitsyn, Gorshkov and these seven officers were each to recruit ten trusted men. While Lieutenant X worked out the ground plan for the rescue, it was Gorshkov's task to find a suitable refuge for the family. He came up with a hiding place – a dacha on the Upper-Isetsk Lake outside Ekaterinburg. The dacha was owned by the father of one of the men in his group named Agafurov, a notable Ekaterinburg merchant family.[60] The lake was 'about twelve miles long and from one to two miles wide'. Located three or four miles away from the villa there were 'two unfrequented islands in the lake covered with dense woods'. Gorshkov suggested they create a camp there, where the Imperial Family could be taken by motorboat after they were rescued and 'could live absolutely out of danger, guarded by eight or ten of our men'. Gorshkov's suggestion was approved, and Agafurov began making preparations at the villa.[61]

In the meantime Kuli-Mirza had made contact with Dr Derevenko, whom he had known when they were both in service with the Imperial Family at Tsarskoe Selo. According to Gorshkov, the doctor managed to secretly pass a note written by Mirza to Tatiana, when he was called to the Ipatiev House to attend Alexey on 2 July, his visit being confirmed in Alexandra's diary. If so, then this letter relating to the second plot – around the same time as the bogus 'officer letters' were arriving – must have created considerable confusion and anxiety in the family.[62]

By the following day the group had seventy men it could count on and sent a message to the Czechs at Chelyabinsk about their rescue plan; word came back that the Czechs were preparing to move on Ekaterinburg on 20 July (in fact it was the 25th when they actually arrived). In the days between 2 and 20 July the group were to gather together the stockpile of arms needed for their operation.

Their plan involved three strategic assembly points: the Kharitonov Gardens attached to the large Rastorguev-Kharitonov mansion opposite the Ipatiev House on Voznesensky Prospekt; the telegraph station down the lane at the back of the house; and the alleyways beyond that. The gardens (which are still there today) were deserted at night and provided the ideal assembly point for fifteen of the group under cover of darkness. A wagon with rifles, machine guns and munitions would drive up and rendezvous with them nearby, and the men would collect them and then hide in the bushes.[63]

It was essential, the group knew, to disable the telegraph station, manned by a couple of sailors, and it was Gorshkov's task to take two officers and capture it at 10 p.m. An hour later, twenty of their group would assemble in the small garden at the back of the station; while a third group of thirty men, led by Kuli-Mirza, would gather in the dark alleys near the house and arm themselves with weapons brought there at midnight. Everything was to be 'accurately synchronized', Gorshkov told Levine, and the attack on the Ipatiev House was to begin 'exactly at 1.20 a.m.' from a signal by whistle given by Major General Golitsyn. After the attack, involving thirty-five men and the use of grenades to kill the guards, and with another fifteen outside keeping guard on the street, the family would be driven away in three waiting vehicles to the Agafurov villa.

That was the plan; it was now a matter of deciding when to enact it.[64]

In early July, just as the Gorshkov plan was being put together, undaunted by the very high odds against success, Little Markov ventured into Ekaterinburg by train from Tyumen to attempt to find out about the 'welfare of my beloved sovereigns'.[65] The railway station was chaotic, crammed with rolling stock and 'extemporized armoured trains, which had been hastily put together from iron coal trucks', and 'crowds of tattered soldiers were strolling about the platforms and on the lines'. They had come in response to posters plastered everywhere exhorting loyal Bolsheviks to head to the front against the Czechs and Whites, in the 'defence of the Red Urals'.[66] The counter-revolution was now at Ekaterinburg's gates.

Markov made his way straight up to the Ipatiev House. 'My heart ached when I saw the building,' he recalled, 'it was surrounded by a high wooden fence which hid the windows; double sentries were posted on all sides.' He remained in the vicinity until the evening, during which time he walked around the perimeter of the house three times. It was final confirmation, were it needed, that he and his fellow monarchists had been hoping against hope for the impossible. He had to 'face the fact that nothing could be accomplished by force ... The house was a trap affording no way of escape.'[67] His fellow monarchists might still be plotting, but for Little Markov the only remaining hope for the Romanovs lay elsewhere, through diplomatic intervention:'A great foreign power, for whom the Bolsheviks felt both fear and respect, must intervene, and this great power could only be Germany.'

In early July of 1918 the grim reality for Russia's last Imperial Family was this: 'If the Germans did not succeed in saving the Tsar and his Family, then they were indeed doomed.'[68]

Chapter 12

'It Is Too Horrible and Heartless'

With Tsaritsa Alexandra and her sister Grand Duchess Ella both imprisoned in Western Siberia, a renewed sense of urgency had been aroused among their German relatives that spring of 1918. For some time, at his brother the Kaiser's request, Prince Henry of Prussia, who was also the two women's brother-in-law, had been monitoring reports from Russia on the plight of their two cousins, but obtaining reliable news of them was frustratingly difficult. The German ambassador in Moscow, Count Mirbach, was thus quick to act when Richard von Kühlmann, the German Foreign Minister in Berlin, passed on news received on 22 June that 'Recent developments in the Urals unfortunately justifies the worst fears for the fate of the Imperial Family.'[1]

Hearing this, Mirbach had made strong representations to the Soviets. 'I told Chicherin outright that I was pretty sure that some harm had come to the Imperial Family in Ekaterinburg.' If this news, which had sparked outrage 'in the widest circles', turned out to be incorrect, he warned Georgy Chicherin, then he 'did not understand why you Bolsheviks do not respond with an outright denial'. The Soviet Foreign Minister had not been able to give Mirbach a clear answer; he 'only protested feebly that false reports were so rife that there was little point in denying each and every one of them'.[2] Even Joffe, the Soviets' own ambassador in Berlin, was rattled by rumours about the Tsar's murder. He wrote to Lenin on 21 June complaining, 'I cannot do my job if I do not know what is going on in Russia ... I know nothing of what is happening to the former tsar. When Kühlmann asked me yesterday, I told him that I had had no news.'[3] Joffe had thought it quite possible that the story of the Tsar's murder was true; Germanophobia was rife in the Urals and people there were, irrationally, convinced that Nicholas was a German sympathiser.

It has been suggested that these false rumours were in fact the work of the Bolsheviks themselves; that Moscow had deliberately circulated them as a means of testing the water on European and domestic reaction to news of the Imperial Family's eventual murder. It is further alleged that the disappearance of Grand Duke Mikhail in June had also been used to sound out the public response to liquidation of members of the Romanov family.[4] The Soviets were certainly getting worried about the gathering threat of the Czech and White forces closing in on Ekaterinburg. Joffe had informed Kühlmann on 22 June of the difficulty in obtaining reliable news because 'the [telegraph] line between Ekaterinburg and Moscow has been interrupted by the Czechoslovakian troops in between'. The Czechs had apparently openly stated that they were 'fighting for and in the name of the Czar', which had served only to heighten hostility towards the Imperial Family among the local population. Joffe predicted that 'should the Czechs score a victory this would be a catastrophe for the family'. Nevertheless, he reiterated to Kühlmann that he had pointed out to Lenin's government in Moscow by telegraph 'how important it was to ensure the safety of the Imperial Family', and told him that they intended bringing them to Moscow as soon as 'the interruption of the railway line by the Czechoslovakians is cleared'.[5] With communications with the Urals extremely weakened, the Germans had no way of getting at the truth of the situation.

Persistent rumours that the Romanovs had been killed were, meanwhile, not helping the German cause among those Russians who had hoped that they would 'get rid of the Bolsheviks' and do all they could to 'save our Imperial Family from their filthy hands', if not restore them to the throne. Russian aristocrat Baroness Hartong expressed the feelings of many in her class when she wrote to Mirbach on 21 June describing their disappointment:

> The people think that it's you <u>who is supporting the Bolsheviks instead of getting rid of them for us. The people are beginning to think that you are here to perpetuate the country's disorder and to undermine everything further, in every way</u>. As to the awful rumour going around about the assassination of the Emperor and His family, the people are convinced that this is the Bolsheviks' doing, committed on German orders.[6]

In conclusion the Baroness warned: 'the Russian people ... now don't expect anything from the Germans and think that it's the Allies who will come to save them'.[7] When her letter to Mirbach was passed on to him, the Kaiser scribbled triumphantly in the margin, 'Tallies completely with my warnings! ... Our frantic clinging to the Bolsheviks inevitably *had* to make us suspect and also *has* done with the Russian people, who believe that we continue to support the revolution, instead of our <u>liberating them from it and imposing order, which is what they expected from us.</u>' It was the Allies who were now seen as Russia's – and the Tsar's – potential liberators. In Wilhelm's view, Mirbach had repeatedly overestimated the Bolsheviks and had not been tough enough with them. Instead he had been propping up their tenuous hold on power, while what Germany should have been doing was more vigorously seeking an alliance with pro-German monarchists that would guarantee the safety of the Romanovs and, more importantly, ensure that the Red menace did not spread from Russia to Germany. Wilhelm was incandescent: his ambassador's 'misjudgment of the domestic Russian political situation' was 'catastrophic'. He had, in fact, for some time been thinking of replacing him with Admiral von Hintze – 'the *only knowledgeable person* in our foreign service'.[8]

The Germans remained equally concerned about the welfare of the other members of the Imperial Family imprisoned in Crimea, so much so that at the beginning of June, a German military attaché was sent there to check on their situation. He passed on an offer from the Kaiser to Dagmar to take refuge in Germany, but she refused; she was adamant that whichever way she got out of Russia, she would not do so with German help.[9] With German troops now occupying Ukraine, and in May taking Crimea – a fact that in itself had greatly alleviated the threat to Dagmar and her family – some monarchists had already made contact.

In Kiev, Alexander Mosolov, former head of the Court Chancellery, met up with two other members of the imperial circle – Prince Kochubey and Duke George of Leuchtenberg – in an effort to secure German help for the Romanovs. Leuchtenberg was distantly related to Nicholas and was also a cousin of the heir to the Kingdom of Bavaria. Using his connections, he managed to obtain an audience with General Eichhorn, Commander in Chief of the German army of occupation in Ukraine, and his chief of staff. They both promised to supply material backing for a mission to rescue the Romanovs, to be undertaken via the Volga and Kama rivers to Ekaterinburg. Knowing that Nicholas – like Dagmar – would never agree to being rescued by the Germans, Mosolov arranged to send a letter to the Kaiser via Baron Alvensleben, German ADC to the Hetman of Ukraine, asking him to guarantee that the Romanovs, once liberated, could live in Crimea and would not be forced to leave for Germany. But he was disappointed. A long-awaited reply merely informed him that Wilhelm was not able to act without his government's agreement. Was this perhaps a veiled admission that Wilhelm could not risk provoking a reaction from the Spartacists – radical German socialists, who even now were plotting an uprising against his throne? Mosolov then appealed to Count von Mumm, the German ambassador to the Hetman, and again received a negative answer. Mumm had, he said, been surprised at the suggestion and had refused assistance. Rescuing the Tsar was not a German priority, he told him.[10]

It would appear from these exchanges, and the meetings that Foreign Minister Kühlmann had with Soviet ambassador Joffe in

Berlin, that the official German line on the Romanovs in the summer of 1918 was restricted to diplomatic appeals that they be properly looked after and put in a safe and suitable place. But then events overtook everyone: German ambassador Count Mirbach was assassinated. On 6 July, Socialist Revolutionaries, intent on provoking a renewal of conflict between Russia and Germany, shot him dead at his embassy in Moscow. Mirbach was replaced by Karl Helfferich, with Dr Kurt Riezler, a diplomat who had been working closely with Mirbach on the Romanov issue, retaining responsibility for the negotiations.

Mirbach's assassination sparked a major crisis for the severely undermined Soviet government, now facing the threat of a coup by the Socialist Revolutionaries and other anti-Bolshevik elements.[11] In retaliation, the Germans demanded that they be allowed to bring a battalion of troops to Moscow to guard their embassy. Even though Lenin refused this demand, the Germans still could not make a move on his government in response, while they were concentrating so many troops on the Western Front. Indeed, the Imperial German Army had recently redeployed more than fifty divisions from the Eastern Front in preparation for a major renewed offensive on the Marne. For now, the Germans had to hang on to the Bolsheviks, however much they disliked them, and continue to juggle their interests between them and the anti-Bolshevik monarchists. That way they could keep Russia divided and take advantage of its present 'military paralysis'.[12]

The British too had by the end of June begun courting the anti-Bolsheviks. Robert Bruce Lockhart had made undercover contact with the National Centre – a secret organisation led by Professor Peter Struve and other cadets and Right Centre politicians who favoured the establishment of a military dictatorship and ultimate restoration of the monarchy. British intelligence officials working under the command of Stephen Alley at Murmansk were also negotiating with monarchists, and other opposition parties such as the Right Social Revolutionaries, for their support for the Allied intervention forces now arriving in northern

Russia. But if the Allies did not move fast, the Germans would beat them to it and 'restore order and proclaim [a] monarchy', warned the British consul in Petrograd, Arthur Woodhouse.[13] The last thing the British wanted was German hegemony in Russia over a puppet tsar. The most effective way to coordinate anti-Bolshevik and anti-German forces – in an attempt to oust the Soviets – might now perhaps be by liberating the Romanovs and using them as a rallying point. But if this realisation had indeed finally hit home, it came too late. The Germans were the ones holding the only trump card left; in Moscow everyone was anticipating a full-scale German invasion.

It is puzzling that beyond the official German Foreign Ministry documents and a few erratic comments by the Kaiser, there is so little surviving evidence of German involvement in the Romanov question in 1917–18, even at this late stage. At a meeting with members of the Ukrainian State Council in Kiev on 5 July, Baron Alvensleben had declared that 'Kaiser Wilhelm wished at all costs to rescue the sovereign, Tsar Nicholas II.' Wilhelm had, according to his daughter-in-law Crown Princess Cecile, been having sleepless nights worrying about the fate of the Romanovs. But Wilhelm's own memoirs are a total blank on the matter; and Alvensleben's papers, which might shed light on these last dramatic days, have not survived.[14] The memoirs of Alexandra's brother Ernie, who was known to be making representations for Alexandra's and Ella's safety, tell us nothing, either. As for the private papers and diaries of Mirbach's assistant, Riezler, these, like those of Mirbach himself, contain no mention at all of German diplomats' efforts on behalf of the Romanovs in 1918. In June 1921, Riezler did however hand over the key diplomatic correspondence discussed here to Sokolov's inquiry.

A greater availability of evidence might have served as a valuable counter to widespread claims that the Germans did nothing to try and help the Imperial Family at this time. All that survives is a cryptic remark made by Mirbach's secretary, Freiherr von Bothmer, in his personal diary for 22 July 1918, stating that 'the German side had tried "certain" things to help the family diplomatically'.[15]

★

With regard to any possible eleventh-hour German efforts, one piece of surviving tangential evidence is a letter in the British Foreign Office archives. It comes from the Swiss section of the League for the Restoration of the Russian Empire and suggests that 'Berlin was considering kidnapping the Tsar and his family and bringing them to Germany.' But who exactly had this plan emanated from, and where is the proof that it was ever more than mere speculation? The Swiss League had been requested to sound out the views of the Allied governments on this, so it claimed, and letters had already been sent to the French and Italian Prime Ministers, Georges Clemenceau and Vittorio Orlando.[16] Those letters have so far not surfaced. Exiled Russian monarchists had also visited the British consul in Geneva with regard to this plan, claimed Summers and Mangold, who concluded that it was actually initiated. But such a rescue seems, like all the others, a fool's errand that is hard to credit. In any event, it would have met with the utmost resistance by the Romanovs, who we know had already indicated loud and clear that they would rather die in Russia than accept German help. As it turned out, the despatch from the Swiss League soliciting the Foreign Office's approval was sent on 17 July and did not arrive till the 21st: rather 'late in the day', as an official noted.[17]

Whatever Kaiser Wilhelm's true intentions, from early July there had certainly been another burst of diplomatic activity, but by a lone Russian, not a German. On the 2nd, Petr Botkin, former Russian ambassador to Portugal and Dr Botkin's increasingly anxious brother, sent yet another anguished cry to the French. Directing his appeal to the Foreign Minister in Paris, Stephen Pichon, he described the state of extreme anxiety in which all Russians devoted to the Romanovs now found themselves. He begged Pichon, in the name of his country's close former alliance with Russia up until the revolution, to take steps to help protect the former Emperor and his family. This was Botkin's last hope – all his efforts to galvanise French help had so far come to nothing: 'every step that I took remained fruitless, and as replies to my letters I have only the receipts of the couriers confirming that my letters reached their destinations'.[18] Botkin was deeply dismayed at this official silence from France, particularly in view of the bonds of Franco-Russian friendship. Even the heavily censored French press had recently alluded to the 'responsibility of the Allies' in the event of the Emperor's murder. Once again he was met with indifference; the French did not reply. Yet they were clearly keeping an eye on the situation, through their agents on the ground in the Urals. On 6 July, a French agent, Commandant Charles Boyard, arrived in Ekaterinburg from Perm to check out rumours about the family's safety and stayed with the consul Thomas Preston at the British consulate, down the road from the Ipatiev House.[19]

Gorshkov's group of conspirators from the Military Academy were also now staking out the house as they continued to prepare for a rescue. On 12 July, they had had a final meeting when it was 'decided to strike the day after tomorrow, the fourteenth'. But then 'an unexpected hitch developed'. The group was warned that two squadrons of Red Guards had just arrived in town, en route to Chelyabinsk. These were vicious, hardened fighters, and the group would have to wait until they had left, which they were told would be on the night of 18–19 July.

And so Gorshkov and his friends fixed their attack on the Ipatiev House for the night after that – 19–20 July.[20]

For the Romanov family at the Ipatiev House, Tuesday, 16 July, in Ekaterinburg was much like any other day, punctuated by the same frugal meals, brief periods of recreation in the garden, reading and games of cards. Over the last three months their lives had become deadened by the extreme constraints placed upon them and by a total lack of contact with the outside world. It was only the fact that they were still together, and in Russia, that kept them going; that and their profound religious faith and absolute trust in God.

Since being brought here they had come to cherish the smallest and simplest of pleasures: the sun had shone; Alexey was recovering from his recent bout of illness and the nuns had been allowed to bring him eggs; they had been granted the luxury of an occasional bath. Such are the few passing, mundane details from the Tsaritsa's diary that have come down to us of the family in their final days and hours. Yet, despite their brevity, they give us a clear and unshakeable image of the family's state of calm – almost pious acceptance – at this time.

We have no way of seeing into the true workings of their hearts and minds, of course, but we do know from everything their guards later said that Alexandra in particular had by now resolutely given herself up to God. She was in almost constant pain – her heart, her back, her legs, everything ached – and her faith was her only refuge. She seemed content to retreat into a state of religious meditation, spending most of her time being read to from her favourite spiritual works, usually by Tatiana. One of the girls always sat with her, giving up her precious recreation time when the others were allowed out into the garden. But, as always, none of the four sisters ever complained. They accepted their situation with incredible forbearance. Nicholas, too, struggled on as best he could, buoyed up by his faith and the loving support of his daughters, although Olga – perhaps, of all the family, consumed by a private sense of despair – had become very thin and morose and was more withdrawn than ever. Her brother and sisters, however, all longed for something to relieve their crippling boredom. In the absence of access to the outside world, their only diversions were snatches of conversation with the more sympathetic of their guards, but even these had been severely curtailed by the new commandant, Yakov Yurovsky, at the beginning of July.

By the evening of the 16th we do not even have Nicholas's few restrained daily comments to go on, for on Sunday, the 13th, he had finally given up keeping his diary. Its closing sentence, coming as it does at the end of a lifetime's reticence, is an extraordinary and very real cry of despair:

We have absolutely no news from outside.[21]

News of the Russia they loved? News of relatives and friends left behind? Or news of would-be rescue by their 'loyal officers'?

If by then Russia's last tsar felt abandoned and forgotten, then the family must have sensed it too and shared in his despair. But they did not show it. And so we continue to ask ourselves: did they, in those final moments, when the guards came and woke them at 2.15 a.m. on the morning of the 17th and led them down the dingy stairs to the courtyard and across to the basement, have any inkling that this really was the end?[22]

In Moscow, Lenin's government had in fact been discussing what to do with Nicholas – and indeed the whole family – on and off since early April. It had become increasingly apparent that the civil war now spreading to Siberia would make it impossible to bring the former Tsar back to Moscow for the long-mooted trial, but Lenin had prevaricated on making a decision until counter-revolutionary forces were on the verge of taking Ekaterinburg. In early July, knowing that sooner or later the city, an important strategic point on the Trans-Siberian Railway, would fall to the Whites and Czechs approaching from the east, a decision was taken that when the time came, the Ural Regional Soviet should 'liquidate' the Imperial Family rather than have them fall into monarchist hands.[23] And they must all perish, in order to ensure, as Lenin insisted, that no 'living banner' (that is, the children) survive as a possible rallying point for the monarchists. But the murder of the children, which the Bolsheviks knew would provoke international outrage, must be kept secret for as long as possible.[24]

On 14 July the Romanovs had unexpectedly been allowed the special privilege of a service, conducted for them at the Ipatiev House by a local priest, Father Ivan Storozhev. He had been deeply moved by their devotion and the enormous comfort they had clearly taken in being allowed to worship together; but he had also been chilled by an eerie sense of doom that had prevailed throughout the singing of the liturgy. It was almost as though the family had been sharing, knowingly, in their own last rites.[25]

Yurovsky had, meanwhile, been planning the family's murder, though with a surprising lack of efficiency for such a ruthless, dedicated Bolshevik. He chose the site in the forest outside

Ekaterinburg where the bodies were to be disposed of, but failed to check how viable it really was as a place of concealment. He selected his team of killers from the guards at the house, but did so without ascertaining whether or not they knew how to handle a gun efficiently; and he investigated the best method of destroying eleven bodies using sulphuric acid or possibly incineration, again without any research into the logistics.

It was decided that the family would be killed there, in the house, in the basement room where any noise of shooting might be muffled. Early on the evening of 16 July, Yurovsky distributed the assortment of handguns to be used. There was one gun for each guard; one murderer for each of the eleven intended victims: the Romanovs and their four loyal retainers, Dr Evgeniy Botkin, the chambermaid Anna Demidova, the valet Alexey Trupp and the cook Ivan Kharitonov. But then, unexpectedly, several of the guards refused point-blank to kill the girls. Having talked with them on many occasions, they had grown to like them; what harm had they done anyone? The intended murder squad was thus reduced to eight or nine who, when Yurovsky gave the order to open fire, launched into a frenzy of wildly inaccurate shooting, several of them disobeying instructions and shooting Nicholas first. The other victims panicked in terror, necessitating the savage bayoneting of any survivors of the first onslaught. One thing is clear: the Romanov family and their servants met their deaths in the most brutal, bloody and merciless way.

The corpses were then unceremoniously thrown into a Fiat truck and taken out to the Koptyaki Forest. But the supposed mine shaft that Yurovsky had selected for them to be dumped in turned out to be too shallow; local peasants would easily find the bodies and seek to preserve them as holy relics. And so, within hours, the mutilated corpses of the Romanov family, stripped of their clothes and the Tsaritsa's jewels, which had been secreted in them, were hastily dug up. Yurovsky and his men then made a botched attempt to incinerate the bodies of Maria and Alexey. Sixty yards away, the rest of the family were hastily reburied in a shallow grave along with their servants.

People still insist, even today, on referring to what happened to the Romanov family as an 'execution'. It was not. Nor was it an assassination, for even that word suggests a degree of planning and skill. There was no trial for any of the family, no due process of law, no possibility of a defence or appeal. What happened in the basement of the House of Special Purpose on Voznesensky Prospekt, Ekaterinburg, in the early hours of 17 July 1918, was nothing less than ugly, crazed and botched murder.*

Despite the grotesque inefficiency with which Yurovsky and his men carried out these killings, and the even greater ineptitude with which they tried to dispose of the bodies, it would be sixty years before these lost graves would be found, in secret, by two local Russians. But it was not till 2007 that the missing remains of Maria and Alexey would finally be discovered.

But let us return to 17 July 1918 ...

British consul Thomas Preston had had surprisingly little intimation, that day in July, of the fulfilment of his worst fears that the Romanov family might be killed, bar the ominous placement of machine guns on Voznesensky Square. In the distance he could hear the boom of the approaching Czech artillery, but from the Ipatiev House itself came only a few audible shots that night. Ever since the family had been brought to Ekaterinburg, Preston had, time and again, made appeals to the Ural Regional Soviet about their welfare, only to be constantly rebuffed and threatened with being shot for his trouble. After the murder of the five children and their parents he was warned that the Bolsheviks were going to come for him; his house was surrounded by a mob shouting, 'That's the man who tried to save the Tsar *Palach* [hangman].'[26] It was only the arrival of the Czechs that saved Preston and his family, when they took the city on 25 July.

---

* For full, forensic details of the murder of the Romanovs and their burial in the Koptyaki Forest, see my book *Ekaterinburg*.

Fifty-four years later, in an article in *The Spectator*, Thomas Preston wrote of his private and continuing agony of regret: 'Ever since then, I have been haunted by the idea that had I been able to argue with the Ural Soviet for a longer period I might have been able to save the Royal family.'[27]

The night after the Romanovs were savagely brought to their deaths in Ekaterinburg, over in Alapaevsk the Grand Duchess Ella, her companion Sister Varvara and her fellow prisoners Grand Duke Sergey, the Konstantinovich brothers Ioann, Konstantin and Igor, and Prince Paley were bundled into a truck by the local Cheka and taken out to a place called Verkhnyaya Sinyachikha twelve miles away. Here they were thrown alive down a disused mine shaft; a couple of grenades were tossed in after them and they were left to die of their wounds, thirst and starvation. Unlike their relatives in Ekaterinburg, Ella and her companions were not even granted the mercy of bullets.

At midday on 17 July, the detailed log of Lenin's official life recorded that he received a telegraph message from Ekaterinburg and wrote on the envelope: 'Received, Lenin'. The contents confirmed that the Ekaterinburg Bolsheviks had carried out the liquidation, acting on Lenin's and the Central Executive Committee's preordained decision.[28] But their message was ambiguous about the family. Moscow asked for clarification. Two hours later a further telegraph to Lenin and Sverdlov from the Ural Regional Soviet confirmed that 'Nicholas Romanov was shot on the night of the sixteenth of July by decree of the Presidium of the [Ural] Regional Soviet.' The URS informed them that it was preparing an announcement to this effect, to which would be added, deliberately misleadingly, that 'the Romanov family ... has been evacuated from the city of Yekaterinburg in the interest of maintaining public security'.[29]

That evening, Beloborodov – Chair of the URS – sent Moscow an encrypted postscript to this message: 'Inform Sverdlov that the entire family suffered the same fate as its head. Officially the family will die during evacuation.'[30] The intention had clearly been to allow a degree of public confusion about the whereabouts of Alexandra and the children, after Nicholas's killing. The URS would only later admit to their perishing during a supposed evacuation to safety. In Moscow, Sverdlov was delegated to make the official announcement, which he did to the Presidium of the All-Russian Central Executive Committee (CEC) on 18 July. Later that day, the government released a printed proclamation stating that Nicholas Romanov, 'the crowned executioner', had been shot, but his wife and son were 'in a secure place'; the four daughters did not merit a mention. When the Ekaterinburg Bolsheviks drafted an announcement for 20 July, stating that the entire family had been shot, it was thrown back at them with the words 'Forbidden to publish' scrawled on it. They were told to stick to the official line of Sverdlov's press release.[31]

It is therefore not surprising that in the days following the Romanov murders intense confusion reigned, not just in Russia, but among their royal relatives in Europe.[32] With so little concrete, reliable information to go on, it would seem at first that the only certain fact was that Nicholas was dead. Until they received confirmation to the contrary, it was imperative that the royals of Europe should now do everything in their power to save the Tsaritsa and her children. Meanwhile the Bolsheviks were already busy throwing up a smokescreen of deliberate disinformation. When challenged by a member of the German diplomatic staff in Moscow about the truth of the rumours about the Tsar, Trotsky had replied: 'I don't know about this, and I am not in the least interested. I cannot really have any interest in the life of an individual Russian bourgeois.'[33]

And so began a hideous, cruel and protracted game of deception; a bizarre diplomatic negotiation over 'resurrected bodies' – in the words of Kerensky – in which the Soviets allowed the Romanovs' relatives and their governments to believe that Alexandra and the children were still alive.[34] It was a cynical ploy to buy the Bolsheviks breathing space from the inevitable worldwide condemnation and to keep any monarchist counter-revolution at bay.

Many of the rumours about the Romanovs that had been in circulation in the West since June had emanated from Stockholm, and from the foreign diplomatic community at Vologda.[35] On 16 July in Copenhagen – the eve of the murders – a Danish newspaper, *Nationaltidende*, had pre-empted that night's events and reported that Nicholas had been killed. The paper's editor sent a telegram directly to Lenin asking for confirmation. At 4 p.m. he received a reply from Moscow that 'Rumour not true ex-czar safe. All rumours are only lies of capitalist press.' Two days later, 18 July, the CEC issued a formal announcement that Nicholas had been executed, 'in view of the threat of the advancing Czechs'; but that was all.[36]

Back in Petrograd, Little Markov first heard the news on 20 July, when he saw a crowd gathering and newsboys 'running in all directions' shouting, 'Special edition! The ex-Tsar shot at Ekaterinburg. Death of Nikolai Romanoff.'[37] The following day the *New York Times* ran the story on its front page, and the day after, 22 July, *The Times* published Sverdlov's official statement. Both articles repeated the Soviet assertion that 'the wife and son of Romanoff have been sent to a place of security' and said nothing about the girls. In Russia, the Soviets maintained a stony silence on any further details.[38] Had the Ekaterinburg Bolsheviks got wind of the Military Academy plot in the days immediately preceding the murders? The local paper, *Uraliskiy Rabochii*, certainly claimed as much, in a story that appeared on 23 July headlined 'White Guardists attempted to abduct the ex-Tsar and his family. Their plot was discovered.' It claimed that the 'execution' of the Tsar had taken place in order to prevent this.[39]

Reliable news from Ekaterinburg was almost impossible to obtain in the present desperate situation there, and with telegraphic communications so unreliable. At 7.15 p.m. on 23 July, the British Foreign Secretary Arthur Balfour, as much in the dark as everyone else and unable to get word from Preston in the city, sent a short, stark telegram to his ambassador in Stockholm, which was also copied to Copenhagen:

URGENT. PERSONAL.
   Have you any definite information as to the death of the Emperor Nicholas?

Please telegraph at once any reliable news which may reach you.[40]

A day later Sir Ralph Paget in Copenhagen responded: 'Royal Family here after making all possible enquiries are of opinion that there no longer exists any doubt as to death of Czar.' Sir Esmé Howard in Stockholm replied soon after, regretting that 'I have no information.'[41]

Although the British government was yet to issue any official pronouncements, the King and Queen were privately informed, even though the details were uncertain. Queen Mary noted in her diary on the 24th that 'The news were [sic] confirmed of poor Nicky of Russia having been shot by those brutes of Bolsheviks last week, on July 16th'. It was, she concluded 'too horrible & heartless'. While she and the King might perhaps have anticipated a violent end for the former Tsar, the anguish of not knowing what had happened to his family was far worse. Languishing under house arrest in Crimea and cut off from any reliable sources, Nicholas's distraught mother Dagmar steadfastly refused to believe the news that trickled through. 'The most gruesome rumours are being spread about my darling Nicky,' she wrote in her diary. 'Won't and cannot believe them, but this tension is unbearable … Oh Lord hear my prayer.'[42]

While the Foreign Office continued to make every effort to verify Nicholas's death, British officialdom had, by necessity, swung into action over the matter of how his demise should be formally acknowledged. A clinical debate thus ensued within the Royal Household over the correct protocol to be observed by the King in mourning his cousin. In an internal memorandum of 23 July, Lord Stamfordham discussed the precedents that should be taken into account:

A. On the death of the Ex-Emperor Napoleon III in 1873 Queen Victoria <u>was</u> represented at the funeral, no member of the Royal Family attended, though the Prince of Wales was present at the lying-in-state at Chiselhurst. There were ten days of court mourning.

B. On the occasion of the assassination of King Carlos of Portugal, King Edward attended a Requiem Mass, which was held in London, and there were four weeks of Court Mourning.

In A there was no relationship between the Sovereign and the deceased and in B there was a distant family relationship.

In the present case the King is a first cousin.[43]

Nicholas may have been a first cousin, but for all that – and let alone the violent circumstances of his murder – British officialdom was far more concerned about the public response. 'Any notice on the part of the King of the Emperor's death might provoke criticism from a small minority that His Majesty was sympathetic towards Czardom, and in favour of Reactionary Government,' Stamfordham argued. On the other hand, Nicholas had been 'a faithful Ally and friend of this country' and 'any lack of respect to his memory would be resented'. Only that day, Stamfordham had sat next to Lord Burnham at a Lord Mayor's Luncheon:

He was most outspoken in deprecating the want of sympathy shown by the Press and by public opinion in this tragedy, and declared most distinctly that in his opinion it would be a great mistake were the King *not* to observe in the usual manner the Emperor's death.[44]

There would certainly have to be a memorial service, which Konstantin Nabokov, the former tsarist ambassador to London, was now arranging with Grand Duchess George* to take place in a

---

* Grand Duchess George was the daughter of King George I of Greece (d. 1913), a niece to the Queen Mother and first cousin to Nicholas. She had been in Harrogate during World War I, running hospitals for the wounded. Her husband, along with the Grand Dukes Nicholas Mikhailovich, Dmitri Konstantinovich and Paul Alexandrovich, was shot by the Bolsheviks at the Peter & Paul Fortress in Petrograd on 30 January 1919, despite heroic efforts by Harald Scavenius to help them.

week's time. Stamfordham presumed that George V would not attend, but 'would be represented'. Indeed, 'Would it not be best to postpone it,' he asked, 'until such a time as the Government can state *officially* that the Ex-Emperor is dead?' He felt that the King should suggest a postponement 'so that His Majesty can continue to act as if he did not believe the news'.[45] Later that day Arthur Balfour contributed his pennyworth in a private letter to Stamfordham. The Prime Minister David Lloyd George was, he said:

quite aware that some comment and criticism might be levelled against the King if he was represented at the Requiem Service and thereafter ordered Court mourning for the late Czar.

But he was clear that taking into account the close relationship of the two Sovereigns and that the Emperor was always loyal to the Entente, and always most friendly to the King, no criticism need divert His Majesty from the natural course of treating the Emperor's memory with the same respect as would be extended to other friendly Sovereigns.

The tragic circumstances of his death appear to render this course more consonant to natural good-feeling than it otherwise would have been.[46]

After another day's hesitation, in order to be certain of at least the Tsar's death, an announcement was published on 25 July in the Court Circular of *The Times*:

The King Commands that the Court shall wear mourning for four weeks, from July 24, for his late Imperial Majesty Nicholas II, first cousin to His Majesty. The Court to change to half-mourning on Wednesday, August 14, and on Wednesday, August 21, the Court to go out of mourning.[47]

On the 26th, from the Marselisborg Palace – the Danish royal family's summer residence – King Christian issued similar orders; the following day the Spanish did likewise.

Whatever opinion their government had in the matter, King George and Queen Mary were most anxious to attend the memorial service for the Tsar, which was held the day after a similar one was conducted at the Russian Church on the rue Daru in Paris. (Other services would follow in Rome, Stockholm, Oslo and The Hague – though surrogates for the Queen of the Netherlands and the Queen Mother attended the latter.) The *panikhida* at the Russian Embassy Chapel on Welbeck Street, Marylebone – the only Russian Orthodox church then in London – was attended by King George, Queen Mary and the Queen Mother, along with many of London's émigré Russian community. No representatives of the British Cabinet were present. 'Why not?' queried Stamfordham. 'Surely not from fear of offending the Bolshevists!' It turned out this was 'out of consideration for the General Election: the announcement of which synchronized with that of the Memorial Service'.[48]

Dressed in the most sombre black, the congregation at the Russian Chapel heard the priest and choir sing the powerful prayers for the dead. 'Their wonderful deep-toned voices broke the silence,' recalled Baroness de Stoeckl, lady-in-waiting to Grand Duchess George; the responses sung *a cappella* by the choir were intensely moving:

> The beauty of the liturgy was too much for the loyal Russians who had come to pay their last homage to their beloved Emperor and all that he represented. They broke into sobs. We tried to restrain our emotions but we, in turn, gave way.[49]

Meriel Buchanan was there with her father, Sir George, and recalled 'the same blue drift of incense, the same wavering golden gleam of candles' that she had seen at funeral services in Russia. The unrestrained emotional response that the Buchanans and Baroness de Stoeckl witnessed that day was not just a farewell to Nicholas; it reflected a profound sense of loss, of it being 'the end of everything'. The old Russia, which so many of those gathered there had known and loved and been forced to flee, was gone. 'With the Emperor so much went that was dear to us in life,' recalled de Stoeckl, and it was a feeling that transmitted itself also to King George and Queen Mary. 'When the choir sang a prayer to the Virgin in farewell to the soul which had fled, tears were running down the Queen's face.'[50]

Never one to record his innermost feelings, even in the privacy of his diary – a characteristic he shared with his cousin Nicholas – George struggled to find something to say that evening. 'It was a foul murder. I was devoted to Nicky, who was the kindest of men and a thorough gentleman,' he wrote. Whatever his faults, his cousin had 'loved his country and people'.[51]

What more could he say? George knew that he had failed Nicholas. But the consequences of that failure were only just beginning to unravel, as too was the final act in the grotesque game of cat-and-mouse being conducted by the Bolsheviks over the fate of Alexandra and the children.

Chapter 13

'Those Poor Innocent Children'

T he memorial service for the former Nicholas II, Emperor of Russia, received scanty coverage in the British press in August 1918. 'So many people do wear black these days,' remarked the society magazine *Tatler*, 'that the Court mourning for the Tsar really made not much difference to the look of things, even at the opera.'[1] 'Most of the newspapers in the countries of the Entente printed the shortest of obituaries and gave the impression that their writers refrained, for motives of delicacy, from expressing their real thoughts,' recalled the former Russian ambassador to France, Alexander Iswolsky. 'One could not help feeling that this reserve veiled an overwhelming condemnation of the character and acts of the late sovereign.' The one 'glaring exception to this "conspiracy of silence",' he noted, was the response of the *Daily Telegraph*, which published a series of articles by Dr Ernest Dillon, full of 'violent accusations against Nicholas II', which Iswolsky found to be 'extreme, misleading and untruthful'.[2]

The Allies were now in the fourth year of a bitter war and in danger of losing it; in Russia a general lack of diplomatic interest about the fate of the Tsar was amplified by the very poor communications, preventing any foreign powers from obtaining reliable news and conveying their outrage to the Soviets. Those diplomats still resident in the country found themselves in an increasingly perilous situation, with many Allied officials in particular in fear for their lives. Violent political reprisals were now becoming widespread as the Bolshevik Red Terror took hold: what was one more death, of a now irrelevant former monarch, in the midst of a growing culture of violence that was taking hold in Russia? The response from ordinary Russians to Nicholas's murder was even more subdued, if not indifferent, although a few services were held in those of Moscow's churches still open to worship. In general, as US ambassador David R. Francis noted, 'The killing of the Emperor, whom the people of Russia once looked upon with affection and reverence as the Little Father, aroused no resentment whatever. In fact, it was forgotten within a short time.'[3]

It was a report in the 'German Wireless' that first pointed the finger of blame – at Britain – for having failed the Tsar:

If England now fulfils the kindred duty of her Court by wearing mourning ... she ought to have fulfilled her duty of granting at least personal protection to the fallen Czar, who was too weak to maintain his position and too weak to take a hand again in the fate of Russia ... Even in the last few weeks she could have protected the Czar if she had so desired. The Czar has been sacrificed to British policy, just like everything else that comes in its way ... Now that Nicholas can no longer do any harm, mourning is worn for him. The English Court makes use of his death, which was welcome to them and for which England herself is partly responsible, in order to make of it before the world a melo-dramatic spectacle.[4]

Over in Britain the levels of official hypocrisy reached new heights in a letter that Lord Stamfordham wrote to Lord Esher on 25 July, in which he bewailed the low-key British response to the Tsar's death. 'Was there ever a crueller murder and has this country ever before displayed such callous indifference to a tragedy of this magnitude?' he asked. 'Where is our national sympathy, gratitude, common decency gone to?'[5]

Callous indifference? Stamfordham seems to have had no sense of his own, when stoking the fires of the King's reluctance to offer asylum, or when debating whether or not the monarch should even attend his own cousin's funeral. 'What were the sufferings of that poor unfortunate Emperor during the past year,' Stamfordham asked, now neatly batting the ball back into the German court: 'Why didn't the German Emperor make the release of the Czar and family a condition of the Brest-Litovsk Peace?'[6] In his response Lord Esher agreed that it was all Wilhelm's fault for not doing so. It all boiled down to a matter of 'Moral cowardice. Fear of insinuation, of criticism, of abuse.'[7]

Moral cowardice was indeed a characteristic of all the failed negotiations for the Romanovs by all the parties involved, except perhaps King Alfonso. Yet, even as the various royals and their governments began pointing the finger of blame at each other, considerable confusion still prevailed about the fate of Alexandra and the children. This was made worse when rumours began circulating that they had been seen being transferred by train out of Ekaterinburg to Perm.[8]

It was this unsubstantiated sighting, told and retold and spun a dozen different ways by conspiracy theorists, that engendered the myths of miraculous escape that would follow over the next century. From Perm, so it was later claimed, the women were separated and sent to different locations in Europe under new identities. The stories rapidly developed a life of their own, feeding into the claims that began in 1920, with the emergence in Berlin of the false Anastasia – Anna Anderson, aka Franciszka Szankowska – not to mention a host of other bogus claimants who followed in her wake.

Acceptance of Nicholas's death, however, was fairly immediate and widespread, although his mother Dagmar refused to believe that her darling Niki was dead till the day she herself died. In the weeks that followed, it was a different matter for the rest of the family. Without tangible proof, without a grave or sight of Alexandra's and the children's bodies, many in their wider European family refused to give up hope that they were still alive. Worse, they were not yet aware that Ella and her fellow captives at Alapaevsk had also been murdered. Indeed, for a while the Germans seem to have been under the impression that Ella was still in Moscow.[9] Even as the acting German consul there, Herbert Hauschild, was making vigorous appeals on behalf of the 'German Princesses', he sensed that the Soviets were lying to him.

There is no doubt that the most shameful episode in this tragic story is the extent to which King Alfonso of Spain was led by the nose by Lenin's government. At the beginning of August his last desperate attempts to help the family were revealed, when Spanish newspapers began reporting that their Foreign Ministry had initiated discussions to 'bring the widow and daughters of the former tsar to Spain'.[10]

Throughout this period of grief and uncertainty, King Alfonso, who had been closely monitoring the Romanov situation since the abdication the previous March, was in close contact with Victoria Milford Haven. The Tsaritsa Alexandra was his wife Ena's and Victoria Milford Haven's first cousin, and they all shared great concern over her well-being and that of the Romanov children. It would appear that on 31 July, the Spanish Foreign Ministry sent instructions to Fernando Gómez Contreras – its business attaché in Petrograd and the sole remaining diplomatic representative in Russia – that at the first opportunity he was to intimate to the Soviets that King Alfonso, out of deep humanitarian considerations, wanted to offer refuge to the 'empress widow and her son', while wishing in no way to interfere in the internal affairs of Russia.[11] A further telegram clarified that the offer was extended to the Dowager and *all* of the children. On 3 August *The Times* broke the Spanish rumours of the proposed 'removal to Spain of the widow and daughters of the ex-tsar', thanks to King Alfonso's 'solicitude'. Three days later it was reporting a rumour in 'political circles in Moscow' that although the 'ex-tsarina is safe', the government intended to 'bring her before a Revolutionary Court owing to her relations with Rasputin'.[12]

On 3 August, Alfonso telegraphed Victoria Milford Haven, confirming he had initiated negotiations

to save empress and young girls, as it seems the tsarevich is dead. The proposal is to move them to a neutral country or have them remain here on my word of honour until the end of the war. I hope that the rest of the sovereigns will help me. I shall inform you of all the news I receive. Affectionately, Alfonso.[13]

He also wrote to the Grand Duchess George in London, who had recently begged him to act for her own husband. Now imprisoned in Petrograd's Shpalernaya Prison by the Soviets, Grand Duke George was receiving very little food, had fallen ill and was in need of medical assistance.[14] Alfonso was, he told her, in the process of making representations on behalf of all their Romanov relatives, but 'it would be of the utmost importance that the King of England telegraphed me in this regard in order to reinforce my petition, which is not easy at all'.[15] It was imperative that he had the British king's support, and Alfonso simultaneously sent word to George, asking, 'May I count on your approval?'[16] Queen Mary – who had also telegraphed King Alfonso about the plight of Grand Duke George – was loath to trouble her husband while he was away visiting the British army in France, but with Alfonso clearly unwilling to act on his own initiative, she discussed the matter with Foreign Office officials.[17] Tiptoeing around the correct protocols, Mary wished 'to be most careful not to compromise herself or our King'. A draft response was discussed with Balfour and then rejected, in favour of the blandest of replies: 'George away', and the additional justification that her brief telegram to Alfonso confirming this had been sent 'with knowledge of Foreign Office'.[18]

Bearing in mind the excruciating degree of royal obsession with the correct procedures demonstrated in this entirely modest exchange, is it likely that the British monarchy could ever have cut through the crippling levels of bureaucratic red tape at any point in this story, to take command of the situation and rescue their Romanov cousins?

Victoria Milford Haven was by now so distraught that she had even considered appealing – woman to woman – to Lenin's wife, Krupskaya.[19] On 10 August she wrote to King George about Alfonso's need for concerted family backing. She was sure he was 'willing and ready' to help; but for 'poor Alix and her girls … any steps to get them out of the country should be taken quickly', otherwise the 'revolutionary fanatics' guarding them might 'do what they like with their prisoners'. But she had no doubt that Ella would refuse to leave her religious work in Russia, to which she had dedicated her life.[20]

Victoria was right on both counts, but sadly, of course, it was too late.

Still ignorant of the truth, Alfonso had now turned his attention to Kaiser Wilhelm, asking him to join in the efforts to save Nicholas's 'unhappy family' and ensure their safe evacuation to a neutral country for the duration of the war.[21] The Germans at this stage seemed as certain as the Spanish that Alexandra and the children were all still alive, and Lenin's government did nothing to disabuse either of them of the fact; indeed, they deliberately played along with them, and all the other Western governments. But there was considerable disquiet in German aristocratic circles that Germany was obliged to conduct pseudo-friendly negotiations with Lenin's government. Princess Lowenstein was horrified with the German conservative press for playing down the Tsar's murder, considering that 'our intimate new friends the Bolsheviks have killed him. How disgusting I find the friendship with these pigs! One day this will exact vengeance.'[22]

For now, the royals and governments of Europe seemed more than happy to allow Alfonso to take the initiative, as they received the telegrams from him that winged their way from Madrid to Berlin, Vienna, Oslo, Paris, Rome, The Hague, London and Copenhagen. With their support, his 'hand would be strengthened', Alfonso told them, 'in an act which can have no political but only humanitarian significance'. In response, words of encouragement arrived from Queen Wilhelmina (who instructed her ambassador in Petrograd to assist in any Spanish negotiations with the Soviets), King Haakon and the Kaiser.[23] With the King still out of the country, London cabled that 'the Government of His British Majesty deeply appreciates the sentiments of His Majesty the King of Spain and sincerely hopes that he shall achieve the intended purpose'.[24] By now, even the Bourbon Prince Jaime – Carlist pretender to the Spanish throne – was also onside and telegraphed: 'hoping quick result salvation unfortunate Russian Imperial Family'.[25] Privately, however, the Spanish were investing little hope in support from the British with regard to a refuge for the former Tsaritsa. The Spanish ambassador in London, Alfonso Merry Del Val, considered that the British court was really only interested in the welfare of the Dowager, and that any efforts to secure the release of Alexandra might be more favourably looked upon if they also included the Queen Mother's sister, Dagmar, in the negotiations. There was still considerable hostility in England towards Alexandra, he noted, in a letter to the Spanish president:

> She is considered to be an agent – conscious or unconscious – of Germany, and the principal cause, although certainly involuntarily, of the revolution ... I must add that the resentment, whether justified or not, but nevertheless very powerful, against the empress Alix, is so extreme that it will ultimately prohibit all possibility of her coming to live in the United Kingdom.[26]

Even in death, Alexandra was still the *bête noire* in this whole sorry story.

It was not until mid-August that the British king himself re-entered the frame. Returning on the 14th from his visit to the front, George V sent a belated but positive response to Alfonso via Sir Arthur Hardinge, his ambassador to Spain:

Would greatly appreciate that you exert all your influence in the most effective way, in order to release the Russian Imperial Family from the deplorable situation they are living in at the present time.[27]

British military intelligence was also enlisting Major General Poole, head of the British forces at Archangel: 'If you have a chance of helping and saving them,' he was instructed, 'Mr Balfour desires that you should do so.'[28]

So British Foreign Secretary Arthur Balfour had finally changed his tune, as had many others in this story who had remained determinedly detached till now. But it had taken confirmation of Nicholas's murder to galvanise them all into this last-ditch action.

Even the Vatican had been drawn into this frantic, concerted campaign to get the Russian Imperial Family to safety. On 11 August, the Vatican newspaper *Osservatore Romano* reported that Pope Benedict XV (who, like Alfonso, had been involved in humanitarian work during the war) 'has offered to defray all costs arising from the move of Nicholas II's family from Russia to Spain, having asked the Cabinets concerned to act as soon as possible on compassionate grounds'.[29] He also offered a refuge to the Dowager and 'an annuity to enable her to live in accordance with the dignity of her position'.[30]

The newspaper announcement was a mercifully short résumé of an excruciatingly obsequious telegram to the German Chancellor, sent by the Pope's nuncio Eugenio Pacelli, informing him of His Holiness's desire to 'help these unfortunate high personages and ... do everything possible so that ... the pain of those poor ruling figures who have been removed from the glory of the throne to the greatest wretchedness may be alleviated'.[31] The Pope's personal petition reached the Soviets on 19 August and received a positive response from the Council of Soviet Commissars. It was all, of course, a sham. Meanwhile the Vatican had assured the German government that, like the Dowager, the Tsaritsa and her daughters would be given 'decent accommodation' and be maintained in the 'proper style'.[32] The Germans were, however, unimpressed by this late papal initiative; it did nothing to help matters. They were now also preoccupied by the fate of the four imprisoned Grand Dukes – George, Dimitri, Nicholas and Paul – and were pressing for them to be released and sent to join their other Romanov relatives in Crimea. The Danish ambassador Scavenius was even attempting to 'buy them out' to safety, in return for a bribe to the Soviets of 500,000 rubles.[33]

It was now more than a month since the Imperial Family's murder, but still the Spanish king was caught, unwittingly, in the ugly charade being manipulated by the Soviets. On 22 August, Fernando Gómez Contreras received orders from Madrid to press on with negotiations for the transfer of the family to Spain. At the beginning of September, he travelled to Moscow with the Dutch ambassador, Willem Oudendijk, to see Chicherin at the Foreign Ministry, which was based at the Hotel Metropole. The minister was clearly annoyed, but acted entirely as though the subjects of their conversation were still alive, telling the two diplomats that he 'could not understand how representatives of countries still ruled by monarchs could intercede for the Imperial Family, which had been responsible for the woes the people had had to endure for centuries'.[34] Nevertheless he played along with the Spanish minister, arguing that allowing the family out to Spain was a considerable risk to the Soviets, as it might foster the growth of a counter-revolutionary movement against Russia there. Contreras had remonstrated that there were few places where the family would in fact be *further removed* from political action than rural Spain. It became apparent to him during their discussion that Chicherin was implying that if neutral Spain finally officially recognised the Soviet government, there might be an advantageous trade-off – the Romanovs. Even in death, the Imperial Family were useful bargaining chips; this demand was one that Alfonso had already anticipated 'as the price of Soviet acquiescence' to his proposal.[35]

Contreras had been deeply uneasy throughout the meeting with Chicherin, even though he left with the promise that his appeal would be passed on to the CEC. He reported his reservations to Madrid, noting in a telling final statement, 'I came out of this meeting utterly convinced of the perversity and bad faith of this people, that surpasses everything that could be imagined.'[36] He could see no easy resolution in sight, and felt that the Germans had a share of responsibility in trying to save the Tsar's wife and children. He later filed an official report in which he observed that despite the many entreaties to the Kaiser to 'stand up for the royal prisoners', Wilhelm had replied that although he greatly regretted the 'pitiful situation of the deposed family', his desire to help had 'run up against the bitter and absolute impossibility of being able to undertake anything to alleviate their fate'.[37]

Contreras was far from convinced of this. Germany, of all the foreign powers, had been in the best position to exert influence over the Bolsheviks. Yet as late as 29 August the Germans still appeared to be hostage to the phoney negotiations being dragged out by the Soviets. At the behest of Karl Radek, liaising on behalf of the Soviet Foreign Ministry, it was now suggested to the German consul, Hauschild, that Alexandra and the children be traded for Leo Jogiches, a Polish Social Democrat and leader of the Spartacists (the German communists now inciting revolution in Germany), who had recently been arrested in Berlin. Soon afterwards Adolph Joffe made the outrageous suggestion of an even bigger trade-off – Karl Liebknecht, founder of the German Communist Party and currently in jail for high treason.[38]

At the end of August, just as Hauschild reported to Berlin that Chicherin and Radek were both angling for some kind of political 'compensation' in return for releasing Alexandra and the children, news finally began circulating in Britain that the entire family had perished.[39] On the 28th a Foreign Office memorandum confirmed the long-awaited news from Archangel. Lord Stamfordham was one of the first to hear it, from Lord Milner at the War Office, on the 31st:

We have just received a very distressing telegram from the Intelligence Officer serving under General Poole at Murmansk to the effect that there is every probability that the Empress of Russia, her four daughters and the Czarevitch were all murdered at the same time as the late Czar. The information reached the Intelligence Officer from a source which he has no reason to doubt. I am much afraid, therefore, that the news is only too likely to prove true.[40]

The King confided a sad little note to his diary that night: 'It's too horrible and shows what fiends these Bolshevists are. For poor Alicky, perhaps it was best so. But those poor innocent children!'[41] He broke the news in person that day to his widowed aunt, Princess Helena, who lived on the Windsor Estate at Cumberland Lodge. It was a Sunday, and the Princess and her daughter Marie Louise were due to have lunch with the King and Queen at the castle, as they often did. But on this occasion they had been kept waiting in the corridor. George and Mary finally emerged half an hour late, looking 'grave and deeply upset'. Indeed, the King seemed so anguished that Helena thought there must have been a major military defeat on the Western Front. Finally, and in a state of deep shock, George told her he had just received confirmation of what they had all dreaded: 'Nicky, Alix, and their five children have all been murdered by the Bolsheviks at Ekaterinburg.'[42]

On 2 September, Marie Louise took the terrible news in person to Victoria Milford Haven on the Isle of Wight. She had been due there on a visit and had volunteered to take a letter from the King. Victoria was profoundly shocked; 'we did not talk at great length about it at all, there was so little one could say,' recalled Marie Louise. 'The horror of this ghastly tragedy was too overwhelming for mere words, and just the ordinary expressions of condolence seemed utterly out of place.'[43]

Victoria herself had, till the last, held out hopes for the four daughters, she wrote to King George the following day: 'Those dear girls were young enough to have recovered from the horrors they went through and happier days might have come to them, yet also there was the chance, that haunted me, of great wrong being done to them.'[44] She was tormented by the fact that she did not know whether Alexandra and her daughters had perished with Nicholas and Alexey or had been killed separately. 'Though her loss is pain and grief to me,' Victoria later wrote of her sister Alexandra to a friend, 'yet I am grateful that I can think of her as being at peace now. She, her dear husband and children removed for ever from further suffering.'[45] It was not until 9 November that Victoria finally learned that her other sister Ella had also been killed, her body and those of her companions recovered from the mine shaft on 29 September, when the Whites took Alapaevsk.*

Lord Stamfordham reacted to confirmation of the murder of the entire family in a letter to a colleague on 1 September: 'Naturally the King is deeply grieved at the ghastly fate which has befallen his relatives,' he wrote, adding that 'it is almost incredible that the innocent children should not have been spared'.[46] The response of George's son and heir, David, Prince of Wales, was rather less charitable: 'How tragic the wretched Czar being shot. What brutes the Bolshevists are … he was a charming man, though of course hopelessly weak' – said by a man who, eighteen years later, would expose his own fatal weakness as king.[47]

On 12 September, the *Daily Express* reported that the 'ex-Czarina and her four daughters' had been assassinated by the Bolsheviks, the assumption already being that Alexey had been killed with his father. The British Foreign Office was unwilling to confirm the story, which the *Express* claimed came from 'a source which is beyond doubt'. It was 'The Foulest of Crimes', remarked the *Aberdeen Evening Express* in its banner headline, and one that would 'arouse a feeling of horror through the whole civilized world'.[48]

---

* Ella and her companions' remains were taken to Irkutsk for safety, but when it became clear that the Whites would lose control of that area, the coffins were sent to Peking to protect them from desecration. In January 1921 Ella's body and that of Sister Varvara were sent to Jerusalem and, in honour of Ella's own long-held wishes, buried at the Russian Orthodox Convent on the Mount of Olives.

Although the British and Spanish royals were by now reluctantly forced to accept that the whole family had died, the Germans were still being led a dance by Chicherin and Radek, who on 13 and 14 September changed their script in order to play for more time. They now claimed that they had received a report from the front that the precise whereabouts of Alexandra and the children, with their Red Guard escort, was unknown, due to the chaotic evacuation of Ekaterinburg when the Czechs had taken the city. But they assured them that 'news of their present location on this side of the front would shortly be received'.[49]

By now the Germans had had enough of Russian stonewalling. In the latest negotiations the Soviets had 'rejected our approach as interference in Russian affairs,' remarked a German Foreign Ministry official, 'unless we equally were to allow Russian intercession on behalf of certain troublesome personalities in Germany [i.e. Jogiches and Liebknecht]'.[50] This political trade-off was something the Germans adamantly rejected; and so they decided to defer to King Alfonso, making ever more desperate suggestions: why not send the family to one of the countries of the Entente? Or to Crimea? Joffe brazenly fielded their suggestions by agreeing to them all, finally conceding that, to the best of his knowledge, the family were all still somewhere in Siberia.[51] The extent to which Soviet misinformation had infiltrated foreign intelligence on the subject is demonstrated by the fact that it took until 5 October before the news was finally confirmed by Sir Charles Elliott, consul-general for Siberia, in a fifteen-page report to the FO. He had travelled to Ekaterinburg to investigate the intelligence at first hand, but came away with very little evidence; he concluded, misguidedly and based only on tenuous rumour, that 'the surviving members of the royal family' had left Ekaterinburg by train to the north or west.[52]

And so the uncertainty continued. Indeed, it never really went away. Count Benckendorff observed in his memoirs, published in London in 1927, the continuing and widespread circulation of stories of survival: 'In spite of the absurdity of the idea that their Majesties, their children, their suite and their servants could have been sent abroad and there hidden without any newspaper mentioning the fact these rumours are credited all over Russia, in all classes.'[53]

It was not till 5 December 1918 that *The Times* formally confirmed the 'Fate of the Tsar's Family'. News had reached Berlin from its officials in Kiev that they had been 'All shot together in a cellar'. By this time the first lurid, tabloid account in English had been rushed into print – by a notorious plagiarist whose books bore very little resemblance to the truth. *The Secret Life of the Ex-Tsaritza* by William Le Queux, published in early November 1918, promised readers a thrill–a–minute account in which the 'grimmer chapters of this stupendous tragedy are reconstructed in the amazing disclosures … based on the statement of Colonel Vassili Gregorieff, who accompanied the Tsar into exile'.[54] Colonel Gregorieff was a fiction; Le Queux's book marked the beginning of a long, false trail of sensationalist claims about the Romanovs and their murder, given further exposure by a *Times* story of the 5th, based on a totally unreliable 'witness'* statement about the last days of the Imperial Family's imprisonment at the Ipatiev House. *The Times* story shocked readers with descriptions of the family being 'locked up in one room, where there was only one bed', being forced to sleep on the floor and woken and interrogated at all hours and, worse, carried insinuations that the four daughters had been sexually harassed.[55]

It would be another eight years before the Soviets finally admitted in print to the deaths of the entire family; forced to do so by the extensive investigative work of Nikolay Sokolov, who

---

* Sensationalist accounts based on the bogus testimony of this witness, named 'Parfen Domnin', were syndicated in the USA. He would appear in fact to have been the Tsar's former valet, Terenty Chemodurov, who went to Ekaterinburg with the family but, when he fell ill in May, was removed from the Ipatiev House to the local hospital. Confused and possibly senile, he was freed from Ekaterinburg jail by the Whites and spoke to some Western reporters about his experiences.

published his findings in French as *Enquête Judiciaire sur l'assassinat de la famille impériale* in Paris in 1924. In 1926, the official, self-justifying Soviet account was released by a member of the Eka-terinburg Soviet, Pavel Bykov. Titled *Poslednye dni Romanovykh*, [*Last Days of the Romanovs*] it was published, appropriately enough, in Sverdlovsk – the new name for Ekaterinburg – honouring Yakov Sverdlov, the key architect of the Romanov murders. It was translated into several languages.

Long before this, in the autumn of 1918, a long saga of accusa-tion and blame had begun to unravel in private letters exchanged within the royal families of Europe. On 1 September, George V, sending a letter of condolence to his cousin Victoria Milford Haven, concluded that 'The awful part is that they might all have been saved if W had only lifted a finger on their behalf.'[56] It is not known how Victoria responded to this, but she made her feelings abundantly clear in a letter of thanks three weeks later to King Alfonso. In it, she painfully admitted that there was 'nothing to hope for' and that death had released her sister Alex-andra and her children 'from further suffering'. They had now 'passed from the cruel hands of man into those of a just and merciful God' and she wanted to thank the Spanish king for all he had 'tried to do to save them from their enemies'. In her mind, much like King George's, it was very clear where the blame lay for the failure to save her family from this hideous end:

> The Sovereign who had most direct influence on the revo-lutionary government in Russia, the one who had known my sister as a child, who had the same blood as hers flowing in his veins, who formerly never failed to claim her as of his nationality deserted her.*

---

* For many years sources have interpreted these comments as an allusion to King George, but this cannot be right, given the context in which it was written. King George's comments in his own recent letter to Victoria Milford Haven quoted above, plus the very specific allusions to their shared German roots, all clearly indicate that she had Kaiser Wilhelm, and not King George, in mind.

Wilhelm: the fellow German, cousin and childhood playmate (from happy family visits to Hesse) of Victoria, Alexandra, Ella and Irene had betrayed the German-born Tsaritsa. Victoria was convinced that he had failed to capitalise on the upper hand that he had had over the Bolshevik government at the Brest–Litovsk talks and insist on the trade-off of the Romanovs being allowed out of Russia to safety. In contrast, King Alfonso, to whom Alexandra and her children 'were comparative strangers', had done his utmost to help them. 'I shall never forget the gratitude I owe you for this,' she told him.[57]

It is said that King Alfonso ever afterwards deeply regretted the 'lack of solidarity' from his fellow monarchs in his efforts to rescue the Romanovs. He never recovered from the grief and despair of having failed them. But one thing at least would have greatly consoled him, for word did in fact reach Nicholas of the efforts Alfonso had been making on his behalf. With the help of Baroness Buxhoeveden, a message from the Spanish king to this effect was passed on to Nicholas at the Governor's House in Tobolsk. The Tsar was deeply moved: 'that is truly one loyal friend', he was heard to say to Alexandra. A true friend indeed, for Alfonso and Nicholas had, in fact, never met.[58]

As the political and moral consequences of the murders began to unravel in the years that followed, we come to the most ignominious part of this complex story – the deliberate bowdlerisation and redaction of the official record. There were reputations to be protected, and the machinery of government set about ensuring that this happened.

Chapter 14

'His Majesty Would Much Prefer that Nothing ... Be Published'

The murder of the Romanovs was one of so many tragedies during a world war that saw millions dead, wounded, displaced and dispossessed. Nevertheless, to those most closely associated with the Imperial Family, their violent end would be a wound that never healed. Frequent and contradictory stories about the survival of some or all of the family continued to reach their relatives in Western Europe for many decades afterwards. Time and again the revival of discussion about the deaths of the Romanovs brought with it bouts of remorse and recrimination over who was to blame for the failure to save them.

King George's grief remained deep, but totally private. 'He never made any public reference to it,' recalled his friend the Aga Khan, 'but more than once in our private talks he had no hesitation in opening his heart to me and telling me of his sorrow.'[1] When Colonel Paul Rodzianko, who had entered Ekaterinburg with the British Expeditionary Force soon after the murders, returned to England in 1920, George invited him to lunch, anxious to 'hear my account of the Siberian Expedition and the murder of his cousins'. Rodzianko had been reluctant to go into details – 'the episode was so intimate' – and recalled that it was 'a somewhat painful conversation'.[2] Four years later, the short-lived Labour government under Ramsay

MacDonald sought to re-establish links with Russia, now renamed the Soviet Union. The King could not, of course, veto this, but he did refuse to receive any Soviet delegates, and insisted that he should not be made to 'shake hands with the murderers of his relatives'.[3]

All these painful discussions had been revived with the arrival of Dagmar and her daughter Xenia in England on 9 May 1919. It had broken the Dowager Empress's heart to leave Russia, clinging to the belief that Nicholas and the family had somehow miraculously survived, and still knowing nothing of the fate of her other son, Mikhail. But with the Russian Civil War now spreading to Crimea, her sister the Queen Mother had begged Dagmar to leave while she still could. George V's sending of a battleship, HMS *Marlborough*, to evacuate the Dowager, Xenia and other members of the Romanov family and their retainers from Yalta in April 1919 probably saved them from being murdered by the Bolsheviks. But the gregarious Dagmar did not take to the dreary tête-à-têtes with her widowed sister at Marlborough House and Sandringham. She soon decamped to Denmark, where she lived at the expense of her nephew, King Christian, unrepentantly running up mountains of unpaid bills. Even when the rest of the world had given up on her son and his family as 'irrefutably dead', Dagmar would not abandon hope. At her window in Copenhagen she kept a small lamp burning, so that 'Nicky will know I'm still awaiting his return.' Dagmar's own lamp went out in 1928.[4] In 2006 her body was repatriated to St Petersburg and reburied with her husband's at the Saints Peter and Paul Cathedral.

The evacuation of the Dowager and her relatives had been an obvious – and no doubt necessary – cathartic act of redemption on George's part, to compensate for his failure to save his Romanov relatives.[5]* But the painful reminders continued to

---

* In 1922, after an insurrection against the Greek throne, the British government sent a warship to rescue King George's cousin, Prince Andrew (the Duke of Edinburgh's father), who was being held under arrest. A British ship also safely evacuated the deposed Emperor Charles I of Austria–Hungary across the Black Sea in November 1921.

haunt him, even as Dagmar arrived in Britain. On 11 April 1919, he received a despatch from Colonel D. S. Robertson, acting British High Commissioner in Siberia based in Vladivostok, enclosing a preliminary report on the murders. Lord Stamfordham wrote to the Foreign Office that the King had read it 'with horror'; he was adamant that 'His Majesty would much prefer that nothing of this account be published.'[6] Stamfordham reiterated this on the front cover of the relevant FO file – entitled 'Murder of the Ex-Czar' – that was circulated to him. 'HM prefers that nothing should be published.'[7] And indeed none of this *was* made public, although the relevant FO file was later made accessible to researchers for consultation at the National Archives.

In contrast, former Russian Prime Minister Alexander Kerensky had no compunction about publishing a series of self-exculpatory accounts in the years after the war. The most widely circulated was his apologia 'Why the Tsar Never Came to England', published in the *Evening Standard* in July 1932, but as early as 1921 Kerensky had sought to explain in the émigré Russian press what went on behind the scenes of his own and Milyukov's attempts to get the Romanovs out of Russia. This greatly incensed the British government's mouthpiece, the *Daily Telegraph*. Blaming Kerensky for his 'futile attempts at statesmanship', which handed power to the Bolsheviks, the paper accused him in 1921 of insinuating that the British government was 'entirely to blame' for the tragic end of the Imperial Family. The paper rightly pointed out that:

There is absolutely no proof that Kerensky, in the event of a favourable answer, would have been able to get his prisoners over the border without imperiling their lives … In 1917 the German submarines had become most deadly, and had sunk several ships around Murmansk. This alone would have been reason enough for a desire to delay the crossing of the Imperial captives.

It was the 'pusillanimity of Kerensky and his colleagues in dealing with the Bolsheviki' that had been the 'real cause of the

Ekaterinburg murders'.[8] Kerensky retaliated by accusing the Allied governments of a 'game of duplicity' played against his own government; the *Telegraph* had attempted to 'soften down the categorical nature of the [British] refusal' to facilitate and provide safe asylum, when by June 1917 it had completely reversed its original offer.[9] In the end, however, as even Kerensky conceded, 'even if the Provisional Government had wanted to remove the former Tsar abroad, it would not have been able to do so, because the Council [Petrograd Soviet] would not have allowed it'. During the lull of July, however, when the Bolsheviks had been discredited and were in retreat, 'it became quite possible to remove Nikolas II from Tsarskoye-Selo', and he had done so. Technically, the Tsar's evacuation north to the Finnish border and out on a British ship, Kerensky now claimed, 'would have been no more difficult than his journey to Tobolsk'.[10] He was backed up in this by Milyukov, and would repeat his claims in numerous articles in the émigré press for the next fifteen years or more, at all times denying any responsibility in the failed asylum initiative.[11] The publication of his memoirs – *The Catastrophe: Kerensky's Own Story of the Russian Revolution* – in London and New York in 1927 aroused another storm of indignation and protest, this time from the Foreign Office.[12]

Inevitably, during the 1920s and 1930s, a succession of political and private memoirs of the last days of imperial Russia followed in quick succession. In 1921, after serving as ambassador for a final two years in Rome, Sir George Buchanan retired and began work on an account of his seven-year service in Russia. He was assisted in the task by the author and literary editor Edmund Gosse, and destroyed all his papers on completing it; in 1923, the two-volume *My Mission to Russia* was published in London.

Throughout the compilation of these memoirs Buchanan was under considerable Foreign Office pressure not to reveal anything that exposed it, the King or his government to undue criticism. Indeed, Diplomatic Service Regulation no. 20 insisted that the Foreign Secretary would have to give permission with regard to any classified information that was obtained in a diplomat's official capacity and used in a subsequent memoir. Thus Buchanan's ability to speak freely about what went on behind the scenes of the Romanov asylum was severely curtailed.[13] In her later book, *The Dissolution of an Empire*, his daughter Meriel revealed how her father was pressurised into covering up details of the King's change of heart and of giving 'a rather ambiguous and misleading account of the facts'.[14] According to her, Sir George was 'told at the Foreign Office, where he had gone to examine some of the documents', that if he did publish the truth:

> he would not only be charged with an Infringement of the Official Secrets Act, but would have his pension stopped … The account he gives of the promise of the British Government to receive the Emperor in England … is therefore a deliberate attempt to suppress the true facts.[15]

To make matters worse, in 1923 – shortly before his memoirs were published – Sir George was forced to respond to malicious accusations made against him in the serialisation of Princess Paley's *Souvenirs de Russie* in the *Revue de Paris*.[16] Paley, the morganatic second wife of Grand Duke Paul Alexandrovich, was one of Sir George's most vocal critics. She nursed a deep-seated antipathy towards the British ambassador as having somehow had a hand in fomenting the February Revolution and, with it, the downfall of the Tsar. Her vitriolic accusations that he had personally betrayed the Romanovs came perilously close to libel. But Sir George's 'guilt by default', as alleged by Paley, was sadly a view shared by Pierre Gilliard and some other members of the Russian aristocracy.[17] He was also accused of having failed to secure the evacuation out of Russia of Grand Duke Kirill and his wife, Victoria Melita – a granddaughter of Queen Victoria – with whom he and his wife had been friends.[18] In truth, Sir George had found himself in a very difficult position at the time, forced to consider the safety of his own family in revolutionary Petrograd and also mindful of the threat to his embassy if he did not cut off his friendship with the Kirills.

In response to Princess Paley's allegations, Sir George published an extended extract from his forthcoming memoirs in the same *Revue*, under the heading 'Nicolas II et la Révolution Bolcheviste', adding a qualifier, clearly made under duress, exonerating both Milyukov's and his own governments:

> I did not call in question the good faith of the Provisional Government … it was they who took the initiative in the matter by asking us to offer the Emperor and his family an asylum in England … Our offer remained open and was never withdrawn. If advantage was not taken of it, it was because the Provisional Government failed to overcome the opposition of the Soviet. They were not, as I asserted and as I repeat, masters in their own house.[19]

When Buchanan's extract was published, Milyukov protested at this closing statement. The controversy did not die down: Paley reasserted her insinuations about Sir George's 'nefarious' dealings over the Romanovs, in a response published again in the *Revue de Paris* on 15 April 1923.[20] Unfortunately, she overreached herself this time, claiming that Sir George had deliberately withheld George V's telegram of support sent to Nicholas II shortly after his abdication. The King, she insisted, had personally telegraphed Nicholas, 'urging him to come as soon as possible to England, where he and his family would find a sure and peaceful retreat'.[21]

It is interesting to note how long this particular misapprehension – that King George had freely and openly offered asylum to the Romanovs – persisted. The accusation against Sir George was, as Meriel Buchanan wrote, all part of 'that old but persistent rumour that my father never tried to save the Imperial Family', and moreover that he did so 'deliberately, and with intent'. Writing in *Dissolution of an Empire* in 1932, she hoped that some day 'somebody will publish the true story of those proceedings, backed by documentary proof in the official archives'.[22]

But back in 1922–3, Paley's ill-conceived attack, and Buchanan's dignified but hamstrung self-defence, took its toll on the ambassador's already-failing health. He died a year after publishing his memoirs, his name and his reputation sullied. His daughter carried the torch of his defence against the 'hurtful' rumours with an energetic militancy over the next thirty years, through her own memoirs and various magazine articles. Sir George's editor, Edmund Gosse, congratulated Meriel on having done so in her book *Diplomacy and Foreign Courts*, published in 1928, recalling that Sir George had 'talked to me much and often of those terrible last months in Russia' when they had worked together on his memoirs.[23] Long after her father's death, Meriel was still repeatedly asked whether her father could not have 'done something to get the Emperor and family out of Russia?'[24] Finally, in her autobiography of 1958, *Ambassador's Daughter*, she was at least able to publish in full the telegram sent by her father on 22 March 1917 to the Foreign Office, relating how Milyukov had told Sir George how anxious he was to 'get the Emperor of Russia out as soon as possible' and how, in response, Sir George had urged the Foreign Office that '*the Emperor should leave before the agitation has time to grow*', and asking for the government's authority '*without delay to offer His Majesty asylum in England* [my italics]'.[25] What more could Buchanan, as ambassador, have done?

Despite her best efforts, Meriel Buchanan was forced to admit that her defence of her father's reputation had been hampered throughout by lack of access to the official records. She had therefore written her accounts 'from my own personal recollections and from impressions left on my mind by my father's actual words and actions'.[26] The problem was compounded, she claimed, by the fact that, with regard to the official record, in 1917–18 Lloyd George:

had a habit of *sending telegrams direct* [my italics] to the various Embassies, and not through the usual source of the FO, so that in the official archives there is nothing to show that he was directly instrumental in preventing the Emperor being given sanctuary in England.[27]

This is an important point, which might explain some of the presumed 'absence of evidence' that perhaps has sent commentators down false trails in this story.

Nevertheless, publication of Meriel Buchanan's *Dissolution of an Empire* in the summer of 1932 aroused considerable press interest and inevitable questions were asked of David Lloyd George. What was his recall of the Romanov asylum affair? His response was vague and evasive; a statement was released through his secretary that the former Prime Minister (who had fallen from power in October 1922) had:

> no clear recollection of what happened at the time but that 'if the question of allowing the Tsar to come here did arise he probably did advise against it, because at that time we were trying to persuade Kerensky to go on fighting for the Allies, and to have allowed the Tsar to come here would have prejudiced the representations we were making to Kerensky'.[28]

As such, this was a retrospective admission that behind the scenes David Lloyd George had no more wanted the Romanovs to come to England than his king had. With the King's reputation under close and unassailable guard, the finger of blame was therefore inevitably redirected at him. Officialdom was aware, but was keeping quiet: 'I understand that Mr Lloyd George was not responsible for the decision,' noted a senior Foreign Office official, 'but that it is not expedient to say who was.'[29]

Two years later, when Lloyd George was busy writing up the 1917–18 period of his six-volume *War Memoirs*, it was his turn to experience at first hand the extent of the continuing government hush-up.

Until now, discussion of the Lloyd George memoirs relating to the Romanov asylum has had little to say beyond a bald statement of the fact that he was prevailed upon to remove an entire chapter relating to the matter, in order to protect the King's reputation. The assumption has always seemed to be that the typescript of that redacted chapter had been destroyed. It was not; it survives in the Parliamentary Archives at Westminster. I found it there, after some searching, thanks to a brief discussion of it by a former Foreign Office official, Keith Hamilton, in a 2013 collection of academic essays.[30] The chapter itself is entirely plodding and unremarkable, but it is the comments pencilled in the margin by the officials who vetted it that are revealing. As is so often the case, the real story is to be found in the marginalia – in what was left unsaid or removed from the record – and it was exciting to receive a copy of this important piece of evidence.

When drafting his chapter entitled 'Czar's Future Residence', Lloyd George enquired about the extent to which he could quote from official documents, for he knew that it would be closely scrutinised. It was, in fact, the responsibility of Cabinet Secretary Maurice Hankey to go through the chapter with a fine toothcomb. After adding his own comments in the margin in pencil, Hankey passed the chapter on to Sir Robert Vansittart, the Permanent Under-Secretary at the Foreign Office, who did likewise. Even though the chapter itself is little more than a chronological résumé of the facts, quoting official telegrams and letters, it was enough to alarm them both for, despite its blandness, it nevertheless implied that the King had had a direct role in the British change of heart.

Hankey was, in particular, concerned that the text showed a clear change in the government's position between the meeting of the War Cabinet on 21 March 1917 when doubt was expressed as to the suitability of Great Britain being the 'right place to go', and the meeting held by the larger Imperial War Cabinet (including representatives of the Dominions) on 22 March, when 'we admittedly changed our mind' and decided to offer asylum, but only for the duration of the war. Opponents would 'fasten on that point and will say that the grounds were not strong enough [to renege on this asylum offer at a later date] and that we were not very courageous.'[31] Objection was also raised to the inclusion of Buchanan's 'pitiless' comment in his 2 April letter to Balfour, in which he spoke of the Tsaritsa having been 'the Emperor's evil genius ever since they married' – 'which rather overstates the case and therefore weakens it'.[32] Of greatest concern, however, was Lloyd George's assertion that there was:

> a strong feeling hostile to the Czar in certain working class circles in this country, *and that articles tending to associate the King with the Czar had appeared in the Press* [my italics]; it was felt that if the Czar should take up his residence here, there was a danger that these tendencies might be stimulated and accented.[33]

Hankey and Vansittart immediately took exception to the phrase above in italics: these words '*must* be omitted'. Overall, they felt that the chapter demonstrated an embarrassing weakening of the King and his government's position, if not downright timidity on their part – 'not very courageous' being a damning admission of their collective lack of will. The telegram to Sir George of 13 April explaining the 'considerable anti-monarchical movement' developing in Britain also had to go; as, too, did Lloyd George's quotation of Buchanan's reluctant agreement that 'it would be far better that the ex-Emperor should not come to England' and that France should be approached instead.[34] This information would 'carry little conviction to the public now, who will not readily believe that there was any real danger to the throne here, and will of course fasten on the obvious point that we confessedly tried to pass the responsibility and risk – if any – to France!'[35] Yes, conceded one of the notes in the margin: 'we admittedly changed our own minds. That is what the accusers say. Will they think the grounds strong enough? I feel sure of the contrary – at this stage.'[36]

After consultation with others in the Cabinet Office, the consensus was that the whole chapter – seven pages of typescript – should be suppressed, in the belief that George V would object to it. Lloyd George was irritated by the news; the court, he noted, seemed 'very jumpy and nervy'.[37] Two months later he removed the chapter and wrote a new one, omitting all reference to the King and stating that 'The invitation [to come to England] was not withdrawn.' The ultimate decision in the matter, he instead insisted, came from the Russian government, 'which continued to place obstacles in the way of the Czar's departure'.[38]

It was not until the 1975 publication of the diary of Lloyd George's private secretary, A. J. Sylvester, that further clarification on the subject was made public, with the entry for 26 June 1934:

> LG has decided to write another chapter about the Tsar. The other one has been scrapped because of objections to it from Hankey, Baldwin and the Court. The new material is not to refer to the movements which were regarded as anti-monarchical in this country.[39]

In the end, it was the King's assistant private secretary, Sir Clive Wigram, who turned the screw on Lloyd George. To further distance the King's role in the whole ignominious affair and cover up the lack of British resolve, Lloyd George therefore concluded in his published version that:

> the fact is that at no time between his abdication and his murder was [Nicholas II] free to leave Russia. An invitation to take refuge here was extended by the British Crown and Government. The Czar was unable in the event to avail himself of it, even had he been anxious to do so – and of that we had no evidence.[40]

For the time being, George V's honour had been saved, protected by the redaction of both Buchanan's and Lloyd George's memoirs. After the King's death in 1936 the inevitable official biography would follow, and in 1948 the author and former diplomat Harold Nicolson was invited to take on the task. He was instructed from the outset that, at all costs, his job was to protect the King's reputation and he should 'omit things and incidents which were discreditable to the royal family'.[41]

Summers and Mangold later claimed that in his account Nicolson 'slithered past the subject [of the Romanov asylum] as quickly as possible, quoting highly selectively'. Not true, countered former court correspondent Daniel Counihan, in a letter to *The Listener* on 7 October 1976: Nicolson had revealed the King's opposition in four pages on the subject; his biography was the product of the severe constraints placed upon him, and 'written at a time when some things simply could not be said'. King George's opposition to the Romanovs coming to England had been that of a 'great constitutional monarch conscientiously doing his job'.[42]

To his dying day in March 1931, Lord Stamfordham also fiercely protected George's position, so much so that he took the most extraordinary of defensive measures not long beforehand. Drawing on his unique position of trust, he obtained access to the Foreign Office papers dealing with the Romanov asylum and, at the bottom of his original letter of 6 April 1917 in which he explained the King's change of heart to Balfour, he added a handwritten note: 'Most people appear to think the invitation was initiated by the King whereas it was *His Govt* who did so.'[43] Ruthless to the last, Stamfordham, the devoted royal servant, was even prepared to doctor the record.

And so the endless game of buck-passing continued. Ultimately, it was historian Kenneth Rose who best summed up King George V's position in his revealing 1983 biography. Unlike other historians, Rose was, apparently, given 'a free hand as regards the royal archives' and access to all of Harold Nicolson's papers. Eventually the typescript had to be submitted to Queen Elizabeth II for her approval. Having read the contentious section in which Rose pulled no punches on George's own failings in the Romanov asylum, the Queen wrote with a flourish at the bottom: 'Let him publish.'[44] Perhaps by 1983 she had come to the conclusion that the Windsors could no longer continue to dodge their responsibility in the affair. It was Kenneth Rose, in fact, who best summed up the extraordinarily difficult position in which the Queen's grandfather had found himself:

> The first principle of an hereditary monarchy is to survive; and never was King George V obliged to tread the path of self preservation more cautiously than in 1917.[45]

From the moment that news of the murder of Nicholas II was announced, impregnable official defences were thrown up around the reputation of King George and are still largely in place to this day. Over the years, both the National Archives and the Royal Archives have responded to numerous Freedom of Information requests from writers and journalists with repeated assertions that there is no relevant material hidden away that has not already been made public. The first challenges to official insistence that nothing had been removed from the record were concertedly made in the 1970s by Summers and Mangold during the research for their TV documentary and controversial bestseller, The File on the Tsar. *They contended, through three editions of their book over the next thirty years, that some official British records had been carefully and selectively weeded of potentially embarrassing or compromising material relating to the Romanov asylum. While the unsealing of Cabinet papers in 1986 showed that David Lloyd George, and to a degree Sir George Buchanan as well, had taken the rap for the King's share of responsibility, there is still the question of Secret Service files. These are of course an entirely different matter: any such MI1(c) files relating to SIS activities in Russia in 1917–18 might reveal behind-the-scenes attempts to help the Romanovs that have never been admitted to. But if they do exist, they will probably never be released.[46] It is, of course, every historian's ultimate nightmare – knowing that there may well be material that will shed valuable light on a complex story, but to which he or she will never be granted access. Sadly, the Romanov story is full of such frustrations.*

Despite the nagging gaps in the record with regard to some aspects of this story, over the last century numerous books and articles, TV documentaries and, latterly, blogs and internet discussions have all repeatedly raked over the coals, many of them in a determined attempt to lay the blame at King George's door in particular. But perhaps the time has come to accept that responsibility should be more widely, and equally, apportioned. The hindsight of 100 years allows us to assess the situation today from several very different perspectives: of political alliances, wartime expediency, personal antipathies, family loyalties, logistics, geography, and even the weather. All of these elements had a part to play in the failure of all and any rescue plans. But back in 1917–18 by far the most pressing aspect, for all the royal families and governments involved, was that of the internal political considerations then prevailing.

In the final analysis, King George V was faced with reaching a highly reluctant decision about his Romanov cousins. Russophobia was nothing new in the UK; indeed, anti-Russian hatred had been whipped up in the reign of George's grandmother, Queen Victoria, from the Crimean War of 1854–6 to Russian encroachments in Afghanistan in the 1880s. In 1908, George's father Edward VII had been widely condemned for meeting the 'blood-stained' Nicholas at Reval, and Labour Party members had signed a petition against the visit. By 1917, the Labour Party and its leadership, not to mention much of the British press, were so vehemently opposed to any possibility of the former Tsar and his family settling in the UK that, like it or not, King George had no alternative but to consider the potentially dire political consequences for his monarchy. It mattered not that Nicholas would have wished to live in quiet domestic obscurity in the countryside; his need for a refuge came at totally the wrong time politically, when many left-wing groups in Britain were hoping that the British throne might go the same way as the Russian one. The King clearly panicked at the exaggerated prospect presented to him by Lord Stamfordham of worker-led strikes and mass protests across the country.

George's scrupulous attention to the position of the constitutional monarch – or, more accurately, parliamentary monarch – meant that he was obliged to respect the Coronation Oath that he had sworn in 1910 to put the national interests first at all times. His government had been voted into power by the will of the people, and the will of the British people in 1917–18 was seemingly that the Romanovs were not welcome. And while it might be easy retrospectively to say that the threat to his throne was exaggerated and that a republican-style uprising on the streets of London was in fact highly unlikely, one has to view the King's reaction in the context of 1917 and not that of 100 years later.

In all his decision-making, King George V's forceful and uncompromising wife Queen Mary supported him quietly but firmly behind the scenes. She, if anything, was even more determined to preserve the continuity and stability of the British throne, in much the same way that Tsaritsa Alexandra had vigorously defended it in Russia. Would Nicholas ever have capitulated and signed the abdication if Alexandra had been in the room at the time? No. Never.

Many years after the events of 1917–18 the former King Edward VIII, now Duke of Windsor, recalled taking breakfast with his parents in the spring of 1917 when an equerry suddenly entered the room – something that was never normally done. 'I mean this was *breakfast*, for heaven's sake! We looked, I hope, suitably horrified at this breach.' His father was furious, the Duke recalled:

But the man went straight up to him with this note, which the king read and gave to my mother, and she read it and gave it back and said, 'No'. The king gave it to the equerry and said 'No.' Later that day I asked my mother what that was all about and she said the government was willing to send a ship to rescue the czar and his family but she did not think it would be good for us to have them in England.[47]

In recounting this story in his book, *The Last Kaiser*, author Tyler Whittle added – from 'private information' given to him – that Queen Mary, whom George V considered his most trusted adviser, conceived it her 'prime duty to protect the English throne' and that 'it could not be put at risk even for dear cousins'.[48] It was for this reason that in July 1917 King George had distanced himself and his family from their German roots by adopting the family name of Windsor; the wider British royal family had also dropped all their German honours and titles.[49]

The suggestion has also been made that much deeper personal feelings coloured Queen Mary's attitude to the Romanov asylum: that her adamant opposition was influenced by her own intense dislike for the Tsaritsa. This, so the story goes, was born of Mary's own sense of inferiority to the 'real royalty' of the tsars, an elevated position to which her modestly born German cousin Alexandra had risen and in which she revelled. In private conversations with the American author Gore Vidal, the late Princess Margaret suggested that Queen Mary had a 'pathological jealousy' of the status of most of her grandchildren: they were Royal Highnesses, whereas she, as the daughter of the Duke of Teck from the obscure Kingdom of Württemberg (and who had contracted a morganatic marriage to boot), was a mere Serene Highness. There is nothing to substantiate Princess Margaret's view, beyond the fact perhaps that Mary's spendthrift parents had lived in straitened circumstances and her relatives had rubbed into her during her childhood a sense of being the poor relation.[50] Alexandra was a crashing snob with an unshakeable sense of her superiority and it is little wonder if Mary felt humiliated by her; particularly when, in 1891, Mary became the lower-ranking second-choice fiancée for Bertie's son Eddy, Duke of Clarence, after Alexandra had rejected him.[51]

Such private feelings may have been in the back of Queen Mary's mind, but neither she nor the King, nor even his insidious adviser Lord Stamfordham, could ever have had an inkling of the terrible murders to come. This in itself is demonstrative of their own and the British government's lack of understanding, at this stage, of the brutal new communist regime that they were dealing with. Nevertheless, Stamfordham's decisive Machiavellian influence over the King was first noted in 1934 by Stephen Gaselee, the official in control of the vetting of diplomatic memoirs: 'the truth of the matter is that Lord Stamfordham suddenly "got cold feet", and induced a couple of rather timid telegrams to be sent from here'.[52] Such was the power of the King's private secretary at that time.

★

There remains one final dimension to this story that till now has not been fully explored – and that is the position of the Kaiser. The subject was first publicly broached when a row broke out in 1935 between former French ambassador Maurice Paléologue and Dr Kurt Jagow, co-director and archivist at the Brandenburg Royal Prussian Archives. It was sparked by publication in Paris that year of Paléologue's *Guillaume II et Nicolas II*, in which he vilified Wilhelm for betraying his cousin and the Imperial Family, claiming that he could – and indeed should – have made their release a prerequisite of the Brest-Litovsk Treaty, and citing at length the accusatory open letter of General Leontiev.*

Jagow rose to the Kaiser's defence in a long article entitled 'Die Schuld am Zarenmord' (The Blame for the Tsar's Murder) published in Berlin.[53] It seemed to him that Paléologue was intent on blaming Germany not only for the Romanovs' deaths, but also for the entire war. As for Wilhelm's responsibility as a cousin of the Tsar, Jagow contended that monarchs have never been particularly famous for their solidarity, and Nicholas and Wilhelm had not had a particularly deep friendship; by 1917, as even Paléologue himself admitted, 'the mutual trust of the two sovereigns [was] dead'.[54] Nicholas and Alexandra, argued Jagow, 'did *not* see the Germans as having a moral obligation to help them; on the contrary, they were actively opposed to such help and refused it point-blank, even when their situation was most desperate'.[55] He then turned his attention to the failures of Britain and France and of Milyukov's government. The Tsar's allies knew from the beginning that his life was in great danger and in 1917 they had the power to save him; yet ambassador Paléologue's sympathy for the imprisoned Tsar and his family had never extended further than 'sentimental entries in his diary and their literary use later' in his memoirs.[56] Jagow pointed out that right at the beginning of this crisis, through the offices of Scavenius

---

* See chapter 9, page 166–7.

at the Danish embassy in Petrograd,* the Germans had promised to allow a ship to evacuate the Imperial Family under a white flag and without threat from their torpedo boats; that in the spring of 1917, Germany 'would not have stood in the way of the Entente to get them out'.[57] He then went on to quote in detail from the various diplomatic exchanges with the Soviet government in efforts to protect the 'German princesses'; how the Germans had liaised with King Christian of Denmark, and later with their Spanish counterparts, to secure the release of the Tsaritsa and her children, who they thought were still alive.[58] But the German government had been 'fobbed off with [Soviet] lies until the end, without being able to do anything'. Jagow had no doubt about who carried the burden of blame in all this: it was 'the Bolshevik government of 1918'.[59]

Jagow's defence of the Kaiser in response to Paléologue's accusations was welcome, but revealed nothing of the Kaiser's own personal feelings. Even in his memoirs, published in English in 1922, Wilhelm had hardly a word to say about Nicholas, beyond noting that 'he ha[d] been murdered'.[60] There is no sense of any regret, let alone outrage, and little or no empathy for his late cousin either, so it is no surprise that many have assumed that Wilhelm had made no real efforts to save the Romanov family.

There was, however, one person to whom the Kaiser *did* speak at length and in confidence about the subject: his old friend Brigadier General Wallscourt H.-H. Waters. The two men had become acquainted during 1900–3, when Waters had served as British military attaché in Berlin. After Wilhelm's wife died in 1921, Waters had visited the Kaiser often at his manor house in Doorn in the Netherlands, where Wilhelm had taken refuge

---

* The Danish diplomat Harald Scavenius is without doubt one of the unsung heroes in this story. If only more information on his diplomatic efforts on behalf of *all* the Romanovs trapped in Russia were available to us. Unfortunately, aside from official correspondence, they probably languish in the Royal Danish Archives, which are closed to researchers.

in 1920. Between 1928 and 1935 the two men had had many
long conversations about the war, which Waters later recounted
in his 1935 memoir *Potsdam and Doorn*. He had proved a willing
listener to Wilhelm's endless and frequent tirades about the 'ocean
of abuse, vilification, infamy, slanders and lies' that he fulminated
had been directed at him from London during and since that
time.[61]

At Doorn in 1935, Wilhelm had insisted on reading Waters the
long Jagow article in full. 'It appeared to me,' Waters wrote, 'that
the conversation on the subject between the Kaiser and myself
should be recorded as spoken at the time.' And so Waters diligently
took notes of the whole 'mendacious accusation' made by Paléologue, along with Jagow's 'withering refutation'.[62] Crucially he
also stated in his memoirs that he had drawn on the Kaiser's own
notes on the matter, for his book.[63]

But where were those observations now? In File on the Tsar, *Summers
and Mangold claimed that Waters's 'full unedited notes' on these conversations with the Kaiser had been lodged with the Royal Archives after
Waters's death in 1945. But on enquiry in 1975, the two authors were
informed that there were 'insuperable administrative difficulties' in making
the papers available to them.[64] More than forty years later, when I too
contacted the RA about these papers, I was informed that the archives
held no such papers, but only a group of letters to Waters from the Kaiser
and his wife that it had purchased from Waters's cousin. There were no
notes on conversations with the Kaiser about the Romanovs. So what
had happened to the supposed notes deposited with the archives in 1945,
I wondered? Were the Kaiser's comments to Waters deliberately weeded
and destroyed at some point, by the RA, to protect King George? Summers and Mangold seemed to think so, and that there was a conspiracy
at work, because in* Potsdam and Doorn *Waters had 'published only
his notes on the German emperor's attitude immediately after the tsar's
abdication in 1917'; and that 'the key period in 1918 is omitted alto-
gether'.[65] But is this really the case?*

*I sought clarification by ordering a copy of Waters's will. In fact it
only makes one brief reference to personal papers – specifically his*

correspondence – instructing his 'residuary legatee', Colonel Lyster Taylor, to dispose of various items as he saw fit. These included 'letters of appreciation from distinguished persons and letters from the Emperor William'. This is the material that Colonel Taylor subsequently sold to the Royal Archives. There were no notes; and no conspiracy by the Royal Archives to hide any such material from the public.[66]

The Kaiser did, however, preserve his own notes. They finally surfaced during research for this book – having been lost to history since the 1930s.

In 2016, a brief internet announcement in German was spotted by a friend of mine, regarding an obscure, small-scale exhibition coming up at the Burg Hohenzollern Archive, entitled '300 Jahre Romanow & Hohenzollern'. Even obtaining a copy of the rudimentary catalogue proved difficult, but when it finally arrived, there – buried under item 64 – was this listing:

'Questions and Reflections concerning Rescue of the Tsar'. Records of William II of April, 1931, concerning his trying to save the Tsar and his family in the summer of 1918* Lead on paper.[67]

A concerted effort to track down the relevant archivist and then obtain permission from HIRH the Prinz von Preussen to see these papers took some time, but finally produced a result. Digital scans pinged into my inbox from Burg Hohenzollern of twelve pages of documents covered with the Kaiser's characteristic, tense pencil scribbles. The first document in the sequence, the 'Questions and Reflections', is written in English in pencil – perhaps for the benefit of Waters. It is not dated but it is, in part, an exact mirror of what Waters recounts on pages 259–61 of Potsdam and Doorn. However, with regard to the claim by Summers and Mangold that the notes on the 'key period

---

* Note that the archival dating of the file is rather misleading. The notes in the Kaiser's hand are not dated. The date of 1931 and another of 1934 in the file both relate to letters sent to the Kaiser about the Romanovs, on which he had scribbled his responses.

in 1918' had been removed from the RA, it seems unlikely there ever were any.[68] *The original documents at Burg Hohenzollern are fundamentally a discussion of the early plans in 1917 for a German evacuation of the Romanovs from Russia. There is little or no mention by the Kaiser of events in 1918.*

In his list of ten points relating to the matter, Wilhelm made numerous angry observations: why had the Danish king taken the step of contacting him direct in the spring of 1917 about the plight of the Romanovs, rather than acting in concert with the British king? Was it because the Danes sensed that the 'desultory treatment of this urgent question' by the British government would get them nowhere? Did news of the growing resistance to the Tsar's asylum in England prompt fears that any rescue 'was being jeopardised' and that it would be more effective to address their appeals to the German emperor direct?[69] Why had Copenhagen not shared the details of the negotiations between London and Petrograd – of which the Danes' ambassador, Scavenius, was well aware – with the Kaiser? And why had the Danes not told the British about the military and naval arrangements that he, Wilhelm, was willing to make for effecting a safe evacuation of the Romanovs? Wilhelm had, he claimed, 'expressed his readiness to co-operate with London for the rescue of the Tsar and his family', but neutral Denmark had not transmitted this information to London. Was Sir George Buchanan not informed of Wilhelm's generous offer?[70] And why had it not been properly acknowledged? He was not just affronted that he had not been consulted, but was furious that 'no steps were taken to ask Copenhagen to express the British Government's grateful appreciation to the German Chancellor at this offer'.[71]

Reading these notes, one's immediate sense is that this is as much about Wilhelm's fragile ego and his imperial sense of honour as it is about his desire to help his relatives. He expected the world to fall at his feet and acknowledge the nobility of his gesture, but instead he had been ignored. Why had his initiative been rejected? Was he deluding himself or was Wilhelm right to ask the question, made in his final point, no. 10:

> If the British people had ... learnt of the offer of cooperation on the part of the German Emperor for the rescue of the Tsar, would they not out of the spirit of chivalry toward their ally have encouraged their Government to rescue the Tsar and his family?[72]

Alas, Wilhelm's mind was stuck in a mythical age of Teutonic heroism; such a 'spirit of chivalry' did not exist in the real world, and certainly not in wartime. Nor was anyone interested in responding to his obsessive attention-seeking.

But that is not the end of the Burg Hohenzollern documents; the file contains another lengthy annotation by the Kaiser, again in pencil, but this time in German. It comes at the end of a letter sent to him on 14 March 1931 by an émigré Russian journalist, Anatoly Gutman, at the end of which the Kaiser added his own impassioned observations. Quotations from this do not appear in the Waters published account, suggesting that Waters either was not privy to this exchange when writing his book (which seems unlikely given his close friendship with the Kaiser) or that he chose not to use it.

Does this explain the absence of evidence that Summers and Mangold interpreted as evidence of absence?

At the time, Gutman – who wrote under the pseudonym Anatol Gan and was resident in Berlin – was working on a book about the murder of the Romanovs (which appears never to have been published) and asked the Kaiser for clarification on several points relating to his knowledge of the negotiations in the spring of 1917. Wilhelm responded that he was kept informed by his then Chancellor, Theobald von Bethmann-Hollweg,* who told him

---

* Note that Bethmann resigned in July 1917.

of appeals that he had received from the Danish king via Stockholm. In response, Wilhelm had agreed that if the Imperial Family were to be evacuated by sea:

> The fleet in the Baltic and in the North Sea would *secretly* have to be informed of this at once, so that the ship – also eventually under a British or Danish flag – could be escorted. I would give the order as soon as the route was certain.[73]

In the event of an evacuation by land, Wilhelm was ready to order a 'brief ceasefire with opposing Russian troops' in that section of the Eastern Front where the Tsar's handover would take place. Nicholas would be brought ceremoniously through 'the lines of his mutinous army' to the German ones, where he would be allowed to pass with dignity, 'among salutes due to a sovereign'. What is more, Wilhelm would 'personally travel to the location and monitor the handover and receive the Imperial Family with all due honour'. 'I was willing to be of assistance to the Tsar in any way – any dignified way,' he insisted. But until the very day this happened 'everything was to remain secret'.[74]

Wilhelm goes on in these notes to claim that 'after some considerable time' Bethmann informed him that he had '*favourably discussed a journey via Scandinavia with the Kerensky government* [my italics], which seemed not unwilling to allow the Tsar to leave the country'. Wilhelm insisted to Kerensky, via Bethmann, that he 'be informed of the chosen route as soon as possible to make the preparations', to which Kerensky responded that he 'would do everything to facilitate and support the departure of the Tsar', placing a special train at his disposal; '*for the presence of the Tsar was a serious impediment for him* [my italics].'[75]

The Germans were still awaiting further news from Kerensky when suddenly the announcement came: 'The British had invited the Tsar to come to England and would take care of his departure.'[76] The German rescue offer was stymied.

★

This till now unknown account by Wilhelm raises important questions. If true, it implies, first, that Kerensky was playing both governments – British and German – at the same time over the Romanov evacuation/ asylum; and, second, that the British, perhaps having got wind of the German plan for an evacuation, had rushed to gain a political advantage and pre-empt them, by making their telegram offer of 23 March. It also begs a final important question: if the British and Germans could have temporarily buried their political differences and acted in concert in March 1917, might this have been the best and only chance of a safe passage for the family?

'What an abyss of personal and political infamy this reveals,' concluded Wilhelm in his notes to Gutman's letter, 'to consign an ally and friend to a certain death so that his chivalrous cousin – even though his opponent – should not be allowed to perform an act of chivalrous service that might possibly have had political disadvantages for England after the war.'[77]

In the end, this entire story comes down to politics, expediency and strategy – not to mention the wounds to the Kaiser's monumental ego – and not to any genuine humanitarian concerns.

If Kerensky did indeed conduct secret negotiations with the Germans in the spring of 1917 to evacuate the Romanovs, no further surviving evidence has come to light, any more than there is proof that the British offer to bring the Tsar and his family out of Russia was a cynical attempt to score points over a hated enemy.

Was it all the workings of the Kaiser's deluded mind, or could there be some truth in this claim? The record, as in so many other aspects of this perplexing and tortuous story, is silent.

Postscript

'Nobody's Fault'?

Whatever the degree of responsibility of the King of Great Britain, the Kaiser of Germany and their various European royal relatives in the terrible fate of their Russian cousins, there is no doubt that the murder of the Romanovs at Ekaterinburg in 1918 was a pivotal event in the long history of European monarchy. It dealt a body blow to an institution that had persisted against the odds, through centuries of revolution, acts of terrorism and the constant threat of republicanism. The Great War that set its stamp on the twentieth century, destroying so many of these seemingly inviolable monarchies, proved that their days were numbered. In the post-war years they would all have to adapt as constitutional monarchies or be forced from power.

Undoubtedly the most profoundly hostile threat to this old order had come from Bolshevism and its manifestations then threatening elsewhere in Europe. The murder of the Romanovs 'helped produce an intense, almost visceral hatred' among the European aristocracy for this new political scourge, for this was an ideology that sought the total annihilation of their kind.[1] The rise of communism in its wake signalled to monarchies everywhere that the 'divine right' of kings and royal personal diplomacy, of the kind promoted by King Edward VII, was a thing of the past. Their continuation would only be possible with the consent of the people over whom they had dominion. Socialism and democracy were the new watchwords everywhere, and monarchs now had to resist their own inbred autocratic instincts and modernise.

In November 1918, the Dutch monarchy fought off overthrow by the extreme left and in 1920 gave asylum to the deposed Kaiser; in Sweden, by 1919 King Gustav had been forced to capitulate to a centre-left administration; after a political crisis at Easter 1920, Christian X of Denmark conceded to abandoning his use of constitutional prerogatives; having survived the traumas of occupation in World War I, the Belgian king Albert I sought to unite the French and Flemish halves of his country as King of *all* Belgians; and in Norway, the consistently pragmatic King Haakon accepted the need for change, declaring in 1927: 'I am also King of the Communists.'[2] In April 1931, however, after a republican and socialist landslide in municipal elections, there was no hope of compromise for King Alfonso of Spain. Holed up with his family at the Escorial Palace in Madrid with an intimidating mob massing outside, waving their red flags and screaming 'Death to the King! ... We want the head of a son!', Alfonso was terrified that a repetition of the fate of his Romanov relatives would be visited upon his own family. Although he did not formally abdicate, he had no option but to flee the country.[3] A second Spanish Republic was proclaimed, and Alfonso eventually took refuge in Rome.

Having seen their fellow royals come crashing down across Europe, and undoubtedly haunted by the murder of their Russian relatives, King George and Queen Mary were among the first monarchs to recognise the need for a dramatic refashioning of their public image. The republican contagion inspired by revolution in Russia had threatened to sweep them aside, and they knew it was essential that they won and retained the hearts of the British working classes. It was necessary also to defuse the threat of republicanism within the Labour Party itself, by promoting the legitimacy of the monarchy as a hands-on partnership with the people. In the post-war world, George V and Queen Mary shrewdly set out to entrench their more personal style of monarchy at the centre of national life, a trend that was continued by their son George VI and has probably reached its apotheosis in the reign of their granddaughter, Elizabeth II.[4]

★

In 1855–7, when writing his 'J'accuse'-style novel *Little Dorrit* – a fierce indictment of government accountability and responsibility – Charles Dickens gave it the working title *Nobody's Fault*. It was an ironic reflection on the complacency of officialdom and the passing of responsibility from one department to another during the debacle of the Crimean conflict of 1854–6, and of society's collective guilt towards the downtrodden poor. The miseries of war and all it brought with it were 'Nobody's fault'. One might apply the same remark retrospectively to the collective guilt of the European monarchs and governments in the fate of the Romanovs. For in truth, their murders were Everybody's – and Nobody's – Fault.

A persistent theme in the many accounts of the Romanovs in 1917–18 is the desire – if not compulsion – to apportion blame, often based on incomplete or faulty evidence. Some of the political participants in their own lifetimes were mindful of exonerating themselves while they still had the chance. Sir George Buchanan did his best to defend his position in 1922, hamstrung though he was by the Official Secrets Act. 'The failure to rescue [the Imperial Family] did not lie at Lloyd George's door,' his secretary A. J. Sylvester assured the former Prime Minister's son in 1983.[5]*

In contrast to his fellow monarchs – King George, King Alfonso, King Haakon and King Christian – who kept their own counsel and never made any public statements, the Kaiser loudly protested his own purity of intent. Wilhelm's conscience was clear: 'I did all that was humanly possible ... The blood of the unhappy Tsar is not at *my* door; not on *my* hands,' he insisted to General Wallscourt Waters in 1935.[6] What written records may or may not have

---

* An interesting point of comparison can be found in the plight of the late Shah of Iran, who until his fall from power in 1979 had many friends and supporters in the West and the USA. After the Iranian Revolution, however, these supposed allies turned their backs on Mohammad Reza Shah. Already dying of cancer, he managed to escape to the West, where he was shuttled back and forth like an unwanted package, in search of medical treatment and asylum. Only Anwar Sadat (the Alfonso of this story) stood by him and offered a refuge.

existed in their private archives to enlighten us have either been destroyed or are still −100 years later − off-limits.

Perhaps we should leave it to the Russian people themselves to best convey the continuing burden of guilt that they carry. When the Romanov remains were first discovered in the Koptyaki Forest outside Ekaterinburg and excavated in 1991, huge crowds made their way out to the site, in what seemed a spontaneous 'collective act of penitence'. 'This is the place where the suffering of the Russian people began,' remarked the Archbishop of Eka- terinburg. Seven years later, President Boris Yeltsin − no doubt atoning for having ordered the demolition of the Ipatiev House in 1977 − made a significant speech on the subject. This came on 18 July 1998, when the remains of the Imperial Family (though without those of the still-missing Maria and Alexey) were buried at a high-profile ceremony at the Saints Peter and Paul Cathedral in St Petersburg, in front of an impressive gathering of surviving Romanovs. Now was the time, Yeltsin declared, for the Russian nation to acknowledge that 'we all bear responsibility for the historical memory of the nation'. 'The Yekaterinburg massacre' was, he went on, 'one of the most shameful episodes' in Russian history. 'Those who committed this crime are as guilty as are those who approved of it for decades. We are all guilty.'[7]

Ultimately, the Russian people also bear a share of responsibil- ity for what happened. It is a burden of which they are profoundly aware, as testified by the huge influx of pilgrims into Ekaterinburg every July. It can also be seen, more poignantly, in the posters of Nicholas II that are erected across Ekaterinburg during those July Days of pilgrimage and remembrance, which bear the words: *Prosti menya, moi Gosudar!* Forgive me, my Emperor.[8]

Having sought out and analysed as much surviving evidence as possible on the Romanov murders in the course of writing this book, one thought in particular persists and it is a crucial one, with which we all need to come to terms. As the *Daily Telegraph* noted as early as 1921: 'It remains ... to be proved, whether Nikolas II desired to leave Russia.'[9]

If they had actually been presented with a real and viable evacuation or escape plan, what would the Romanovs have done?

In the spring of 1917 they might have been prevailed upon to accept the offer of a temporary refuge in England *for the duration of the war*, although no doubt with a grudging regret. In 1934, writing from Lausanne to the Russian diplomat Nicholas de Basily, Pierre Gilliard had no doubt that the Romanovs had had no regrets about not being sent to England.* 'The Empress in particular repeated to me on several occasions that it would have been an intolerable torture for her and especially the Emperor to live as deposed monarchs in London,' he told de Basily.[10]

The fantasy that Alexandra in particular seemed to have nursed was of a liberation that would have allowed them to remain in Russia – hidden away somewhere remote, until a possible White victory facilitated a restoration of the monarchy. Right up until July 1918, she and Nicholas might well have responded positively to rescue by loyal Russian monarchists. But whatever the manner of their liberation, it had to be bloodless. They were absolutely insistent on that, which in itself made rescue virtually impossible. It is clear that during their imprisonment at Tobolsk and Ekaterinburg the entire Imperial Family recoiled in horror at the prospect of anyone being killed or injured as a result of any rescue. And they showed great concern, always, about having to leave their loyal servants behind to face the consequences of their escape.

Would the family ever have countenanced being freed, if it meant being forced to abandon their beloved Russia for ever? This seems highly unlikely; Alexandra told Gilliard they would have been utterly 'desolate' to have had to do so; and the children

---

* Gilliard, who was not allowed to join the family at the Ipatiev House in Ekaterinburg, remained in Siberia, where he gave valuable testimony to the Sokolov enquiry. In 1919 he married the childen's former Russian nanny, Alexandra Tegleva, and in 1920 the couple settled in Gilliard's home town of Lausanne, where he taught at the university.

also said as much to him many times when he was with them at Tobolsk.[11] To leave Russia would have been an act of betrayal of Mother Russia and a final acceptance of the irrevocable destruction of their world. They would not have been able to reconcile leaving with their devoutly Russian Orthodox consciences.

Looking at the sequence of events today, one cannot help thinking this: if only Alexandra had acted quickly and decisively and had got her children out to safety immediately after the revolution had broken in Petrograd, no matter how sick they were. The bitter truth is that there was one – and only one – real window of opportunity for escape and that was before Nicholas abdicated on 15 March 1917. Till that moment, as Tsaritsa, she still had the power to do something, before the net tightened around them all at the Alexander Palace.

Ultimately – and whether or not we are Romanov sympathisers or detractors – there is one enduring, painful truth, which is that Russia's last Imperial Family almost certainly would have refused to leave Russia under any circumstances, preferring to die together in the country they loved. By July 1918 they were reconciled to their fate; they had each other and that was all that mattered. Whatever the future held for them, whatever the suffering, it had to be shared – together, and in Russia. Ekaterinburg was their Calvary.

As their reply of 11 June 1918 to the second 'officer letter' stated so plaintively:

Nous ne voulons et ne pouvons pas FUIRE …
We do not want to and cannot *ESCAPE* …[12]

Acknowledgements

A ny book attempting to tread fresh ground in a familiar story needs to plough a very broad furrow in order to uncover new, unseen or overlooked sources. Yet even the Romanov story has not been fully told – certainly not in terms of its closing stages – and it was a thrill to find so much previously uncited material. In taking on the challenge of *The Race to Save the Romanovs* I knew that the key to new perspectives lay in foreign-language sources that had been virtually untouched in English-language studies till now. In order to find this new material I had to draw on a team of translators and researchers able to access material scattered all over the world. The task would otherwise have been impossible for me to undertake in the relatively short time I had to write the book, and bearing in mind that I was not familiar with all the languages involved.

In the United Kingdom I called on the advice and wisdom of numerous friends and historians of long standing, but by far the most crucial contributor to this entire project was my colleague Phil Tomaselli. As an expert in World War I military and intelligence material, with many years' knowledge of the enormous range of War Office and Foreign Office sources at the National Archives on this subject – and, crucially, how to find his way around their erratic filing system – I deferred to Phil's greater experience in this regard. I was not disappointed. He knew where to look and saved me an enormous amount of time. At Cambridge, Peter Day kindly searched through the papers of Lord Hardinge in the University Archives; Jane Wickenden, a specialist naval librarian, offered useful advice; Nick Forder and Tim Pickles of the Cross & Cockade International First World War Aviation Historical Society both responded helpfully to my appeals for information on World War I aviation; Michael Hargreave Mawson and Norman Gooding provided information on orders and medals of the World War I period. Tim Giddings and Felix Jay shared what they knew of Stephen Alley; Philip Kerin told me of the exploits of his grandfather, Stephen Berthold Gordon-Smith, in World War I. The following writers and historians all sent helpful answers to questions: Charlotte Zeepvat, Christopher Warwick, Douglas and Susan Ronald; Dr J. F. Pollard; Hugo Vickers and Julian Fellowes.

Once again, my fellow Russianist and brilliant French translator David Holohan helped me with Russian handwriting and French translation; my valued colleague Richard Davies, Archivist at the Leeds Russian Archive, was always ready and willing to answer any queries. Julie Crocker at the Royal Archives was most helpful and accommodating in answering my requests for material; and Emily Bourne at the Parliamentary Archives helped me locate an important document there.

In the USA my friends Mark Andersen and Ilana Miller helped me lay hands on obscure articles and offered advice; Rebecca Adaire Ramsay at Emory University, Atlanta, made a most efficient and thorough search of the Isaac Don Levine Archive on my behalf; I am grateful to archivist Kathy Shoemaker for introducing me to her. Tanya Chebotarev was most kind and helpful in providing material for me at the Bakhmeteff Archive in New York; and my stalwart researcher at the Hoover Institution, Ron Basich, searched long and hard for new and overlooked material. I am also grateful to fellow historians Doug Smith, Griffith Henniger and Professor Norman E. Saul for sharing information. In writing this book I have also greatly appreciated the support and interest in my work shown in the USA by John David Cofield, Dominic C. Albanese, Candace Metz-Longinette Gahring, and Paul Gilbert in Canada.

For Russian sources I could not have managed without the indispensable contribution of my Finnish friend Rudy de Casseres, a fluent Russian speaker who on his many frequent trips to St Petersburg sought out obscure material and was always willing to make that extra effort to try and locate hard-to-find sources on my behalf. I simply could not have gone to GARF or AVPRI myself to tackle their difficult archival systems, or the Russian handwriting of original documents, and gratefully delegated this work to the wonderful Anna Erm, who found material that I could never have hoped to locate.

In pursuing Spanish sources I was given a wonderful start by royalty historian Ricardo Javier Mateos Saínz de Medrano, who pointed me in the right direction for the best material on King Alfonso and Spanish attempts to help the Romanovs. Laura Otal at my agency, PFD, kindly gave up time to translate a long article from Spanish, before I found the wonderful Blanca Briones González, who has helped me enormously in tracking down and translating Spanish material for this story.

Scandinavia was very much virgin territory for me and I knew none of the languages, but it was somewhere that I most particularly wanted to search for new material. I was fortunate to find translator John Irons, who helped check for potential sources and translated material from Danish, Swedish and Norwegian. John also tackled the horrendous German Foreign Ministry documents on the blurred and darkened 1940s microfilm from the National Archives at Kew – but not until Phil Tomaselli had first heroically searched through it for what looked like the most important documents. In Switzerland, Karen Roth also tried to decipher some of these pages for me, as well as translating from Danish and German sources. My Dutch friend Marianne Kouwenhoven offered many helpful leads on the Scandinavian royals, as did Professor Bent Jensen, Stig Sivebæk Nielsen and Trond Norén Isaksen. Tor Bomann-Larsen generously shared his knowledge of King Haakon and, with it, copies of his four-volume biography of him. Per Gisle Galåen at the Norsk Maritimt Museum kindly sent me scans of Jonas Lied's diary; Marit Werenskiold told me of her research on Jonas Lied and sent me a copy of her book; and from Denmark, Bernadette Preben-Hansen sent me much valuable information on Harald Scavenius and advised on the difficulties of Danish royal archival sources. Anna von Lowzow also passed on her thoughts in this regard, and Nigel Holden kindly sent me his article on Harald Schou Kjeldsen.

German royalty historian Karina Urbach generously shared her knowledge and expertise and put me in touch with Jörg Schüttler, who obtained material from the Hesse Archives for me and helped me track down the archivists at Burg Hohenzollern. I am deeply grateful to Stefan Schimmel at the Burg Hohenzollern archive for sending me scans of the relevant documents that I needed from this valuable and previously unseen source.

In Winnipeg, Canada, my wonderful and super-efficient researcher Elizabeth Briggs looked long and hard for documents in the Hudson's Bay Company's archive relating to the possible Murmansk house for the Romanovs, and my thanks go to archivist Lisa Friesen for making copies available to me.

Finally – having been determined to explore every possible avenue – I contacted Keishi Ono at the National Institute for Defense Studies in Tokyo, in my attempt to verify rumours about possible Japanese interest in helping the Romanovs. Alas, we could find nothing.

In the case of much of the archival material I have drawn on, it is now impossible, at a remove of 100 years, to trace any surviving copyright holders, but I value being able to quote from documents provided to me by the various archives listed in the Bibliography. I am grateful to Her Majesty Queen Elizabeth II for permission to quote from material in the Royal Archives; to SKH Georg Friedrich Prinz von Preussen for the Kaiser's notes in the Burg Hohenzollern Hausarchiv; to Tanya Chebotarev at the Bakhmeteff Archive, Columbia University, New York; to the Archivo Histórico Nacional, Madrid; to AVPRI and GARF in

Moscow; the Syndics of Cambridge University Library; the Hoover Institution, California; the Hudson's Bay Company Canada Archives; Isaac Don Levine Archive at Emory University, Atlanta; the Leeds Russian Archive; the Parliamentary Archives at Westminster; the Oslo Maritime Museum; and the National Archives at Kew. Victor Buchli kindly granted permission for me to quote from Anastasia's letters to Katya Zborovskaya held at Hoover. The executors of the John Wimbles estate – David Horbury and Sue Woolmans – generously allowed me exclusive access to these papers before they were donated to Spain.

Several good and trusted friends, who are both Russian and Romanov specialists and enthusiasts, read and commented on the text of this book: I am indebted to Sue Woolmans, Ruth Abrahams, David Horbury, Nick Nicholson, Rudy de Casseres and Phil Tomaselli for their time, their support and their helpful notes.

Once again, I have had the pleasure of working with my American publisher Charlie Spicer at St Martin's Press, whose never-failing enthusiasm and encouragement make it such a joy to be seeing yet another book through to publication with him. Charlie's team at St Martin's Press are all tremendously supportive and hard-working, and I thank April Osborn, Kathryn Hough, Jason Prince and all those in PR and marketing who put in such a phenomenal effort in the promotion of my work in the USA.

In London, my editor and publisher Sarah Rigby and Hutchinson Publishing Director Jocasta Hamilton both provided warm and supportive back-up in the writing and production of this book, as too has my wonderful publicist Najma Finlay, with whom I am lucky to have such a fruitful partnership. Laurie Ip Fung Chun offered considerable enthusiasm in overseeing the book through to the paperback edition with Windmill. Mandy Greenfield gave my text the most scrupulous copy edit, for which I am enormously grateful.

Throughout I have had the never-failing reassurance of a caring and supportive agent, who believes in my work and has been an absolute rock in the writing of this difficult and challenging book. My love and thanks and deepest respect, as ever, go to Caroline Michel at PFD and the exceptional team of people who look after every aspect of my work there, from books to broadcast media to foreign and dramatic rights. Thank you Jon Fowler, James Carroll, Tessa David, Dan Herron, Jonathan Sissons, Alexandra Cliff, Marilia Savvides, Laura Otal, Janelle Andrew – I know you all have my back, and it is truly a privilege to have you in my professional life. I look forward to a few more books together yet.

Finally, and on a poignant note, I managed to finish the text of this book and deliver it on time, despite the heartbreaking loss in the final stages of the writing of my mother, Mary, and my former husband, Irving. In their very different ways they have both left their stamp on my life, experiences and worldview; on the things that have moulded me as a writer and that have made me the person I am now. This book is dedicated to them, and also my late father, Kenneth, who sadly never lived to see me take up my writing career. I hope he would have been proud. They and my dear family – brothers Mike, Chris and Pete, and daughters Dani and Lucy – have all helped see me safely through to the end of this, my fourteenth book.

Helen Rappaport
West Dorset, March 2018

Notes

ABBREVIATIONS

Ambassador	Maurice Paléologue, *An Ambassador's Memoirs*
AVPRI	Arkhiv Vneshney Politiki Rossiiskoy Imperii
Dissolution	Meriel Buchanan, *The Dissolution of an Empire*
Dnevniki	V. M. Khrustalev, *Dnevniki Nikolaya … i Alexandry*, 2 vols
Fall	Mark Steinberg and Vladimir Khrustalev, *Fall of the Romanovs*
FO	Foreign Office
FOT	Anthony Summers and Tom Mangold, *File on the Tsar*, 2nd edn, 1987
GARF	Gosudarstvennyi Arkhiv Russkoy Federsatsii
HBCA	Hudson's Bay Company Archives
Last Days	P. M. Bykov, *Last Days of Tsar Nicholas*
LP	Andrei Maylunas and Sergei Mironenko, *Lifelong Passion*
Mission	Sir George Buchanan, *My Mission to Russia*, vol. 2
Murder	Captain Paul Bulygin and Alexander Kerensky, *The Murder of the Romanovs*
Nicholas II	Robert Service, *The Last of the Tsars: Nicholas II*
RA	The Royal Archives
Revolyutsiya	Genrikh Ioffe, *Revolyutsiya i semya Romanovykh*
Ross. Arkhiv	L. A. Lykova (ed) and N. A. Sokolov, 'Predvaritelsnoe sledstvie'

Sudba	Sergey Melgunov, *Sudba Imperatora Nikolaya II posle otrecheniya*
Thirteen Years	Pierre Gilliard, *Thirteen Years at the Russian Court*
TNA	The National Archives
Tsarism	Semion Lyandres, *The Fall of Tsarism*
Tsaritsa	Sergey Markov, *How We Tried to Save the Tsaritsa*

Full bibliographic references are only given if the title does not appear in the bibliography.

Chapter 1: Happy Families

1 *Ambassador*, 80–1.
2 *LP*, 47.
3 *Ambassador*, 86, 89.
4 Christopher Hibbert, *Queen Victoria in Her Letters and Journals*, London: Viking, 1985, 329.
5 Röhl, *Young Wilhelm*, 326.
6 Ibid., 333.
7 Poore, *Memoirs of Emily Loch*, 154.
8 Mosolov, *At the Court of the Last Tsar*, 203; *Nicholas II*, 141.
9 Carter, *Three Emperors*, 290.
10 Urbach, *Royal Kinship*, 114.
11 Princess of Battenberg, *Reminiscences*, London: Allen & Unwin, 1925, 236, 237.
12 Aronson, *Grandmama of Europe*, 185, quoting Sir Henry Ponsonby.
13 Ibid., 118.
14 See Bomann-Larsen, *Kongstanken*, 118, 153, 314.
15 King, *The Court of the Last Tsar*, 426–7.
16 *LP*, 129.
17 Ibid., 127.
18 Isaac Don Levine, *The Willy–Nicky Letters between Kaiser Wilhelm and the Czar*, London: Hodder & Stoughton, 1920, 73.
19 John C. G. Röhl, *Kaiser Wilhelm II, a Concise Life*, Cambridge: Cambridge University Press, 2014, 83.

20 Mosolov, *At the Court of the Last Tsar*, 209.
21 Isaac Don Levine, review of the *Reminiscences of the Princess of Battenberg*, in *Salt Lake City Tribune*, 7 March 1926. See also Paléologue, *Guillaume II*, 76.
22 Egan, *Ten Years Near the German Frontier*, 51, 52.
23 See Helen Rappaport, 'Mister Heath: The English tutor who Taught Nicholas II to be the Perfect Gentleman', *Royalty Digest Quarterly*, 2016: 2, 10–16.
24 *LP*, 204, 213.
25 Barbara Tuchman, *The Guns of August*, New York: Bantam, 1962, 22.
26 Carter, *Three Emperors*, 351.
27 Ann Morrow, *Cousins Divided: George V and Nicholas II*, Stroud: Sutton Publishing, 2006, 94.
28 Hardinge papers, vol. 18, 28 March 1909, quoted in Roderick R. MacLean, *Royalty and Diplomacy in Europe, 1890–1914*, Cambridge: Cambridge University Press, 2007, 168.
29 See Buxhoeveden, *Life and Tragedy*, 121–2.
30 Viscount Esher Reginald, *Journals and Letters*, vol. 2, London: Ivor Nicolson & Watson, 1934, 460.
31 Aronson, *Grandmama*, 191.
32 Van der Kiste, *Crowns in a Changing World*, 87, 88.
33 Carter, *Three Emperors*, 385.
34 Tomaszewski, *A Great Russia*, 50, 51.
35 *Ambassador*, 91.
36 Virginia Cowles, *1913: The Defiant Swan Song*, London: Weidenfeld & Nicolson, 1967, 62.
37 Catrine Clay, *King, Kaiser, Tsar*, London: John Murray, 2006, 302.
38 Margot Asquith, *Margot Asquith's Great War Diary: The View from Downing Street*, Oxford: Oxford University Press, 2014, 93.
39 Bomann-Larsen, *Makten*, 61.
40 HRH Prince Nicholas of Greece, *Political Memoirs 1914–1917*, London: Hutchinson, 1928, 20.
41 Platen, *Bakom den Gyllne Fasaden*, 295–6.
42 Egan, *Ten Years near the German Frontier*, 16.
43 Holden, 'Harold Schou-Kjeldsen', 14, 19–20.
44 *Fort Wayne Sentinel*, 5 June 1915.

Chapter 2: 'Some Catastrophe Lurking in the Dark'

1   The papers are now lodged at the Archivo Orleans-Bourbón, Fundación Infantes Duques de Montpensier Sanlúcar de Barrameda, the archive of the granddaughter of the Queen of Romania's sister, Beatrice.

2   Letters of 12 February 1913; 7 February 1914, John Wimbles Papers.

3   Egan, *Ten Years near the German Frontier*, 318.

4   Aronson, *Grandmama of Europe*, 144–5.

5   Mosolov, *Court of the Last Tsar*, 78.

6   Alexandrov, *The End of the Romanovs*, 156.

7   See e.g. *Ambassador*, 619–20.

8   Smith, *Rasputin*, 527.

9   Hardinge, *Old Diplomacy*, 83.

10 Letter of 12 February 1913, John Wimbles Papers.

11 Letters of 31 January 1910; 26 June 1912, John Wimbles Papers.

12 Letter of 12 February 1913, John Wimbles Papers.

13 Ibid.

14 Letter of 12 April 1914, John Wimbles Papers.

15 John W. Davis, *The Ambassadorial Diary of John W. Davis: The Court of St James's 1918–1921*, Morgantown: West Virginia University Press, 1993, 56.

16 De Angelis, *Personality of Nicholas and Alexandra*, 65–6.

17 Ibid., 60.

18 *Ambassador*, 740.

19 *LP*, 530, letter to Nikolay Mikhailovich of 14 February [OS] 1917.

20 Almedingen, *Empress Alexandra*, 184–5; Shulgin, 'Dni', in Haugolnykh, *Beloemigranty*, 72.

21 Patrick Buchanan, *Later Leaves of the Buchanan Book*, Montreal: E. Garand, 1927, 277.

22 Marie of Romania, *Story of My Life*, vol. 2, London: Arno Press, 1971, 123.

23 Hall, *Little Mother of Russia*, 279.

24 Alexander, *Once a Grand Duke*, 284.

25 *Tsarism*, 106.

26 De Angelis, *Personality of Nicholas and Alexandra*, 36, 38; *LP*, 534.

27 Van der Kiste, *Crowns in a Changing World*, 136.

28 De Angelis, *Personality of Nicholas and Alexandra*, 46.

29 Bomann-Larsen, *Makten*, 121.

30 Mironenko, 'Romanov Family Tensions', 146.

31 Letter of 29 December 1916, John Wimbles Papers.

32 Jamie Cockfield, *White Crow: the Life and Times of the Grand Duke Nicholas Mikhailovich Romanov, 1859–1919*, Santa Barbara, CA: ABC Clio, 2002, 182; Stopford, *Russian Diary*, 94.

33 Neklyudov, *Diplomatic Reminiscences*, 400, writing in 1916.

34 *LP*, 477.

35 Bokhanov et al., *The Romanovs: Love Power & Tragedy*, London: Leppi Publications, 1993, 282–3.

36 *LP*, 475.

37 Egan, *Ten Years near the German Frontier*, 319–20.

38 *LP*, 527.

39 Rodzianko, *Reign of Rasputin*, 247. Van der Kiste, *Princess Victoria Melita*, 117.

40 Yusupov, *Lost Splendour*, 266; Rodzianko, *Reign of Rasputin*, 244; *Tsarism*, 58.

41 Pipes, *Russian Revolution*, 269.

42 *Tsarism*, 58.

43 Ibid., 264, 271. For further details of pre-revolutionary conspiracies against N&A, see Lyandres's valuable collection of contemporary interviews, and especially 271–2.

44 *Mission*, 41.

45 TNA FO 800/205/16, 5 January 1917.

46 TNA FO 800/205/17–18, 7 January 1917.

47 Ibid.

48 TNA FO 800/205/22.

49 See *Mission*, 43–9, for his description of this final audience with Nicholas on 12 January 1917.

50 Sir George Buchanan to Sir Charles Hardinge, 13 January 1917, quoted in McKee, 'British Perceptions', 283.

51 Lange, *Jorden er ikke Større*, 86.

52 Ibid., 86, 87; Egan, *Ten Years near the German Frontier*, 106. Egan observed at the time that the feeling in court circles there was that 'If Prince Valdemar of Denmark had been the son instead of the brother of the Dowager Empress, Russia would have a future.'

53 RA PS/PSO/GV/C/Q/1550/XVIII/215.

54 Ibid.

55 RA PS/PSO/GV/C/O/1177/218.

56 Lange, *Jorden er ikke Større*, 86.

57 TNA FO 800/205/39.

58 RA PS/PSO/GV/C/Q/1550/XVIII/220.

59 Lange, *Jorden er ikke Større*, 89.

60 *Tsarism*, 104–5, 284–5.

61 Ibid., 108.

62 Letter of 11/24 February 1917, John Wimbles Papers.

63 Buxhoeveden, *Life and Tragedy*, 250–1.

64 Voiekov, *S Tsarem I bez tsarya*, 165–7; *Dnevniki*, 1: 212.

65 Buxhoeveden, *Life and Tragedy*, 252.

66 Fuhrmann, *Wartime Correspondence*, 697.

67 *Dnevniki*, 1: 254.

68 Buchanan telegram to FO, 17 March, TNA FO 371/2995; *Tsarism*, 289.

69 De Angelis, *Personality of Nicholas and Alexandra*, 2; *Dnevniki*, 1: 264.

70 *LP*, 550; Sukhanov, *Russian Revolution*, 172.

71 Nicholas, diary of 15 March 1917, *Dnevniki*, 1: 254.

Chapter 3: 'Alicky Is the Cause of It All and Nicky Has Been Weak'

1 Diary for 13 March 1917, Rose, *King George V*, 209.

2 Van der Kiste, *Crowns in a Changing World*, 138.

3 Urbach, *Go-Betweens for Hitler*, 100–1.

4 AVPRI F. 133. Op. 470. D. 32. 1917. L. 20 and 21, quoted in Mednikov, 'Missiya Spaseniya', 65–6.

5 Regrettably none of the many books on Alfonso by the distinguished Spanish historian Carlos Seco Serrano are

available in English, but see *Alfonso XIII en el centenario de su reinado*.

6. Jensen, *Zarmoder*, 29–30.
7. Dorothy Seymour diary, 3/16 March 1917 (NS), in Imperial War Museum, Documents 95/28/1.
8. Mordvinov, *Iz perezhitogo*, 2: 146.
9. Notes of the Meetings of the Provisional Government, March–October 1917, 1: 385, notes for 15/2 March, quoted in Mironenko et al. (eds), *Gibel semi imperatora Nikolaya II*, 83.
10. TNA FO 371/2995, 16 March 1917.
11. Balfour to Buchanan, 17 March 1917, TNA FO 800/205 and FO 371/2995.
12. *LP*, 552.
13. According to Zhukov, see mironenko et al., *Gibel semi imperatora*, 287; *Sudba*, 76.
14. TNA FO 371/2995 ciphered telegrams of 15 and 16 March.
15. Ibid..
16. Basily, 'Notes on Departure', 4. Basily cites 'Mr Paléologue telegram no. 354 to the French Foreign Office'. See *Ambassador*, 834–5.
17. Basily, 'Notes on Departure', 5; citing 'unpublished documents furnished by Mr Paléologue'.
18. Alexander, *Once a Grand Duke*, 288.
19. Fuhrmann, *Wartime Correspondence*, 652, 653.
20. TNA CAB/24/8/147–8; Williams to Alexeev, 19 March; *Sudba*, 79.
21. Ibid., 78. According to Alexander Kerensky, speaking many years later in exile, shortly after Nicholas arrived back at Stavka, General Mannerheim – future commander of the Finnish army and President of Finland, who was devoted to the Tsar – had suggested a secret mission to send him on a special train to Sweden via Finland, but Kerensky had thought it too risky.
22. Ibid., 79–80; TNA CAB 24/8, 23 March 1917, 281.
23. Hanbury-Williams, *Emperor Nicholas II*, 169–70.
24. Zhuk, *Voprositelnye znaki*, 30.

25 Basily, 'Notes on the Departure', 3.

26 Buchanan, *Ambassador's Daughter*, 152.

27 Levine, *Eyewitness to History*, 112; Browder, *Russian Provisional Government*, 179.

28 Hanbury-Williams, *Emperor Nicholas II*, 171; TNA CAB 24/8.

29 Basily, 'Notes on Departure', 5; *Russkoe slovo*, 21 March 1917; Kerensky, 'Tsarskaya Semya', in Haugolnykh, *Beloemigranty*, 192.

30 TNA FO 371/2998.

31 TNA FO 371/2995, FO 371/2998.

32 Stamfordham note of meeting, 22 March 1917, *LP*, 559.

33 Lloyd George, *War Memoirs*, III: 3616, quoted in Rose, *King George V*, 209.

34 *LP*, 560; Nicolson, *King George V*, 299.

35 Buchanan, *Ambassador's Daughter*, 152; *Dissolution*, 193; FO 371/2998.

36 *Ambassador*, 845.

37 FO 371/2998, 22 March 1917.

38 Basily, 'Notes on Departure', 6.

39 Alexander, *Once a Grand Duke*, 288–9; *Dnevniki*, I: 341, 358.

40 Dagmar diary quoted in *Dnevniki*, I: 338.

41 *Dnevniki*, I: 365.

42 For a detailed discussion of the motives for the arrest of Nicholas and Alexandra, see *Sudba*, 80–5.

43 Benckendorff, *Last Days at Tsarskoe Selo*, 19. See also Puchenikova, 'Deyatelnost Britanskikh diplomaticheskikh … ', 45, quoting Shulgin.

44 TNA FO 800/205 f. 53. For Paléologue misinterpretation, see *Ambassador*, 864.

45 TNA FO 371/2998, 25 March; *Mission*, 103.

46 Francq, *Knout and the Scythe*, 239–40; Nicolson, *King George V*, 300; Buchanan, *Ambassador's Daughter*, 154–5.

47 TNA FO 800/205/50, draft of message, 19 March 1917.

48 TNA FO 800/205/51–2, 27 March 1917.

49 TNA FO 566/1199 Political Signals, 60126, Buchanan to FO, 19 and 21 March 1917.

50 Buchanan, *Ambassador's Daughter*, 153; *Dissolution*, 194.

51 *Dissolution*, 194–5.
52 Buchanan, *Ambassador's Daughter*, 154.
53 *Ambassador*, 850.
54 *Dissolution*, 194.
55 TNA CAB/24/8/265, 22 March 1917.
56 Ibid.
57 TNA CAB 281, 23 March 1917.
58 TNA CAB 23/40, minutes of Imperial War Cabinet 22 March; *FOT*, 241. Sir Charles Hardinge, 1st Lord Hardinge of Penshurst, was a cousin of Sir Arthur Henry Hardinge, British ambassador to Madrid at this time.
59 *LP*, 560.
60 AVPRI Op. 470. 1917. D. 5. L. 87, 273 March, Nabokov to Milyukov; in Mironenko et al., *Gibel semi imperatora*, 86.
61 Rose, *King George V*, 211.
62 *Mission*, 105.
63 Pierre Gilliard to Nicholas de Basily, Lausanne, 29 April 1934, De Basili Papers, Hoover Institution.
64 Official note of 25 March, on front of file no 3743, marked 'Ex-Emperor of Russia', TNA 371/3088.
65 23 March 1917, TNA 371/3088.
66 AVPRI F. 133. Op. 470. D. 32. 1917. L. 25; quoted in Mednikov, '*Missiya Spaseniya*', 70
67 Kerensky and Milyukov, 'Light on the Murder of Tsar Nikolas', 642.
68 *Liverpool Echo*, 31 March 1917.
69 GARF F. 579. Op. 1. D. 3879a. L. 1–2. The document can be seen at: http://statearchive.ru/assets/images/docs/13a/
70 Basily, 'Notes on Departure', 7. See Rose, *King George V*, 211.
71 *Dissolution*, 194–5.

Chapter 4: 'Every Day the King Is Becoming More Concerned'

1 Sukhanov, *Russian Revolution*, 220.
2 *Tsarism*, 139; *Krasnyi Arkhiv*, 1:21, 1927, 67. Online at http://istmat.info/files/uploads/33041/krasnyy_arhiv_22–1927.pdf

3   Sukhanov, *Russian Revolution*, 197, 199; Pipes, *Russian Revolution*, 333; *Last Days*, 33. See also the transcript of the document in Russian in Mironenko, *Gibel semi imperatora*, 130.

4   *Pravda*, 28 March 1917.

5   *Dnevniki*, 1: 384; *Tsarism*, 160; Grand Duchess George, *Romanov Diary*, 183.

6   *Tsarism*, 140.

7   Levine, *Eyewitness to History*, 122–3; *Tsarism*, 140; Wilton, *Last Days*, 173.

8   *Tsarism*, 139; Executive Committee of the Petrograd Soviet resolution of 21 March 1917 in Kokovtsov, 'La verité', 860.

9   *Murder*, 109–10.

10 *Ambassador*, 862; *Mission*, 105.

11 *Murder*, 112.

12 *Mission*, 105.

13 See 'Instructions … to the head of the garrison', 17 March, in *Fall*, 133–5.

14 Gilliard letter to Nicholas de Basily, 29 April 1934, Nikolai de Bazili papers, Hoover Institution; Buxhoeveden, *Life and Tragedy*, 276. The Mannerheim story is to be found in 'Prakh Tsarskoe semi', *Komsomolskaya Pravada*, 24 July 2001, 132.

15 *Liverpool Echo*, 29 March 1917.

16 TNA FO 800/205/63; *LP*, 561–2.

17 *LP*, 566.

18 See 'Russia Free! Ten Speeches Delivered at the Royal Albert Hall London on 31st March 1917', London: The Herald Office, 1917.

19 Quoted in Prochaska, 'George V and Republicanism, 1917–1919', 33; RA/GV/O/1106/1; Marr, *Diamond Queen*, 27.

20 RA/GV/O/1106/3. See Prochaska, 'George V and Republicanism', 34.

21 Marr, *Diamond Queen*, 26.

22 *Murder*, 112; Browder, *Russian Provisional Government*, 202–3; Egan, *Ten Years near the German Frontier*, 346.

23 Kerensky, *Memoirs*, 331–2.

24 *Dnevniki*, 1: 410–11.

25 Ibid., 424.

26 N. P. Karabchevsky, 'Chto glaza moi videli', in Haugolnykh, *Beloemigranty*, 190.

27 *Dnevniki*, 1: 414; *LP*, 565.

28 *Dnevniki*, 1: 413–14; *LP*, 561; TNA FO 800/205/58, 28 March; /68, 4 April.

29 TNA FO 800/205/68; see also 9 April, Buchan to Balfour, FO 800/205/82.

30 TNA FO 800/205/71, 6 April.

31 TNA FO 800/205/76 and /78, 6 April.

32 Stamfordham to Balfour, 6 April 1917, *LP*, 567; TNA FO 800/205/80. See also Lloyd George Papers F3/2/19, Parliamentary Archives.

33 *LP*, 568.

34 Ibid., TNA CAB 23/2, WC 118, 13 April 1917, available online.

35 Quoted in Lacey, *Monarch*, 61.

36 *Sudba*, 214–15; the quotation also appears in *Revolyutsiya*, 191–2, with the same incorrect attribution.

37 https://www.britishnewspaperarchive.co.uk/titles/globe

38 TNA FO 800/205/82, 9 April 1917.

39 Sir Clive Wigram to Sir William Lambton, quoted in Anthony Lambton, *Elizabeth and Alexandra*, New York: Dutton, 1986, 389.

40 *LP*, 569.

41 Ibid.; see Nicolson, *King George V*, 301–2.

42 *Dissolution*, 196.

43 Ibid., 195, published 1932; the same error in the date is repeated in her 1958 memoir *Ambassador's Daughter*. Meriel Buchanan also claims that the telegram told her father to 'tell the Provisional Government to cancel all arrangements', but it is clear that at this stage the British had not made any overt statement of refusal. Buchanan appears to have conflated events of March/early April with those of May/June, when the British position was finally made clear.

44 TNA FO 800/205/88.

45 TNA FO 800/205/90, 15 April.

46 See Meriel Buchanan, *Queen Victoria's Relations*, London: Cassell, 1954, 224.

47 TNA FO 800/205, 90–91.

48 TNA FO 800/205/105.

49 Hardinge to Lord Bertie, 17 April 1917, Hardinge Papers, vol. 31, ff. 293–4.

50 Peter Jackson, *Beyond the Balance of Power: France and the Politics of National Security, 1914–1918*, Oxford: Oxford University Press, 2013, 147–8.

51 Bertie to Balfour, 22 April, TNA FO 800/78, 22 April; Bertie to Hardinge, 22 April, Hardinge Papers, vol. 31: 165–6. There is a striking absence of comment in French sources on the Romanov asylum issue, even in British and French Foreign Office archives for the period. Ambassador Maurice Paléologue is also strangely silent on France's failure to help its ally, and has nothing at all to say about this suggestion in his memoirs.

52 Hardinge to Bertie, 27 April 1917, Hardinge Papers, vol. 31, f. 299.

Chapter 5: 'Port Romanoff by the Murmansk Railway'

1 *Thirteen Years*, 217–18.

2 Wallscourt Waters, *Potsdam and Doorn*, 245.

3 *Murder*, 107.

4 Botkin, *Real Romanovs*, 140.

5 Information from Phil Tomaselli.

6 *Murder*, 116.

7 Kerensky, 'Why the Tsar Never Came to England'.

8 *Dissolution*, 195.

9 GARF 553. Op. 1. D. 42. L. 1–2 Ob; partially quoted in Exhibition Catalogue 131.

10 Aide-memoire from British Embassy Petrograd to Milyukov, 24 March 1917, AVPRI Sekretnyi arkhiv ministra, Op. 467 D 662/693. L. 40; in Mironenko, *Gibel semi imperatora*, 131.

11 All discussion of a possible evacuation scenario from here to the end of this chapter is based on conversations and email exchanges with Phil Tomaselli, an expert on WWI sources at the National Archives, plus a great deal of speculative searching in these archives.

12 TNA ADM 137/1386.

13 Information on Archangel in May, from the diaries and letters of Graham Romeyn Taylor, a US diplomat who was there in May 1918, private collection.

14 AVPRI F. 133 (Kantselariya). Op. 470 Polit. D. 5. L. 105. 30 March 1917.

15 *LP*, 560.

16 For details, see British Embassy note to Provisional Government, 23 March 1917, AVPRI F. 133. Op. 470. Nepolit. D. 25 (Angliiskoe posolstvo). 1917. L. 19. The Bergen service was soon being taken full advantage of: Sergey Sazonov, the new Russian ambassador to the UK appointed by the Provisional Government, was due to travel to England by the Bergen route via Christiania to Denmark, as confirmed by Sir George Buchanan in a despatch to England of 14 April. TNA FO 371/3010.

17 Simon Sebag Montefiore, *The Romanovs*, London: Weidenfeld & Nicolson, 2016, 628.

18 *Murder*, 116.

19 Ibid., 117.

20 Basily, 'Question of the Departure of the Emperor Nicholas II', 24 February 1933, 11, Nikolai de Bazili Papers, Hoover Institution.

21 *Revolyutsiya*, 182; *Dnevniki*, 1: 408.

22 TNA GFM 139/6, 20 May 1917.

23 TNA GFM 139/6, 14 June 1917.

24 Dehn, *The Real Tsaritsa*, 170.

25 *Tsaritsa*, 79.

26 Ibid., 70.

27 Ibid., 83.

28 *Sudba*, 183, 238.

29 *Tsaritsa*, 87–8.

30 Ibid., 88–9.

31 Ibid., 90.

32 Markov II, in *Vestnik vyschego monarkhicheskogo soveta*, Berlin, 28 April 1924, quoted in *Revolyutsiya*, 183.

33 Stephen Locker Lampson, *Nothing to Offer But Blood*, TS of Oliver Locker Lampson's memoirs, 214, Leeds Russian Archive RUS 30.

34 Ibid., 215.
35 *Dnevniki*, 1: 601.

Chapter 6: 'I Shall Not Be Happy till They Are Safely out of Russia

1 *FOT*, 244; TNA CAB 23/2.
2 Lloyd George, *War Memoirs 1916–1917*, 514; see also Bertie to Hardinge, 22 April, Hardinge Papers, vol. 31: f. 165.
3 Leal, 'Alfonso XIII y Su Actuación Humanitaria', 57; *Dissolution*, 195.
4 TNA CAB 23/2/WC118, 13 April 1917, 2; Leal, 'Alfonso XIII y Su Actuación Humanitaria', 58.
5 TNA CAB 23/2 WC118 13 April 1917, 2.
6 Allied microfilm of captured German Foreign Ministry documents, TNA GFM 6/139 Bd 66. Madrid, 29 March 1917. The microfilm of these documents, copied after they were captured by the Allies in Berlin, is extremely variable. Some frames are so blurred or dark as to be illegible, while many have darkened borders and top and bottom edges, making dates and reference numbers indistinct. Where possible, dates and references are given, but many of these are missing on the original microfilm.
7 *Ambassador*, 904.
8 Bessie Beatty, *Red Heart of Russia*, New York: Century Co., 1918, 32.
9 Letter of 17 May 1917, Miller, *Four Graces*, 153.
10 *Thirteen Years*, 227; Benckendorff, *Last Days at Tsarskoe Selo*, 47–8.
11 Benckendorff, *Last Days*, 48–9.
12 Milyukov, *Vospominaniya*, 487.
13 See Milyukov, quoted in Kokovtsov, 'La Verité', 862; Kerensky and Milyukov, 'Light on the Murder of Tsar Nikolas', 642.
14 In his 1932 article 'Why the Tsar Never Came to England' Kerensky claimed that the British FO 'sent a conditional refusal, stating that "the British Government does not insist upon its former offer".'

15 'Informations données par M. M. Tereshchenko à M. N. de Basily à Paris le 23 Avril, 1934 au sujet de la question du départ de Nicolas II et de sa famille pour l'étranger après son abdication', 1, de Bazili Papers, Hoover Institution, Box 27, folder 11.

16 *Dnevniki*, 1: 503.

17 *Revolyutsiya*, 179; *Izvestiya*, 21 May 1917, quoted in *Revolyutsiya*, 180; *Dnevniki*, 1: 548.

18 Quoted in David Lloyd George, 'Tsar's Future Place of Residence', 4.

19 *Revolyutsiya*, 179.

20 See Benckendorff, *Last Days at Tsarskoe Selo*, 50–3.

21 Document no. 152, 'Resolutions Adopted at the Congress of Delegates at the Front, April 12, 1917', in Browder, *Russian Provisional Government*, 1: 184.

22 23 May 1917, Donald Thompson, *Donald Thompson in Russia*, New York: Century Publishing, 1918, 238–9.

23 4 April, Pourtales to Berlin; 4, 5 and 7 April, Lucius von Stoedten to Berlin, TNA GFM 6/139.

24 Rose, *King George V*, 216.

25 Document no. 77, 28 May 1917, Browder, *Russian Provisional Government*, 186.

26 Spanish ambassador in Petrograd, 9 June 1917, in Ministerio de Exteriores H: Guerra en Europa, Correspondencia con la Embjada de Espana en Russia, Bundle 2993, File 16, N6.8.

27 *Revolyutsiya*, 190–1.

28 *Murder*, 118.

29 'Informations données par M. M. Tereshchenko', 2, Nikolai de Bazili Papers, Hoover Institution.

30 *Murder*, 118.

31 Lloyd George to Hardinge, David Lloyd George Papers LG/F/5, Parliamentary Archives.

32 *Revolyutsiya*, 189, 192–3.

33 Kerensky, *Memoirs*, 336.

34 Kerensky, 'Why the Tsar Didn't Come to England'; *Murder*, 118.

35 Zhuk, *Voprositelnye znaki*, 47; partially quoted in 'Pereezd Tsarskoy Semi v Angliyu byl vozmozhen: beseda "I. R." c A. F. Kerenskim', *Vozrozhdenie*, no. 3331, 17 July 1934.

36 Jagow, 'Die Schuld am Zarenmord', 389.

37 Information from Bernadette Preben Hansen; *FOT*, 346.

38 Sir Esmé Howard to Lord Hardinge at the Foreign Office, 29 May 1917, Howard Papers DWH. 5/6, quoted in Ronald W. Clark, *Lenin: The Man Behind the Mask*, London: Faber & Faber, 1988, 347–8.

39 *FOT*, 361.

40 Neklyudov, *Diplomatic Reminiscences*, 502.

41 Ibid., 503.

42 Ibid.

43 Neklyudov's letter to Prince Lvov, Madrid, 3 July, GARF F. 601. Op. 2. D. 13. L. 1–4.

44 Ibid.

45 Alban Gordon, *Russian Year: A Calendar of Revolution*, London: Cassell & Co., 1935, 182.

46 Hanbury-Williams, *Emperor Nicholas II*, 223.

47 *Murder*, 118; *Dnevniki*, I: 587.

48 *Murder*, 119; *Revolyutsiya*, 193.

49 *Murder*, 120; *Revolyutsiya*, 194.

50 *Murder*, 119–20.

51 Ibid., 120.

52 *Revolyutsiya*, 195. For a detailed discussion of Kerensky's thinking on the Romanov evacuation, see King and Wilson, 'The Departure of the Imperial Family', 112–30.

53 *Murder*, 118; King and Wilson, 'Departure of the Imperial Family', 20.

54 25 July 1917, *Fall*, 155; TNA FO 371/3015/2, 4–5.

55 *Ross. Arkhiv*, 277.

56 Ibid.

57 *Murder*, 121.

58 Paléologue, 'Le Drame d'Ekaterinebourg', 1107.

59 TNA FO 800/205/225, 13 August 1917.

60 For a detailed description of the departure of the Romanovs from Tsarskoe Selo, see Rappaport, *Four Sisters*, 316–21.

61 Sanvoisin, 'Comment Nicolas II a quitté Tsarskoie-Selo'.
62 Ibid.

Chapter 7: 'The Smell of a Dumas Novel'

1 Draft letter in French to the Dowager Empress, 2–8 August 1917, in Chernovniki pisem P. K. Benkendorfa raznym litsam, GARF f. 553 Op.1 D. 40. This letter can also be found in Kseniia Aleksandrovna Papers, Box 8, no. 80011 9.39 Hoover Institution.
2 *Thirteen Years*, 255; Wilton, *Last Days of the Romanovs*, 190.
3 Captain Harry de Windt, 'Tobolsk', *The Globe*, 18 August 1917.
4 Dolgorukov letter to Benckendorff, 27 August 1917, in Vinogradoff Collection, Hoover Institution; Benckendorff, *Last Days at Tsarskoe Selo*, 114.
5 *Fall*, 171.
6 *Last Days*, 61.
7 *Tsaritsa*, 100.
8 Ibid., 106, 110.
9 *Murder*, 137.
10 Ibid., 137. For a discussion of the Khitrovo incident, see Rappaport, *Four Sisters*, 329–3; *Revolyutsiya*, 201–7.
11 *Tsaritsa*, 105; *Murder*, 195.
12 *Fall*, 174; *Nicholas II*, 85.
13 *Thirteen Years*, 245.
14 *Tsaritsa*, 111.
15 Ibid., 113.
16 Radzinsky, *The Last Tsar*, 208.
17 *Tsaritsa*, 129.
18 Smith, *Rasputin*, 523.
19 Cook, *Murder of the Romanovs*, 134–5.
20 Benckendorff, *Last Days at Tsarskoe Selo*, 118–19.
21 Ibid., 120.
22 Ievreinov, 'Poezdka v Tobolsk', 15, Bakhmeteff Archive.
23 McNeal, *Secret Plot to Save the Tsar*, 59–60; Ross, *Gibel tsarskoy semi*, 497; *Murder*, 198.
24 *Last Days*, 51.

25 Alexandra to Vyrubova, 22 January 1918, in Vyrubova, *Memories*, 322.
26 *Murder*, 199.
27 *Nicholas II*, 135.
28 *Last Days*, 52–6; see *Nicholas II*, chapter 20.
29 *Fall*, 177–8; *Thirteen Years*, 256.
30 Radzinsky, *Last Tsar*, 168; Ross, *Gibel tsarskoy semi*, 498.
31 *Last Days*, 59.
32 Ross, *Gibel tsarskoy semi*, 499; *Murder*, 199.
33 *Murder*, 199; Ross, *Gibel tsarskoy semi*, 499.
34 *Nicholas II*, 135–6; *Last Days*, 59–60; Botkina, *Vospominaniya*, 79–80.
35 Pares, *Fall of the Russian Monarchy*, 486. Francq, *Knout and the Scythe*, 112; *Revolyutsiya*, 216–17.
36 *Sudba*, 314, 316–17; Sokolov, 'Popytka osvobozhedeniya', 288.
37 *Sudba*, 315.
38 Pares, *Fall of the Russian Monarchy*, 487; Botkina, *Vospominaniya*, 78–9.
39 Wilton, *Last Days of the Romanovs*, 194–5.
40 Trubetskoy, 'Istoriya odnoy popytki', 114–15: 32.
41 Ibid.
42 Ibid., 118–19: 29.
43 Ibid., 120: 21.
44 Ibid., 22.
45 Ibid., 23.
46 'The Tsar's Abandoned Family' became the title of the Russian edition of Markov's subsequent book, *Pokinutaya tsarskaya semya*.
47 *Tsaritsa*, 126.
48 Ibid., 146, 129.
49 Ibid., 131; *Sudba*, 332.
50 *Tsaritsa*, 145–6.
51 Ibid., 152–3.
52 Ibid., 154–5.
53 Ibid., 156; *Sudba*, 332.
54 *Tsaritsa*, 157; *Dnevniki*, 2: 331.
55 *Tsaritsa*, 158–9.

56 Ibid., 163.
57 Ievreinov, 'Poezdka v Tobolsk', 3, Bakhmeteff Archive.
58 Ibid., 6–7.
59 Ibid., 10–11.
60 Ibid., 15.
61 Ibid., 12.
62 Ibid., 13, 14, 16.
63 Ibid., 17. See Alexandrov, *End of the Romanovs*, 184–5.
64 Ibid.
65 Gleb Botkin, *Real Romanovs*, 169–71.
66 Tatiana Neumova-Teumina, 'Poslednye dni poslednego tsarya', *Uralskii rabochii*, 1950, 7: 5. See also S. Zakharov, 'Poslednii put poslednogo tsarya', *Oktyabr*, 1967: 3, 204.
67 Ibid.

Chapter 8: 'Please Don't Mention My Name'

1 TNA FO 800/205/219, 8 August 1917.
2 TNA FO 800/205, 215, 5 August 1917; ibid., 217, telegram of 8 August.
3 *FOT*, 247.
4 Letter of 5 December 1917, in Olivier Coutau Begari sale catalogue no. 106, 2007.
5 Letters of 13 and 154 October to Katya Zborovskaya, Hoover Institution.
6 Trewin, *Tutor to the Tsarevich*, 89–90.
7 Ibid., 90.
8 Zeepvat, Charlotte, *From Cradle to Crown: British Nannies and Governesses at the World's Royal Courts*, Stroud: Sutton, 2006, 257–8.
9 Robert Wilton, confidential report: 'Russia Still the Greatest Factor in the War. German Plans – The Need of Urgent Measures', 27 December 1917, TNA 371/3018, 3, 4.
10 Ibid., 4.
11 Ibid., 5.
12 Occleshaw, *Dances in Deep Shadows*, 155.
13 HBCA, RG 22/26/5/10, telegram 520, 9 October 1917.

14 In her book *The Secret Plot to Save the Tsar*, 47, Shay McNeal claimed that 'the house detailed in the Hudson's Bay Company files was provisioned with dishes, food, beds, blankets etc. in quantities of seven [for the seven members of the Romanov family], and stressed luxury items that … were strikingly different from a normal provisions list'. Unfortunately she does not give the HBCA reference for this in her notes, and an extensive search of the archives at Winnipeg, commissioned for this book, failed to locate the document(s) in question.

15 HBCA RG 22/26/5/6, telegram 368, 9 November 1917.

16 TNA ADM 137/1714f 138. This crucial document was discovered by my colleague Phil Tomaselli in 1996.

17 Kuznetsov's bill for the house came to 5,896 rubles. It can be found in HBCA RG 22/26/10/6.

18 Telegram no. 358 of 29 October, Hudson's Bay Company, London; McNeal, *Secret Plot*, 46, is not clear about her precise sources; see the original documents in HBCA RG 22/26/10/16.

19 Report on the Murmansk consulate, 5 February 1917, TNA FO 369/950.

20 Graham, *Part of the Wonderful Scene*, 97.

21 I am indebted to Karen Roth for translating this valuable Norwegian article on Lied, for whom there is very little material in English; http://ww-article-cache-1.s3.amazonaws.com/no/Jonas_Lied

22 Graham, *Part of the Wonderful Scene*, 96.

23 'The Kara Sea Passage', TNA 137/2844.

24 Graham, *Part of the Wonderful Scene*, 96; Marit Werenskiold, *Consul Jonas Lied and Russia*, 15.

25 For further details, see Terence Armstrong, *The Northern Sea Route: Soviet Exploitation of the North-East Passage*, Cambridge: Cambridge University Press, 2011, 11–13, 16, 17, 18.

26 Ibid. For further information, see also Per Gjendem, 'Jonas Lied and the Siberian Trading Company', http://www.pergjendem.com/?p=898; Lied, *Return to Happiness*, 214–15.

27 Letter to Henry Armitstead of 18 February 1918, from unnamed Hudson's Bay official, HBCA RG 22/4/2.

28 *FOT*, 250. Information from Phil Tomaselli, who from his research confirms that British intelligence did have an interest in Lied dating from about the right period and that MI5 had an (unreleased) file on him.

29 See entry for 4 March 1918, Jonas Lied Arkivboks nr. 28, Dagboker 1917–21, Norsk Maritimt Museum, Oslo. The original entries are in English.

30 *FOT*, 251.

31 Jonas Lied, *Siberian Arctic: The Story of the Siberian Company*, London: Methuen, 1960, 118–19. Lied, *Return to Happiness*, 217.

32 McNeal, *Secret Plot*, 116. McNeal claims Urquhart was part of this supposed secret Romanov rescue plan, but this is an absurd suggestion, although the economic mission itself may have been covertly counter-revolutionary. As a man with considerable lead- and zinc-mining concessions in Siberia, Urquhart was a businessman first and foremost, looking out for his own commercial interests and eager to recover his mines that had been confiscated by the Bolsheviks. In the summer of 1918 he was 'recruited by the British Foreign Office to run the Siberian Supply Company – a Whitehall-funded agency which was intended in the short term to relieve shortages in Siberia through trade, but which had clearly been designed with the longer term aim in mind of securing for Britain as much of a monopoly of Siberian trade as possible'. The mission landed at Murmansk on 20 June, but was in fact delayed, first by pack ice on the White Sea and again in Vologda as they waited for permits from the Soviets to proceed. It finally set off on 17 July – the day the Romanovs were murdered – and proved fruitless, returning to London by 13 August. For details on Urquhart in Siberia, see Jonathan D. Smele, *Civil War in Russia: The Anti-Bolshevik Government of Admiral Kolchak, 1918*, Cambridge: Cambridge University Press, 2006, 117. The mission is described in K. H. Kennedy, *Mining Tsar: The Life and Times of Leslie Urquhart*, London: Allen & Unwin, 1986, 129–33.

33 TNA FO 368/1970. The flax shortages are described in a report entitled 'Department of the Surveyor General of Supplies. Flax Control Board', at TNA MUN 4/6506.

34 1 March 1918 memorandum in FO 368/1970.

35 Lied, *Return to Happiness*, 218.

36 Ibid.; *Revolyutsiya*, 254.

37 *FOT*, 251; Lied, *Return to Happiness*, 218–19.

38 Ibid., 219.

39 Ibid.; *FOT*, 251.

40 Ibid, 220.

41 Ibid., 162–3.

42 *FOT*, 394.

43 Anthony Summers, letter to the *Independent*, 3 August 1999.

44 Lied, *Return to Happiness*, 211.

45 *FOT*, 250.

46 Email from Wilhelm Wilkens to the author, 9 July 2017.

47 Letter from unnamed HBC accountant, 18 February 1918, TNA RG 22/4/2.

48 Private email to the author, 25 October 2016.

49 My informant's adoptive Russian grandmother confirmed that the rescue was indeed genuine, 'but that some of the details in Patricia Eykyn's letter weren't correct'. But his grandmother 'wouldn't be drawn on the subject of who cancelled it', and 'changed the subject' when he asked. He concluded that 'There was a clear reluctance on her part to discuss anything more about it, other than to confirm that it had been planned', but he was never able to clarify what the reluctance amounted to.

50 Unpublished TS notes by Mrs Patricia Eykyn, courtesy of Philip Kerin. These notes are also cited in Occleshaw, *Romanov Conspiracies*, 94. Occleshaw interviewed Patricia Eykyn for his book, but her additional comments about the Gordon-Smith mission are so garbled factually – including talk of flying the entire Romanov family to Archangel – that they make little logical sense. According to George Alexander Hill, Warrender had been on Poole's staff in Petrograd in July 1917, when Hill met him on his arrival at the Finland Station. If Patricia Eykyn's story is correct, Warrender must have returned to the UK at some point between July 1917 and January 1918.

51 Information by email from Philip Kerin, 11 October 2014.

52 Ibid.

53 *Mail on Sunday*, 20 November 1988.

54 Information from Phil Tomaselli.

55 Unpublished TS notes by Mrs Patricia Eykyn, courtesy of Philip Kerin.

56 Ibid.

57 Supplement 30720 to the *London Gazette*, 31 May 1918, 6512. The annotated Honours Gazette in the Military Cross files in TNA WO 389 give no further information on the award, 3 June 1918. Warrender's Medal Card is at TNA WO 372/21/18972.

58 Information from Phil Tomaselli. TNA WO 160 Military Operations and Intelligence files relating to Major-General Poole's Mission 'reveal a sudden and unexplained flurry of activity in Siberia from April 1918' onwards, according to Michael Occleshaw. This, he says, came via the activities of Rusplycom. Does it suggest they were involved in planning a Romanov rescue? See Occleshaw, *Armour Against Fate*, 266–8.

59 Robert Wilton, confidential report: 'Russia Still the Greatest Factor in the War. German Plans – The Need of Urgent Measures', 27 December 1917, TNA 371/3018, 4.

Chapter 9: 'I Would Rather Die in Russia than Be Saved by the Germans'

1 Paléologue, *Guillaume II et Nicolas II*, 237.

2 Leontiev, 'Otkrytoe pis'mo Imperatora Vil'gelmu', 2.

3 Ibid., 6–7.

4 Jagow, 'Die Schuld am Zarenmord', 389.

5 Service, *Nicholas II*, 129.

6 Röhl, *Wilhelm II: Into the Abyss of War and Exile 1900–1941*, 1161.

7 Ibid.

8 For a discussion, see Röhl, *Wilhelm II*, 1155–6.

9 Wilton, *Last Days of the Romanovs*, 25.

10 *Murder*, 202.

11 Alexandrov, *End of the Romanovs*, 68.

12 Gilliard, *Thirteen Years*, 257; Prince Nicholas of Greece, *Political Memoirs*, 20.

13 Testimony to Sokolov in August 1919, in Ross, *Gibel tsarskoy semi*, 422–3.

14 *Nicholas II*, 141.

15 *Thirteen Years*, 257; Wilton, *Last Days of the Romanovs*, 70.

16 Pierre Gilliard notes on Nicholas II, sent from Lausanne to Nicholas de Basily, 29 April 1934, 2, Nikolai de Bazili Papers, 65017–9.23, box 2, Hoover Institution.

17 Bitner testimony in Ross, *Gibel tsarskoy semi*, 422–3; Wilton, *Last Days of the Romanovs*, 70.

18 *Fall*, 275–6.

19 GARF. F. R-130. Op. 2. D. 1109. L. 2.

20 TNA GFM 6/139 telegram no. 256, 12 March 1918. See also Hall, *Little Mother*, 303–4.

21 Aksel-Hansen, 'Breve fra Petrograd', 201.

22 TNA GFM 6/139 telegram no. 256, 12 March 1918.

23 TNA GFM 6/139 AS 1356, 15 March 1918.

24 Ibid.

25 TNA GFM 6/139 telegram, 17 March 1918.

26 See https://www.ippo-jerusalem.info/item/show/271.

27 Crawford, *Michael and Natasha*, 344–5; Larsen, *Makten*, 187.

28 *Revolyutsiya*, 249.

29 Steinberg, *In the Workshop of the Revolution*, 142.

30 Ibid.

31 Ibid.; *Fall*, 225. See also GARF F. R-130. Op. 2. D. 1. L. 85, 89; GARF F. R-130. Op. 2. D. 1. L. 135.

32 Konstantin Melnik testimony, in Ross, *Gibel tsarskoy semi*, 491.

33 *Last Days*, 62–3.

34 Ibid., 64.

35 *Fall*, 229; *Revolyutsiya*, 254; Pares, quoted in Francq, *Knout and the Scythe*, 113.

36 Gilliard, *Thirteen Years*, 257–8.

37 *Dnevniki*, 2: 352–3; and Khrustalev, *Last Diary of Tsaritsa Alexandra*, 95.

38 Buxhoeveden, *Life and Tragedy*, 325–6. For a discussion of the political rivalries between the Omsk and Ekaterinburg Red Guards, their attempts to take control of the Romanov family and the turbulent political situation in Tobolsk, see *Nicholas II*, chapters 24 and 25, which provide a concise and lucid overview.

39 *Dnevniki*, 2: 351.

40 *Nicholas II*, 156.

41 *Fall*, 230; GARF F. 1235 (VTsIK). Op. 34. D. 36. L. 9; Service, *Nicholas II*, 153; Alexeev, *Last Act of a Tragedy*, 75.

42 *Fall*, 231; *Revolyutsiya*, 255.

43 Radzinsky, *Last Tsar*, 233.

44 Plotnikov, *Gibel tsarskoy semi*, 53; Radzinsky, *Last Tsar*, 234.

45 Plotnikov, *Gibel tsarskoy semi*, 39.

46 *Revolyutsiya*, 261.

47 Ibid.

48 *Fall*, 231–2. GARF F. 601. Op. 2. D. 33. L. 1; *Nicholas II*, 154. The directives are very clear about Ekaterinburg as the intended, albeit temporary, destination. See also Ioffe, *Revolyutsiya*, 261.

49 Gilliard, *Thirteen Years*, 258, 259.

50 Ievreinov, 'Poezdka v Tobolsk', 21.

51 Kobylinsky testimony in Wilton, *Last Days of the Romanovs*, 202; Botkin, *Real Romanovs*, 194.

52 Kobylinsky testimony in Wilton, *Last Days of the Romanovs*, 202.

53 Botkin, *Real Romanovs*, 194.

54 Yakovlev, 'On the Transfer of the Former Tsar', in *Fall*, 255; *Revolyutsiya*, 266.

55 *Thirteen Years*, 258; *Dnevniki*, 2: 252.

56 *Revolyutsiya*, 265.

57 *Murder*, 222.

58 Klavdiya Bitner testimony in Ross, *Gibel tsarskoy semi*, 422.

59 Kobylinsky testimony in Wilton, *Last Days of the Romanovs*, 205.

60 Rappaport, *Four Sisters*, 359. See also Yakovlev's account in *Fall*, 256; *Thirteen Years*, 259–61.

61 *Thirteen Years*, 260.

62 Neidgart, *Ross. Arkhiv*, 266; Krivoshein, *Ross. Arkhiv*, 271; *Tsaritsa*, 222–3.

63 Neidgart, *Ross. Arkhiv*, 266.

64 Ibid., 26. Krivoshein, *Ross. Arkhiv*, 272.

65 Ibid., 272, 265. For another version, see *Murder*, 221.

66 Ibid.

67 Krivoshein, *Ross. Arkhiv*, 273.

68 Jagow, 'Die Schuld am Zarenmord', 391.

69 *Murder*, 202, 219–20.

70 Krivoshein, in *Ross. Arkhiv*, 274; Neidgart, in *Ross. Arkhiv*, 265.

71 Krivoshein, in ibid., 272, 273.

72 Neidgart in ibid., 265.

73 Trepov, *Ross. Arkhiv*, 274.

74 Ibid., 274–5, 10.

75 Ibid., 275.

76 TNA GFM 6/139 PA, Ru 82, Nr 1, Bd 65; see also Baumgart, *Deutsche Ostpolitik*, note 13, 337.

77 Ibid.

78 Ibid.

79 Krivoshein, *Ross. Arkhiv*, 273; a variant form of this quote is in *Murder*, 227; see also Jagow, 'Die Schuld am Zarenmord', 391.

80 Mirbach to GFM in Berlin, 11 May 1918, TNA GFM 6/139 A 19964, quoted in Occleshaw, *Romanov Conspiracies*, 56. Although Occleshaw's book claiming the miraculous escape of Grand Duchess Tatiana has been superseded by DNA proof to the contrary, his chapter 7, 'The Kaiser's Will', contains valuable research in German Foreign Ministry documents for 1917–18, which are notoriously difficult to access and work with.

81 Zenzinov, 'Ubiistvo Tsarskoy Semi', Nicolaevsky Collection, Hoover Institution, 1; Jagow, 'Die Schuld am Zarenmord', 392–3.

82 Countess Alexandra Olsoufieff, 'HIH Grand Duchess Elisabeth Feodorovna', London: John Murray, 1923. Available online at http://www.alexanderpalace.org/palace/GDElisabeth.html

83 TNA FO 566/1201 ref. 78031 Petrograd no. 142, 26 April 1918.

Chapter 10: 'The Baggage Will Be in Utter Danger at All Times'

1   Summers and Mangold argue in *FOT*, 257–62, that Yakovlev wanted to get the Romanovs to England, but the claim has no foundation in any British sources, any more than a similar one by Victor Alexandrov that Yakovlev was a British agent tasked with 'watching over the Russian Imperial Family'; see Alexandrov, *End of the Romanovs*, 211.

2   For a discussion and adamant denial of the unlikely German rescue scenario, see Jagow, 'Die Schuld am Zarenmord', note 81, 391.

3   See Appendix Five: 'Rescuing the Tsar', in Andrew Cook, *Ace of Spies: the True Story of Sidney Reilly*, Stroud: Tempus, 2004, 281–4.

4   GARF documents ranging from February 1917 to the end of August 1918, and also including a selection of material relating to the subsequent Sokolov investigation, can be found online at http://statearchive.ru/docs.html. The best source for these documents in English remains Steinberg and Khrustalev's excellent 1995 edition, *Fall of the Romanovs*, although it is selective.

5   *Revolyutsiya*, 269; *Nicholas II*, 162. Robert Service, an expert in Bolshevik politics of this period, provides an excellent summary of the Yakovlev mission in his *Nicholas II*, which cuts through a lot of the confusion about the story. See chapters 26–30. A useful map of the route that Yakovlev took can also be found in *Nicholas II*, xvi, and *Fall*, 247.

6   *Fall*, 186.

7   Ibid., 245.

8   *Revolyutsiya*, 269–70.

9   *Fall*, 246; *Nicholas II*, 174.

10   See *Last Diary of Tsaritsa Alexandra*, 112; *Dnevniki*, 2: 382–3.

11   *Fall*, 248; *Nicholas II*, 175.

12   *Fall*, 248; *Nicholas II*, 174.

13   *Fall*, 248.

14   Ibid., 246.

15   Ibid., 249; *Revolyutsiya*, 271.

16   *Dnevniki*, 2: 385.

17   Kozlov, *Last Diary of Tsaritsa Alexandra*, 116.

18 *Revolyutsiya*, 270–71.

19 *Fall*, 250.

20 Ibid., 251.

21 Ibid., 251, 252.

22 Ibid., 252.

23 Yakovlev's statement 'On the Transfer of the Former Tsar from Tobolsk to Yekaterinburg', 16 May 1918, in *Fall*, 258.

24 For more on Yakovlev's career, see Plotnikov, *Gibel tsarskoy semi*, 38–52, and *Fall*, 183–5.

25 Rappaport, *Four Sisters*, 363–4.

26 TNA FO 371/3938, 273.

27 3 May 1918, TNA FO 371/3329, 163.

28 TNA FO 371/3329/78031.

29 3 May 1918, TNA FO 371/3329/165.

30 Russia file, 'The Imperial Family', May 1918, TNA FO 371/3329/78031.

31 Harald Scavenius report of 14 May 1918, in Bent Jensen, *Harald Scavenius' Syn på Omvæltningerne i Rusland 1917–1918*, Copenhagen, Eget Forlag, 1973, 188–9. Also in TNA GFM 6/139/99.

32 Ibid.

33 Ibid.

34 Thomas Preston, telegram of 10 May 1918, TNA FO 371/3325/422–3.

35 Note on Summers and Mangold documentary, October 1971, in TNA FCO 12/122.

36 Alexandrov, *End of the Romanovs*, 212.

37 See Occleshaw, *Armour Against Fate*, 256–7.

38 Clarke, *Lost Fortune of the Tsars*, 108.

39 A two-seater bomber such as the DH4 or the DH9 had a maximum flying distance of about 235 miles before it would need to land and refuel, although the recently introduced Handley Page V/1500 had a range of 1,300 miles, but none of these were based in Russia in 1918 and DH9s were not delivered to the anti-Bolshevik forces till 1919; information from Nick Forder and Andrew Pentland of Cross and Cockade International: The First World War Aviation Historical Society. Re. Fellowes: see Richard

Palmer. 'Royal Blog: Prince Michael bids to Clear George V's name over Tsar's death', *Sunday Express*, 2 February 2010; information on Fellowes's RNAS career from Phil Tomaselli and Nick Forder. Occleshaw's claims re. Meinertzhagen and the mythical air rescue can be found in *Romanov Conspiracies*, 98–9, which quotes from Meinertzhagen's diary of 18 August 1918, but does not mention Fellowes. Clarke, *Lost Fortune of the Tsars*, also quotes the diary on 107–9, but does not mention Fellowes, either. For Summers and Mangold's now dubious claim that the Meinertzhagen account 'is one more addition to the growing pile of evidence that the British did mount an operation to save the Romanovs', see the 2002 edition of *File on the Tsar*, 366–7. Fifteen years on from this revised edition, this entirely unsubstantiated claim has still not been rescinded.

40 Information on Peregrine Fellowes from Lord Fellowes, by email to the author, 13 April 2017.

41 Information from Phil Tomaselli.

42 *FOT*, 2002 edn, 367.

43 See Smith, *Rasputin*, 631.

44 Information from Phil Tomaselli, based on his extensive research in TNA files. See also Andrew Cook, *Murder of the Romanovs*, 152–6, for a discussion of the Alley mission.

45 See TNA WO 157/1215 Intercepted Telegrams.

46 John Crossland, 'British Spies in Plot to Save Tsar', *Sunday Times*, 15 October 2006. UK readers can view the documentary, *Three Kings at War*, at http://www.channel4.com/programmes/three-kings-at-war/on-demand/41616–001.

47 Thomas Preston report, 17 September 1918, TNA FO 371/3938/158859/274. Preston, *Before the Curtain*, 102.

48 Cook, *Murder of the Romanovs*, 152. This request was confirmed in a follow-up telegram from Alley in Murmansk on 29 May, asking for urgent sanction of the £1,000 he had requested.

49 Ibid., 153. Additional information on SIS agents from Phil Tomaselli.

50 Ibid., 154. This fragment of a memorandum from Alley is unfortunately undated and incomplete.

51 Preston, *Before the Curtain*, 111; see also McNeal, *Secret Plot*, 141.
52 Lindley to WO, 27 August 1918; Digby Jones's 'Claim for Travelling Expenses, Major-General Poole's Military Mission Russia', made posthumously in TNA WO 374/19738.
53 Alley telegram, 29 May 1918, TNA FO 371/3325/53740. Telegram to Lindley at Archangel, forwarding telegram from Irkutsk of 15 August.
54 Digby Jones's tragic death does at least provide us with unexpectedly valuable detail, for afterwards a parsimonious British army tried to reclaim money from his estate that he had been given to fund his mission in Russia, as well as alleged overpayment of his salary. In order to prove their case, the War Office drew up a schedule of his journey, showing how long it would take an actual agent to make the trip to Archangel and then on to Ekaterinburg, and the likely way in which it was made. Information from Phil Tomaselli. See also Digby Jones's file at TNA WO 374/19738.
55 Buxhoeveden, *Life and Tragedy*, 78; Wilton, *Last Days of the Romanovs*, 151.
56 William Black, *The Platinum Group Metals Industry*, Cambridge: Woodhead Publishing, 2000, Appendix 2.
57 Cook, *Murder of the Romanovs*, 168; *A Collection of Reports on Bolshevism in Russia*, HMSO: London, 1919, 43.
58 Preston, *Before the Curtain*, 68; see TNA FO 368/1970.
59 Occleshaw, *Romanov Conspiracies*, 128.
60 John Crossland, 'British Spies in Plot to Save Tsar', *Sunday Times*, 15 October 2006. See also Occleshaw, *Romanov Conspiracies*, 127–8.
61 Cook, *Murder of the Romanovs*, 156; Occleshaw, *Armour Against Fate*, 279–81.
62 Preston, *Before the Curtain*, 98.

Chapter 11: 'Await the Whistle around Midnight'

1 Victoria Milford Haven, letter to Arthur Balfour, 23 May 1918, FO 371/3329/93852.
2 Ibid.
3 Ibid.

4 Ibid.

5 Ibid.

6 TNA FO 371/3329/93852.

7 TNA FO 371/3329/93852/171.

8 TNA FO 371/3329/93852.

9 Thomas Preston, 'The Vigil', TS, 1, Levine Papers, series 5, box 36/136. Thomas Preston affidavit, 22 January 1960, in Vorres, *The Last Grand Duchess*, 243.

10 Preston, 'The Vigil', 2.

11 Ibid., 3.

12 Ibid.

13 *Last Days*, 76.

14 Semchevskaya, 'Vospominaniya o poslednykh dnyak Velikikh Knyazey'; Avdeev, 'Nikolay Romanov', 202.

15 Vorres, *Last Grand Duchess*, 243; *Last Days*, 76.

16 Wilson, 'Memoirs of Princess Helena Petrovna', 55.

17 *Last Days*, 776; Plotnikov, *Gibel tsarskoy semi*, 118–19.

18 Plotnikov, *Gibel tsarskoy semi*, 479; *Last Days*, 78; King and Wilson, 'The Officer Letters', 85.

19 Preston, *Before the Curtain*, 98.

20 Wilson, 'Memoirs of Princess Helena Petrovna', 58–9.

21 Preston, *Before the Curtain*, 99; *Dnevniki*, 2: 577.

22 *Last Days*, 79; *Dnevniki*, 2: 430. The plan, which is in GARF, can be seen in Vitalii Shitov, *Dom Ipatieva*, Ekaterinburg: Avto Graf, 2013, 161.

23 Buxhoeveden affidavit, 4, Bakhmeteff Archive.

24 Radzinsky, *Last Tsar*, 261; Rappaport, *Ekaterinburg*, 117.

25 GARF F. 601 Op. 2 D. 48 letter c 30 April 1918.

26 Thomas Preston affidavit, 22 January 1960, in Vorres, *The Last Grand Duchess*, 243.

27 Buxhoevden affidavit, 4. Buxhoeveden testified that the Tsar's former valet, Chemodurov, who had been set free from the Ipatiev House, identified Dologrukov's clothes.

28 *Revolyutsiya*, 334.

29 Ibid., 335.

30 Ibid.

31 Ibid., 336; *Fall*, 320.

32 Avdeev, 'Nikolay Romanov', 202.

33 *Revolyutsiya*, 331; Plotnikov, *Gibel tsarskoy semi*, 125.

34 King and Wilson, 'The Officer Letters', 79.

35 *Last Days*, 78; Zhuk, *Ispoved Tsareubiits*, 420–1. In her 2007 study of original documents connected with the Romanov murders, *Sledstvie po delu ob ubiistve* …, the Russian historian Lidiya Lykova discussed the bogus 'officer letters', concluding that they were all in Rodzinsky's handwriting; see 271–5. See also Rodzinsky interview in *Ogonek*, no. 2, 1990, 27. For a full transcript of the original letters in French and the response to them, see Pipes, *Russian Revolution*, 766–70. The authorship of the original first letter is still disputed. For a discussion, see Pipes, footnote to 767.

36 *Fall*, 310.

37 Ibid.

38 Ibid., 315.

39 *Ekaterinburg: Entsiklopediya*, Ekaterinburg: Akademiya, 2002, 7.

40 Plotnikov, *Gibel tsarskoy semi*, 115; Ross, *Gibel tsarskoy semi*, 369.

41 Ibid.

42 *Fall*, 315–16.

43 Ibid., 316–17.

44 Ibid., 317.

45 *Dnevniki*, 2: 497

46 *Fall*, 320.

47 Ibid.

48 Plotnikov, *Gibel tsarskoy semi*, 122.

49 *Fall*, 322.

50 Lykova, *Sledstvie po delu* …, 275. Lykova, 'Neizvestnyi otvet tsarskoy semi na pismo "Ofitsera" Yul 1918g Ekaterinburg', *Otechestvennye arkhivy*, 2006, at http://naukarus.com/neizvestnyy-otvet-tsar-skoy-semi-na-pismo-ofitsera-iyul-1918-g-ekaterinburg.

51 See *Sudba*, 266–8; Carl Ackerman, *Trailing the Bolsheviki: 12,000 with the Allies in Siberia*, New York: Scribner's, 1919, 100; discussed in King and Wilson, 'The Officer Letters', 82–3.

52 *Murder*, 163–4.

53 A. Korneev, *Russkiy vestnik*, 28 May 2005.

54 *Tsaritsa*, 244.

55 Diterikhs quoted in Plotnikov, *Gibel tsarskoy semi*, 116–17.

56 *Last Days*, 76–7; see also Semchevskaya, 'Vospominaniya', 192.

57 Levine, *Eyewitness to History*, 142.

58 Ibid., 143. Levine gives the precise publication date of 23 August 1923, but fails to say where the article was published, though it would appear to have been in a New York journal or newspaper. He states that he sent the original document and the map to the publisher. They are nowhere to be found in his archive, despite a concerted search by the author, and are presumed lost.

59 Ibid., 144.

60 For more on the Agafurovs in Ekaterinburg, see http://www.1723. ru/read/dai2/dai-2–31.htm.

61 Levine, *Eyewitness to History*, 144–5.

62 Ibid., 145; Kozlov, *Last Diary of Tsaritsa Alexandra*, 184. There is no evidence confirming its contents or whether the Romanovs actually received the letter from Gorshkov's group. The facts in the description of the mission have been checked, in so far as this is possible, and seem to correlate.

63 Levine, *Eyewitness to History*, 145.

64 Ibid., 146.

65 *Tsaritsa*, 252.

66 Ibid., 254; see also *Revolyutsiya*, 331.

67 *Tsaritsa*, 254–5.

68 Ibid., 245, 255.

Chapter 12: 'It Is Too Horrible and Heartless'

1 TNA GFM 6/139 no. 664, 22 June 1918.

2 TNA GFM 6/139, no. 338, 21 June 1918; *Ross.Arkhiv*, 333–4.

3 Joffe to Lenin, 21 June 1918, *Ross.Arkhiv*, 380.

4 Zenzinov, 'Ubiistvo tsarskoy semi', Nicolaevsky Collection, Hoover Institution, 2; Jagow, 'Die Schuld am Zarenmord', 395.

5 TNA GFM 6/139, 664, 22 June 1918, von Kühlmann to von Grunau. McNeal, *Secret Plot to Save the Tsar*, 103, quoting Von Kuhlman to von Grunau, TNA GFM 6/139, A 26851.

6   Baumgart, *Deutsche Ostpolitik*, 387–8.

7   Ibid., 388.

8   Ibid.; *Nicholas II*, 221–2.

9   Jagow, 'Die Schuld am Zarenmord', 394. Hall, *Little Mother*, 308–9.

10 Mosolov, *At the Court of the Last Tsar*, 260–1; *Nicholas II*, 225.

11 Occleshaw, *Romanov Conspiracies*, 58–9.

12 Ibid., 62.

13 Occleshaw, *Dances in Deep Shadows*, 161.

14 *FOT*, 279, 275.

15 See Bothmer, *Mit Graf Mirbach in Moskau*, 97.

16 *FOT*, 276; Letter of 18 July, British Consulate, Geneva, TNA FO 371/3328.

17 *FOT*, 276.

18 Petr Botkin, letter to Stephan Pichon, French Foreign Minister in Paris, 2 July 1918, *Ross.Arhkiv*, 279–80.

19 Boyard's presence in Ekaterinburg was not revealed until Sokolov's later investigation. See Ross, *Gibel tsarskoy semi*, 216.

20 Levine, *Eyewitness to History*, 145–6.

21 *Dnevniki*, 2: 522.

22 For a full account of the murder of the Romanov family at the Ipatiev House on the night of 16/17 July, see Rappaport, *Ekaterinburg: The Last Days of the Romanovs*.

23 See Rappaport, *Ekaterinburg*, chapter 10, 'What is to be Done with Nicholas?', which describes the dicussions that took place in Moscow.

24 Ibid., 141.

25 Ibid., 162–3.

26 Preston, 'The Vigil', 3.

27 Preston, 'Sir Thomas Preston Recalls Ekaterinburg'.

28 Lenin, *Khronika* V, 642, quoted in Pipes, *Russian Revolution*, 781.

29 *Fall*, 337.

30 Ibid.; Pipes, *Russian Revolution*, 781.

31 *Fall*, 341; Pipes, *Russian Revolution*, 784.

32 The best summary of the chronology of events following the murders can be found in Pipes, *Russian Revolution*, 780–5.

33 Bothmer, *Mit Graf Mirbach in Moskau*, 98.

34 Orlano-Erenya, 'Ispanskii korol', 156.

35 For a discussion of the rumours, see Salisbury, *Black Night, White Snow: Russia's Revolutions 1905–1917*, London: Cassell, 1977, 714. See also *Sudba*, 390–400.

36 *Fall*, 341; Leal, 'Alfonso XIII y su Actuacion', 63.

37 *Tsaritsa*, 259.

38 Pipes, *Russian Revolution*, 782–3.

39 Ibid., 784.

40 TNA FO 800/205/307, 23 July 1918.

41 TNA FO 800/205/313, 24 July 1918; /314, 25 July.

42 Preben Ulstrup, *Kejserinde Dagmars fangenskab på Krim: Dagbøger og breve 1917–1919*, Copenhagen: Gyldendal, 2005, 222, 223.

43 23 July 1918, RA PS/PSO/GV/C/M/1344a/2.

44 Ibid.

45 Ibid.

46 23 July 1918, RA PS/PSO/GV/C/M/1344a/6, 7.

47 *The Times*, 25 July 1918.

48 Stamfordham to Rt Hon. George Russell, 26 July, RA PS/PSO/GV/C/M/1344a/8.

49 Baroness de Stoeckl, *My Dear Marquis*, London: John Murray, 1952, 179.

50 Ibid.

51 George V diary, 25 July 1918, quoted in Rose, *King George V*, 216.

Chapter 13: 'Those Poor Innocent Children'

1 *Tatler*, 7 August 1918, 144.

2 Alexander Iswolsky, *Recollections of a Foreign Minister*, New York: Doubleday, 1921, 252.

3 David R. Francis, *Russia from the American Embassy*, New York: Scribner's, 1921, 328.

4 *German Wireless*, 4 August 1918, RA PS/PSO/GV/C/M/1344a/13.

5 Lord Stamfordham to Lord Esher, 25 July 1918, quoted in Rose, *King George V*, 217.

6 Ibid.

7 Lord Esher to Stamfordham, 28 July 1918, quoted in Rose, *King George V*, 217.

8 For a discussion of the rumours, see *FOT*, chapters 24 and 25. Sadly, *The File on the Tsar* went a long way to perpetuating the unsubstantiated claim of survival of Alexandra and her daughters.

9 Occleshaw, *Romanov Conspiracies*, 62.

10 *FOT*, 361. For a useful discussion of the Spanish and German mediation attempts in August/September, see Occleshaw, *Romanov Conspiracies*, 61–6.

11 Mednikov, 'Missiya spaseniya', 71; *FOT*, 362.

12 *The Times*, 3 and 6 August 1918.

13 8 August 1918, in Summers and Mangold, *El Expediente sobre el Zar*, 325. The Spanish translation of *FOT* contains material on Alfonso's role, in a postscript on 319–33, that was not included in the English editions of the book. See also Rey y Cabieses, 'Alfonso XIII, Jorge V, y el Frustrado Rescate de la Familia Imperial de Rusia', 123; Cortes Cavanillas, *Alfonso XIII y la Guerra*, 149.

14 *The Times*, 8 August 1918.

15 TS of telegram in French from Alfonso to Grand Duchess George, 8 August 1918, in TNA FO 800/205/325–6.

16 Edward Wallington to Harry Verney, 8 August 1918, TNA FO 800/250/320.

17 Buckingham Palace, 8 August 1918, TNA FO 800/205/402.

18 TNA FO 800/205/323–5.

19 Miller, *Four Graces*, 155.

20 Ibid., 156.

21 *FOT*, 362.

22 Letter of 25 July 1918, quoted in Urbach, *Go-Betweens for Hitler*, 131.

23 Cortes-Cavanillas, 'Alfonso XIII en la Guerra del Catorce'.

24 Rey y Cabieses, 'Alfonso XIII', 124.

25 Ibid., 125.

26 Seco Serrano, 'Alfonso XIII y la Familia del Zar', 2.

27 TNA FO 800/205/424, 15 August 1918.

28 Telegram from Directorate of Military Intelligence to Major-General Poole Archangel, 9 August 1918. RA PS/PSO/GV/C/M/1344a/20.

29 Summers and Mangold, *El Expediente sobre el* Zar, 326–7. See comments on this Spanish chapter mentioned at note 13 above; *FOT*, 363. See also Occleshaw, *Romanov Conspiracies*, 72–6.

30 Clarke, *Lost Fortune of the Tsars*, 112.

31 Monsignor Eugenio Pacelli, Apostolic Nuncio Munich to Herr Count von Hertling Reichskanzler, 12 August 1918, TNA GFM 6/139.

32 See Summers and Mangold, *El Expediente sobre el Zar*, 327; Clarke, *Lost Fortune of the Romanovs*, 112.

33 Occleshaw, *Romanov Conspiracies*, 74–5; Grand Duchess George, *A Romanov Diary*, 231, 238.

34 Cortes-Cavanillas, 'Alfonso XIII en la Guerra del Catorce'.

35 *The Times*, 8 August 1918.

36 Ibid.; Contreras reported on his meeting to Polo de Bernabe, Spanish ambassador to Berlin, who in turn sent the details in a ciphered telegram no. 111, 6 September 1918, to Madrid. See also the account of the meeting in Carlos Seco Serrano, 'Alfonso XIII y la Familia del Zar'.

37 Orlano-Erenya, 'Ispanskii korol', 155.

38 Pipes, *Russian Revolution*, 783; Occleshaw, *Romanov Conspiracies*, 63; Jagow, 'Die Schuld am Zarenmord', 398–400; Orlano-Erenya, 'Ispanskii korol', 156.

39 Zenzinov, 'Ubiistvo tsarskoy semi', 6.

40 Director of Military Intelligence to Lord Stamfordham, War Office, Whitehall, 31 August 1918, quoted in Hough, *Louis & Victoria*, 326.

41 Report from Intelligence Coordinator for British Forces and Missions in Russia and Siberia, 28 August 1918, TNA FO 800/205; George V diary, 31 August 1918, in Rose, *King George V*, 216.

42 Princess Marie Louise, *My Memories of Six Reigns*, London: Evans Brothers, 1956, 186.

43 Ibid., 187. Note that an examination of this source, in comparison with the account of how Victoria Milford Haven received

the news from Marie Louise, reveals that the story does not relate to when the King and Queen first received news of Nicholas's death on the 24th, as has been widely assumed – for there was no word at that time on the fate of the rest of the family. Her story relates to 31 August, when George and Mary received the distressing confirmation, via the Foreign Office, that the entire family had been killed. See Hough, *Louis and Victoria*, 326, which clearly states that Marie Louise's visit with the letter from King George was on 2 September, and not a month earlier, when news of Nicholas's murder only was first received.

44 VMH to King George, 3 September 1918, in Miller, *Four Graces*, 157.

45 14 September 1918; Hough, *Louis and Victoria*, 326; Miller, *Four Graces*, 157.

46 Lord Stamfordham to Milner, Windsor Castle, 1 September 1918, RA PS/PSO/GV/C/M/1344a/31.

47 Letter to Freda Dudley Ward, 25 July 1918, Rupert Godfrey (ed.), *Letters from a Prince*, London: Warner Books, 1999, 76.

48 *Aberdeen Evening Express* quoting a report in *Yorkshire Evening Post*, 12 September 1918.

49 Occleshaw, *Romanov Conspiracies*, 64. Jagow, 'Die Schuld am Zarenmord', 400.

50 Occleshaw, *Romanov Conspiracies*, 66.

51 Jagow, 'Die Schuld am Zarenmord', 401. Zenzinov, 'Ubiistvo Tsarskoy Semi', 6, Nicolaevsky Collection, Hoover.

52 See Elliot's report of 5 October 1918 to Balfour, TNA FO 371/3977, and an interim summary in TNA FO 371/3335.

53 Benckendorff *Last Days at Tsarskoe Selo.*, 132–3.

54 *Birmingham Mail*, 14 November 1918.

55 'Fate of the Tsar's Family. All Shot Together in a Cellar', *The Times*, 5 December 1918

56 *FOT*, 26.

57 Victoria Milford Haven to King Alfonso, 22 September 1918, Madrid Archives, quoted in Miller, *Four Graces*, 161.

58 Summers and Mangold, *El Expediente Sobre El Zar*, 328. Carlos Seco Serrano, 'El Relato de la Baronesa Buxhoeveden A. D. Franciso Gutierrez de Agüera', *Diario ABC*, Madrid, 6 March 1980. Buxhoeveden's father Carlos Matthias von Buxhoeveden was in the Russian diplomatic service in Copenhagen and passed on this message from his colleague, Gutiérrez de Agüera, a Spanish minister based there. When she travelled to Tobolsk, Baroness Buxhhoeveden was not allowed to enter the house to visit the Romanovs but Alfonso's message was smuggled in by Anastasia Hendrikova.

Chapter 14: 'His Majesty Would Much Prefer that Nothing ... Be Published'

1 Aga Khan III, *The Memoirs of Aga Khan: World Enough and Time*, New York: Simon & Schuster, 1954, 113.
2 Rodzianko, *Tattered Banners*, 271.
3 Christopher Hibbert, *The Court of St James*, London: BCA, 1983, 72.
4 'Europe Harbors Hapless Queens', *Louisville Courier-Journal*, 3 October 1927.
5 For an account of the evacuation, see Frances Welch, *The Russian Court at Sea: The Voyage of HMS Marlborough, April 1919*, London: Short Books, 2011.
6 Stamfordham's comment, front cover of TNA file FO 371/3977/ Part I, no. 98898. Quoted in FCO 12/158, Rohan Butler memo dated 22 February 1974. 4 July 1919, Lord Stamfordham to Sir Ronald Graham, Acting Permanent Under-Secretary in the FO during the Paris Peace Conference.
7 TNA FO 371/3977, Part I, no. 98898.
8 *Daily Telegraph*, 7 September 1921.
9 Kerensky, 'The Provisional Government's Responsibility', Part IV of Kerensky and Milyukov, 'Light on the Murder of Tsar Nikolas', 643.
10 Ibid., 645.

11 For Kerensky and Milyukov's defence of their position, see 'Light on the Murder of Tsar Nikolas', 638–45, which is a résumé of various articles they had written in the Russian émigré press.

12 TNA FO 370/273 1928. See correspondence between the FO occasioned by this.

13 Keith Hamilton, 'Addressing the Past', 101. The Librarian's Department of the Foreign Office carried out the vetting of diplomatic memoirs.

14 Buchanan, *Ambassador's Daughter*, 159.

15 *Dissolution*, 192–3.

16 The Paley memoirs were published over several issues of the *Revue de Paris*. See 1 and 15 June, 1 July, 15 August, 1 and 15 September 1922.

17 Van der Kiste, *Princess Victoria Melita*, 130.

18 Ibid., 124.

19 *Revue de Paris*, 15 March 1923.

20 Ibid., 690.

21 *Dissolution*, 189.

22 Buchanan, *Ambassador's Daughter*, 154; see also *Dissolution*, 193–5.

23 Buchanan, *Ambassador's Daughter*, 159.

24 *Dissolution*, 198.

25 Buchanan, *Ambassador's Daughter*, 154.

26 *Dissolution*, 193.

27 Ibid., 198.

28 *Western Daily Press*, undated cutting *c.* June 1932, Meriel Buchanan Archive, Nottingham University. This and many other reviews of *Dissolution of an Empire* were carefully collected by Buchanan, but in cutting them out she failed to append any dates of publication, and very few of the sources from which the reviews were taken.

29 Note by Laurence Collier, head of Cabinet Office's Northern Department, 5 July 1932, quoted in Hamilton, 'Addressing the Past', 114–15.

30 See Hamilton, 'Addressing the Past'.

31 David Lloyd George, 'Tsar's Future Place of Residence', LG/G/212/3/7, Parliamentary Archives

32 Ibid., 4.

33 Ibid., 5.

34 Ibid., 6.

35 Ibid., 6.

36 Ibid., 7.

37 Rose, *King George V*, 218.

38 Lloyd George, *War Memoirs*, 3: 514. For an enlightening discussion of the suppressed chapter, see Hamilton, 'Addressing the Past'.

39 Sylvester, *Life with Lloyd George*, 110.

40 Lloyd George, *War Memoirs*, 3: 1638.

41 David Cannadine, 'The Context, Performance and Meaning of Ritual: The British Monarchy and the Invention of Tradition *c.* 1820–1977', in Eric Hobsbawm and Terence Ranger, *The Invention of Tradition*, Cambridge: Cambridge University Press, 1992, 142, note 156. Lacey, *Majesty*, 333. For a discussion of George's position, see E. F. Benson, 'The King and His Reign: XII. The King and Democracy', *The Spectator*, 19 April 1935, 648–9.

42 Daniel Counihan, 'The Romanov Riddle', letter to the editor, *The Listener*, 7 October 1976, 444.

43 LG MSS F/3/2/19, Parliamentary Archives; quoted in Suttie, *Rewriting the First World War*, 192.

44 Lacey, *Majesty*, 62.

45 *The Listener*, 110, 7 July 1983, 26.

46 See *The Listener*, 30 September 1976, 3.

47 Story as told by the Duke of Windsor to the writer Gore Vidal, in Vidal, *Palimpsest, A Memoir*, London: Abacus, 1996, 207–8.

48 Michael Tyler Whittle, *The Last Kaiser: A Biography of William II, German Emperor and King of Prussia*, New York: Times Books, 1977, 285.

49 *London Gazette*, 17 July 1917.

50 See http://www.royalfoibles.com/the-british-queen-partially-to-blame-for-the-murder-of-tsar-nicholas-ll-and-his-family/.

51 See Deborah Cadbury, *Queen Victoria's Matchmaking*, London: Bloomsbury, 2017, 151–2.

52 Gaselee to Sir Robert Vansittart, 16 April 1934, quoted in Hamilton, 'Addressing the Past', 115.

53 See Jagow, 'Die Schuld am Zarenmord', 363–40, and Semenovsky, 'Popytki Spaseniya Romanovykh'.

54 Jagow, 'Die Schuld am Zarenmord', 369.

55 Ibid., 371.

56 Ibid., 373, 388.

57 Ibid., 389.

58 Ibid., 392–3, 399.

59 Ibid., 400–401.

60 Wilhelm II, *The Kaiser's Memoirs*, New York: Harper & Bros, 1922, 130.

61 Lamar Cecil, *Wilhelm II*, vol. 2: *Emperor and Exile 1900–1941*, Chapel Hill: University of North Carolina Press, 1996, 322.

62 Waters, *Potsdam and Doorn*, 252–3.

63 Ibid., 253.

64 *FOT*, 275.

65 See *FOT*, 275.

66 Wallscourt Waters's will, dated 28 May 1942; probate 1 August 1945, p. 4; www.probaterecords.co.uk.

67 '300 Jahre Romanow & Hohenzollern', Ausstellungsfuhrer, Burg Hohenzollern 22 Okt 2016–29 January 2017, no page numbers. I am grateful to Mark Andersen for passing on this information to me.

68 *FOT*, 275.

69 Wilhelm II, 'Questions and Reflections Concerning the Rescue of the Tsar', points 1–3, Burg Hohenzollern Archive, résumé in Waters, *Potsdam and Doorn*, 259–60.

70 Ibid., notes 5–9, fo. 2.

71 Ibid., note 8, fo. 2.

72 Wilhelm II, 'Questions and Reflections', note 10, fo. 2.

73 Ibid. fo. 11.

74 Wilhelm notes to Gutman letter, 'Wilhelm Written Records', ff. 11–12.

75 Ibid., fo. 12.

76 Ibid.

77 Ibid.

Postscript: 'Nobody's Fault?'

1 Jonathan Petropoulos, *Royals and the Reich: The Princes von Hessen in Nazi Germany*, New York: Oxford University Press, 2008, 199.

2 See official site of the Royal Norwegian House at http://www.kongehuset.no/artikkel.html?tid=27613&sek=27060. I am grateful to royalty historian David Horbury for a detailed discussion of this issue and for his helpful notes.

3 Ana de Sagrera, *Ena y Bee: En defensa de una amistad*, Madrid: Velecío Editores, 2006, 362. María Teresa Puga, *La vida y la época de Alfonso XIII*, Barcelona: Editorial Planeta, 1997, 176.

4 For an excellent study of George and Mary's reinvention of the British monarchy, see Frank Prochaska, *Royal Bounty: the Making of a Welfare Monarchy*, London: Yale University Press, 1995.

5 Letter to Earl Lloyd George, 26 October 1983, quoted in Suttie, *Rewriting the First World War*, 193.

6 Wallscourt Waters in 1935, *Potsdam and Doorn*, 257–8.

7 Yeltsin speech in *New York Times;* http://www.nytimes.com/1998/07/18/world/address-by-yeltsin-we-are-all-guilty.html.

8 See, for example, http://3rm.info/main/24366-ekaterinburg-prosti-menya-moy-gosudar.html.

9 *Daily Telegraph*, 7 September 1921.

10 Gilliard notes to de Basily, 29 April 1934, p. 2, Nikolai de Bazili Archive, Hoover Institution.

11 Ibid.

12 Pipes, *Russian Revolution*, 769.

Bibliography

ARCHIVES

Archivo Histórico Nacional, Madrid
AVPRI: Arkhiv Vneshney Politiki Rossiiskoi Imperii: Sekretnyi
  Arkhiv Ministra
Bakhmeteff Archive, Columbia University, New York

  Benckendorff Family Papers
  A. I. Ievreinov memoir, 'Poezdka v Tobolsk'
  Olga Ivanovna Subbotina Papers – Buxhoeveden and Gilliard
    affidavits

Burg Hohenzollern Archive: 'Questions and Reflections Concern-
  ing the Rescue of the Tsar', eigen-händige Aufzeichungen
  Nicholas II. vom April 1931 bezüglich seines Versuches, den
  Zaren und seine Familie in Sommer 1918 zu retten
Cambridge University Library: Lord Hardinge Papers, 1917–18,
  vols 30–38
Emory University Archives, Atlanta: Isaac Don Levine Papers for
  1917–18

  Thomas Preston, 'The Vigil', undated TS, series 5, box 136

GARF: Gosudarstvennyi Archiv Russkoy Federatsii

German Foreign Ministry Berlin (GFM): Auswartiges Amt, Abteilung A. Akten betreffend: die russische Kaiserfam. Microfilmed documents at TNA

Hechingen, Burg Hohenzollern, Hausarchiv des vormals regierenden preussischen Königshaus: 'Records of William II of April 1931'

Hessian Staatsarchiv, Darmstadt

Hoover Institution, California:

Nikolai de Bazili Papers: 'Informations données par M. M. Tereshchenko a M. N. de Basily à Paris le 23 Avril, 1934, au sujet de la question du départ de Nicolas II et de sa famille pour l'étranger après son abdication', box 27, folder 11; Pierre Gilliard notes on Nicholas II sent to de Basily, 29 April 1934, box 2, folder 62

Boris I. Nikolaevsky Collection:Vladimir Zenzinov, 'Ubiistvo Tsarskoy Semi: po materialiam Politicheskogo Arkhiva nemetskago ministerstva inostrannykh del', unpublished TS, box 788, folder 2

Igor Vinogradoff Collection: typescript of letters sent from Tobolsk by Prince Vasili Dolgorukov 1917–18; Alexander Lukomsky, 'Question of the Departure of the Emperor Nicholas and His Family', box 27, folder 11

Ekaterina Erastovna Zborovskaia letters, 1917–18

Hudson's Bay Company Canada Archives, Winnipeg

John Wimbles Papers, private archive of transcribed letters now donated to: Archivo Orleans-Bourbón, Fundación Infantes Duques de Montpensier Sanlúcar de Barrameda

Leeds Russian Archive at Leeds University Library

National Archives, Kew: Cabinet Papers (CAB), Foreign Office (FO) and War Office (WO) papers

Oslo Maritime Museum: Jonas Lied Diary

Parliamentary Archives, Westminster:

David Lloyd George: 'Tsar's Future Place of Residence', redacted chapter from his *War Memoirs*, Lloyd George Papers LG/G/212/3/4

Royal Archives, Windsor: various papers relating to King George V and Lord Stamfordham 1917–18

UNPUBLISHED SOURCES: DISSERTATIONS, PAPERS AND ARTICLES

Asgarov, Asgar, M., 'Reporting from the Frontlines of the First Cold War: American Diplomatic Despatches about the Internal Conditions in the Soviet Union, 1917–1933', University of Maryland dissertation, 2007.

Chap, Olivia, 'Skeletons in the Soviet Closet: Russia's Last Tsar and his Family in the Early Soviet Era, 1918–1937', thesis, Connecticut College, 2015.

Holden, Nigel, 'Harald Schou-Kjeldsen: A Young Danish Entrepreneur in Early Soviet Russia', unpublished TS, 2000.

McKee, Claire Theresa, 'British Perceptions of Tsar Nicholas II and Empress Alexandra Feodorovna 1894–1918', PhD thesis, University College London, 2014.

Puchenikova, Lyubov: 'Deyatelnost britanskikh diplomaticheskih predstavitelstv v Rossii v 1917 godu', Historical Sciences dissertation, St Petersburg, 2005.

PUBLISHED SOURCES: BOOKS, ARTICLES AND NEWSPAPERS

Note: In view of the fact that a wide range of sources in eight languages have been drawn on for this book, it seemed most logical – and useful – to group them by the language in which they were written.

English

Alexander, Grand Duke, *Once a Grand Duke*, New York: Garden City Publishing, 1932.

Alexandrov, Victor, *The End of the Romanovs*, London: Hutchinson, 1966.

Alexeev, V. V., *The Last Act of a Tragedy: New documents about the Execution of the Last Russian Emperor Nicholas II*, Ekaterinburg: Urals Branch of Russian Academy of Sciences Publishers, 1996.

Almedingen, E. M., *The Empress Alexandra 1872–1918*, London: Cassell, 1973.

Aronson, Theo, *Grandmama of Europe: The Crowned Descendants of Queen Victoria*, London: Cassell, 1973.

Basily, Nicolas de, *The Abdication of Emperor Nicholas II of Russia*, Princeton, NJ: Kingston Press, 1984.

Benckendorff, Pavel, *Last Days at Tsarskoe Selo*, Ontario: Gilbert's Books 2012 [reprint 1927].

Botkin, Gleb, *The Real Romanovs*, London: Putnam, 1932.

Browder, Robert Paul, and Kerensky, Aleksandr Fyodorovich, eds, *The Russian Provisional Government, 1917: Documents*, 1: chapter 4, section on 'The Former Tsar and the Imperial Family', Stanford University Press, 1961, 177–90.

Buchanan, Sir George, *My Mission to Russia,* vol. 2, London: Cassell, 1923.

Buchanan, Meriel, *Dissolution of an Empire*, London: John Murray, 1932.

—— 'The Foulest Crime in History – The Truth', *Saturday Review*, *CLIX*, 18 May 1935, 616.

—— *Ambassador's Daughter*, London: Cassell, 1958.

Bulygin, Captain Paul, and Kerensky, Alexander, *The Murder of the Romanovs*, London: Hutchinson, 1935.

Buxhoeveden, Baroness Sophie, *The Life and Tragedy of Alexandra Fyodorovna*, London: Longmans Green, 1928.

Bykov, P. M., *Last Days of Tsar Nicholas*, New York: International Publisher, 1934.

Carter, Miranda, *The Three Emperors*, London: Penguin, 2009.

Clarke, *The Lost Fortune of the Tsars*, London: Orion, 1996.

Cook, Andrew, *The Murder of the Romanovs*, Stroud: Amberley, 2010.

Crawford, Rosemary and Donald, *Michael and Natasha: The Life and Love of the Last Tsar of Russia*, London: Weidenfeld & Nicolson, 1997.

De Angelis, Stephen R., ed. and trans., *The Personality of Nicholas and Alexandra Feodorovna: The Historical Bulletin, April* 1917, Volume CXLVIII, *According to the Testimonies of their Relations and Those Close to Them*; CXLVIII, USA: Bookemon, n.d.

Dehn, Lili, *The Real Tsaritsa*, London: Thornton Butterworth, 1922.

Dillon, E. J., 'The ex-Tsar Nicholas II: an imperial tragedy. A tragic history of opportunities missed', *Daily Telegraph*, 22 and 24 July 1918.

Duff, David, *Hessian Tapestry: The Hesse Family and British Royalty*, London: David & Charles, 1979.

Edwards, Anne, *Matriarch: Queen Mary and the House of Windsor*, London: Coronet Books, 1984.

Egan, Maurice Francis, *Ten Years near the German Frontier: A Retrospect and a Warning*, New York: George H. Doran Company, 1919.

Francq, Henri G., *The Knout and the Scythe: The Story of the Hyenas*, New York: Vantage Press, 1980.

Fuhrmann, Joseph T., *The Complete Wartime Correspondence of Tsar Nicholas II and the Empress Alexandra, April 1914–March 1917*, Westport, CT: Greenwood Press.

George, Grand Duchess, *A Romanov Diary*, New York: Atlantic International, 1988.

Gilliard, Pierre, *Thirteen Years at the Russian Court*, London: Hutchinson, 1921.

Graham, Stephen, *Part of the Wonderful Scene: An Autobiography*, London: Collins, 1964.

Hall, Coryne, *Little Mother of Russia*, Teaneck, NJ: Holmes & Meier, 2006.

– '"An Energetic and Chivalrous Protector": Danish Efforts to Help the Imprisoned Romanovs', *Royal Russia Annual* no. 6, Summer 2014, 29–41.

Hamilton, Keith, 'Addressing the Past: The Foreign Office and the Vetting of Diplomatic and Ministerial Memoirs during the Years between the World Wars', in Christopher Baxter et al., *Britain in Global Politics, 1: From Gladstone to Churchill*, Basingstoke: Palgrave Macmillan, 2013, 99–131.

Hanbury-Williams, Major General Sir John, *The Emperor Nicholas II as I Knew Him*, London: Arthur L. Humphreys, 1922.

Hardinge of Penshurst, Lord, *Old Diplomacy*, London: John Murray, 1947.

Hennessy, James, *Queen Mary, 1867–1953*, London: Allen & Unwin, 1959.

Horbury, David, 'Half a Century of Royal Letters, 1899–1946', *Royalty Digest Quarterly*, 2016: 3, 58–63.

Hough, Richard, *Louis and Victoria: The First Mountbattens*, London: Hutchinson, 1934.

Kerensky, A. F., 'Why the Tsar Never Came to England', *Evening Standard*, 4 July 1932.

—— *The Kerensky Memoirs: Russia and History's Turning Point*, London: Cassell, 1965.

—— and Milyukov, P., 'Light on the Murder of Tsar Nikolas', *Living Age*, 311, 1921, 638–45.

King, Greg, *The Court of the Last Tsar: Pomp, Power, and Pageantry in the Reign of Nicholas II*, Hoboken, NJ: John Wiley & Sons, 2006.

—— and Wilson, Penny, 'The Departure of the Imperial Family From Tsarskoye Selo', *Atlantis Magazine*, 4: 5, 2003, 12–30.

—— 'The Officer Letters', *Atlantis Magazine*, 4: 5, 2003, 73–86.

'King could Have Saved the Tsar', *Mail on Sunday*, 20 November 1988.

Kozlov, V. A., and Khrustalev, V. M., *The Last Diary of Tsaritsa Alexandra*, London: Yale University Press, 1997.

Lacey, Robert, *Majesty: the Life and Reign of Elizabeth II*, New York: Free Press, 2002.

Levine, Isaac Don, *Eyewitness to History: Memoirs and Reflections of a Foreign Correspondent for Half a Century*, New York: Hawthorn Books, 1973.

Lied, Jonas, *Return to Happiness*, London: Macmillan, 1943.

Livak, Leonid, *Russian Émigrés in the Intellectual and Literary Life of Inter-War France: A Bibliographical Essay*, Montreal: McGill-Queen's University Press, 2010.

Lloyd George, David, *War Memoirs,* vol. III, London: Ivor Nicolson & Watson, 1934.

Lyandres, Semion, *The Fall of Tsarism: Untold Stories of the February 1917 Revolution*, Oxford: Oxford University Press, 2014.

McNeal, Shay, *The Secret Plot to Save the Tsar: New Truths Behind the Romanov Mystery*, London: Perennial, 2003.

Marie, Queen of Romania, *The Story of My Life*, New York: Scribner's, 1934.

Marr, Andrew, *The Diamond Queen, Elizabeth II and Her People*, London: Pan Macmillan, 2011.

Maylunas, Andrei, and Mironenko, Sergei, *A Lifelong Passion: Nicholas and Alexandra, Their Own Story*, New York: Doubleday, 1997.

Miller, Ilana, *The Four Graces: Queen Victoria's Hessian Granddaughters*, East Richmond Heights, CA: Kensington House Books, 2011.

Mironenko, Sergey, 'Romanov Family Tensions on the Eve of the First World War and the Revolution', *1917 Romanovs & Revolution: The End of Monarchy*, exhibition catalogue, Amsterdam: Hermitage Amsterdam, 2017, 140–6.

Mosolov, A. A., *At the Court of the Last Tsar*, London: Methuen, 1935.

Nabokov, C. [Konstantin], *The Ordeal of a Diplomat*, London: Duckworth & Co., 1921.

Neklyudov, Anatoly, *Diplomatic Reminiscences before and during the World War 1911–1917*, New York: Dutton, 1920.

Nicholas of Greece, HRH Prince, *Political Memoirs 1914–1917*, London: Hutchinson, 1928.

Nicolson, Harold, *King George V: His Life and Reign*, London: Constable, 1984.

O'Conor, John F., *The Sokolov Investigation*, New York: Robert Speller & Sons, 1971.

Occleshaw, Michael, *Armour Against Fate: British Military Intelligence in the First World War*, London: Columbus Books, 1989.

———— *The Romanov Conspiracies*, London: BCA, 1993.

———— *Dances in Deep Shadows: Britain's Clandestine War in Russia 1917–20*, London: Constable, 2006.

Paléologue, Maurice, *An Ambassador's Memoirs, 1914–17*, London: Hutchinson, 1973.

Pares, Bernard, *Fall of the Russian Monarchy: A Study of the Evidence*, London: Cassell, 1988.

Pipes, Richard, *The Russian Revolution 1899–1919*, London: Fontana Press, 1992.

Poore, Judith, *The Memoirs of Emily Loch: Discretion in Waiting*, Forres, Moray: Librario Publishing, 2007.

Preston, Robert, 'Sir Robert Preston Recalls Ekaterinburg', *Spectator*, 11 March 1972, 19.

Preston, Thomas, *Before the Curtain*, London: John Murray, 1950.

'Prince Michael bids to clear George V's name over Tsar's Death', *Daily Express*, 2 February 2010.

Prochaska, Frank, 'George V and Republicanism, 1917–1919', *Twentieth Century British History*, 10: 1, 1999, 27–51.

Radzinsky, Edvard, *The Last Tsar: The Life and Death of Nicholas II*, London: Hodder & Stoughton, 1992.

Rappaport, Helen, *Ekaterinburg: The Last Days of the Romanovs*, London: Hutchinson, 2008.

—— *Four Sisters: The Lost Lives of the Romanov Grand Duchesses*, London: Macmillan, 2014.

Robertson, Anne, 'Kings, Queens, Tsars, and Commissars: Russia Gets the Royal Treatment', *Demokratizatsiya* (Washington DC), 4: 2, 1996, 201–22.

Rodzianko, Mikhail, *The Reign of Rasputin: An Empire's Collapse: Memoirs of M. V. Rodzianko*, London: A. M. Philpot, 1927.

Rodzianko, Count Paul, *Tattered Banners*, London: Seeley, Service & Co., 1939.

Röhl, John C. G., *Young Wilhelm: The Kaiser's Early Life, 1859–1888*, Cambridge: Cambridge University Press, 1998.

—— *Wilhelm II: Into the Abyss of War and Exile 1900–1941*, Cambridge: Cambridge University Press, 2014.

Rose, Kenneth, *King George V*, London: Phoenix Press, 2000.

Service, Robert, *The Last of the Tsars: Nicholas II and the Russian Revolution*, London: Macmillan, 2017.

Shelking, Evgeniy, *Recollections of a Russian Diplomat: The Suicide of Monarchies (William II and Nicholas II)*, New York: Macmillan, 1918.

Smith, Doug, *Rasputin*, London: Macmillan, 2016.

Soroka, Marina, *Britain, Russia and the Road to the First World War: The Fateful Embassy of Count Aleksandr Benckendorff 1903–1916*, London: Routledge, 2016.

Steinberg, Isaac N., *In the Workshop of the Revolution*, London: Gollancz, 1955.

Steinberg, Mark, and Khrustalev, Vladimir, *The Fall of the Romanovs*, London: Yale University Press, 1995.

Stopford, Albert, *The Russian Diary of an Englishman, Petrograd 1915–1917*, London: Heinemann, 1919.

Sukhanov, Nikolai, *The Russian Revolution 1917: A Personal Record*, Princeton: Princeton University Press, 1984.

Summers, Anthony, and Mangold, Tom, *The File on the Tsar*, 2nd edn 1987 and 3rd edn 2002.

Suttie, Andrew, *Rewriting the First World War: Lloyd George, Politics and Strategy 1914–18*, Basingstoke: Palgrave Macmillan, 2005.

Sylvester, A. J., *Life with Lloyd George: The Diary of A. J. Sylvester 1931–1945*, London: Macmillan, 1975.

Taylor, Edmond, *The Fall of Dynasties: The Collapse of the Old Order 1905–1922*, New York: Doubleday, 1963.

Tomaszewski, Fiona K., *A Great Russia: Russia and the Triple Entente, 1905–1914*, New York: Praeger, 2002.

Trewin, J. C., *Tutor to the Tsarevich: Charles Sydney Gibbes*, London: Macmillan, 1975.

Urbach, Karina, *Royal Kinship: British and German Family Networks 1815–1914*, Munich: K. G. Saur Verlag, 2008.

—— *Go-Betweens for Hitler*, Oxford: Oxford University Press, 2015.

Van der Kiste, John, *Princess Victoria Melita: Grand Duchess Cyril of Russia 1876–1936*, Stroud: Sutton, 1991.

—— *Northern Crowns: Kings of Modern Scandinavia*, Stroud: Sutton, 1998.

—— *Crowns in a Changing World: The British and European Monarchies 1901–36*, Stroud: Sutton, 2003.

Vorres, Ian, *The Last Grand Duchess*, London: Hutchinson, 1964.

Vyrubova, Anna, *Memories of the Russian Court*, New York: Macmillan, 1923.

Waters, Brigadier Wallscourt Hely-Hutchinson, *Potsdam and Doorn*, London: John Murray, 1935.

Werenskiold, Marit, ed., *Consul Jonas Lied and Russia: Collector, Diplomat, Industrialist Explorer 1910–1931*, Oslo: Unipub, 2008.

Wilson, Penny, 'From the Memoirs of Princess Helena Petrovna of Serbia', *Atlantis Magazine: In the Courts of Memory*, 4: 3, 2003, 53–60.

Wilton, Robert, and Telberg, George Gustav, *The Last Days of the Romanovs*, London: Thornton Butterworth, 1920.

Yuuspov, Prince Felix, *Lost Splendour*, London: Adelphi, 2016.

French

Botkin, Petr, 'Le Massacre de la famille impériale en Russie', *Le Gaulois*, 45691, 19.IX.1920, 1.

Buchanan, Sir George, 'Nicolas et la Révolution Bolcheviste', *Revue de Paris*, 15 April 1923, 225–52.

Chantecler, 'Les Derniers jours des Romanof', *Soir*, 326, 22 December 1921, 1.

Combaluzier, L., 'M. Bourtzeff évoque la fin tragique de tsar Nicolas et de sa famille impérial de Russia', *Journal*, 13982, 28 January 1931, 1, 4.

Kokovtsov, Vladimir, 'La vérité sur la tragédie d'Ekaterinbourg', *Revue du Deux Mondes*, LIII, 1 October 1929, 506–31; 15 October 1929, 847–65.

'La Mort d'un empereur – A propos du vingtième anniversaire du massacre de la famille imperial russe', *Marianne*, 299, 13 July 1938, 1, 4.

'L'Assassinat du tsar – Une controverse entre MM Kerensky et Jacoby', *Sept. L'hebdomadaire du temps present*, 148, 25 December 1936, 16.

'Le Massacre des Romanoff – Une version inédite', *Le Gaulois*, 16107, 9 November 1921, 3.

Lukomsky, Georgiy, 'Comment Nicolas II a quitté Tsarskoe Selo', *Le Gaulois*, 18353, 4 January 1928, 1–2.

Lvovsky, Zinovy, 'Il y a vingt ans, le tsar Nicolas II était massacré avec tous les siens – La Tragédie d'Ekathérinbourg. Document historique inédit', *Candide*, 747, 7 July 1938, 3.

Milyukov, Pavel and Vladimir Kokovtsov, 'Aurait-on put sauver Nicolas II?', *Le Soir* [Belgium], 48, 17 February 1936, 4.

Paléologue, Maurice, 'Les dernier Jours de j'impératrice de Russie', *Revue des Deux Mondes*, 8 series, II, 1932, 59–70.

——— 'Le Drame d'Ekaterinebourg', *Documentation catholique*, XXXIV: 774, 19 December 1935, 1107.

——— *Guillaume II et Nicolas II*, Paris: Librairie Plon, 1935.

Paley, Princesse, 'Réponse à Sir George Buchanan', *Revue de Paris*, II, 15 April 1923, 689–90.

Sanvoisin, Gaetan, 'Comment Nicolas II a quitté Tsarskoie-Selo: Un entretien avec M. Loukomski, ancien conservator du Palais impériale', *Le Gaulois*, 4 January 1928.

Savvich, Sergey, 'L'Abdication de l'empereur Nicolas II – souvenirs d'un témoin oculaire', *Revue universelle*, XXXVII: 1, 1 April 1929, 1–10.

Sederkholm, Boris, 'Qui est responsible de l'arrestation et de la mort de Nicolas II?', *Figaro*, 270, 27 September 1921, 3–4.

Semenov, Evgeniy, 'L'Assassinat de la famille impérial russe', *Mercure de France*, CLXXXVI: 665, 1 February 1926, 460–68.

Sokolov, Nikolay, *Enquête judiciaire sur l'assassinat de la Famille Impériale Russe*, Paris: Payot, 1924.

German

Baumgart, Winfried, *Deutsche Ostpolitik 1918: Von Brest-Litowsk bis zum Ende des Ersten Weltkrieges*, Munich: Oldenbourg R. Verlag GmbH, 1982.

Bothmer, Karl Freiherr Von, *Mit Graf Mirbach in Moskau*, Tübingen: Osiander'sche Buchhandlung, 1922.

Jagow, Kurt, 'Die Schuld am Zarenmord', *Berliner Monatshefte Ausgabe*, May 1935, 363–401.

Machtan, Lothar, *Prinz Max von Baden: Der Letze Kanzler des Kaisers*, Berlin: Suhrkamp Verlag, 2013.

Russian

Avdeev, A., 'Nikolay Romanov v Tobolske I Ekaterinburge', *Krasnaya Nov, 5*, 1928, 185–209.

Botkin, Petr, 'Chto bylo sdelano dlya spaseniya Imperatora Nikolaya II', *Russkaya Letopis*, 7, Paris, 1925, 207–23.

Botkina, Tatiana Melnik-, *Vospominaniya o tsarskoy semi*, Moscow: Zakharov, 2009.

'Doklad Vremennomy Pravitelstvu komissara ... S. G. Svatikova o kontr-revolyutsionnom dvizhenii za granitsei', *Krasnyi Archiv*, no. 1, 1927, 25–38.

Haugolnykh, E. A., ed., *Beloemigranty o Bolshevikakh i proletarskoy revolyutsii*, vol. 1: *Fevralskaya Revolyutsiya v vospominaniyakh pridvorniykh, generalov, monarkhistov i chlenov vremennogo pravitelstvo* [Moscow, 1926], reprinted Perm: n.p., 1991.

Ioffe, Genrikh, *Revolyutsiya i semya Romanovyk*, Moscow: Algorithm, 2012.

Khrustalev, V. M., *Dnevniki Nikolaya II i Imperatritsy Aleksandry Fedorovny, 1917–1918*, 2 vols, Moscow: Vagrius, 2008.

Krasnyi Arkhiv: Istoricheskii Zhurnal 1923–41, online at https://igorkurl.livejournal.com/449647.html

Leontiev, Maxim Nikolaevich, 'Otkrytoe pis'mo Imperatora Vil'gelmu', Paris: n.p., 1918 [copy in Hoover Institution, Nikolaevsky Papers, box 784, folder 6].

Lykova, Lidiya, *Sledstvie po delu ob ubiistve rossisskoi imperatorskoy semi*, Moscow: Rosspen, 2007.

Lykova, L. A. (ed.), and Sokolov, N. A., 'Predvaritelnoe sledstvie 1919–1922', *Rossisskiy Arkhiv: Istoriya Otechestva v svidetelstvakh I dokumentakh XVIII–XX vv.*, VIII, 1998; online at: http://next.feb-web.ru/text/rosarc_8_1998/go,0;fs,1/

Markov, N., 'Popytka spaseniya Tsarskoy Semi', *Vestnik Vysshego monarkhicheskogo soveta*, (Berlin), 28 April/11 May 1924.

Mednikov, I. Yu., 'Missiya Spaseniya: Alfonso XIII i Rossiiskaya Imperatorskaya Semya', *Vestnik RUDN: Rossiya i Ispaniya*, 2011, 1, 65–75.

—— 'Missiya Spaseniya:Alfonso XIII i Rossiiskaya Imperatorskaya Semya', *Vestnik RUDN: Vseobshchaya istoriya, 1*, 2011, 65–75.

Milyukov, Pavel, 'O vyezde iz Rossii Nikolaya II', *Golos Rossii*, Berlin, 15 September 1921.

Milyukov, P. N., *Vospominaniya, 1859–1917*, vol. 2, Moscow, 1990.

Mironenko, Sergey et al., *Gibel semi imperatora Nikolaya II: Sledstvie dlinoyu vek. Katalog vystavki*, Moscow: Indrik, 2012.

Mordvinov, A. A., *Iz perezhitogo: vospominaniya fligel-adyutanta imperatora Nikolaya II*, vol. 2, Kuchkovo Pole, 2004.

Naryshkina, Elizaveta, 'S Tsarskoy semey pod arestom: Dnevnik ober-gofmeisteriny', *Poslednye Novosti*, 10 May and 28 June 1936.

Orlano-Erenya, A., 'Ispanskii korol I popytki spaseniya semi Nikolaya II', *Novaya i noveishaya istoriya*, 5, 1993, 152–65.

'Pereezd eks-imperatora', *Russkoe Slovo*, 3 (16) August 1917.

Plotnikov, Ivan, *Gibel tsarskoy semi: Pravda istorii*, Ekaterinburg: Izdatelstvo Uralskogo Universiteta, 2005.

Ross, *Gibel tsarskoy semi: materialy sledstviya po delu ob ubiistve tsarskoy semi*, Frankfurt am Main: Posev, 1987.

Semchevskaya, Elizaveta, 'Vospominaniya o poslednykh dnyak Velikikh Knyazey v g Ekaterinburge', *Dvuglravyi Orel*, 10, 15 (28) June 1921.

Semenovsky, L. G., 'Popytki Spaseniya Romanovykh. Po Doneseni-yam Germanskikh Diplomatov', *Vozrozhdenie*, 15 June 1935, 4.

Sokolov, Konstantin, 'Popytka osvobozhdeniya tsarskoy semi', in *Arkhiv Russkoy Revolyutsii*, vol. 17, Berlin, 1926, 280–92.

'Sudba Doma Romanovykh', *Russkoe Slovo*, 8 (20) August 1917.

'Sudba Otrekshegosya Tsarya', *Novoe Vremya*, 10 (23) March 1917.

'Tragediya Tsarskoi Semi', *Vozrozhdenie*, 11: 3885, 22 January 1936.

Trubetskoy, Alexander E., 'Istoriya odnoi popytki', *Chasovoi*, nos 114–15, 1 December 1933, 31–3; nos 118–19, 15 January 1934, 29–30; no. 120, 1 February 1934, 21–3. A shortened version of this original article can be found in A. E. Trubetskoy, 'Kak my pytalis spasti tsarskuyu semyu', *Dvoryanskoe Sobranie*, 2, 1995, 61–8.

Voiekov, V. N., *S Tsarem I bez tsarya: vospominaniya poslednogo dvortsogo komendanta gosudarya-imperatora Nikolaya II*, Moscow: Rodnik, 1995.

Zakharov, S., 'Poslednii put poslednogo tsarya', *Oktyabr*, no. 3, 1967.

Zhuk, Yuri, *Ispoved Tsareubiits: podlinnaya istoriya velikoy tragedii*, Moscow: Veche, 2008.

—— *Voprositelnye znaki v 'Tsarskom dele'*, St Petersburg: BKhV, 2013.

Scandinavian: Danish, Swedish and Norwegian

Bomann-Larsen, Tor, *Haakon & Maud*: vol. 1, *Kongstanken*; vol. 4, *Makten*, Oslo: Cappelen Damm, 2010–11.

Jensen, Bent, *Danmark og det Russiske Spørgsmål 1917–24*, Unknown Publisher, 1979.

—— *Zarmodere Blandt Zarmodere 1917–1918: Enkekejserinde Dagmar og Danmark 1917–1928*, Copenhagen: Gyldendal, 1997.

Kamstrup, Jørgen, *H. N. Andersen – En ØK-logisk livsberetning*, Copenhagen: Books on Demand, 2012.

Kulavig, E., *Two Danes in Revolutionary Russia: Danish-Russian Cultural Relations 1700–1900*, Frederiksborg: Museum of National History at Frederiksborg, 2011, 147–52.

Lange, Ole, *Jorden er ikke Større*, Copenhagen: Gyldendal, 1988.

Platen, Gustaf von, *Bakom den Gyllne Fasaden*, Stockholm: Albert Bonniers, 2002.

Preben Hansen, Bernadette, ed., 'Esther Aksel-Hansen: Breve fra Petrograd 1917–1918', Copenhagen, 2007; available online at http://www.preben.nl/EAH.pdf

Scavenius, A. S., *Diplomatfrue ved zarhoffet*, Copenhagen: Martins Forlag, 1960.

Scavenius, Harald, Official reports to the Danish Foreign Office from Petrograd: 'Syn på omvæltningerne i Rusland 1917–1918: Belyst gennem depecher og telegrammer fra den danske gesandt i Petrograd', *Danske Magazin*, 1973, Række 8, Bd. 4, Hæfte 2.

Zahle, C. Th., *Konseilspræsident C. Th. Zahles dagbøger 1914–17*, Aarhus: Universitetsforlaget, 1974.

Spanish

Cortés Cavanillas, Julián, *Alfonso XIII y la Guerra del 14*, Madrid: Editorial Alce, 1976.

—— 'Alfonso XIII en la Guerra del Catorce: Los Intentos para Salvar a la Familia del Zar', *ABC Sevilla*, 5 December 1976.

Leal, Guillerma Calleja, 'Alfonso XIII y Su Actuación Humanitaria para el Rescate de la Familiar Imperial Rusa 1917–1918', *La Coronelía Guardas del Rey*, III: 16, 2005, 53–71.

Rey y Cabieses, D. Amadeo-Martin, 'Alfonso XIII, Jorge V, y El Frustrado Rescate de la Familia Imperial de Rusia', *Junta Sabatina de Especialidades Historicas*, 3, 2003 (Argentina), 99–131.

Rives, Luis Garcia, 'La Tragedia de la Familia Imperial Rusa: Gestiones de Espana para Salvarla', *Diario ABC*, Madrid, 19 March 1964.

Seco Serrano, Carlos, 'Alfonso XIII y la Familia del Zar', *Diario ABC*, Madrid, 21 October 1979.

—— *Alfonso XIII en el centenario de su reinado*, Madrid: Real Academia de la Historia, 2002.

Summers, Anthony, and Mangold, Tom, *El Expediente sobre el Zar*, Barcelona: Plaza & Janes, S.A., 1978.

Index

Index

Index

Index

Index